Literary Practice III

American University Studies

Series XIX
General Literature

Vol. 34

PETER LANG
New York • Washington, D.C./Baltimore • Bern
Frankfurt am Main • Berlin • Brussels • Vienna • Oxford

Dushan Bresky
WITH THE COLLABORATION OF
Miroslav Malik

Literary Practice

Volume III

Esthetics of Literary Subjects

PETER LANG
New York • Washington, D.C./Baltimore • Bern
Frankfurt am Main • Berlin • Brussels • Vienna • Oxford

Library of Congress Cataloging-in-Publication Data

Bresky, Dushan.
Esthetics of literary subjects / Dushan Bresky
with the collaboration of Miroslav Malik.
p. cm. — (Literary practice; 3) (American university studies.
XIX, General literature; vol. 34)
Includes bibliographical references.
1. Literature—Aesthetics. I. Title. II. American university
studies. Series XIX, General literature; vol. 34.
PN45 .B7254 801'.93—dc21 2001029115
ISBN 0-8204-5519-9
ISSN 0743-6645

Die Deutsche Bibliothek-CIP-Einheitsaufnahme

Bresky, Dushan.
Literary practice / Dushan Bresky.
With the collab. of Miroslav Malik.
–New York; Washington, D.C./Baltimore; Bern;
Frankfurt am Main; Berlin; Brussels; Vienna; Oxford: Lang.
Vol. 3. Esthetics of literary subjects.
(American university studies: Ser. 19, General literature; Vol. 34)
ISBN 0-8204-5519-9

The paper in this book meets the guidelines for permanence and durability
of the Committee on Production Guidelines for Book Longevity
of the Council of Library Resources.

Printed in the United States of America

ACKNOWLEDGMENTS

The research leading to the gradual completion of the *Literary Practice* trilogy was supported by the Killam Resident Fellowship (the University of Calgary Endowment Fund), by two grants from the Humanities and Social Sciences Research Council of Canada and by two University of Calgary sabbatical leaves. The Vice-Presidents (Academic) contributed to the publication subsidy of the trilogy's three volumes. Final work on this third volume was facilitated by a University of Calgary Research Grant. To these institutions, their representatives and committees I extend my thanks. Dr. Miroslav Malik, my late collaborator, recorded the biometric measurements reproduced in this volume at the Dr. Myer Pollock Communication Research Laboratory at Concordia University, Loyola Campus, Montreal. I would like to express my gratitude to this university as well as to Dr. Malik's colleague, Dr. Michael Thwaites. My appreciation also goes to Louise Bresky for her steady editorial guidance; to Mrs. Violette Clemente, who typed the manuscripts of all three volumes and prepared the camera-ready manuscript of this volume, and to the team at University of Calgary Printing Services. Finally, I would like to acknowledge the valuable support offered me throughout the project by Dr. Michael Bishop and Dr. James Brown of Dalhousie University and Dr. Henri Mydlarski of the University of Calgary.

TABLE OF CONTENTS

List of Tables xi

I LITERARY SUBJECT: ITS CONCEPT, KINDS AND STIMULATIVE POWER 1

The Catonian Imperative. Goals and Limits of Literary Mimesis. Writers' Favorite Subjects. Drever's and Fletcher's *Instinct Man* and his "Innate Faculties." Clynes' "Sentics." Breitenberg, Bergström, Pribram Explore Physiology of the Brain. The Durable Lure of Sex, Violence, Laughter and Miracles. Voltaire's "Immortal" Satire of 18th Century Characters and Intrigues. Journalistic and Literary Stimuli Have Much in Common. News in Fiction. Gide's First Reading of Proust. "Un Somnifère." Signifiers, Signifieds, Referents: Theory, Practice, Neurology. Scholes Argues with Derrida's Disbelief in Perception. A Biocybernetic View on Referents and Signifieds. A Humanist's Deduction. "Full" and "Empty" Signifieds. Mr. Jingle's Concrete Information "Very." Intangibles, their Signifieds and Referents.

II LITERARY CONTENT: ITS MICRO- AND MACRO-STIMULI 33

Heroes: From Homer to Carlyle. Villains and Antiheroes. Recurrent Characters. Plots. Epical Constants in Macrostimulative Fairy Tales and Myths. Microstimuli Quantified. One Thousand *Cinderellas*: Scholars Debate Deep Structure. Microstimuli in an Epical Macrostimulus: *Le Colonel Chabert*. Microstimuli in Kipling's Macrostimulative "If." Lyrical Stimuli. Humanistic Implications—*Écriture*. Didactic Stimuli.

III CONFLICTS 63

Creator vs. Creation, Eve's Inner Conflict. Achilles Kills Hector: *Deus ex machina*. Esthetics of Violence, Fear, Risk. Cycles of Mimesis: Voltaire on Shakespeare and Rabelais. Mock Violence in Rabelaisian Utopia. War and Duels in Voltaire's Satire. Regicide in *The Heptameron* and *Lorenzaccio*. Executions: Anatole France. Stendhal. Sartre. Zikmund Winter. Terrorist Tchen: Malraux' Communist Martyr. Psychological Conflicts: Biblical and Ancient. Inner Conflict: Medieval and Classical. Sacrifice of a Patriotic Prostitute. White Man's Burden French Style. Rutherford's Thesaurus of Russian Atrocities. The Tatar. Ivan. Intensified Conflicts. "Gut" Reactions.

IV EROTIC JOYS AND SINS 107

Incompatible Creationist Mythologies: Gaia and Eros. Jehovah's Single-handed Genesis. Christianity and Sinful Sex. Mimesis of Sensual Love: Erotic Micro- and Macrostimuli. Religious, Ethnic, Statistical Biases in

* * *

TABLES

* * *

I

LITERARY SUBJECT: ITS CONCEPT, KINDS AND STIMULATIVE POWER

"Rem tene, verba sequuntur."[1]

The Catonian Imperative. Goals and Limits of Literary Mimesis. Writers' Favorite Subjects. Drever's and Fletcher's *Instinct Man* and his "Innate Faculties." Clynes' "Sentics." Breitenberg, Bergström, Pribram Explore Physiology of the Brain. The Durable Lure of Sex, Violence, Laughter and Miracles. Voltaire's "Immortal" Satire of 18th Century Characters and Intrigues. Journalistic and Literary Stimuli Have Much in Common. News in Fiction. Gide's First Reading of Proust. "Un Somnifère." Signifiers, Signifieds, Referents: Theory, Practice, Neurology. Scholes Argues with Derrida's Disbelief in Perception. A Biocybernetic View on Referents and Signifieds. A Humanist's Deduction. "Full" and "Empty" Signifieds. Mr. Jingle's Concrete Information "Very." Intangibles, their Signifieds and Referents.

The Catonian Imperative

Budding occidental orators, poets, politicians, jurisprudents used to

1 Cato Maior Censorius, *Fragmenta*, Jordan, 2nd ed., p. 180. See *LP II*, p. 25. At the outset of *Literary Practice III*, I would like to point out that *Literary Practice I* and *II* (subsequently *LP I*, *II*) outline the characteristic esthetic stimuli related to content or style (*LP I*, ch. III, especially pp. 62–66) as well as the criteria distinguishing the "informative" and the stylistic stimuli identifiable in the micro- and macrocontext (*LP I*, ch. V, pp. 91–111). *LP II*, ch. I, pp. 9–12 draws a clear line between style and content. *LP I*, ch. VII, pp. 135–58 discusses the common esthetic aspect of all stimuli and categorizes their contentual and stylistic features. Miroslav Malik comments on "Esthetic Stimulations of Literary Text from the Biometric Point of View" (*LP I*, ch. IX, pp. 177–202). He stresses that biometric polygraphs, so far, cannot isolate content from style. Only appropriate cross-references direct the reader to these relevant comments and tables in *LP I*, and *II*. Like *LP I* and *II*, *LP III* also draws from my previous books, *The Art of Anatole France*, (The Hague: Mouton, 1969, hereafter *The Art of A.F.*) and *Cathedral or Symphony, Essays on Jean-Christophe* (Bern: Lang, 1973, hereafter *Essays on J.-C.*). First references to my articles are footnoted *passim*.

hear *ad nauseum* the Catonian oracle: "stick to your subject, words [will] follow." Whenever they lost sight of the *res*—the matter at hand—their tutors hastened to remind them that in any communication, be it between the speaker and listener or the writer and reader, the substance is its main goal. Digression, profusion, logorrhea tend to obscure the issue under scrutiny. In our culture, most of us value the contents more than the container. In his prolog to *Gargantua*, Rabelais urges readers to go to the core of his text and crack it the same way a dog cracks a bone and thoroughly sucks its marrow, "la substantifique mouelle." Fancy jars or bottles are merely amusing shells; only what is inside counts; the same applies to unshapely human flesh concealing a genius:

> Alcibiades, in...Plato's...Banquet...said that [Socrates] resembled the Silenes. Silenes of old were little boxes...in the shops of apothecaries, [decorated] with...satyrs, bridled geese...and other such-like counterfeited pictures, to excite people unto laughter, as Silenus himself, who was the foster-father of good Bacchus...; but within those capricious caskets were...kept many fine drugs, such as balm, ambergris, amomon... Just such another thing was Socrates... He had...the look of a bull, and countenance of a fool; he was...boorish in his apparel...the better by those means to conceal his divine knowledge.[2]

Today as in the days of Rabelais, literary substance and its quality rather than the form still drives our main interest: if we tell an average reader that he "simply must read" a book which he has not yet read, his first instinct makes him ask what it is about. While the "storage" of literary content in its artistic form differs from the safekeeping of spices in ceramic jars, most readers would agree that our interest in and the impact of subject matter are basic criteria of literary qualities. Naturally, this assumption does not imply that the form and style are less essential than content in either creating or perceiving art; nor does it ignore the fact that the degree of esthetic surprise, which we individually experience as we read and imagine the text's stimulative content, is not an invariable and exact intensity quantum. The level of our esthetic delectation (i.e., vital energy we discharge to initiate and sustain delectation) is preconditioned

2 *The Works of Rabelais*, transl. Urquhart and Motteux (London: Trade, [n.d.]), p. 9. Collaborator Miroslav Malik suggests that, in the biocybernetic sense, "container" is the physical information source, e.g., book; "content" is the sum of the psycho-physiological stimuli discernible as temporal neural pathways in the brain of the reader/receiver of information. Since author and reader are separated in time and space, certain rules must be observed in the process of neurophysiological decoding. Such a system of rules is called "software."

by our neurological make-up and by our individual reactivity. In the broad context of art perception, such a disposition seems to be a multi-faceted interaction of our inborn and acquired faculties, energized first by the textually evoked topics and also by their stylizations. The faculties involved in perceiving, storing and responding to the literary content include our memory, intelligence, instincts, curiosity, imagination, erudition (broad knowledge able to relate the known to the unknown), refinement, world outlook and wisdom, as well as a sensitive taste able to distinguish, appreciate and even rate the qualitative distinctions and nuances implied by the communicated substance, its verbal (formal) correlates, their accuracy, vagueness, number, syntactic integration and overall tone. Our fleeting moods—expectation, lethargy, distraction, somnolence—also affect the unstable intensity and duration of our esthetic stimulation. And, of course, some of our esthetic responses may be immediate and rather preliminary, others delayed, often corrective and possibly more permanent second thoughts.

Goals and Limits of Literary Mimesis

Clearly no verbal mimesis can replicate the referents to which it alludes—whether concrete, imaginary or abstract.[3] The verbal/literary signifiers designating specific beings, things, actions, relationships, ideals, rules, obligations, fantasies, etc., replace them with written or spoken words familiar to the intended audience/readers. When in doubt, we consult dictionaries to clarify the connotative range of unfamiliar words/signs. The authors adjust the applied mimetic means to their informational goals—journalistic, political, commercial, judicial, literary (epical, dramatic, lyrical). In literary discourse, political, moralistic, didactic objectives often overlap with the prevalent esthetic goals. Artists invoking *l'art pour l'art*, for example Baudelaire or Mallarmé, are uncompromising esthetes; existentialists such as Sartre are *engagé* politically and morally, and religiously motivated writers such as Paul Claudel or Chesterton subordinate their esthetica to faith in God and to the catechism. To attract the attention of their public, authors orally

3 Aristotle's concept formulated in *Peri Poietikes*, (approx. 344 B.C.); Erich Auerbach adopts the term in *Mimesis—Dargestellte Wirklichkeit in der abendländischen Literatur*, Bern 1946; Engl. transl. Princeton, 1953. Concrete referents are visual, acoustic, olfactory, gustative and tactile. The flying carpet, Plato's cave, Dante's Devil exemplify imaginary referents; abstract referents allude to ideals such as "freedom," "pursuit of happiness," etc.

articulate or textualize their chosen subjects in appropriately stylized language. In artistic texts, the esthetically motivated semantics, rhetoric, syntax, macrosyntax (composition) and prosody (versification) are the stylistic tools of transformative artistic representation—mimesis.

Presenting their subject matter in an amalgam of content and form, writers try to achieve the highest informative and stylistic impact. Critics as well as average readers simultaneously savor the two kinds of power; qualified readers can distinguish them and appraise each separately before rendering an overall judgment on the two qualities of the text. We may theorize that the contentual impact equals the overall intensity of unified content/form minus the esthetic force generated by formal elements.[4] This premise is a logical derivation from my earlier reflections on the possibility of enjoying and analysing the esthetic information independently of its artistic stylization and, vice versa, the style independently of content. Throughout the 20th century scholars have debated this issue.[5] According to Gerald Graff, the divisive controversy began before World War I. On one side John Erskine advocated English courses covering the Western classics' Great Books in translation, on the other hand, his "angry colleagues had objected that to read a great work in translation [stripped of its original style] was not to read it at all". Erskine put this adage in perspective by pointing out "that were this so, very few of his colleagues had read the Bible."[6] Naturally, his opponents' argument was not entirely without merit. Translations of works in which stylistic density and intensity are very high, for example, translations of Goethe's or Verlaine's lyrical poems, can rarely reproduce the verbal music characteristic of the original and its artistry. But such works were not on Erskine's list. While the loss of the original stylistic component and its replacement by the translators' signifiers (semantic and rhetoric

4 This equation explains the order of volumes in this trilogy: a thorough understanding of all stylistic factors seemed prerequisite to isolating and analyzing subject matter and its impact. We may add that any appraisal of stylistic as well as informative intensity, at best, can only be an erudite, empirical ad hoc estimate. This does not, however, prove that such value judgments are invalid nor does it imply that such impact will *never* be measurable . I assume that our creative production as well as its perception (delectation or provocation) have, today still latent but one day quantifiable, biophysical and biochemical correlates. The subsequent comments on the signifiers, signifieds and their referents and on the "full" and "empty" signifiers complement these reflections on mimesis.

5 See n. 1, cross-references to *LP I, II*.

6 *Professing Literature. An Institutional History* (Chicago Press, 1987, 89), p. 134.

options) is frequently regrettable, our contact with other cultures, their thoughts, art and visions, would be very limited without qualified translations. But even in merely adequate translation, the ancient myths—their characters and their actions—retain most of their original power.

Readers' and Writers' Favorite Subjects

We look for stimulation in any kind of information, personal, public or artistic. Our individual responses to the broad range of stimulating subjects—whether presented as fact in a private letter, magazine or fiction (art)—depend on our expectations. Some newspaper subscribers seek full local, national and international news coverage. Others devote their reading time to obituaries and horoscopes. Still others merely glance at the sports section or the stock-market quotations. A comparable range of subject-oriented preferences, interests and indifference can also be attributed to those who write, publish/sell, buy/read, study and judge literary works. Each participant in this chain estimates literary style and subject matter according to his/her conscious and instinctive choices and biases. Writers/sportsmen like Ernest Hemingway or Henri de Montherlant are likely to treat topics and themes other than those offered by an asthmatic Emile Proust as a refined mimesis of his own social life, remembered in his cork-panelled room. Readers like the late President J.F. Kennedy generally prefer LeCarré's spy novels to Beckett's *Waiting for Godot*. Readers like Rolland Barthes might opt for the opposite. Simone de Beauvoir loathed Henri de Montherlant's aggressive machoism; she condemned his "virile" humanistic contempt for compassion and tolerance.[7] Rabelais' childish delight in anal and genital anatomy filled the puritan Jean Calvin with apocalyptic wrath but merely provoked the bemused disdain of a critic as accomplished as Voltaire.[8] Commenting on Karel Čapek's antimystical pragmatism, the Czech Catholic poet Jaroslav Durych[9] allegedly said that the well known novelist and playwright would try to solve the tragedy of the Crucifixion by sending an ambulance to Calvary. Like the previous reflections, this anecdote[10] fur-

7 *The Second Sex*, (translated H.M. Parshley, New York, A.A. Knopf, 1957), "Montherlant or the Bread of Disgust" pp. 199–214.

8 Rabelais II, *Classiques Larousse*, p. 103 citing *Opera*, 1555, vol. XXVII; see *LP I*, ch. I, pp. 22–3.

9 Author of, e.g., *Panenky*, *Žebrácké písně*, *Nejvyšší naděje*, etc.

10 Told by my gymnasium professor Eduard Beneš in 1938 in one of his lectures on modern Czech writers.

ther illustrates how individual outlook affects both perception and representation of historical events as powerful as the alleged mystical sacrifice and resurrection. One writer's overwhelming faith may transpose the brutal paradox of divine will as proof of infinite love whereas the other's charitable pragmatism could represent it as a regrettable case of human or cosmic bestiality demanding constructive intervention by a civilized society. The first has its roots in Christian mysticism, the other in pagan materialistic positivism willing to struggle like Prometheus against the brutality of an indifferent cosmos. Like our instincts, knowledge, memory and individual dispositions, such discrepant world views predetermine whatever we think or however we respond to various communications and experiences which either challenge or concur with our individual teleology and its valuatory scales.

Just like moral or market values, esthetic values must never be confused with physical or chemical values derived from physically quantifiable materials. Critical, humanistic evaluations are empirical appraisals, not scientific evidence. They can be subjective and usually inspired by individual empirical experience or preference, or they can be teleological or normological arguments approved by, for example, legislative political consensus, common law or recognized cultural (e.g., religious) commandments. The esthetic norms such as, for example the expected unity of action, could at best be designated as objective empirical conventions or options. Invoking them as creative "laws" would be an overstatement.[11]

Our definite or vague preferences, favoring or resenting certain kinds of content, spring from our heterogeneous biological, intuitive and intellectual make-ups and from our inherited or adopted biological, psychological, social, political, religious, cultural (etc.) tendencies. They form a labyrinth of individual and collective concepts, opinions and tastes. Medieval scholars shied away from this labyrinth. Fearing they would get lost in it, they pragmatically proscribed value judgments in matters of individual taste. Hence the ultimate negative oracle: *de gustibus et coloribus non est disputandum*—let's not dispute tastes and colors.[12]

11 Karel Engliš, *Malá logika* (Prague: Melantrich, 1947), p. 451–81. Also see philosophical reflections on the relativity of value judgments in E.J. Bond, "The Concept of Value: The Old Orthodoxy and the New," *The Humanities Association Review*, vol. XXXI, No. 1/2, 1980, pp. 1–16

12 In the cultural context the Latin *gustus*—taste—always had a broader metaphorical connotation than exclusively gustative likes and dislikes. Descriptive literary

Five centuries of literary creation and scientific progress, along with modern marketing and advertising, have changed this view. Not only writers and critics but many modern laymen want to dispute the "indisputable". We are curious about the nature and evolution of individual and collective tastes, about the sources, nature and scope of our stimulation, esthetic and non-esthetic. Scholars want to describe and ultimately record the impact of all stimuli.[13] The current monitoring of our imagination, activated by various stimuli in the content and style of commercial or artistic texts, is still in the early stages of development. Nonetheless, no theorists examining the primary goals of any art can neglect the results of neurological and psychological exploration of the human innate faculties and instincts which perceive and spontaneously judge whatever life or art (which is part of life) present or represent. In this respect, successful writers, as well as their pragmatic editors and publishers are more in tune with the realities of art production than those in academia who view art from many narrow theoretical perspectives—Marxist, Freudian, anthropological, semiotic, linguistic…

Drever's and Fletcher's *Instinct Man* and his "Innate Faculties"

During this century two scholars, James Drever and Ronald Fletcher, identified the instincts and impulses which motivate us and which we, as inhabitants of this planet, have in common. Fletcher classifies our basic impulses as "the instincts proper" and as "general instinctive tendencies." He distinguishes ten specific instincts: 1. breathing; 2. eating; 3. drinking; 4. maintaining comfortable temperature; 5. sleeping; 6. caring for comfort of body surface; 7. fearing; 8. excretion; 9. general "spontaneous "and vital" activities a) play, b) curiosity, c) hunting; 10. sexual activity: a) eroticism and courtship; b) sexual fighting, c) parental activity, d) homemaking. Among the "general instinctive tendencies (ego-tendencies)" he considers the pleasure/pain dichotomy as the most significant and defines it as a "polarity [which] derives from seeking for gratification of all instincts proper; and includes the fundamental tendency to safeguard individual survival." It springs from "the desire for

---

scholarship—structuralist and deconstructionist—however, still seems to adhere to the medieval proverb.

13 *The Calgary Herald* (June 12, 98, p. A3) quotes the London *Telegraph* report that a University of Pennsylvania researcher, Brian Salzberg, had for the first time photographed the electrical signals forming a thought. These signals "travel across brain cells" faster than 402 km/h. See *LP I*, ch. X, p. 195, n. 4.

pleasure; for a state of overall satisfaction and well being. The desire for physical and mental harmony. The desire to resolve pain, conflict, dissatisfaction, frustration." The other tendencies include the binary correspondence—attachment/avoidance (manifesting itself in loyalty or antipathy to one's society, surrounding, social values)—and positive/negative ego-tendencies seeking rational solutions to problems.[14]

Fletcher's classifications assist the critic in categorizing the vast reservoir of contentual stimuli into several homogeneous and characteristic domains of artistic subject matter. Further, Fletcher's hierarchy of instincts makes us assume that the perennial magnets such as violent conflicts, erotic affinities, comical or supernatural subjects, address the most urgent faculties such as the instinct of self-preservation, fear of death, the correlated sexual drive, or propensities such as faith, hope, reasoning, doubting, curiosity, quest of pleasure and play.

As part of a mankind consisting of many races, nations, countries, communities and myriads of individuals, each of us is subject to heterogeneous influences—geographical, climatic, social, economical, cultural, etc. While we have many physical, physiological and intellectual faculties in common, we do not always concur in our individual standards, our cultural or political attitudes, interests, joys, or in our responses to different stimuli experienced directly or indirectly through art or communications; often, in fact, we are diametrically opposed. What each of us is used to seeing, hearing, tasting, touching, reading, remembering, doubting, enjoying, resenting, determines our esthetic criteria. The ideals which we are taught to cherish motivate and color our expectations and reactions to everything we confront. Thus the same contentual stimulus hardly ever provokes, even in the same reader, a stable, equally intensive response.

Clynes' "Sentics"

What Drever and Fletcher identified as "instincts and innate faculties" Manfred Clynes has recently described as "non-extricable elements of human thinking" which he labelled as "sentics." He speculates that, while other "mammals or macrobiological systems" may be endowed with comparable sentics, only mankind has an innate, genetic and partly externalized (through writing and speech) "systemic coding ability." This

14 *Instinct in Man* (New York: International Universities Press, 1957), pp. 308–315. Fletcher's concepts are based on the premises of James Drever's *Instinct in Man* (Cambridge University Press, 1917).

sentic ability is essential to human thinking. Thus sentics plays a significant role in all literary works. Sentic activities are detectable in the EEG signal from the hypothalamic region of the human brain. Clynes categorizes the perceivable polycultural subjects, "eternal themes," into three "groups" according to the "sentics" which they activate and the degree of stress they generate: 1. "egotropic" information alluding to spontaneous basic activities (related "automatically, i.e., with minimal awareness, to the body's own mechanisms"), such as breathing, sleeping, eating, etc., triggers the lowest information impact; 2. "egosentic" group of themes provoking, e.g., fear, joy, surprise, grief, pain, frustration, "initiates stress waves which amplify their information impact"; finally, 3. "egospatial" group of topics conveying environmental and personal concerns. A subdivision within this group, the "egosocial" theme, refers to work, play, erotic and parental activities, etc., or to social attitudes, such as love, alienation, loyalty, avoidance.[15]

Breitenberg, Bergström, Pribram Explore Physiology of the Brain

The German neurologist Valentin Breitenberg discusses the interdependence of our brains' physiologically predetermined instinctive reactions and the stimuli's variable and unpredictable informative potentials in the following context. "Instinct is largely functional, not the structural feature of the [animal's] brain. It has a certain time segment, where the response to the stimuli is predetermined by the genetical and ontological structure of the brain, but the final outcome is dependent very much on the stimuli's information potentials."[16] This observation suggests that both the physiological quality of the individual brain, its intelligence and memory, as well as the intratextual potential of the perceived

15 *Theory of Emotions* (Sydney: NWS Conservatory Press, 1976), pp. 26–34 and "Sentics: Biocybernetics of Emotion Communication," *Annnals of the New York Academy of Sciences,* 1974, 220, 3, pp. 55–131; see also V. Breitenberg, "Hypothalamische Systeme,"*Neurolgische Berichte*, May 1977, pp. 34. These and other comments concerning the physiological and neurological aspects of general as well as esthetic perception are written by M.F. Malik and edited by Dushan Bresky and Louise Bresky. Most of them form Ch. VIII, "A Biocybernetic Epilog." Cross references in subsequent chapters direct the reader to the relevant passages in the "Epilog." The paper by M.F. Malik and H.M. Thwaites, "Form and Content of Artistic Work: a Biocybernetic View" (7th Conference on Crosscultural Information Impact, Miami, Florida, 1991), offers a more extensive resume of Clynes' research.

16 Gehirngespinste/Neuroanatomie für kybernetisch Interesierte (Berlin: Springer, 1975), p. 85.

stimulus jointly determine the refinement and intensity of the brain's extratextual response to the informative stimulus at a given moment. Bergström's research focuses on the judgmental spontaneity of our instinctive responses and on the individual limits of the brain's ability to assimilate new information. He states that instinct is "sometimes called the feedforward of the brain information network" and detects "some features of fight-flight responses [in our] instinctive behaviour." According to him, instincts activate "protective measures of the brain's network" or even protect "neuronal nets against information overload."[17] More recently, K.H. Pribram has formulated a theory of the genesis of our instincts and thus throws additional light on the gradual development of our intuitive propensities and tastes: "Psychologically, instincts belong to the group of brain mechanisms which we usually call stereotypes...they encompass the routes of temporal neural pathways; their fixations are usually routed through the brain's hypothalamic and recticular formation regions. If certain stereotypes are maintained for several generations, they become archetypes."[18] Having experienced an "overload" or misfits of ancestral stereotypes, we usually reject or at least modify them.[19] From the traditional perspective, we can see any stable period as a social and cultural cycle during which certain collective beliefs and fashions and tastes take root, prevail, become banal and the reaction against them initiates a new cycle with its "fresh" sociocultural orientation. Each generation's collective taste for certain themes and certain categories of subject matter is challenged not only by posterity but even by contemporary critics crusading against the fashions of their time[20] or by artists not following the prevalent trends of their era.[21] The recurrent poetic themes, plots, characters, their prototypical conflicts, as treated by classical and modern writers of all cultures and favored by their readers, have become "information skeletons," (clichés). Their variants have fused into "information matrices" which characterize past and recent civilizations. Biometric tests which analyze such matrices can be compared to the Human Genome Project, which gathers, classifies and codifies essential genetic

17 E. Bergström, *Adaptive Behavioural Features* (n. p., Umea Press, 1983), pp. 23–4.

18 *Language of the Brain* (Berkeley Press, 1983), p. 122.

19 E.g., Victor Hugo's rejection of the classical doctrine, the Parnassian and Naturalist rejection of Romanticism and the Decadent rejection of Naturalism, etc.

20 E.g., Molière ridiculing the fashionable *préciosité* of the "sophisticated" cultural establishment.

21 E.g., A. France's *roman livresque* blossoming during the heyday of Zola's naturalism.

information on the human species.

The Durable Lure of Sex, Violence, Laughter and Miracles

Modern moralists often blame the media for the corruption of humanity: the press, television and films incessantly bombard adults and children with farce, sex, violence and freakish fantasies. The newspapers devote their prime space and largest headlines to brutal wars, crimes, scandals. The entertainment programs, financed by commercial sponsors selling everything from luxury cars to diapers, brainwash us, offer free lessons in depravity and destroy public taste. Social critics also complain that many contemporary writers imitate the venal media in trying to conquer (in whichever order) the book market and Hollywood. Before we succumb to such a gloomy vision, we should remember that works such as *The lliad*, *The Odyssey*, the Greek tragedies, would be dull and Boccaccio's, Rabelais', Shakespeare's, Molière's, Goethe's masterpieces could never become "immortal" without generous doses of murder, laughter, licence and the supernatural.

Sex? Flaubert's *Madame Bovary* and Baudelaire's *Les Fleurs du mal* are highly rated not only because they reflect the writers' consummate craftsmanship but also because of erotic subjects so "daring" in 1857 that both provoked judicial prosecution as potential pornography offending public mores.[22] In the ever relaxed French erotic climate both these works and the trials attracted a great deal of public interest long before we were "corrupted" by modern communications.

Violence? Malraux's tragic novel *La Condition humaine* (1934) could never become the artistic transposition of Chiang-Kai-Sheks's and Mao-Tse-Tung's precarious alliance turning into a bestial war without the spectacular atrocities of fictionalized Communist terrorists and their brutal rivals. We may well ask what subjects other than tragic conflicts, human comedy, erotic adventures and absurd miracles could writers represent in their works without dealing a death blow to the millennial tradition of literary commerce. In any case, neither journalists, screen dramatists nor the literary trade seem to contemplate a radical ban on "corruptive" subject matter.

While covering the professional activities of a former Miss India inside and outside of British Parliament, a Canadian correspondent offered his recipe for what sells papers. "It is the stuff scandal-sheet

22 See comments in ch. IV.

dreams are made of—a former beauty queen, Libyan connection, jobs with MP's, sex for money and liaisons with the rich and powerful," he proclaims with a nod to Shakespeare in the lead of his story.[23] *Time* Magazine squanders precious column inches on the same "Pamela affair," also borrowing from the Bard to call it "Much Ado About—What?"[24] Like his Canadian colleague, the *Time* writer sees the affair as a prototype of a never boring journalistic stimulus: "For Britons, political sex scandals seem to be as popular as May poles, marmalade and Miss Marple. The genre demands a beautiful woman of at least ambiguous repute, highly placed public figures and, ideally, a shadowy foreign agent who may be on the trail of state secrets." The article also cites, with some nostalgia, the London shocker of the 60's—Christine Keeler's tantalizing simultaneous liaisons with the British Minister of Defense and a Soviet naval attaché.

Voltaire's Immortal Satire of 18th Century Characters and Intrigues

If we compare the contentual formula for the ideal modern scandal with the topics Voltaire treated in *Candide* in the mid-18th century, we find little difference. There are obvious parallels between the modern journalistic gravitation to the secret amours of celebrities and Voltaire's characters embroiled in melodramatic, violent and erotic actions. Although digressive in the context of Candide's *picaresque*, romantic and violent pilgrimage, the episode discussed below serves to satirize the doctrine claiming that whatever is, is right. It relates the turbulent life story of Cunégonde's elderly chambermaid. One day, when Cunégonde starts bemoaning her own tragic fate, the maid suddenly reveals not only that she is of even nobler descent than Cunégonde, but also that the mistress' martyrdom is a mere trifle compared to her servant's past suffering. "Je n'ai pas toujours été servante," she opens. "Je suis la fille du pape Urbain X,[1] et de la princesse de Palestrine."[25] (Note 1 within the citation is Voltaire's own remark revealing that Urbain X is poetic licence dictated by the author's *savoir faire*. It reads as follows: "Voiez l'extrême discrétion de l'auteur! il n'y eut, jusqu'à présent, aucun Pape

23 James Ferrabee, "Friendly Beauty Queen Giving MP's a Scare," *The Calgary Herald*, March 23, 1989, p. A5.

24 April 3, 1989, p. 29, by Daniel Benjamin, reported by William Mader and Frank Melville.

25 *Les Oeuvres complètes de Voltaire—Candide ou l'optimisme*, ed. René Pomeau (Oxford: The Voltaire Foundation at the Taylor Institute, 1980), p. 153.

nommé Urbain dix. Il craint de donner une bâtarde à un pape connu. O la circonspection! ô la délicatesse de conscience!" In his critical note on Voltaire's ironic note, René Pomeau, editor of the original MS, somewhat rectifies Voltaire's facetious compliments to himself—"[dans] le dernier MS Voltaire n'avait pas craint de donner un bâtard à un pape connu: Clément XII...qui régna de 1730 à 1740." Pomeau's note 2 clarifies that Palestrina is a name of a principality near Rome.

At the age of 14 the noble child becomes engaged to Prince Massa-Carrara.[26] In spite of a splendid prenuptial celebration, "des fêtes carousels, des opera-buffa continuels," the wedding does not follow. The engaged prince is poisoned by a cup of chocolate offered to him by his vindictive mistress who objects to the projected betrothal. To limit the social inconvenience of this fatal blow, the Princess of Palestrina and her daughter sail back to the family domain situated on the Italian coast. Their boat is attacked by Moroccan pirates and the bereaved bride-to-be and her mother are both raped: "J'étais ravissante et j'étais pucelle. Je ne le fus pas longtemps: cette fleur réservée pour le beau prince me fut ravie par le capitaine corsaire. C'était un nègre abominable, qui croyait encore me faire beaucoup d'honneur." (Political correctness was not Voltaire's creative forte.) When they disembark in North Africa they become victims of the civil war and of the combatants' ferocity. "Cinquante fils de l'empereur Mulei-Ismaël avaient chacun leur parti: ce qui produisait en effet cinquante guerres civiles, de noirs contre noirs, de noirs contre basanés, de basanés contre basanés, de mulâtres contre mulâtres..."[27] O.R. Taylor, editor of another critical edition of this text,[28] identifies Voltaire's historical source, the Moroccan emperor Mulei-Ismaël (1647–1727). He points out that only two of the emperor's sons were involved in the succession struggle. Civil war is a hyperbolic *mimesis* of historical events which Voltaire chose and transformed into his subject. In the subsequent discourse of his invented character, Voltaire further unbridles his satirical fantasy:

> Je [la fille du pape] fus témoin d'un combat tel que vous n'en voyez jamais dans vos climats d'Europe...c'est du vitriol, c'est du feu qui coule dans celles des habitants du mont Atlas et des pays voisins. On combattit avec la fureur des lions, des tigres et des serpents de la contrée, pour savoir à qui nous aurait. Un

26 Ibid., p. 154; not a fictitious name: it is a name of a minor Italian principality—princedom.

27 Ibid., pp. 154–56.

28 (Oxford: Blackwell, 1942), p. 92.

> Maure saisit ma mère par le bras droit, le lieutenant de mon capitaine la retint par le bras gauche; un soldat maure la prit par une jambe, un de nos pirates la tenait par l'autre. Nos filles se trouvèrent presque toutes en un moment tirées ainsi à quatre soldats. Mon capitaine me tenait cachée derrière lui. Il avait le cimeterre au poing, et tuait tout ce qui s'opposait à sa rage. Enfin, je vis toutes nos Italiennes et ma mère déchirées, coupées, massacrées par les monstres qui se les disputaient. Des scènes pareilles se passaient, comme on sait, dans l'étendue de plus de trois cents lieues, sans qu'on manquât aux cinq prières par jour ordonnées par Mahomet.[29]

The fictional descendant of Christ's vicar is finally saved by an equally fictional former Neapolitan who was castrated as a child to become a singer in the chapel of the heroine's mother. Later, a Christian monarch discovers the singer's diplomatic talent and sends him to negotiate an insidious commercial treaty with the Moroccan ruler. When the heroine recovers from her coma the first thing she hears are the memorable words of her unknown countryman. "O che sciagura d'essere senza coglioni."[30] Hearing again her native Italian she is moved to tears to find at last a trustworthy benefactor. The compassionate diplomat promises to transport her to her native Italy but instead sells her to a Janissary[31] chieftain in Algiers. Again, according to one of the text's previous editors, A. Morize cited by Pomeau, the chambermaid's "savior" may have been modeled after "Carlo Broschi, dit Farinelli" born in Naples in 1705 who, following his career as a singer, played an influential role at the Spanish court.

The above citations from *Candide* and of some of the historical sources identified by the text's erudite editors not only illustrate the nature, range and genesis of Voltaire's subjects, they also show that "the stuff scandal-sheet dreams are made of" in 1989 resembles the contentual stimuli in his best known satire (1759). "Women of ambiguous repute, liaisons with rich and powerful highly placed public figures," have their titillating counterparts in his text: the ravished daughter of Christ's Vicar, betrayed by a castrated singer turned Machiavellian envoy serving an unprincipled Christian ruler; Voltaire's brutal Moroccan exoticism is a precedent of the Libyan connection in the Miss India intrigue. Algiers was a metropolis of pirates in his era and is an asylum of terrorists today. The modern sex for money has its Voltairean parallel in the slavery of the heroine, who throughout her life had to offer sex for nothing to

29 Ibid., Ed. cit., n. 23, p. 156.

30 Ibid., p. 157. "Oh what a disaster to have no balls." (My transl.)

31 Janissaries were the Sultan's mercenaries.

whoever owned her. This mock *mimesis* of 18th century violent crime, erotica and black farce exemplifies the imaginative conversion of an author's direct (life) and indirect (e.g., reading) experiences into the stimulating subjects of his literary art.

Journalistic and Literary Stimuli Have Much in Common

While evaluating the content of the news or topical features, reporters, editors and electronic-media producers empirically estimate the degree of newsworthiness, timeliness and factual evidence of the gathered material. Naturally, practical criteria for the esthetic impact triggered by literary content cannot be identical because the goals of literary art and journalism differ: in choosing their literary subjects, poets and writers consider mainly the potential stimulative power of the invented or fictitionalized material and the possibility of increasing it by stylistic techniques. Veracity and timeliness of the content are at best only secondary factors.[32] Yet it is relevant to compare the two disparate approaches to quality: in true subjects reported by the media or in those transposed or entirely invented in fiction by writers of poetry and prose. The principle of newsworthiness dictates coverage of timely events (and persons involved in them) which have sufficient informative significance to stimulate the reader's curiosity. Vice-versa, the fictionalized, imaginatively enriched subjects, in addition to being esthetically surprising, attractive or shocking, have to emanate at least an illusion of reality and credibility even if they are, for instance, utopian (e.g., *Brave New World*) or supernatural (e.g., *La Révolte des Anges*).[33] On the whole, journalistic and artistic contentual stimuli could be categorized under the same headings and subheadings.

Fictionalizing the initiation of Quoyle—novice reporter on the *Mockingburg Record*, the Pulitzer Prize winner E. Annie Proulx illustrates the media hunger for a scoop where there is none. Her reporter hands in his copy on the revision of the city by-law to the black deskman Partridge. "'Your lead,' said Partridge. 'Christ!' He read aloud in a high-pitched singsong. 'Last night the Pine Eye Planning Commission voted...to revise earlier recommendations for amendments to the

32 There are exceptions: the (temporarily) anonymous *roman à clé* by Joe Klein, *Primary Colors* (New York: Random House, 1996). While fictionalizing key campaigners in the 1992 presidential primaries, it perfectly coincides with the 1996 election campaigns. This does not hurt sales.

33 See ch. VII, ref. to Coleridge and the "suspension of disbelief".

municipal zoning code that would increase the minimum plot size...'" Not beating around the bush, the copy editor tells Quoyle what is wrong with his story. "It's like reading cement. Too long. Way, way, too long... No human interest. No quotes. Stale." Partridge requires short sentences. "Break it up." The material is dull but Quoyle's final reference to the resignation of a dissenting commission member offers a spark of hope. "Move it up," says the editor recommending the following improvement: "Pine Eye Planning Commission member Janice Foxley resigned during an angry late-night Tuesday meeting. 'I'm not going to sit here and watch the poor people of this town get sold down the river,' Foxley said. A few minutes before [her] resignation the commission approved a new zoning law by a vote of 9 to 1." The self-critical Partridge recognizes that his rewrite would still have to go a long way to become a scoop. "Not very snappy, no style, and still too long,...but going in the right direction. Get the idea? "[34]

News in Fiction

In modern literature, stimulating non-fictionalized reality and fictional subject matter often overlap. In his *U.S.A.*, John Dos Passos reproduces fragments of daily news in his artistic vision of America and arranges the unaltered headlines and selected clippings into narrative units (chapters) entitled "Newsreel" and/or "the Camera Eye." The result is an experimental mosaic of material reported by press or radio fused with the material transposed by the author's imagination. John Updike often makes his fictional characters watch or listen to the news reports reflecting the era. In modern literary genres such as the screenplay or *ciné-roman*, this kind of mimesis has become common: Ingmar Bergman, in his film *Persona*, presents his fictitious character Elizabeth Vogler, an illustrious stage actress, at a moment when she suffers mental/spiritual paralysis during her performance of *Elektra*. Suddenly, in the middle of the second act, she becomes mute, unable to continue. She recovers to finish the performance, but once off stage, cannot (or will not) speak. Temporarily hospitalized, she watches television in her room. Surprisingly, Mrs. Vogler tends to avoid television theatre; she is fascinated by images of the real world. One evening she watches a political report which shows a Buddhist monk burning himself to death

34 *The Shipping News* (New York, London, Toronto, Sydney, Tokyo, Singapore: S. Schuster, 1993), p. 7.

in the street to protest the government's religious policy. Horrified by this scene, Mrs. Vogler suddenly starts to scream.[35] Bergman does not transpose this shocking reality reported through images and commentary on television; he injects the live footage directly into his drama. The ensuing scream of the fictional actress links her with real global violence—creating a quintessential image of contemporary life.

Original documentary material plays an important esthetic role in the film version of Milan Kundera's novel, *The Unbearable Lightness of Being*,[36] which relates the tragic absurdities of life behind the Iron Curtain. The novel and the film tell the story of the 1968 Soviet invasion of then Communist Czechoslovakia. In the film, the original tapes and photographs smuggled out of the country by refugees are blended with fictional scenes to serve the artistic goals of the film. Juxtaposed with cinematic fiction, they offer a historical record of the shock and despair experienced by the real citizens of Prague along with the fictional characters of Kundera's novel and in the screenplay. This increasingly common meshing of documentary images with cinematic fiction, however, does not imply that the post-Goethean *Dichtung* and *Wahrheit* are becoming indistinguishable: poetic mimesis has to leave many transposed facts to our imagination, but whatever is transformed into literary or cinematic content will always reflect the author's very personal perceptions.

Gide's First Reading of Proust

We may assume that each perceived intratextual subject/stimulus has its specific degree of excitive potential conditioned by and variable according to the reactivity and general[37] background of each individual reader. Although, due to the difficulties related to probing such a potential, it may seem that the impact of any stimulative content is, at least for the time being, an indeterminate quantity, our common bio-

35 *Persona and Shame* (London: Calder and Boyars, 1972), pp. 35, 36.

36 Transl. M.H. Heim (New York, Cambridge,...: Harper and Row, 1985). Malik comments that Kundera's use of cinematic information skeletons exemplifies a frequent 20th century literary *cliché*. Readers accustomed to the rich, multilayered information environment of film easily follow the novel's juxtaposition of real and fictional events; literary-minded readers expecting epical cohesion may find the narrative fragmented. The same applies to *Kolja* by Jan Svěrák, only in reverse order: *Kolja*, first conceived as a film script, was re-written as a novel, in which dialog was condensed and descriptive passages were added.

37 Biological, intellectual, intuitive, educational, social, psychological, etc.

graphical experiences suggest the opposite. As critics we are sufficiently aware of our own and other people's predilections, tastes and idiosyncrasies; some domains of subject matter either attract or repel us. Relating Marcel Proust's initial setbacks in getting his 2,000-page typescript of *A la recherche du temps perdu* accepted for publication, Derric Leon alludes to André Gide's resentment of the lengthy psychological novel written by the young socialite who submitted his opus to *La Nouvelle Revue Française.*

> For a long time Proust's...typescript lay neglected on an office table. Readers occasionally came...and went away. After further appeals from Prince Antoine Bibesco, Gide himself opened the bundle somewhere about the middle, only to be confronted by a long string of ducal and princely names. Dubiously he shook his head... Society novels were not much to his taste. After a further long wait, the manuscript was returned. Proust was dumbfounded. He had offered even to pay all the printing expenses, and still they had rejected his book—the *Nouvelle Revue Française*,...he had expected might...appreciate his ideas.[38]

According to this testimony, the experienced writer and the director of the avant-garde publishing house did not even muster enough professional patience to read at least a few more chapters before reaching a fair decision. The kind and the bulk of subject matter were sufficient to undermine, at least for a while, Gide's interest in the work: shortly after the 1913 publication of *Du Côté de chez Swan,* Gide declared the rejection of Proust's manuscript as the "gravest error on the part of the *N.R.F.*"[39]

The apparently subjective nature of such responses seems to compromise their significance, especially in the eyes of literary theorists. Yet they explain why certain kinds of content are predestined to stimulate only an exclusive circle of readers to which a seasoned literary practitioner like Gide certainly belonged. But his first reaction to the "bundle" makes two things clear: as a director and reader for the publishing house, he found it too ponderous and the few pages on the French *monde*, which he managed to read, too trivial. His second reaction humbly acknowledges that his blitz diagnosis was a professional blunder. In this context, it may be pertinent to add a personal anecdote

38 *Introduction to Proust* (London: Routledge and K. Paul, 1940), p. 132. See also publisher Ollendorf's response, *LP II*, p. 198, n. 9.

39 Germaine Brée, Carlos Lynes, eds., in M. Proust's *Combray* (New York: Appleton-Century-Crofts, 1957), p. 7.

documenting how experienced readers respond to literary texts.

"Un Somnifère"

Some 20 years ago, a graduate student, who had finished her M.A. thesis on Henri Troyat's debt to Racine, came to consult me on her next academic step. She was trying to find a convenient Ph.D. project—meritorious enough but not too time-consuming. She inquired which among the then contemporary authors had not yet been so over-researched that a young scholar like her could hardly add anything significant to current crititicism.

I suggested several representatives of the *nouveau roman*. She read a few texts by Robbe-Grillet and found them too monotonous. In the next round of our consultation she followed my second proposal and read my copy of *La Modification* along with a few monographs on Butor. Three weeks later I found my book in the mail box with a "merci" note followed by a laconic one-liner—"un autre somnifère!" Her dictum immediately provoked some fleeting reflections on what a literary "somnifère" is, at least in the mind of a relatively sophisticated conservative reader who for several months analysed *Les Eygletières*, relating the tragic actions and conflicts leading to an incestuous adultery between a young stepmother and her adult stepson, to his homosexuality and to his tragic death. Yet she was reluctant to devote her scholarly zeal to Butor's refined psychological analysis of the adulterous liaison between a Parisian businessman and a Roman secretary.

Assuming that the Francophone student would be encouraged rather than discouraged by Butor's innovative form or even by his stylistic, easily satirizable affectations, I mainly attributed her rejection to the limited impact produced by the dreary subject matter: the 235 pages outline the deliberations which lead Léon Delmont not to divorce his loyal wife Henriette as he had planned, and not to marry his mistress Cécile Darcella who works for the U.S. Embassy in Rome.[40] Generally, the novel's material can be divided into three distinct domains of subject matter: the first includes Léon's reminiscences of various episodes leading to his infidelity and to his decision to divorce Henriette and marry Cécile. As an ultimate result of his contemplations during the Paris-Rome journey—a journey intended to separate him for good from his family—Léon rejects the projected marriage to Cécile and decides to

40 *La Modification* is summarized in *LP II*, pp. 209–10.

return to his wife and children. The second contentual sphere is a travelog-like *pot pourri* of livresque remembrances alluding to Roman and Parisian galleries, museums, churches, statues, paintings and the history of landmarks visible from the train. This cultural *contaminatio*, constantly digressing from the conjugal drama, is enriched by bookish references to Virgil's *Aeneid* (like Aeneas, Léon travels to Rome) and to the railroad timetables to which the travelling art dilettante and fictionalized reader of the Roman epos returns from time to time. The train itself constitutes the third sphere of contentual features: a multitude of microscopically described but not very thrilling glimpses of the train milieu such as the compartment's sliding doors, windows, upholstery, digressive sketches of anonymous passengers getting on and off the train or of the conductor passing back and forth with his punch, railroad platforms, landscape visible from the train, comments on the changing weather, light giving way to symbolical darkness. Such an abundance of tedious subjects is likely to weaken the reader's interest unless the writer saves them by his stylistic skill, his wit or by a fast dramatic pace and gradation. Naturally, the novel's intersecting streams of content produce many contrasts, but the dull atmosphere of the would-be symbolic train and the traveller's compartment prevails for the duration of the trip (and the novel). The humorless psychological vacillations of a solitary brooding businessman during his 22-hour Paris-Rome pilgrimage is the main esthetic information Butor offers to his readers during their reading time which, like his hero's travelling time, approximates 20-25 hours. (Even if read ironically, the "subtext's" humor is dull.) Butor's excessive descriptive material (modern rediscovery of Rome, travelog/train) and his psychologically convincing yet epically overstated account of an adulterous bourgeois love affair may indeed strike many readers as a monotonous "somnifère."

No scholar reflecting on his own extratextual fascination or boredom elicited by the subject matter can consider such individual responses of two qualified readers as reliable empirical indicators of the content's intensity and value, yet neither Gide's nor my student's reactions were unworthy of a sufficiently serious bibliophile. In addition, we may compare the livresque material and erotic subjects in Butor's *roman-puzzle* with other analogical topics: Anatole France's *Le Lys rouge*, fictionalizing his own liaison with Mme de Caillavet and unfolding the plot, first in the express leaving Paris and then in the poetic setting of Florence as France saw it during his era, exemplifies a successful topical fusion of ironic vision, descriptive poetry and erotic tension. Or, John Updike's recent *Roger's Version*[41] creates a high stimulative impact through dramatic point-counterpoint of Roger Lambert's reading the Latin original of Tertullian's *De resurrectione carnis* and his imagining the flesh of his second wife Esther and her adultery with a graduate student who tries to find scientific proof of the existence of God with the help of sophisticated computers.

Finally and above all, most of us assume that professional writers have a pragmatic (normative) sense of measure which reins in any author "trop plein de son sujet."[42] In a work of art, the quality of content is often conditioned by its quantity: optimal dosage is usually more effective than excessive,[43] or too sketchy transposition of subject matter. This sense manifests itself in all creative cuts or amplifications of contentual factors. Empirical stylistic skill determines any final choice of a specific subject, its quality, scope ("quantity") and its details. The experienced writer chooses and tailors the subject matter to achieve an optimal esthetic balance between the highest impact of the content and the greatest economy of form. The author seeks the maximum stimulative power presentable within the lightest stylistic frame.[44] The reader's sense of measure tends to reject everything that is dispensable. The Roman *multum, non multa*[45]—much, not many—is a universal norm. In artistic mimesis and its condensation of material, it is an imperative.

Signifiers, Signifieds, Referents: Theory, Practice, Neurology

The preliminary comments on the nature and significance of literary content—as well as individual readers' extratextual responses to it—allow us to assume that writers first perceive or imagine they perceive and then transform extratextual materials into intratextual content, literary product. These materials include concrete or intangible life experiences, for example, war adventure, social gossip, the fiction or news they read, personal relationships, thoughts, dreams or fantasies. The markets transmit the finished literary product, initiating the conventional writer/reader communication. This either leads to a

41 New York: Fawcett Crest, 1986, Part III, ch. I, pp. 160–194, paperback edition.
42 N. Boileau, *l'Art poétique*, Chant I, l. 49.
43 See above Bergström's comments on instinctive self-defense against "information overload."
44 *LP II*, ch. I, p. 10 considers this creative phase as the "first (negative) stylistic act."
45 Plinius (jun.) *Epistulae*, bk 7, par. 15.

sufficient mutual understanding between them or the reverse if the reader attributes to some signifiers different meaning than the author had intended. The specific scope of individual stimulation triggered by exciting subjects depends on their provocative potential, on their density and on the reader's overall refinement and instantaneous responsiveness. Readers oversaturated with certain types of subjects offered to them again and again in stale form or those nursing private idiosyncrasies, will reject the text. The parallel stimulative potentials of both content and style are subject to a relatively slow multilevel evolution. From the general esthetic perspective, the stimulating subjects represented in artistic texts include any natural or supernatural beings or things, any event, action, illusion, abstract thought, concept, fantasy, any allusion to real or imagined life and existence in the broadest sense which is capable of stirring up the readers' imaginations and thus, their innate faculties. Each single word—signifier—is merely a graphic or acoustic symbol (stylization). When we hear (signal) or read (sign) and understand it, it evokes the correlated signified from our memory. The writer and the reader independently determine whether to write or read a given signifier in a given microcontext denotatively or figuratively—in its semantically conventional or, for example, metaphorical or ironic sense. Discrepancies between the writers' implications and the readers' interpretations are possible. Thus activated signifieds provoke our thought and our imagination: we fancy and are stimulated, for instance, by Rolland's or King Arthur's legendary swords, Hamlet's or the Cid's code of honor, or the sick child's mortal hallucination in Goethe's "Erlenkönig". The Rhine in *Jean-Christophe* denotes the river dividing France and Germany but, on the macrocontext level it also allegorizes the hero's birth, life and death. While the text's stylistic impact springs from the signifiers (their rhetoric, prosodic, syntactic and macrorhetorical adaptations), the esthetic power of the subject matter originates in the signifieds evoking the referents. It also depends on our direct or indirect (e.g. bookish, schoolish) knowledge of real things or ideal notions which may or may not have been stored in our memory. Generally, literary critics favor credible esthetic illusions minimally distant from life and its verbal transposition; they prefer "real life" characters to artificial phantoms and convincing plots to contrived cabals. Writers often relate their tale in the first person singular to resemble an autobiographical testimony rather than a fictitious narrative. Linguists and semiotists reflecting on the language of literary texts pay little attention to the reader's esthetic need for strongly felt links between reality and the words which stylize them. Verbal transposition of things into sounds or signs has been preoccupying scholars for centuries. Are spoken signals and written signs linked with the objects, or even with intangible thoughts to which they allude?—that is the question which contemporary theorists argue in published disputations echoing the "hypostatizing abstractions" of the medieval "realists and nominalists."[46]

Scholes Argues with Derrida's Disbelief in Perception

In the seventies, the neo-Marxist review *Tel Quel* was a forum not only for the pioneers of the *nouveau roman* but also for avant-garde theorists such as Roland Barthes, Jacques Lacan, Jacques Derrida and Julia Kristeva.[47] This circle of intellectuals and their followers developed an unprecedented pedantic jargon and formulated abstract interdisciplinary hypotheses designed to replace "bourgeois" (and thus *eo ipso*) reactionary literary history, criticism and philology. Just as Marxist politicians (such as Marchais in France or Berlinguer in Italy and their lucky comrades behind the Iron Curtain) tried to destabilize the Western democratic legal order and liberal capitalist economy, Marxist intellectuals publishing in *Tel Quel* endorsed a long-range ideological campaign against "idealism common to bourgeois materialism." This initiative consisted of twelve scholarly commandments. One of them targeted conventional "language which believes to be the language." Its destabilization, the reformers hoped, would facilitate the "destruction" of capitalist *status quo* and "its mechanistic, revisionist mirror-image—the university establishment."[48]

One of the *Tel Quel* strategists was Jacques Derrida (author of *De la grammatologie*, 1967), who developed Saussure's speculations on signification, claiming that every signified (as defined by Saussure) was in turn a signifier for another signified.[49] Once legitimized, such an assumption affects the relationship between the denoted concrete or

46 *Mot juste* used by A.S. Pringle-Pattison in "Scholasticism" *Encycl. Brit.* 11th ed. (reprint 1920) vol. XXIV., pp. 346–56. They argued if "universalia", i.e., concepts of *genera* or *species*, exist either *in re, ante or post rem*. Today, deconstructionist Derrida postulates that the signifieds (concepts) may exist *sine re*, independently of perceivable things (*res*, referents); see the comments below.

47 See *LP I*, ch,.IV, pp. 73–4, and Peter Demetz' comments, ibid, p.48.

48 L.S. Roudiez, "Twelve Points from Tel Quel," *L'Esprit Créateur*, 1974, XIV No 4, pp. 297–303.

49 Ibid., p. 299.

abstract subjects and the corresponding verbal signs. It frees spoken and written words from their intended pre- and post-verbalized substance and thus not the substance but the autonomous verbal medium becomes the McLuhanesque message. A rigorous embrace of such a theoretical premise, for example in political and judicial life, could put the social, legal substance at the mercy of word-twisting rhetors and demagogues. Robert Scholes is one of the critics who challenge the contemporary confusion of tongues. In the following (here abridged) table he roughly projects our linguists' discrepant approaches to the conventional trichotomy (1) signifier (speaker's, writer's word) (2) signified (speaker's, writer's listener's, reader's concepts concurrent or discrepant) based on (3) external referent (real object or abstract idea, e.g., a common ideal such as freedom) designated by the intratextual signifier:

TABLE 1

Frege's	Ausdruck	Sinn	Bedeutung
Ogden/Richard's	Symbol	Thought (reference)	Referent
Peirce's	Sign	Interpretant	Object
Saussure's	Signifier	Signified	———

Saussure's disregard for perceivable substance in the schematized chain of communication provokes Scholes' amazement; "The Saussurian formulation, like most 'linguistic' views of language eliminates the third column and with this gesture erases the world." When Derrida elevates the same "Saussurian" neglect to a full-fledged hypothesis, Scholes rejects his apodictic allegations that "reference is a mirage of language" and that "the world is always already textualized by an arch-writing or system of differentiation which...sets aside the questions of reference." To suggest that the philosopher's unsustainable axiom reflects a serious noetic gap, Scholes quotes a ridiculous confession which, if sincere, illustrates Derrida's empirical anemia or his sophistry if seriously invoked to justify his linguistic guess: "*I don't know* what perception is and *I don't believe* that anything like perception exists" (my italics). Scholes argues that our words carry with themselves a "semantic field of potential meanings...partly governed by social code and partly individualized." To Derrida's disbelief in perception and referents he opposes his belief in a non-linguistic semantic sphere pertaining to our signifiers and signifieds: "*I believe* this is the most important and controversial part of what I am suggesting—it seems to me self-evident that *the semantic field for many verbal signs is not exclusively verbal.* That is, we carry with us...as part of language itself—...much information that is not...linguistic."[50] If Derrida's disbelief in perception were justified and if, contrary to Scholes' belief, perception did not exist, its definitions by reputable lexicologists would have to be dismissed as untenable. One of Webster's connotations, "awareness of object...through the medium of the senses," would have to be judged as a semantic illusion and Robert's "verbes de perception—regarder, voir, sentir" as incorrect examples. One would wonder why Descartes, Leibnitz, Rousseau, Condillac, Merleau-Ponty (cited by Robert) consider perception as a basic human faculty, if its existence is so dubious and why H.R. Jauss sees the evolving "human sensory perception" as one of the perennial "functions of art to discover new modes of experience in changing reality"?[51]

Elsewhere[52] Derrida parts with the "world textualized [in] arch-writing" to throw new light on the referents which teasingly appear and disappear in a small talk about the weather. He imagines that he is in a room with an "interlocutor" who (somewhat like the prisoners in the Platonic cave) cannot see the window and the sky outside. Perhaps to break the silence the theorist who does not believe in perception looks out and tells his handicapped interlocutor that "the sky is blue." For such an auditor, according to Derrida, the referents are "not present" and they would be "absent" even for the informer, if for instance, he lied and tried to "mislead [his] interlocutor." I find such a speculation unconvincing. The relevant question in such an argument is not whether the visual referents appear to be "present" or "absent" (absent when and where?) but whether the two colloquialists have ever become familiar with them.

50 In *On narrative*, ed. W.J.T. Mitchell, U. of Chicago Press, 1980, "Language, Narrative and Antinarrative." In this entry (pp. 201–8) Scholes alludes to Derrida's *Grammatology* and cites "Structure, Sign and Play in the Discourse of Human Sciences" in *The Structuralist Controversy; The Languages of Criticism and the Sciences of Man*, ed. R. Macksey and E. Donato (Baltimore: London, 1970), p. 272.

51 *Aesthetic Experience and Literary Hermeneutics*, (Minneapolis: U. of Minnesota Press, 1982), p. 63 q.s.

52 In J. Derrida, *Limited Inc.*, "Signature Event Context," transl. Samuel Weber and Jeffrey Mehlmtin (Evanston: Western University Press, 1988, 90), ed. Gerald Graff, pp. 1–23. In this translation the editor sums up "Reply to Derrida. Reiterating the Differences"in which J.R. Searle addresses 1. "Derrida's assimilation of oral speech to writing"; 2. his claim that what speakers or writers state does not reflect the intended meaning, 3. Derrida's concept of iterability (repeatability); and 4. his critique of J.L. Austin's distinction between speech acts conveying fiction and nonfiction (pp. 25–7).

Have they ever seen (perceived) and can they still remember any sky and any blue objects? Such past empirically perceivable visions of day and night, blue and cloudy skies, and of the pale, royal and navy blueness (once perceived, neurologically codifiable reality[53] serving as a material precedent of all potential subsequent semantic applications) are normally stored in and are recallable from human memory. The latent, more or less permanent physiological trace of the once or oft repeated sensory contact with the referent—seeing the sky and its varying shades of blueness—is reactivated if the interlocutor decides to verify the deconstructionist's potential deception, goes to the window and says:" The first referent you have mentioned—the sky—is indeed there. Under the circumstances it would be cataclysmic if it vanished regardless whether or not you try to see it. But in any case, at this moment, the sky is not blue, it is grey because it is raining cats and dogs." The interlocutor could not express his *argumentum ad hominem*, if he relied only on his conceptual signified and couldn't perceive the window and the color of the sky. Naturally, the referents are not stored in our brains like pickles in a jar, but the signifiers and signifieds implying them more or less intensely cannot be entirely divorced from the once or frequently observed precedential, encoded and remembered percepts either.

As scholarly as it may be, the theorist's disbelief in perception implies his disbelief in seeing, hearing, reading, listening, smelling, touching. Inevitably, such impediments make one wonder how, while seeing and hearing nothing, the theorist ever gets from Paris to Harvard to deliver a guest lecture; how can he find his passport, air ticket or his way to the men's room? And what does he do, if he tries to cash the cheque covering his honorarium and the bank interlocutor informs him that the monetary "referent has to be set aside"; and that, yes, the grammatological signifier is correct but that it is just the "mirage of [his host's] language [i.e., scription]." Clearly, if perception did not exist and if the "question of reference [could be] set aside," life, could become a Babel more absurd than Heidegger's and Sartre's universe.

The disagreement between the two theorists, one specialized in philosophy and the "grammatology" which "he had fathered" and the other in comparative literature and semiotics, cannot be settled by arguments based on their theoretical disbeliefs and/or beliefs. It is up to neurologists to determine if perception exists, if what we perceive is electro-chemically encoded and retained in our neural pathways and if, in

53 Perhaps Scholes characterizes it as non-linguistic information.

the process of thinking and imagination, our encoded percepts of referents can be activated.

A Biocybernetic View on Referents and Signifieds

Malik offers the following biocybernetic clarification of the above conjectures on the perception of referents, the origin of the signifieds and their nexus with the acoustic or graphic words/signs.

When information stimulus (heard, seen, read, etc.) enters the recipient's brain, it triggers an energetic reaction with catalytic characteristics in the brain's complete neural system. This system transmits with impressive speed the information quanta to the recipient's whole neocortical web (mindscape). An intensive, recurrent and/or stressful information impact may also penetrate deeper in the subcortical region and mark (or remain imbedded) in the neural pathways' envelopes. Seen from the biocybernetist's perspective, multiple information chains interact in stimulating responses which parallel their many variants, intensities and directions. Normally, information-chain energy flows from its source—speaker/author—(who selects more or less functional words/signifiers relating to the described subject matter) to the listener/reader (whose brain links the heard/read message with the corresponding signified stored in his/her own brain). There is a subtle but irrefutable systemic link between the referents once biologically retained in the writers' and the readers' mindscapes and the signifiers written by authors and read by readers.

On the margin of my remarks I would like to stress that, while sentics, perennial topics, fictional heroes and plots are today what they were in the past, the informational environment and readers, especially the younger generation, have changed radically. Their environment has become a multi-media information matrix and young readers accustomed to thinking digitally (in pieces and bits of information rarely unified into coherent concepts) have modified and will continue to modify their perception of traditional literary subject matter and its forms.

A Humanist's Deduction

Malik's remarks on the human brain and its functions offer writers and critics some assurance that (1) perception continues to exist and that (2) the signifiers adopted by various cultures not only have their correlated signifieds but (3) also can lead us to the correlated and verifiable material as well as to abstract referents defined in lexicons.[54] Further, we can be sure that (4) these referents, generally, are correlated to our functional semantic choices of either informative or esthetically evocative signifiers regardless of whether we use them denotatively or poetically. Finally, empiricism suggests that (5) the use of signifiers deviating from their conventional connotative range outlined in dictionaries often leads to confusion or demands explanation. When I see my labrador flushing a pheasant; when I pull the trigger, hear the shot, smell the gun powder, see the dog retrieving the bird, or when I glimpse a trout rising above water level, cast my fly, hook the fish, kill it, clean it, smoke it above the smouldering hickory sawdust of my Swedish smoker and eat it with my family, all my senses are involved in a continuing chain of perceptions parallelling my actions. Even the camera may document such a specific slice of my life. And if, one day, I fictionalize some of these past percepts, as a writer or critic, I sincerely hope that my "scription", all *grammata*/signifiers and signifieds will rally to resurrect the vital referents rather than some dim unverifiable abstractions.

"Full" and "Empty" Signifieds

Signifieds either allude to the specific subjects, actions or qualities or merely spell out a specific contentual nexus among them. For example, Giovanni Boccaccio sums up the content of one of his novellae in the following subheading: "Messer Guglielmo Rossiglione makes *his* wife eat *the* heart *of* Messer Guglielmo Guardastagno, *her* lover, *whom he had* slain..."[55] The esthetic intensity of the italicized, indefinite (*kenemes*) factors totally depends on their integration with the *informative* signifiers referring to specific (*pleremes*) signifieds.[56] The suppression of the italicized indefinite signifiers in this summary merely leads to the loss of grammatical cohesion and thus somewhat obscures the content. However, the informative signifiers still offer adequate semantic clues and potential stimulation to the reader confronting the slightly obscured statement. Naturally, the inarticulate content "Messer Guglielmo Rossiglione makes...wife eat...heart...Messer...Guglielmo Guardastagno...lover...slain" does not clearly indicate who had slain Guardastagno or even whose wife is made to eat whose heart. On the other hand

54 See discussion below on abstract signifieds.

55 *The Decameron*, "The Fourth Day, Ninth Tale," transl. Richard Aldington (New York: Garden City Books, 1930), p. 243.

56 Linguistic metaphors: Greek *pleres* means full, *kenos* empty.

the italicized isolated signifier/signifieds...*his...the...of...her...whom he had*" offer only grammatical information and no stimulation. The latter sequence could be a cryptic message in a spy story or in a livresque tale on a damaged document; in such a genre a similar rebus and its ultimate solution could acquire a high esthetic intensity. This comparison illustrates two major categories of signifiers: one referring to concrete and definite signifieds, both within and out of literary context, and the other indefinite, neutral, auxiliary. The concrete signifieds are conveyed by signifiers including nouns, verbs, adjectives and adverbs. The indefinite and stylistically functional signifiers articulate a grammatical and logical nexus among the definite "full" signifieds. They include articles, conjunctions, prepositions; demonstrative, relative, interrogative and possessive pronouns; verbal endings. Out of context, in spite of their important signified component such signifiers are mere grammatical abstractions. They become definite and esthetically intensive only within their specific context.

Mr. Jingle's Concrete Information "Very"

Some passages in *The Posthumous Papers of the Pickwick Club* document the esthetic predominance of the informative signifieds over the auxiliary articulating ones. One of the comical characters in Dickens' novel, Alfred Jingle, Esq., of No Hall, Nowhere, communicates elliptically. Mainly nouns and a few verbs "telegraph" Mr. Jingle's messages. Mr. Pickwick and other club members meet Mr. Jingle at a match between the Dingley Dell Cricket Club and All Muggleton. Entering the spectators' tent at the playground, Mr. Pickwick first hears the yet unknown gentleman's comment: "Capital game—smart sport—fine exercise—very." Shortly after, the mysterious speaker grabs Mr. Pickwick's hand and bombards him with the following words: "This way—this way—capital fun—lots of beer—hog heads; rounds of beef—bullocks; mustard—cart loads; glorious day—down with you—make yourself at home—glad to see you—very." When the surprised Mr. Pickwick inquires how the yet unknown spectator came to the match he receives the following answer: "Come," replied the stranger—"stopping at Crown—Crown at Muggleton—met a party—flannel jackets—white trowsers—anchovy sandwiches—devilled kidneys—splendid fellows—glorious." Later Mr. Jingle sums up the quality of the menu at the Blue Lion Inn as follows: "Devilish good dinner—cold but capital—fowls and pies and all that sort of thing—pleasant fellows these—well behaved, too—very."[57]

Intangibles, their Signifieds and Referents

Mr. Jingle's semantics reflecting his enthusiasm—the hyperbolic adjectives "capital, splendid, glorious, devilish" are abstractions which sufficiently express specific content. Nevertheless that content is not as concrete as "hog heads, anchovy sandwiches" or the metonymical "flannel jackets." Both glory and splendor generally exemplify ideal intangibles of the signifiers referring to ideals such as "freedom," "justice"[58] and so on; such concepts are conditioned by diverse variables. The most obvious among them seem to be (1) the lucidity and scope of the terms' connotations as stored in (speakers', writers', listeners' readers') individual memories; (2) the earlier mentioned communicators' imagination and erudition; (3) the recipients' immediate contemplative alertness; (4) their ability to assess the nature, function and the tone of micro- and macrocontext where such abstractions are mentioned; (5) their cultural inclinations and teleology undoubtedly further modify the esthetics of informative exchanges. Those among us who assume that the abstract referent of the word "freedom" designates one's absolute possibility to do whatever one wants to do including, for example, to commit crimes, have a much broader (anarchistic) concept of liberty than those who pragmatically associate the term with the constitutional guarantee of inalienable rights compatible with restrictive penal and civil taboos. A western jurisprudent generally using the term "justice/*ius*" links its use with the Roman law "definition" *ius est ars aequi et boni* which reflects Ulpian's and Gaius' concepts invoked in *ius gentium* and *ius naturale*. It has a comparable meaning, for example, in the context of Lord Acton's (1834–1902) dictum on the degeneration of any justice administered secretly *in camera*. The same word, however, has an ironic ring in the Ciceronian paradox *summum ius summa iniuria;*[59] in that context it does not allude to the "skill of finding equity and fairness," it satirizes *ius strictum*, restrictive literal interpretation of law or neglect of *aequum et bonum* invoqued by natural law. The often cited aphorism—

57 *The Postumous Papers of the Pickwick Club* (London: Chaptman and Hall, 1866), pp. 93, 94, 97. Among the contemporary novelists frequently using such brachylogies is E.A. Proulx, see above comments and n. 35.

58 Ideals generally known to communicating parties.

59 *De officiis*, bk. I, ch. I, part 33.

fiat iustitia, pereat mundus[60] extends Cicero's irony. On the other hand an empirical concept of justice may crystallize in our conscience and memory long before we study law: a mother dividing food among her children may demonstrate how equity is achieved and why.

This chapter prepares the ground for a detailed discussion on the specific informative stimuli, their categories and on their relative power possibly implied by authors and felt by qualified readers. We can conclude that the imagination of each reader responds not only to the contextual signifiers but also inwardly envisions the signifieds and associated with the previously perceived analogical referents such as characters, events, actions, objects, thoughts, fantasies, abstract concepts. When imagined, such perceptions may, in varying degrees, stimulate, bore or (theoretically) remain indifferent to individual readers. Further, we know that no active perception seen, heard, read, can ever take place without a correlated (and today recordable) discharge of fluctuating energy needed 1) to transfer the informative content and its stylization and 2) to process it in the reader's mindscape. The more we know about this process, the better are we equipped to evaluate the quality of perceived information, including all its artistic domains.

Although neither authors nor readers have ever disputed the stimulative effect of effective artistic subjects, they have never reached any consensus on their highest and lowest stimulative potentials. Is comedy more effective than tragedy? Do we as readers find violence more compelling than erotica? And is there any stimulative scale applicable to all contentual stimuli? We still don't know. Nonetheless, the empirical practice of centuries suggests that perennial topics, if treated in a sufficiently original manner, will always attract characteristic groups of readers. We can easily distinguish these topics and categorize them. Many years of reading, erudition and ever-active instincts make us aware of their diverse intensities in diverse contexts.[61] The main areas of tested contentual stimuli identified in the first volume[62] include extra-ordinary characters, actions, plots, conflicts as well as erotic, comical, supernatural, Utopian, magic, bizarre and poetic subjects. Each chapter of this volume examines one or several of these characteristic domains.

* * *

60 Ferdinand I Hapsburg (1503–64).

61 The overlapping of journalism and art is discussed in detail in the subsequent chapters treating the various types of contentual stimuli.

62 *LP I*, ch. VII, p. 135–57.

II

LITERARY CONTENT: ITS MICRO- AND MACROSTIMULI

"Ihr naht euch wieder schwankende Gestalten!
Die früh sich einst dem trüben Blick gezeigt.
. . . .
Mein Busen fühlt sich jugendlich erchüttert,
Vom Zauberhauch der euren Zug umwittert…"[1]

Heroes: From Homer to Carlyle. Villains and Antiheroes. Recurrent Characters. Plots. Epical Constants in Macrostimulative Fairy Tales and Myths. Microstimuli Quantified. One Thousand *Cinderellas*: Scholars Debate Deep Structure. Microstimuli in an Epical Macrostimulus: *Le Colonel Chabert.* Microstimuli in Kipling's Macrostimulative "If." Lyrical Stimuli. Humanistic Implications—*Écriture.* Didactic Stimuli.

Heroes: From Homer to Carlyle

Musing over Jean de la Bruyère's dictum, "the heroes' life enriched history and history embellished their heroic deeds,"[2] pedantic scholars might question the classic's crediting the embellishments to historians rather than to poets. Prehistory must have had its history but nobody kept reliable records of historical events when, in the opening lines of his two Bronze Age sagas, Homer begged the divine forces to "sing Achilles' Wrath" and "the man of many tricks," Odysseus. Without invoking the

1 J.W. Goethe *Faust* "Zueignung," "Dedication". Again you stagger in my heart,/ Ghostly players on illusion's stage,… ./Once more your spell of soaring art/ Awakens dreams of my youthful age. (*Sit venia traductioni meae*).

2 *Caractères ou les moeurs de ce siècle*, 1688–96 (Paris: Nelson, 1944) p. 89, my transl.

gods or Musae, but in line with the Homeric models, Virgil sang the *man* and his *fights*, "arma virumque."[3]

According to mythological rather than historical sources, Achilles, Odysseus, Agamemnon, Hector are descendants of the Greek gods. With their support they distinguished themselves as intrepid warriors and leaders during the more or less prehistoric Trojan war. The post-Homeric worship of heroic ancestors gave rise to cults which made the family of heroes grow. These cults began venerating as heroes other luminaries than legendary swordsmen and strategists. For example, the premythical singer Orpheus, Homer himself, later Sophocles as well as meritorious women were honored as heroes and heroines. Those who represented and embellished the lives of these new heroes were above all the Greek playwrights. The titles of their tragedies and comedies, such as *Antigone, Electra, Medea, Lysistrata, Prometheus Unbound, Oedipus the King,* and so on suggest that, from the very beginning of our literary tradition, unique heroes, heroines and their epic or dramatic struggles have been the major magnets drawing patrons of the ancient bards and playwrights. Reflecting on various kinds of heroism, Thomas Carlyle (1795-1885) added his own controversial list of heroes to the ancient stock of macrostimulative characters: the Teutonic master of Valhalla, Odin/Wodan ("The Hero as Divinity"); Mohamet ("The Hero as Prophet"); Luther ("The Hero as Priest"); Johnson, Rousseau, Burns ("The Hero as Man of letters); Cromwell and Napoleon ("The Hero as King").[4] Although not a single heroine appears in Carlyle's Victorian synopsis of paragons, his choices confirm what writers have always known: that any historical phase, any culture may produce striking individuals whose deeds the historians, journalists and fiction writers can chronicle, embellish, satirize or demonize.

Villains and Antiheroes

Epical or dramatic power generated by the representations of rivalries between protagonists and antagonists is often heightened by stressing the moral contrast between the two characters: for instance, while the violent duel between Achilles and Hector is vehement, Homer does not try to sway the reader's/listener's sympathies one way or the

3 *The Iliad*, ch. I, l. 1; "Ménin aide, theá, Peléiadou Achiléos..."; *The Odyssey*, I, l. 1 "Andra moi ennepe, Mousa, polytropon hos mala polla plagchthé..."; *The Aeneid*, I, l. 1.

4 *On Heroes—Hero Worship and Heroic History* (New York: T.V. Cromwell, n.d.).

other. The Trojan warrior is no less worthy than the godlike Achaian son of Peleus and the goddess Thetis. On the other hand, in Achilles' non-violent feud with Agamemnon (concerning the captive Briseis), Achilles inspires sympathy while the Greek supreme commander sounds like an arrogant bluffer. To maximize the contrast between clashing opponents, writers thus pit gallant characters against villains: Orestes, son of Agamemnon, murdered by his adulterous wife and her lover Aesisthus, avenges his father's death. David, the Judaic underdog, slings his stone right in the forehead of the boastful Philistine Goliath and then chops off his head with the bully's own monumental sword. The underdog's unexpected victory intensifies the drama of this biblical vision.

Ancient and modern comic genres also developed their own gallery of macrostimulative antiheroes. Homer, for example, offers a hilarious portrait of bandy-legged and foul-mouthed Thersites. Aristophanes' *Knights* satirizes and personnifies the gullible Greek voters in the antihero named Demos (Gr. people) who hires the sly Paphlagonian to manage his household. Paphlagonian, in his turn, is a parody of the historical politician Kleon, an arrivist tanner who, with the support of the corrupt business community, succeeds Pericles as the Athenian leader. Demos' two slaves—Demosthenes[5] and Nikias—persuade their senile master to fire the scheming Paphlagonian and replace him by a flattering sausage seller, the embodiment of vulgar demagoguery. Demos, counselled by Demosthenes, thus goes from the fire into the frying pan.

Molière modelled his "classical" miser Harpagon after Plautus' antiheroic Euclio. Plautus' Sosie (Mercury disguised as a servant in *Amphytrion*) is a literary ancestor of antiheroic valets such as Sancho Panza, Don Juan's Sganarelle, the pragmatic Figaro, Mr. Pickwick's cockney butler Sam Weller, or Hašek's *Putzfleck* Schweik.

Recurrent Characters

The primary models of macrostimulative heroic protagonists and antagonists were not exclusively developed by Greco-Roman and biblical antiquity. Various folkloric cultures also created effective character models such as the magician Merlin, Robin Hood, Bluebeard, Faust, Ahasuerus, the Eternal Jew; Golem, Eulenspiegel, the Pied Piper

5 His ambiguous name echoes both the name of his fictional master as well as the name of a historical military commander *strategos* serving during Kreon's regime. Aristophanes, who died in 388 B.C., does not allude to the orator Demosthenes born in 384. (Greek *theinein* means to strike, beat.)

of Hamlin, the Russian bogatyr, Ilja Muromec; the Slovak Robin Hood, Janošik, Sinbad the sailor, Alladin, and so on.

Each cultural cycle extended the list of immemorial heroes, saints, mentors, rascals. Gargantua, Pantagruel, Ponocrates, Panurge embody the Rabelaisian legacy. Cervantes begot Don Quixote; Hamlet, Lady Macbeth, Othello exemplify the numerous Shakespearean addenda. Inspired by Tacitus' *Annales*, Racine dramatized the Neronian legend of the honest Britannicus (son of Claudius), murdered by his odious step-brother Nero. Molière unmasks Dom Juan and Tartuffe. Madame de Lafayette's *La Princesse de Clèves* (1678) foreshadows the late classical and preromantic mimesis which gradually replaces the archetypal and legendary protagonists and antagonists by historically less distant or contemporary yet universal characters. For instance, Richardson relates the shocking seduction and rape of Clarissa (1748); Goethe portrays the suicidal lover, Werther (1779); on the other hand, his Wilhelm Meister (1795-1821) seeks the path to moral, social and cultural ideals of the post-revolutionary era. Diderot's posthumously published *La Religieuse* (1796) is a fictionalized sketch of Marie-Suzanne Simonin, forced by her parents to become a nun. In the convent she is victimized by a Lesbian Mother Superior. Her long path to freedom is melodramatic.[6] A truly Romantic protagonist and his nemesis are Victor Hugo's ostracized Jean Valjean, haunted throughout his life by the fanatic Inspector Javert. Balzac's Father Goriot is a *bourgeois* businessman ruined (like King Lear) by his pretentious daughters. It would require too long a list to mention all the memorable literary characters—individual or allegorical—ranging from the alcoholic clan of the Rougon-Macquart in Zola's saga to the four complex geniuses interacting in Thomas Mann's *Magic Mountain*: Hans Castorp, *homo Dei*, who listens in the Davos sanatorium to the teleological controversies of the Freemason Settembrini, the Jesuit Naphta (a converted Jew) and the sybaritic Dutchman Mynheer Pepperkorn.[7]

The variety and the role of macrostimulative characters in both classical and modern works leave no doubt that their colorful adventures have inspired the literary content of all typical genres with the exception of lyrical or reflexive poetry or essays. In this study I call these transpositions epical or dramatic macrostimuli; in their specific contexts

6 See ch. IV, "Peyrefitte's debt to Voltaire" and Appendix, Diderot.

7 In any case, chs. II–VII analyse a number of heterogeneous characters and correlated plots created by other authors.

they form integral textual entities consisting of homogeneous informative microstimuli, for instance, comical, supernatural, erotic, etc. Although their stimulative potentials also depend on their stylizations, as subjects (even outside or prior to their literary mimesis) they generate enough autonomous informative power to activate the imagination in real life. Due to individual inclinations, changing tastes and due to the cycles of our biases and nostalgias, the esthetic intensity of any contentual micro- or macrostimulus is unstable.[8] The names of the above characters suggest that these complex single subjects have a very wide range. They portray mythological characters such as Orpheus or Medea; they evoke leaders who have shaped our history—Caesar, Cleopatra, Charlemagne, Henry IV (V, VI, VIII); they put on stage fictitious social archetypes, misanthrope, miser or morons such as Ubu, in Alfred Jarry's burlesque *Ubu roi* (1896). Authors such as Christopher Marlowe, Gotthold E. Lessing, Goethe and Thomas Mann were attracted by the figure of scholar/quack or learned humanist Doctor Faustus and his supernatural escort, Mephistopheles. Each individual mimesis of the demon and of the mesmerizing half historical half-legendary alchemist, astrologer, necromancer, etc. Johannes (or perhaps Jörg allegedly born in Knittlingen around 1480,) reveals yet another vision of the *schwankende Gestalten*—characters haunting in Goethe's creative fantasy. Phillip Melanchthon-Schwarzerd respected as the *praeceptor Germaniae* (1497-1560), described Faust as "turpissima bestia et cloaca multorum [gutter full of] diabolorum." This historical hyperbole concurs with the folkloric representations of Faust as a corrupt charlatan who sold his soul to the devil to gain power, pleasure and wealth. On the other hand, Goethe transformed Faust into an enlightened Promethean sage in search of perfect beauty and his devilish consort into a cynical but cultivated guide. Thomas Mann fictionalized Mephisto's erudite disciple in modern Germany between the two world wars; his Faust is a brilliant student of mathematics and theology, Adrian Leverkühn, who ultimately becomes an avant-garde musical composer. In his schizophrenic seizures, Mann's Faustus argues with a Lutheran vision of the devil about the subtleties of artistic "beauty", its creation and originality. Half a century prior to the publication of Mann's novel, Romain Rolland modelled a comparable character-counterpoint. His Jean-Christophe Krafft like Faust/Adrian, is also a fictitious German composer and he too has mystical visions but his

8 See comments *LP I*, pp. 103–111; *LP II*, pp. 26–29, 99–108, etc.

loyalty to the Creator never wavers.[9]

In their quest of original characters, modern authors often transpose at least some autobiographical propensities into the actions or inner conflicts of their literary characters. For example, André Gide's Edouard in *Les Faux-Monnayeurs* (1925), Michel in *L'immoraliste* (1902) or Jerôme in *La Porte étroite* (1909), mirror the author's own contemplative complexity, esthetic preoccupations, homosexuality and restless "disponibility." To allegorize the absurdity of human existence, Albert Camus modernizes the destiny of the mythological Sisyphus and gives it to his modern characters such as Dr. Rieux in *The Plague* or Daru in *L'Hôte* (discussed and tabulated in the subsequent chapter).

In his best-known, plotless tragicomedy *Waiting for Godot*, Samuel Beckett creates two antiheroic loafers to answer the eternal metaphysical "to be or not to be?" Lost in an absurd vacuum, Vladimir/Didi and Estragon/Gogo contemplate a suicide in each act and then "solve" this forever dead-end dilemma in a laconic finale:

> ESTRAGON: I can't go on like this.
> VLADIMIR: That's what you think.
> ESTRAGON: If we parted? That might be better for us.
> VLADIMIR: We'll hang ourselves tomorrow. (*Pause*) Unless Godot comes.
> ESTRAGON: And if he comes?
> VLADIMIR: We'll be saved.[10]

On one hand, Vladimir's bleak prognosis suggests that their suicide may follow "tomorrow"; on the other hand, its daily deferment and an endless wait for salvation is a more probable alternative.

In her C.B.C. radio interview with Martin Amis about his comic novel, *The Information*, Eleanor Wachtel asks whether the author concurs with his fictitious hero Richard, who predicts "the decline of the literary protagonist." (Like Gide's Edouard above, Richard is a writer.) Admitting this is possible, the British writer speculates that this creative

9 See ch. VI, "Adrian Leverkühn's *illuminatio*" and "Jean-Christophe's mystical visions of the Creator."

10 *Waiting for Godot* (New York: Grove Press, 1954), p. 61. Also see ch. VII, "Beckett's experimental bizarreries." Wallace Fowlie (*Experimental Theater*, "Beckett," pp. 211–17), points out that critical interpretations are prevalently mythical and religious: like Charlot in French refers to Charlie Chaplin, Godot refers to "inscrutable indifferent" God. The critics associate the only prop on the stage, a stylized tree, with the tree of knowledge and also with the cross; the two tramps could allegorize "the fallen state of man." Beckett rejected these hermeneutic speculations.

bias springs from the common sentiment of growing cosmic insignificance: "[A]s we get smaller in the universe, as our centrality is questioned and then abolished, our opinion of ourselves goes down." This may explain why many contemporary novelists demonstrate what Amis confesses doing: "I've often set out to create the worst characters I possibly could, just to see how bad I can make them." Yet the writer foresees a "turnaround"—calling to mind the above-cited "*turpissima bestia*" Faust being "embellished" by Goethe. "As we reach...the end of the milennium," Amis risks a guess: "we've pretty well exhausted turpitude and evil.[11]

Plots

The creation of unique, fascinating characters is only the beginning; for such figures to achieve their full stimulative potential, they must have lives, destinies, unfolding in a sequence of interrelated, captivating actions.[12] This very linkage of characters with their actions, experiences and their fate is what forms a cohesive, powerful plot; gives the text its artistic unity[13]. For Aristotle, the plot was the artistic cornerstone of the Greek play. His normative premise applies not only to dramatic genres: an effective plot is also the macrostimulative nucleus of epical narratives. In both cases, a fateful nexus unifies the characters' endeavors. Without their inadvertent consumption of the magic love potion, Tristan and Isolde could never become poetic models of metaphysically predestined lovers.[14] One can imagine Perceval without evoking his quest of the Holy Grail but any mystically motivated knight without a specific mystical goal would be like an unfinished sentence—a promising subject followed by no informative verb, no direct and indirect objects. Captain Ahab's tenacious chase after Moby Dick in distant antarctic waters is an essential element of the sailor's adventures, culminating in a dramatic denouement. Lautréamont portrays his sadistic Maldoror as a libertine

11 Eleanor Wachtel, *Writers and Company* (Toronto: Vintage Canada, 1997) p. 310.

12 In Plutarch's historical *Biographies of famous men* (*Bioi parallêloi*) the historical characters' caliber corresponds to the caliber of their main acts. On the other hand, in de la Bruyère's "character" sketches (see n. 4), the mediocre social types are satirized but are not integrated in any major plots. E.M. Forster, *Aspects of the Novel* (New York: Harcourtt, Brace, 1954), ch. V. "The Plot" examines the anatomy and the range of original plots.

13 In lyrical and reflexive poetry, maxims or non epical poems in prose, characters or actions rarely figure among such genres' macrostimuli.

14 See ch. VII, "Cocteau's Muse Cinéma."

observer of sundry bizarreries and of episodic, fantastic miniplots hatched in a chimerical universe.[15]

Without separating characters and plots, Tzvetan Todorov outlines the gamut of prototypical plots under three main headings: intrigues of fate, character and thought. In the first category belong the action plot such as Jim Hawkins' adventures in Stevenson's *Treasure Island*; the melodramatic tale of sorrow-torn characters beset by misfortune, and its opposite, the sentimental plot with a happy ending; the tragic plot like that of *Oedipus Rex*, and its adjunct, the apologetic plot, in which the hero surmounts tragedy; the punishment plot ("intrigue de châtiment") exemplified by the despicable scheming and ultimate fall of Tartuffe; the cynical plot, in which villains triumph. The second category covers intrigues of character ("personnage") which portray heroes who seek and find maturity (Joyce's *Portrait of the Artist as a Young Man*); those who are rehabilitated after a major transgression (Hawthorne's *The Scarlet Letter*); those who are severely tested by circumstance, and those forced by failure to abandon their ideals (Chekhov's *Uncle Vanya*). The plot models designated as "intrigues de pensée" include the education plot such as *Huckleberry Finn*; the revelation plot, in which the leading character is unaware of his/her potential; the affective plots, such as *Pride and Prejudice*, in which the hero gains new knowledge of people, but maintains an exemplary philosophy, and the disillusionment plot, tragic opposite of the education plot, in which the hero is doomed by the loss of ideals.[16]

As Torodov makes clear, other ways of classifying plot models can be considered. I have chosen to discuss characters and plots separately as key macrostimuli under the individual chapter headings covering major categories of subject matter—conflicts, inner conflicts, eroticism, humor, supernatural elements and bizarreries including fantasy, utopias and so on. Thus various plots are shown to reflect, for instance, violence, personal turmoil, sexual adventures, social satire, mystical visions, etc., treated either comically or tragically.

General criteria distinguishing effective literary plots from either trivial artificial intrigues or from motley sequences of picaresque, more or less independent adventures experienced by the hero (for instance, Gil Blas, Baron von Münchausen, Maldoror) require (1) a single, engaging,

15 See ch. VII, "Maldoror's nightmarish wanderings."

16 Oswald Ducrot and Tzvetan Todorov in *Dictionnaire encyclopédique des sciences du langage* (Paris: Seuil, 1972), "Texte", pp. 380–82.

homogeneous macrostimulative condensation—not an anemic epical or dramatic accumulation. An enticing plot's core is usually a thrilling conflict or challenge leading to fatal clashes and causing the protagonist's and antagonist's tragic or comical dilemmas. (2) High density and intensity of microstimuli forming the topical and stylistic gradations within the subplots and suspenseful continuity. (3) Optimal epical or dramatic pace suitable to the genre (play, novel, TV series) and increasing the power of its subject matter. The classical esthetics of dramatic plots rested on the three normative unities of action, place and time. The above-mentioned plotless and static *Waiting for Godot* is a recognized experimental challenge to the traditional dramatic gradation of interrelated events building to an effective denouement. Will Beckett's avant garde salvo against tradition render its tested practices obsolete? Not very likely—it merely demonstrates that literary practices are not inflexible "laws."[17]

In many epical or dramatic texts the characters' stimulative power is often balanced or even outweighed by fast-moving macrostimulative accounts of extraordinary events—floods, cholera, revolutions or evocations of strange subjects, bullfights, satanism, utopias and so on. The frame of Boccaccio's *Decameron* (1350-55), Albert Camus' *The Plague* (*La Peste* 1947), Jean Giono's *Le Hussard sur le toît* (1951) confronts the characters with a devastating epidemic. From the represented *vis maior* spring the fictitious characters' conflicts and actions. In Ernest Hemingway's *For Whom the Bell Tolls* (1940) and in J.-P. Sartre's "Le Mur" (1939), it is the absurd brutality of the Spanish civil war which becomes the macrostimulative bond unifying and artistically determining the characters and their missions. In *Les Bestiaires* (1926) it is the glamor and risk of a bullfight around which Henri de Montherlant develops his original plot and which motivates his puerile, macho hero, Alban de Bricoule.[18]

17 It is also possible to gain acclaim with too much, rather than too little plot. Howard Hawk's classic 1946 film version of Raymond Chandler's labyrinthian thriller *The Big Sleep* received four stars and this accolade: "So convoluted even Chandler didn't know who commited one murder but so incredibly entertaining that no one has ever cared." *1998 Movie & Video Guide*, ed. L. Maltin (New York: Signet), p. 116.

18 Assessments of a plot's informative impact should distinguish it from the potential parallel power generated by its style. See *LP II*, ch. VII, pp. 20–8, comments on the composition of Gide's *Les Faux-Monnayeurs*, A. France's and Huysmans' novels.

Epical Constants in Fairy Tales and Myths

Vladimir Propp unravels the main epical threads woven by anonymous narrators into the texts of Russian folk tales, *skazki*.[19] He outlines their creative formula and identifies eight typical "characters" and 31 "narrative functions" forming the tales' plots; we can see them as microstimuli within the macrostimulative wholes. These functions describe the characters' actions or their fates. Like Propp, Lord Raglan looks for common denominators discernible in the plots of various heroic myths. His *The Hero* (1936) lists 22 fixed epical analogies which he calls "features". Although the two theorists' scholarly goals are not identical,[20] Propp's "functions" and Raglan's "features" are comparable: for instance, Propp's eight "characters" include the princess, the hero, the false hero; "function" 31 relates the hero's marriage and his ascendence to the throne; "function" 16 refers to the duel between the hero and the villain; functions 18 and 30 postulate that "the villain [be] defeated [and] punished." Raglan's first "feature" rules that the hero's (prince's) mother is a royal virgin (princess); feature 6 alludes to the father's or grandfather's intention to kill his son/grandson/hero and feature 11 to the final victory over the king and/or a giant dragon or wild beast (villain defeated); according to Raglan's epical model, the mythical hero marries a princess (12) and becomes a king (13) (ascendence to the throne).[21] Today, we may wonder why Propp restricted his epical prescriptions to the Russian folktale and Raglan to myths. Only the relatively rigid order of the macrostimulative information segments and eight stereotypical characters distinguish the Russian fairy tale from other works or literary fiction. Obviously, in the vast domain of *belles lettres* the range of character prototypes is broader; so is the range of all categorizable macrostimuli such as extraordinary actions fusing into plots. But *mutatis mutandis*, all Propp's "functions" as well as Raglan's "features" have been recurrent stimuli in epical and dramatic plots of all eras.

19 [19]*Morphologiya Skazki* (Leningrad: Academia 1928; French transl). See *LP I*, p. 14, n. 4.

20 Propp defines the content and composition formula ("laws") applicable to Russian fairy tales whereas Raglan is a predecessor of Claude Lévi-Strauss' "*mythèmes*." I consider the term "laws" as a terminological overstatement and see Propp's "functions" and Raglan's "features" as stimulative epical denominators prevalent in fairy tales and myths. Naturally, such stimuli have always been commonplace in epical and dramatic genres.

21 Robert Scholes' *Structuralism in Literature* (New Haven and London: Yale University Press, 1974), pp. 63–66, summarizes Propp's and Raglan's observations.

Designating these transpositions of unusual human beings, their deeds, struggles and their profound affinities with a general abstract term such as "functions," or "features" strikes me as terminological generalization ignoring their main esthetic, i.e., (micro- and macrostimulative) goals. Most often these "functions" and "features" form typical stimulative or suspenseful clusters. For example, function 12 "the hero is tested, interrogated, attacked, etc. which prepares the way for his receiving either a magical agent or helper," outlines a recurrent formula of a typical episode: it simultaneously alludes to a danger, a mysterious encounter, to the helper's (risk-taking rescuer's) possible gratitude or debt and supernatural help. Such miscellaneous information also implies dramatic or epical suspense or an illusory conflict obviously related to the hero's continuing macrostimulative struggle. Raglan's two central features prescribe that the hero "(11) after a victory over the King and/or giant, dragon or wild beast," (12) marry "a princess", often the daughter of his predecessor."[22] The specific stimuli in such sequences possibly include the suspenseful prelude to a (secondary) conflict, its culmination, a supernatural rival, or a bizarre hunting danger requiring superhuman courage and admirable force and finally, a paradoxical erotic bond between the princess (heroine) and her father's mortal foe (irony of fate). I consider such clusters of interdependent microstimuli (either overlapping or in sequence) as esthetic glue bonding characters and plots into a distinct macrostimulus.[23]

The theoretical borderline between micro- and macrostimuli is entirely empirical but, generally, also entirely clear. For instance, Michel de Montaigne's well known essay, "Of the Cannibals," forms a concise though occasionally digressive macrostimulative whole. It can be characterized as a skeptical causerie on the relativity of preconceived cultural notions.[24] Cannibalism is a tabu in Western society but it should be considered with tolerance when it comes to the menu of ancient Scythians or to South American aborigines. Montaigne interviewed one of them following Villegraignon's expedition to colonize Brazil in 1557. In his colloquy and its notations, he covered a broad spectrum of subjects idealizing (but not without latent irony) the primitive culture of Indians

22 Ibid. The happy ending is a favorite stimulative "chesnut" common in literary genres of all eras.

23 See comments and tables in *LP I*, pp. 95–106, and *LP II*, pp. 73–7; 102–8. Such concentrations often take the form of gradation or extended climax.

24 See table, comment and n. on one of its passages, *LP II*, pp. 62–5.

living in unpolluted harmony with their natural setting. One of their ethnological approaches to conflicts which Montaigne addressed was tribal warfare; on its margin the humanist also learned how the natives dispose of their prisoners of war.

> ...[T]he captor of each one calls a great assembly of his acquaintances (1). He ties a rope to one of the prisoner's arms, by the end of which he holds him, a few steps away (2), for fear of being hurt (3), and gives his dearest friend the other arm to hold in the same way (4); and these two, in the presence of the whole assembly (5), dispatch him with their swords (6). This done, they roast him (7) and eat him in common (8) and send some pieces to their absent friends (9). This is not, as people think, for nourishment as the Scythians once did (10); it is to betoken an extreme revenge (11).[25]

Obviously, in the essay's broad context, the description of exotic wars and their aftermath forms a sequel of episodic (in 1580, newsworthy) microstimulative shockers: the victor ostentatiously publicizes his prowess (1); bizarre technique of roping the defeated prisoner (2); the ironic correlated precaution (3); exotic privilege reserved for the best friend of the triumphant captor (4); following this prelude, the bloodthirsty tribe is ready to watch and participate (5) in the show's three climactic acts which Montaigne condenses into a brief, dramatic gradation: two officiating victors chop the enemy to pieces with their wooden swords; (6) roast him (7) and share the grisly feast with everyone present (8), even the friends unable to attend will receive a slice—a sardonic echo of the Western custom of sending absent friends a slice of wedding cake (9). After an ironic, livresque comparison with the ancient Scythians, the humanist further qualifies this cannibalistic banquet: its goal is not to feed hungry guests (10), it is a ritual consecrating tribal revenge; thus it could even be ironically read as a barbaric counterpoint to Christian Communion (11).

Microstimuli Quantified

"Une charogne" ("A Carcass") is the shocking title as well as the first microstimulus in one of Baudelaire's best known poems.[26] As an aspiring author, I discussed book titles with an established Czech novelist and reader for a major publishing house. He favored short,

25 *Selected Essays*, transl. and introduction by D.M. Frame (New York: van Nostrand 1943), p. 84.

26 See its text and exegesis stressing the role of Baudelaire's antithesis in *LP II*, pp. 81–86.

euphonious titles promising provocative subjects. Their elementary musicality was to be created by words with the liquid consonants, "r's" and "l's"—*Romeo and Juliet, Die Räuber, Brave New World,* Čapek's onomatopoetic *Krakatit, Le Rouge et le noir, Les Trois Mousquetaires, Treasure Island, Der Zauberberg* (the alliterative English title: *The Magic Mountain).* Any index attached to a comprehensive movie guide seems to support my consultant's esthetic as well as marketing empiricism: *Dracula, Prince of Darkness, Dragonseed, Dr. Jekyl and Mr. Hyde, Intrigue, Invisible Invaders, Man-Eater of Kumao, Paradise Murder, Terror by Night, Terror in the Jungle, Terrorist, Virgin Spring* (Bergman's *Jungfrukallan*). Can microstimuli be reduced to less than a word? Of course. No spectators watching Jarry's *Ubu Roi* will ever forget the first word they hear as soon as the curtain rises: "Merd**r**e![27]. The epenthetic "*r*" in the above "merd*r*e" exemplifies a minor farcical incongruity. Prosodic features such as rhymes and euphonies are most obvious reservoirs of "minimalist" microstimuli: "... je hume ici ma future fumée..." (l. 28 in Valéry's *Le Cimetière marin*), is a minor microstimulative topos ("I breathe here my nearing breath of death," my transl.) cited often for its stimulative alliteration and vocalic and consonantal harmonies. Baudelaire's rich rhyme in "Sed non satiata," Mégère libertine/Proserpine is a stylistic microstimulus crowning the sonnet's anecdotic *pointe*.[28]

Most often, however, the contentual microstimulative elements are coherent, brief segments expressing a surprising description, utterance, observation. The previously cited fictional Scottish prince Bertauld sums up his apostolic tidings in a simple formula which he hopes will enable the pagan peasants of Porcin to see the light without delay: "The God I preach is the only true God. He is single in three persons and his son is born of a virgin."[29]

The macrostimulative power of *Lolita* springs mainly from the novel's high accumulation of erotic (contentual) and comical (both farcical and ironic) stimuli. One of them is the author's definition of a "nymphet." It "microstimulatively" identifies the macrostimulative focus of Nabokov's antihero, Humbert Humbert and his fatal obsession. "Now I wish to introduce the following idea. Between the age limits of nine and

27 See text and comments on epenthesis and etymon, *LP II*, p. 43.

28 See *LP II*, pp. 103–110 and esp. p. 149.

29 See *LP I*, the discourse and tables pp. 94–118, illustrating the breakdown of microstimulative segments within a macrostimulative Francian passage.

fourteen there occur maidens who, to certain bewitched travelers, twice or many times older than they, reveal their true nature which is not human, but nymphic (that is, demoniac) and these chosen creatures I propose to designate as nymphets."[30] Such a semi-didactic bizarrerie heightens the curiosity which will ultimately be gratified when the reader learns that Humbert becomes the stepfather of the 12-year-old nymphet Lolita (Dolores) Haze by marrying the girl's widowed mother Charlotte. His bride is indeed one of convenience: she expires in a car accident before her scheming "Hum" finds enough courage to get rid of her.

Commenting on biometric projections of my microstimulative segments, Malik remarks that my tables[31] and his polygraphic follow-ups are both esthetic as well as biometric precedents of the recent cognitive science research which classifies elementary percepts in an informative discourse as "semanoles—semantic atoms." Like this research, Malik's biometric methods (as practised in the early eighties when he and I were gathering material for this trilogy) also clearly document that usually groups of words rather than single words or letters are, at least at present, discernible and interpretable in his biometric measurements.

One Thousand *Cinderellas*: Scholars Debate Deep Structure

Propp's and Raglan's inventories of recurring epical highlights in myths and fairy tales characterize the descriptive analytical methods of early structuralists. More recently, one of their successors, Seymour Chatman, has contemplated the preliterary roots of prototypical narrative plots. He asserts that "narrative itself is a deep structure quite independent of its (literary, cinematic, musical, etc.) medium." Carl Jung's metaphor "deep" suggests (according to Chapman) that the plot of *Cinderella* somehow sprang from (Jung's concept of) a primordial collective subconscious. To support this unprovable claim, Chatman stresses "translatability" of literary versions into non-literary forms: "*Cinderella* exemplifies a narrative which artists can treat as a verbal tale, as ballet, as opera, as film,...as pantomime and so on." [32] Such

30 *Lolita* (Greenwich, Conn.: Fawcett, 1955), p. 18.

31 Overviews identifying and analysing the contentual and stylistic stimuli and their segmented gradations, leading to synthetic valuatory appraisals of potential impact generated by the microtexts.

32 *On Narrative* (Chicago, London: The University of Chicago Press, 19981), ed. W.J. Mitchell, "Narrative Versions, Narrative Theories," pp. 209–32. Re. metaphor

"translations," of course, provide no evidence of either "depth" or of an atavistic genesis of specific characters and plots. Nor do they compromise Joseph Bédier's polygenic theory[33] documenting that some similar tales may have been imitations of early Oriental narratives (as Gaston Paris had claimed) but others originated in various cultures at various times independently from one another. In a positivist and Aristotelian spirit, Barbara Herrnstein-Smith rejects Chatman's idea of a "Platonic untold story" which would have to be a prehistoric ideal ("pure being") epical nucleus of "about a thousand variants of *Cinderella* collected by folklorists." What attracts me in her essay, perhaps more than her theoretical discard of Chatman's hypothesis,[34] is her illustrative summary of polycultural *Cinderella* variants. Her comments on Marian Roalfe Cox' *Cinderella; three hundred and forty-five variants...abstracted and tabulated; with discussion of medieval analogues and notes,*[35] strike me as indirect but convincing evidence of the esthetic longevity and persistent *esthetic* power of the Cinderella macro-stimulative plot and its archetypal characters. At the same time, she alludes to the limits of the cross-cultural *imitatio* distinguishable in heterogeneous ethnic treatments. (In them microstimulative variants are fitted into the macrostimulative epical mould; Malik metaphorically refers to such recurrent formulae as "information skeletons"). To illustrate the range of Cox' investigation, Herrnstein-Smith recapitulates an Icelandic variant (collected 1866). In it, maiden Mjadveig's dating style differs from the classical Cinderella's ballroom triumph—she does not marry a prince but a sea captain and she delivers an unusual come-uppance to her hated stepmother and scheming stepsisters. Having tied

---

"deep" see J.A.C. Brown, *Freud and Post-Freudians* (Penguin Books, 4th ed., 1964), pp. 44–8.

33 *Les Fabliaux Études de Littérature populaire et d'histoire littéraire*, 3rd ed., Paris, 1911.

34 Nevertheless, while reading an ad promoting "The Real-Life Story of Sylvester Stallone", she whimsically recognizes the "deep" epical contrast of "ur-Cinderella" in one of the universal Hollywood formulae, "rags to riches". She also points out that the Cinderella macrostimulative antithesis (my jargon) inspires Dickens, e.g., in David *Copperfield, Oliver Twist*, etc. (The reverse alternative "from riches to rags" appeals to ironic writers such as Balzac or Twain.)

35 London, British Folklore Soc., 1893, on its 1957 follow-up by Anna B. Rooth's *The Cinderella Cycle* and on the Chinese scholar Nai Tung-Ting's discovery of 18 early Oriental versions *The Cinderella Cycle in China and Indochina*, (Helsinki, 1974), H.S.'s note.

the knot, the Viking bride invites her stepmother to the ship where she and her sailor treat her with "salted meat from...barrels which contain the remains of the ugly stepsisters." Mjadveig's cannibalistic retaliation not only echoes Cinderella but, for surprising good measure, also evokes the sadistic nobleman in the *Decameron* tale, "The Eaten Heart." (Boccaccio's melodramatic triangle portrays the jealous husband who kills his best friend for seducing his wife; and, not fully purged by the lover's death, has his heart cut out, baked and served to the adulterous spouse. Learning what she has eaten, she commits suicide by jumping from the window).[36] If Chatman's "deep narrative structures" were more than a theoretical metaphor, one could ask whether Cinderella's deep structure grew even "deeper" when another shocking plot was "grafted" on it. From my perspective, the fusion of the two plots certainly increases the Icelandic Cinderella's density and for some readers its stimulative potential.

To form an opinion on the impact of literary information, I subdivide all major segments of macrostimulative material into microstimulative units. Such an inventory has to precede any synthesis, in which the specific impact generated by the artistic quality of characters' actions, plots, subplots and details is meaningfully assessed. Generally, a valuatory estimate of isolated stimulative "atoms" without a reference to their macrostimulative context is a sterile exercise; without the overall vitality emanating from vigorous stimulative compounds, the esthetic power of any informative microstimulus separated from its correlated macrostimulus often remains indefinite or more or less latent until the reader finally realizes its initially disguised role when the macrostimulative segment culminates.[37] Modern critical practices leading to a credible appraisal of the texts' global artistic effects are likely to accept the empirical premise that it is above all the concentration of cohesive, mutually supportive, informational microstimuli which provokes our fleeting impressions of their intensity. Such impressions are

36 See ch. I, comments on "Full and empty signifieds. See also a grisly punishment in *The Heptameron*, 32nd novella, in which the lover's skull serves as the adulteress' wine goblet. Also see ch. III, "Voltaire on Shakespeare," (ref. to *Titus Andronicus*) and ch. VII, "Maldoror's nightmarish wanderings."

37 E.g., in *Rabbit at Rest* (see ch. IV, n. 119) the hero's granddaughter tells Rabbit that, at summer camp, she was able to stay under water longer than other girls. Her small talk becomes retroactively stimulative much later only when the teasing display of her skill causes her grandfather's stroke. The first reference in this context is a disguised prelude to the forthcoming suspense and its dramatic peak.

common extratextual reactions which we readers experience when information activates the intricate process of imagination. We do not know how our individual imaginations respond to intensity levels (perhaps calculated by the author) when the stimuli enter and are stored in our memory. We react, however, whenever the macro- or microstimulative charges elicit our more or less distinct valuatory approval or disapproval; we terminate our perception not only when we are, for instance, sleepy but also when we are bored; we are eager to extend it, when the content and style stimulate us. As the anatomy and physiology of our valuatory mechanism continues to be under scientific scrutiny, we do not know yet if the intensity levels which, in the course of our valuatory responses to successive stimuli, are added up arithmetically or at a different rate. Do the intensities decline after a long storage or can they improve up to a point like stored red wine? Gradually, neurological research is bound to clarify the process of our perception and spontaneous reactions to stimulative qualities.[38]

Microstimuli in an Epical Macrostimulus: *Le Colonel Chabert*

The subsequent comments on the content of a well known text reflect my personal reactions elicited by calculated gradations of successive microstimuli, condensed in original macrostimulative sketches of three main characters playing an essential role in a fascinating macrostimulative plot. (The third character, the hero's wife remarried to Count Ferraud, is merely mentioned in the cited passages).

In epical and dramatic texts a fight or a violent act usually marks the climax of the heroic conflict. In Honoré de Balzac's *Le Colonel Chabert* (1832) it is the reverse. This cavalryman commanded a regiment in the 1807 battle of Eylau in Eastern Prussia. During the charge a Russian Cossack split the colonel's helmet and skull with his saber (microstimulative violent conflict) and the military surgeons, who found the officer's body, erroneously (although microstimulative, it is a key tragic mistake) declared him dead (heroic death), and had him buried alive in a collective military grave (bizarre tragedy). Nevertheless, as a

38 See the previous comments on the rapport between micro- and macrocontext in *LP I*, pp. 95–107. So far neurological research has not determined whether the growing impact created by progressive gradation of several consecutive microstimuli triggers a cascade of energy changes which are, or are not, fully stored in our memory. And, if so, what is the volume of impact stored? Is it an echo of the very first impact or of delayed reminiscing—"sinking in"?

result of unique circumstances he survives his burial (an almost "miraculous" paradox) and gradually regains his memory and reason (extraordinary recovery). After Napoleon's fall, the change of regime and following the marriage of his "legal widow" (a former prostitute, irony of fate) to Count Ferraud, Chabert emerges in Paris and tries to have his death certificate annulled (rare legal entanglement). This struggle is the core of Balzac's macrostimulative plot and its dénouement.

Balzac first introduces his elderly hero, clad in a shabby coachman's coat and looking like a pathetic half-wit, in the moment when he comes to seek legal help from the young *Maître* Derville. The lawyer's mischievous clerks are mistrustful and sarcastic when this future client tells them that he is a colonel who had died years ago in the memorable battle (contrasting farcical and tragic stimuli). They advise him to return to the lawyer's office one hour after midnight (a rather incredible bizarrerie). To Chabert's surprise the eccentric attorney (also an extraordinary figure) receives him at the agreed-on ghastly hour. The dialog preceding the nocturnal appointment is calculated to entice the reader's curiosity and to prepare the ground for the disclosure of a shocking mystery. Derville's first impressions are negative and misleading. This heightens the reader's anticipation when Derville's scepticism gradually turns into trust.

> En voyant l'avoué...[l]e vieillard se leva pour saluer le jeune homme; le cuir qui garnissait l'intérieur de son chapeau étant sans doute fort gras, sa perruque y resta collée sans qu'il s'en aperçût [farcical detail], et laissa voir à nu son crâne horriblement mutilé par une cicatrice transversale [the comic vision becomes dreadful] qui prenait à l'occiput [*mot juste*] et venait mourir à l'oeil droit, en formant partout une grosse couture saillante... [repulsive bizarrerie, gradation] La première pensée que suggérait l'aspect de cette blessure était celle-ci: — Par là s'est enfuie l'intelligence!...[(a) the mutilation provokes (b) the lawyer's ironic and entirely incorrect *blitz* diagnose which (c) sets the scene for an effective reversal].
>
> — Monsieur, lui dit Derville, à qui ai-je l'honneur de parler?
>
> — Au Colonel Chabert.
>
> — Lequel?
>
> — *Celui qui est mort* à Eylau, répondit le vieillard [absurd mystery].
>
> En entendant cette *singulière* phrase [ironic contradiction], le clerc et l'avoué se jetèrent un regard qui signifiait: — *C'est un fou*! [The lawyer's first conclusion strengthened; gradation; however, readers may anticipate a reversal—trusting the lucid character and his honesty.]

Chabert's engaging description of the battle at Eylau follows the attorney's silent assessment. Its opening takes Derville to the battlefield in Eastern Prussia. Paradoxically, the "crazy" officer's statement reflects no folly. On the contrary, in spite of its bewildering nature, his version of the combat and of his "death" gradually becomes credible.

> Monsieur, *dit le défunt* [author's paradox, black humor], peut-être savez-vous que je commandais un régiment de cavalerie à Eylau. J'ai été pour beaucoup dans le succès de la *célèbre charge* que fit *Murat* [Napoleon's brother-in-law, King of Naples, etc.], et qui décida le *gain de la bataille* [heroic courage]. *Malheureusement pour moi, ma mort est un fait historique* consigné dans les *Victoires et Conquêtes*, où elle est rapportée en détail [historical highlight]. Nous fendîmes en deux les trois lignes russes, qui, s'étant aussitôt reformées, nous obligèrent à les retraverser en sens contraire [additional strategic risks]. Au moment où *nous revenions vers l'Empereur* [legendary historical leader emerges], après avoir dispersé les Russes [false illusion of victory], je rencontrai un gros de cavalerie ennemie [new danger; gradation]. Je me précipitai sur ces entêtés-là [heroism]. *Deux officiers russes, deux vrais géants, m'attaquèrent* à la fois [impressive military superiority]. L'un d'eux m'appliqua sur la tête un *coup de sabre* qui fendit tout jusqu'à un bonnet de soie noire que j'avais sur la tête, et *m'ouvrit* profondément *le crâne* [details of violent combat explaining the dreadful scar; anatomy of heroism]. Je tombai de cheval [mortal wound]. *Murat vint à mon secours, il me passa sur le corps lui et tout son monde, quinze cents hommes...* [The hero's apparent death; irony of fate; absurd friendly help tops the brutality of the enemy attack].

Balzac's character further extends his dramatic flashback by imagining the Emperor's hasty effort to save the brave officer whom he respected.[39]

> Ma mort fut annoncée à *l'Empereur*, qui, par prudence (*il m'aimait un peu, le patron*!), voulut savoir s'il n'y aurait pas quelque chance de sauver l'homme *auquel il était redevable de cette vigoureuse attaque* [Derville's desperate client had belonged to the elite imperial entourage]. Il envoya, pour me reconnaître et me rapporter aux ambulances, deux chirurgiens en leur disant, peut-être trop *négligemment, car il avait de l'ouvrage*: "Allez donc voir si, par hasard, mon pauvre Chabert vit encore?" [A more urgent order would have been desirable].] Ces *sacrés carabins* [millitary medics cursed], qui venaient de me voir foulé aux pieds par les chevaux de deux régiments, *se dispensèrent sans doute de me tâter le pouls* [careless helpers; fateful négligence] et dirent que *j'étais bien mort* [tragic medical error]. *L'acte de mon décès* fut donc

39 *Le Colonel Chabert*, ed. A.G. Lehmann, London, Toronto, Wellington, Sydney, Harrap, 1955, p. 46. See an illustrative biometric polygraph of Bresky's reading this passage in ch. VIII, Table 8. The table also contains Bresky's estimates of the fluctuating intensity of the narrative and Malik's interpretations of the recorded data. The following six citations refer to pp. 47–9. Yves Angelo's film version (1994) starring Gérard Depardieu introduced Balzac's melodramatic conflicts to modern movie goers.

> probablement dressé d'après les règles établies par *la jurisprudence militaire* [gradation: tragic legal error; military red tape ultimately seals the hero's destiny].

The lawyer no longer believes that the grotesque visitor is a fool. He interrupts Chabert's flashback to let him know that he, Derville, may be in conflict because he handles the business affairs of the remarried Countess Chabert. This sudden allusion to the hero's former conjugal life and to a potentially serious legal and human complication obviously links the macrostimulative character portrait to the beginning of an extraordinary plot. However, Chabert is not yet ready to address his present troubles and quickly returns once more to his "death" and survival. From Balzac's point of view the stimulative potential in his character's past has not yet reached its climax. "*Ma femme*! Oui, Monsieur. Aussi, *après cent démarches infructueuses* chez des gens de loi qui m'ont tous *pris pour un fou*, me suis-je déterminé à venir vous trouver. Je vous parlerai de mes malheurs plus tard. Laissez-moi d'abord vous établir les faits, vous expliquer plutôt comme ils ont dû se passer..." Acknowledging that only God knows how he survived, Chabert speculates what may have happened following his burial: "Donc, Monsieur, les blessures que j'ai reçues auront probablement produit *un tétanos*, ou m'auront mis dans une crise analogue à une *maladie nommée, je crois, catalepsie* [mot juste: didactic bookish elucidation]. The *rare* catalepsy is a condition of peculiar muscular rigidity which the military medics failed to diagnose. Since he was declared dead, the colonel was undressed and buried in a trench with other war casualties heaped any which way on top of one another.

To secure an adequate testimony, Balzac invents a witness, a former sergeant, whom Chabert met several years after the battle when he was institutionalized as a madman in Stuttgart. His second credible flashback explains the "miracle" of Chabert's surviving his injury and Murat's cavalry charging to rescue his threatened regiment.

> J'ai rencontré, en 1814 [seven years later], à Stuttgart un ancien maréchal des logis de mon régiment. Ce cher homme, le seul qui ait voulu me reconnaître [unexpected helper], m'expliqua le phénomène de ma conservation ["miracle" clarified], en me disant que mon cheval avait reçu un boulet dans le flanc au moment où je fus blessé moi-même. *La bête et le cavalier* s'étaient donc *abattus comme des capucins de cartes*. [Fate's lucky strike]. En me renversant, soit à droite, soit à gauche, j'avais été sans doute couvert par le corps de mon cheval qui m'empêcha d'être écrasé par les chevaux [Murat's "rescue" operation], ou atteint par les boulets [incredible chance].

Returning to the interrupted first flashback, the animated narrator then attempts to describe the atmosphere in the collective grave following his awakening. The novelist rehabilitates his hero's senses. In the tomb Chabert could see nothing but, due to the rare circumstances, he could smell (air pockets) and imagined he could hear.

> Lorsque *je revins à moi* [resurrection], Monsieur, j'étais dans une position et dans une atmosphère dont je ne vous donnerais pas une idée en vous en entretenant jusqu'à demain. Le peu *d'air* que je respirai était *méphitique* [mot juste; allusion to decomposing bodies; hopeless situation]. Je voulus me mouvoir, et ne trouvai point d'espace. En ouvrant les yeux, *je ne vis rien...* Mes oreilles tintèrent violemment. *J'entendis*, ou *crus entendre*, je ne veux rien affirmer, *des gémissements* poussés par le monde *de cadavres* au milieu duquel je gisais [traumatic hallucination]. Quoique la mémoire de ces moments soit bien *ténébreuse*...il y a des *nuits* où je crois encore entendre ces *soupirs étouffés*! [recurrent nightmare] Mais il y a eu quelque chose de plus horrible que les cris, un silence que je n'ai jamais retrouvé *nulle part, le vrai silence du tombeau* [mysterious contradiction? What did the colonel hear in his quasi-mortal agony?].

In this situation, ironic fate literally lends him a hand: a (microstimulative) morbidly bizarre tool found in the military grave helps the buried man to get his wounded body out from under the soil and the corpses loosely heaped above him. A breathtaking struggle for survival begins.

> En furetant avec promptitude, car il ne fallait pas flâner, je rencontrai fort heureusement un *bras qui ne tenait à rien*, le bras d'un Hercule! un *bon os* auquel je dus mon salut [triple gradation; bizarre function of a limb ripped off by the firing guns]. Sans ce secours inespéré, je périssais! Mais, avec *une rage* que vous devez concevoir, je me mis à *travailler les cadavres*, qui me séparaient de la couche de terre...jetée sur nous,... J'y allais ferme, Monsieur, car *me voici*!

Finally, Chabert returns among the living; now the annulment of his death certificate and recovery of his lost assets can be considered. Derville, who had returned to his office after a successful gambling party, is so moved by Chabert's prodigious survival that he offers to split his 300-franc win and offer free legal aid to the destitute old man.[40]

The uninterrupted gradation of such informative microstimuli has

40 Ibid., pp. 47–52. A pedantic reader may see the last detail as a *collisio officiorum*: appealing to Balzac's fantasy. Derville, who handles the legal matters of Chabert's remarried wife, would face a conflict of interest, should litigation between Chabert and the wealthy countess Feraud follow.

several esthetic functions: on the microcontext level the reader perceives their immediate independent impact;[41] as they are interrelated yet heterogeneous and arranged climactically, they shield the microcontext against the curse of monotony. On the macrocontext level the concentration of epical details increases the overall esthetic intensity generated by the gradually emerging portrait of a unique character. Further, Chabert's gruesome subplot and its collateral stylistic symbolism, help to underscore the main plot's Romantic macroconflict between a *de facto* living but *de iure* dead man and a skeptical society and its intransigent laws: in spite of his astonishing rescue the hero continues to be "buried," not underground but in a legal labyrinth where there is no way out.

The microstimuli identifiable in the long dialog between Chabert and Derville indirectly portray the two male characters who join to overcome the consequences of medical and legal blunders. The microstimuli in Chabert's evocation of the battle of Eylau fuse to reveal the panorama of a dramatic historical event. Details linked to form an ascending topical gradation include cavalry attack, brief combat with two Russians, fall from the horse, Murat's "rescue" aggravating Chabert's grave injury, Napoleon's possible help, the medics' misjudgment of Chabert's condition, premature burial in a mephitic mass grave and the narrator's hallucinatory memories of sighing corpses and the silent dead.[42] These incidents experienced by the then young and dashing colonel are seamlessly yet contrastingly unified with the main plot, i.e., the cruel misfortune of the now old, forgotten officer sporting a comical overcoat. The shocking scar on his occiput, suddenly visible under an errant wig, Derville's strange timetable, his gambling passion and generous streak are relatively indivisible contentual microstimuli which link the two characters (hero/helper) and set the sarcastic anticlimax characteristic of intrigues treated in *The Human Comedy:* Chabert's calculating wife, now

41 E.g., the unknown war victim's severed arm used as a spade by the survivor to dig out his own body from the loose soil—bizarrerie.

42 A stunning resurrection is the climactic subject in Proulx' *Shipping News* (see ch I, "Journalistic and literary stimuli have much in common." and n. 35): the *News* publisher drowns while fishing. Minutes before his funeral, he comes out of apparent *rigor mortis* under the intense gaze of a girl with psychic vision. Charles Frazier's hero, Inman (*Cold Mountain*, n.p., A Scepter Book, 1997, pp. 178–80), seemingly executed by vigilantes during the Civil War, was buried alive. Feral hogs, "drawn by the tang in the air…dug out arms, feet and heads" of the executed "outliers" and miraculously saved the survivor of the massacre.

mother of two children from her marriage to Count Ferraud, not only persuades her "rescued" first husband not to claim the restitution of his estate; she even succeeds in making him give up his legal identity without any compensation. When Derville learns what his client had signed, he finally locates him in a dismal suburban shelter for senile or disowned paupers. Approaching the colonel, the lawyer calls him with his name and rank but the old soldier rejects his own name: "No, not Chabert! My name is Hyacinthe...I am no more a human being, just Number 164, Ward seven." (my transl.) Thanks to his own selfish wife and her heartless milieu, the traumatized stoic elects to remain thus buried alive until he dies.[43]

Microstimuli in Kipling's Macrostimulative "If"

Our physical life could not follow its course without seemingly immaterial rational reflections, or instinctive impulses preceding, paralleling and succeeding our actions. But all of our deliberations, fleeting feelings, desires, joys or fears are not always accompanied by physical actions. Many of our inner reflections remain immaterial but many of them enter into the vast domain of literary subject matter as soon as a qualified author articulates them in poetic form. Naturally, such representations of our inner life do not address the same innate faculties as epical or dramatic stimuli. While representations of artworthy heroes and heroines and their struggles merge in the excitive content of epical and dramatic genres, the mimesis of the human soul—its humanistic elan, its longings, triumphs or deliria—prevails in poetic, lyrical and reflexive texts. Such subjects acquire macrostimulative scope and intensity, especially in concentrations of cohesive lyrical or reflexive microstimuli framed in tightly written and stylistically effective forms such as sonnets, ballads, reflexive poems, maxims, etc. Rudyard Kipling summed up his popular creed of chivalrous integrity in a short paternal sermon entitled "If." The fictionalized listening "son" (you), emerges after hearing his father's breviary of humble but unbending "manliness."

If you can keep your head when all about you
Are losing theirs and blaming it on you,
If you can trust yourself when all men doubt you,

43 In this denouement Balzac reveals that Countess Chabert, now Countess Ferraud, used to earn her living in the streets...where her first husband hired her like a cab. S'il [Chabert] est dans cet hospice au lieu d'habiter un hôtel, c'est pour avoir rappelé à la jolie Comtesse Ferraud qu'il l'avait prise comme un fiacre, ed. cit., p. 95.

But make allowance for their doubting too;
If you can wait and not be tired by waiting,
Or being lied about, don't deal in lies,
Or being hated, don't give way to hating,
And yet don't look too good, nor talk too wise;
If you can dream—and not make dreams your master;
If you can think—and not make thoughts your aim;
If you can meet with Triumph and Disaster
And treat those two impostors just the same.
If you can make one heap of all your winnings
And risk it on one turn of pitch-and-toss,
And lose, and start again at your beginnings
And never breathe a word about your loss.
If you can talk with crowds and keep your virtue,
Or walk with Kings—nor lose the common touch,
If neither foes nor loving friends can hurt you,
If all men count with you, but none too much;
If you can fill the unforgiving minute
With sixty seconds' worth of distance run,
Yours is the Earth and everything that's in it,
And—which is more—you'll be a Man, my son!

To spell out his main imperatives Kipling needed 24 lines (six rhymed quatrains) which he rhetorically unified by eleven "if" anaphorae and epanaphorae (ll. 1, 2, 5, 9, 10, 11, 13, 17, 19, 20, 21); by 16 distinct antitheses (ll. 1, 2, 3, 5, 6, 7, 9, 10, 11, 13, 14, 15, 17, 18, 19, 20); a double "punchline" further strengthened by a triple gradation (ll. 23, 24). These prosodic and rhetoric features infuse poetry in Kipling's didactic creed, which consists of about a dozen commandments outlined as moral preconditions of achieving a single macrostimulative ideal. The eleven microstimulative "if's" call for (1) calm, *sang froid* (ll. 1, 11, 12), critical self-confidence (ll. 2, 3, 4), patience (l. 5), high code of honor (ll. 6–8), humility (ll. 8, 11, 12), tolerance (l. 7), vision combined with contemplative vigor (ll. 9–10), firm resistance to pressure (l. 17), ability to take a worthwhile risk (l. 11), social ease and understanding (ll. 17–18), unassailable integrity (ll. 19–20), and a thorough use of one's precious time (ll. 21–22).

Kipling's brand of uncompromising virtue understates the pathos of Horace's ode to *vir probus:* "Neither a base mob hurling wild insults nor an irate tyrant's threats can shake a just man's rock-like will." The Roman poet's staunch stoic would rather die than stain his honor: "Should the round sky collapse around him, he will perish fearless in its ruins."[44] Today, no critic contemplating the poetry of *virtus* can forget either Horace's or Kipling's prescription. As "If" is addressed to everybody, its elaborately printed versions are often tacked on the shabby walls of sport-club locker rooms; its integral text has made the *Concise Oxford Dictionary of Quotations* while its editor found only six lines of Dante's *Comedia* worthy of the same honor. As a daughter—not a "son"—, my wife found a framed copy hanging in her Scottish grandmother's home; at the age of twelve she was so fascinated by it that she learned it by heart (as had her grandmother!) and wished to acquire moral stamina à la Kipling. As I was drafting this chapter, I watched a televised interview with one of the British commanders participating in the 1991 liberation of Kuwait. Discussing the military challenge his troops faced during the protracted waiting for the operation Desert-Shield, he quoted the poem written a century ago. All of these "proofs" may seem to be trivial, nevertheless, like the ancient model, Kipling's catechism of manly probity ages quite gracefully.

Lyrical Stimuli

Like the comical dichotomy, irony/farce, lyricism also has its stylistic as well as informative side: its stylistic precedents are the prosodic forms developed to sing the ancient *melika*, i.e., monodic (solo) and choric performances accompanied by the flute or lyre. Ancient lyrical poets such as Sappho, her contemporary, Alcaeus (about 600 B.C.), and later Pindare (522–442 B.C.) began practising various prevalently iambic metres contrasting with traditional Homeric dactylic hexameters. *Melika* further introduced recurrent strophic structures common to folk songs. The miscellaneous stimulative topics of these poetico-musical stanzas corresponded to the cultural or social functions which they fulfilled at weddings, funerals, drinking parties and so on.[45]

The pioneers of this post-Homeric poetry, especially Sappho and Pindare, "discovered how with the maximum of art to pour forth strains of personal magic and music... The ecstasy...of lyrical poetry could go

44 III, iii, 1, 7. ": "Justum ac tenacem propositi virum / non civium ardor prava iubentium / non vultus instantis tyranni / mente quafit solida." The ancient fearless stoic will *die* for his principles: "Si fractus illabatur orbis / impavidum ferient ruinae." [My transl.]

45 E.g., *epithalamia* were sung at weddings; *threnoi* were mournful laments; marching or fighting incitements were framed in the martial *embateria;* victory odes in *epinikia*, farewell songs in *propemtika*.

no higher than it did in [their]...harmonies." This at least is the opinion of Edmond Gosse; elucidating the concept of lyricism, he refers—not without some reservations—to Hegel's opposing the subjective discourse of lyrical poets to the "objective" mimesis prevailing in epical masterpieces. He sees the later developed elegy, sonnet and the ballade as typical prosodic molds in which lyrical poets often, though not always, cast their deeply felt emotions—joyful elan, nostalgia, despair, tedium, spleen... In their literary tradition, the main stimulative goals of lyrical communication had become revelatory rather than dictated by conventional occasions. They disclose in "terms of pure art, the secrets and the inner life, its hopes, its fantastic joys, its sorrows, its delerium."[46] Integral citations and detailed interpretations of various lyrical poems in the first two volumes of this trilogy sufficiently illustrate not only lyrical but also reflexive and even satirical stimuli.[47]

In the broad esthetic perspective of literary practice, lyricism is not a monopoly of lyrical poetry. It may be less pervasive in the novels and short stories but the 19th and 20th century prose writers, ranging from Chateaubriand and Hugo to Zola, Thomas Mann, Giono, Camus, Updike, et al., benefit wherever functional from all stimulative features which help to extend the range of their excitive material. Several previously cited and stylistically analyzed fragments of prose document this common practice. Among them are the following three (here cross-referenced) excerpts which exemplify powerful lyrical stimuli in prose discourse. The first is Flaubert's rhythmical account of the irresistible breath of aristocratic traditions which overwhelms Emma Bovary as she walks through the resounding hallways of the Château de Vaubeyssard (an echo of her girlhood reading of Sir Walter Scott). In the second, Anatole France's rhythmical prose transposes a wave of melancholy which suddenly depresses the aging Franciscan abbot Fra Mino when he remembers his bygone student love in Bologna. The third relates the poetic pilgrimage to a solitary mountain cottage already drowned in the evening shadows cast by the still sunlit mountains; in it, Gide's *pasteur*

46 E. Gosse "Lyrical Poetry" *Encycl. Brit.*, 11th ed.

47 See Verlaine's elegiac *ariette*, "Chanson d'automne" (*LP I,* 114–122); Rimbaud's elegy, "The Stolen Heart" (*LP II*, pp. 50–6); Ronsard's mournful sonnet, Malherbe's baroque *threnos/oraison funèbre* (pp. 95–7); Nerval's and Baudelaire's sonnets (pp. 98–110); Villon's ballade (p. 240); Verlaine's "Clair de lune" (p. 240)' Baudelaire reflexive "Une charogne" (pp. 81–6) and "Spleen" (pp. 220–1); Mallarmé's "Brise marine" and "Don du poème"" (pp. 231–2)' Charles d'Orléans' "Le Printemps" (p. 236), and Paul Valéry's "La Dormeuse" (pp. 238–9).

encounters death and a hidden "treasure."[48]

Humanistic Implications—*Écriture*

The three mentioned texts are not only lyrical: each of them enriches the content with another level of meaning. Flaubert's extended antithesis contrasting the ancestors, who died on the battlefields, with their billiard-playing descendants who vy for victory in cozy salons, satirizes the young aristocrats. The counterpoint of the Francean Abbot's sad erotic souvenir is Anatole France's own humanistic regret that ascetic Christianity destroyed the pagan joy of life. André Gide's poetic as well as gravely ironic account of the pastor's charitable love is also the first hint of his future love for Gertrude, an erotic bond which will ruin his family's happiness. The subjects implied by stylistic features such as extended antitheses, sublime ironic undertone, allegories or poetic ambiguities often reflect the author's humanistic outlook which, like any stimulus, has its connotation and potential intensity.

Roland Barthes draws a line between language, style and its function, which he metaphorically designates as *écriture*/handwriting. Without defining this concept, he comments on his theoretical distinctions as follows: "Langue et Style sont des objets; l'écriture est une fonction: elle est le rapport entre la création et la société, elle est le langage littéraire transformé par sa destination sociale, elle est la forme saisie dans son intention humaine et liée ainsi aux grandes crises de l'Histoire."[49] Analyzing writing techniques of modern French authors who use the customary literary *passé simple* (preterite tense) obsolete in spoken French, Barthes (a critic close to the Marxist *Tel Quel* group) claims that such writing is not an innocent stylistic procedure but a crypto-bourgeois support of the cultural and capitalistic status quo. Such criticism is, of course, a personal and politically colored opinion which Barthes was never able to document.[50]

In this study, depending on their context and their micro- or macrostimulative scope, I consider major teleological implications in literary art as didactic or humanistic themes and minor reflections of authorial opinion as microstimulative subjects, usually didactic, ideological or satirical.

48 See *LP II*, pp. 158–60; 161–3; and 34–5.

49 *Le Degré zéro de l'écriture* (Paris: éd. du Seuil, 1953), pp. 19–25.

50 See *LP I*, pp. 46–49 and nn. 10, 19 and pp. 73–4, nn. 6, 7, 8; also see Terence Hawkes, *Structuralism and Semiotics* (London: Methuen, 1977), pp. 106–22.

Didactic Stimuli

Addressing our curiosity and contemplative faculties, effective didactic stimuli mainly advance our knowledge. However, such sparks of intellectual and spiritual enlightenment may enrich not only our individual erudition but also our wisdom.

La Rochefoucauld's "Maxime 377, on the shortcomings of sharp intelligence [51], is a microstimulus in his macrostimulative comments on human reason, intelligence ("esprit") and judgment. Such a context covers, for instance, the "pre-freudian " maxime 102, "L'esprit est toujours la dupe du coeur"; the paradoxical maxime 415, "L'esprit nous sert quelques fois à faire hardiment des sottises," which reiterates the author's lack of confidence in high brow intellectualism lacking intuitive skeptical wisdom and his maxime 425, "La pénétration a un air de deviner qui flatte plus notre vanité que toutes les autres qualités de l'esprit." In genres consisting of proverbial axioms, common sense and pragmatic criteria determine when and how many microstimuli form a macrostimulus. What counts is the bulk, thematic unity and nature of aphoristic accumulations. No matter how profound its humanistic counsel, an isolated maxim woven into an epic or dramatic plot cannot suddenly become a macrostimulative feature. For instance, the Homeric "aíèn aristeuein kai hypeírochon émmenai állōn" (*Iliad*, VI, 208)—always to be best and distinguished above the rest," is a *topos* memorized in schools by many generations of students whose teachers tell them that this line sums up man's competitive drive, his goal of life. In spite of this pedagogic emphasis, in its context, this bit of wisdom is not macrostimulative: heroes Glaucus and Diomedes meet on the battlefield. Before slaughtering one another, Diomedes prudently checks whether or not his rival is a god. (He does not fight gods). Outlining his family tree with epical width Glaucus, grandson of Bellerophon, casually alludes to the above proverbial advice which his father Hippolochus gave him before sending him to Troy. Paradoxically, the legendary dictum, instead of presaging a deadly fight, leads to friendship. At the mention of Hippolochus, son of Bellerophon, Diomedes announces that his ancestor, the godlike Oeneus, entertained and exchanged gifts with Bellerophon and declares Glaucus an old family friend. The projected duel never takes place and in the context of this reversal the cited imperative is

51 Le plus grand défaut de la pénétration, n'est pas de n'aller point jusqu'au but, c'est de le passer." Extensively discussed in *LP I*, pp. 80–7.

esthetically secondary. A socio-critic reading this passage may be stimulated more by the mythical formula of diffusing the threat of a violent confrontation than by Homeric's didactic postulate of competitive excellence: the ancient exchange of gifts is an embryo of peace on the international level. Thus the passage would fit (as an illustrative footnote) in Marcel Mauss' sociological arguments outlined in his *Essai sur le don* (1923–24).

On the other hand, the three climactic hexameters in the prophetic vision of Rome's future which Aeneas has in Hades (*The Aeneid* VI, 851–3), sum up the chant's macrostimulative significance; they read like a solemn breviary of Roman imperialism. Students in the classical lycées also had to learn this *topos* by heart because it sums up the highest historical mission of ancient Rome—"to rule over nations, impose peace, spare the humble and battle the arrogant foes." Pascal's *Pensées* (numbered apodictic axioms) on art, style or on miseries of agnostics, or La Rochefoucauld's maxims on human reason subservient to domineering passions (instincts) are microstimulative if they are isolated and examined each on its own merit. When read as homogeneous catechism of wisdom they spell out two humanistic (macrostimulative) creeds, one Jansenist the other skeptical.[52]

* * *

52 The tables in the previous and this volume, tables identifying topical and stylistic stimuli in prose, poems or essays, suggest how to assess the incitive features in any literary genre including aphorisms or reflexive essays. In the interest of editorial economy the macro- and microstimuli are discussed jointly under the pertinent chapter headings. Macrostimuli with the highest density of, for example, supernatural microstimuli will be treated in the chapter analyzing the supernatural incongruities on both micro- as well as macro-stimulative levels. In my exegesis, marginal, say erotic or comical accents within prevalently supernatural macrostimulative material, have to be deemphasized, wherever digression could obscure the main issue under scrutiny.

III

CONFLICTS

"War is the Father of all, the King of all."
"O baby. Violence today is *hot.* It is what people *want."*[1]

Creator vs. Creation, Eve's Inner Conflict. Achilles Kills Hector: *Deus ex machina.* Esthetics of Violence, Fear, Risk. Cycles of Mimesis: Voltaire on Shakespeare and Rabelais. Mock Violence in Rabelaisian Utopia. War and Duels in Voltaire's Satire. Regicide in *The Heptameron* and *Lorenzaccio.* Executions: Anatole France. Stendhal. Sartre. Zikmund Winter. Terrorist Tchen: Malraux' Communist Martyr. Psychological Conflicts: Biblical and Ancient. Inner Conflict: Medieval and Classical. Sacrifice of a Patriotic Prostitute. White Man's Burden French Style. Rutherford's Thesaurus of Russian Atrocities. The Tatar. Ivan. Intensified Conflicts. "Gut" Reactions.

Creator vs. Creation, Eves's Inner Conflict

No sooner had God created Adam and Eve than he had a conflict with them. Because they violated his house rules and sought self-education, He expelled them from the Garden of Eden. On one side the Omniscient may have granted them free will but on the other He somewhat sadistically forbade them to eat the fruit of the Tree of Knowledge, which he nonetheless had placed temptingly within their reach. Did He wish to entrap them with the help of the satanic snake, whom He first created and then punished? The first inner (psychological) conflict was born—to know or not to know, to enjoy the tasty fruit or let it rot, to obey or disobey the jealous Lord. The Biblical pair suffered another blow in terrestrial exile when Cain, their firstborn, killed his

1 Heraclitus of Ephesus (530–470 B.C.), *Peri fyseos (On Nature)* cit. and transl. by G.H. Clark, "The Beginnings of Greek Philosophy" in *History of Philosophical Systems*, ed. Vergilius Form (New York: Philosophical Library 1950), p. 73; and Salmon Rushdie (his ital.), *The Moor's Last Sigh* (London: J. Cape 1995) p. 306.

younger brother Abel out of resentment over the preference Jehovah showed to Abel.[2]

Hesiod also relates a primordial conflict between the mankind-loving demiurge Prometheus and the gods jealously guarding their Olympian fire, the mythological key to technological progress and to a higher, perhaps divine power.[3]

Achilles Kills Hector: *Deus ex machina*

One does not have to be a literary scholar to know that any battle, whether between gods and mortals or whether in war, politics or love, thrills the participants and fascinates observers and posterity. Since the very beginning of our poetic tradition, literary transposition of diverse conflicts has been a major stimulant. The *Iliad* represents the whole range of heroic, tragic, comic, collective or personal clashes which have served as models of fundamental esthetic subjects. In addition, many literary protagonists and antagonists also experience traumatic inner conflicts. Among the highlights of the Trojan war as told by Homer is the memorable duel between Achilles and Hector (chant XXII). Following Hector's victory over Patrocles, Achilles overcomes his hatred of Agamemnon (who usurped his war-prize concubine Briseis) and returns to the battlefield to avenge his friend's death. His decision changes the war's tide and invigorates the fading Achaean ranks. The final stage of a long war begins. (1). After slaying a number of Trojan defenders, he is eager to challenge Troia's prince, the fearless Hector. While the stunned Trojan warriors rapidly seek shelter behind the city walls (2), Hector, insidiously encouraged by the ruse of Pallas Athena, gives no ground and without any support faces his mortal foe (3). Prior to his attack, Achilles boasts that Pallas Athena will help him to defeat the hated Hector (4). Several suspenseful ups and downs (5–9) precede the last four (10–13) climactic segments relating Achilles' retaliation: Achilles' first blow fails—Hector dodges his "long-shadowed spear"(5); however, the godess intercepts it and gives it back to her protégé (6). During this miracle the Trojan has enough time to mock the "godlike" and "glib-tongued" Achaean: it is now Achilles' turn to dodge the bronze spear of Hector (7). He does not miss but his spear rebounds from Achilles' shield which was especially made for him by the god Hephaestus (8). Hector's divine

2 *Genesis*, chs. 3,4.
3 *Theogony*, 507–616.

protector, Apollo, fatefully fails to safeguard him.[4] With only his sword in hand, Hector has to face Achilles who, with supernatural help, regains his deadly weapon (9). After the dramatic reversal Achilles plants his spear right in Hector's throat, but without piercing his windpipe (10). This allows the poet to prolong the dialog between the "swift-footed" victor and the Trojan prince. "Dog, beseech me neither by my knees nor by my parents. Would that my angry heart would let me cut off your raw flesh and eat for what you have done to me," Achilles says (11). Before "his soul flees from his limbs to the house of Death", Hector has enough time to forebode that his divine ally, Phoebus Apollo, will slay Achilles for all his valor (12). Achilles pulls out his spear from Hector's throat, makes a few heroic comments and punctuates his mythical triumph by a brutal show of power (13):

> He [Achilles] spoke, and devised foul treatment for godlike Hector. The tendons of both feet he pierced behind from heel to ankle and threaded them with ox-hide thongs and tied them to his chariot and allowed the head to drag. He mounted the chariot, held aloft the glorious armour, and lashed the horses to a gallop, and not unwillingly the pair flew off. A cloud of dust rose from the dragging Hector.[5]

Without such brutal triumphs no fascinating characters, plots or epic or dramatic genres could be created. Without them poetry would not only be impoverished, it would become dull. "War makes rattling good history; but peace is poor reading."[6] Homer speculated that our longing to be the best and superior to others[7] is an urgent force behind our destinies; our ambitions drive us to seek victories and risk the defeats. The proverbial Horatian *topos* "Lovely and honorable it is to die for one's fatherland"[8] mythifies the glory of death on the battlefield.

The numbers within the paraphrased macrostimulative gradation mark my responses to 13 successive microstimuli. Table 2 schematizes the gradual intensity growth within the epical climax.

4 See ch. VI, "God of *Genesis* and the Greek Gods."

5 *The Iliad*, transl. A.H. Chase and W.G. Perry Jr., Bantam Classics, 1972, p. 343.

6 Thomas Hardy, *The Dynasts* (II, ch. V). Critics of all eras assume that without conflict there is no tragedy. See Hegel's comments in nn. 10 and 65. Roland Barthes, *Sur Racine*, (Paris, Seuil 1963), p. 34: "Le conflit est fondamental chez Racine. On le trouve dans toutes ses tragédies."

7 See *LP I*, p. 54, n. 4 and above ch. II, "Didactic stimuli."

8 *Carmina, II*, 2, 2, l. 13.

TABLE 2

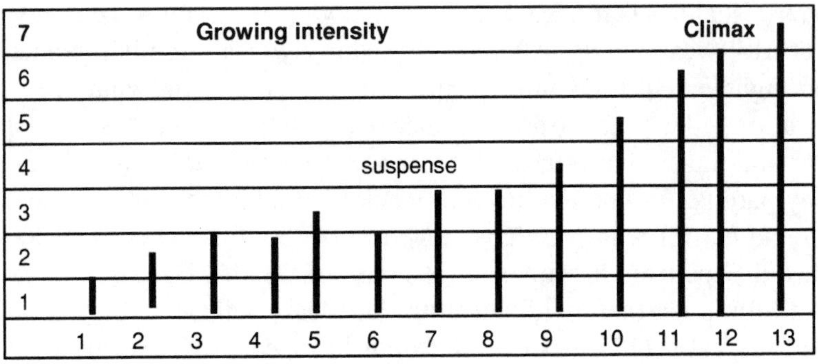

Esthetics of Violence, Fear, Risk

The fights which overwhelm us in life, thrill us when we observe them from a safe distance: "How sweet to watch raging battles when no danger threatens you!"[9] No doubt, mimesis provides a cozy lookout for colorful confrontations, epic, dramatic, comic or tragic. Melvin Raeder identifies "the Hegelian-Marxian exhilaration of conflict" as one of the six "root values in art"; indulgence in conflicts is one of our inborn tendencies which motivate our artistic creation and its perception.[10] But evidence more convincing than all the historical and scholarly observations is the vast corpus of works over the ages in which conflicts form the main artistic substance. The omnipresence and density of micro- and macroconflicts in major genres prove that their transposed rivalries and inner struggles constitute the broadest category of recurrent stimuli sought by writers and readers throughout all stages of our literary tradition. We can define their mimesis as the artistic description of collective or individual clashes between two or several opposite wills or forces, or accounts of human struggles with Nature. The radical esthetic contrast in typical conflicts between protagonists and antagonists essentially comes down to moral or metaphysical polarities between good and evil, love and hatred, freedom and slavery, decency and

9 T. Lucretius Carus *De rerum natura*, II, 1: "Suave etiam belli certamina magna tueri / Per campos instructa tua sine parte pericli."

10 See earlier comments on Raeder's assumptions, *LP I*, ch. III, p. 55 and n. 5. G.W. Hegel (*Hegel on Tragedy*, Garden City, N.Y., 1962, Eds. Anne and Henry Paolucci, pp. 114–5) distinguishes three categories of "collisions" originating in 1. "natural...physical" conditions, 2. in "natural spiritual conditions and 3. "divisions...caused by disruption in the spirit alone." See below n. 56.

falsehood. Extended and coherent mimesis of wars, revolutions, regicides, memorable duels, executions, suicides, human fights against nature, floods, epidemics, earthquakes generates macrostimulative impact.[11] The above-discussed chant XXII of the *Illiad* is a macroconflict full of epical details relating the mythical duel between Achilles and Hector. The episodic references to such specific details of the epically unified macroconflict are microstimulative: the chant's climactic finale evoking the triumphant Achilles' "foul treatment"—demeaning Hector's corpse—is a powerful naturalistic gradation consisting of three microstimuli describing how Achilles 1. pierced Hector's heels to thread them with oxhide thongs, 2. attached the dead body to his chariot and 3. dragged it ostentatiously through the dusty battlefield. The gamut of micro- and macroconflicts in art could be even broader than their scope in life: imaginative authors keep inventing fresh variations of physical and inner conflicts. Like the real conflicts, their literary representations are tragic when causing a heroic death or welcome when terminating the villain's life; they are violent, erotic, comical (mock-violence), bizarre, fabulous, legal, political, social and so on. Like our life struggles, their fictionalizations usually culminate in dramatic confrontations marking the climax of a tale or play, a victory or a defeat, physical or moral. In some plots a conflict, which strikes the opening note, initiates a long chain of hostile actions and reciprocal retaliations.[12] Inner (psychological) conflicts transpose the characters' complex often traumatizing deliberations over the solution to fatal dilemmas.

Whether participants in or observers of real conflicts or readers of their transpositions, we may be indifferent, neutral or sympathize either with the attacker or defender. In epical macroconflicts attackers try to extend their power or try to regain power previously lost. The defenders protect their power base, which of course could have been gained "legitimately" or acquired violently or fraudulently. The outcome depends on the rivals' strength, courage, determination, self-confidence.

11 E.g., *The Illiad*, Tolstoy's *War and Peace*, many of Maupassant's short stories, Ernest Hemingway's *A Farewell to Arms* and his anthology, *Men at War*; Jules Romain's *Verdun* (1952–47), Joseph Kessel's *L'Armée des ombres* (1945) draw from the history of ancient and modern wars. Anatole France offered a livresque panorama of the French revolution in *Les Dieux ont soif* (1912). Malraux' *La Condition humaine* (1933) and *l'Espoir* (1937) fictionalize the Chinese and Spanish civil wars. (See also struggles against the cataclysms discussed in ch. II, "Plots," re Boccaccio, Camus, etc.).

12 See ref. to Propp and Raglan (ch. II) and *LP I*, p. 73, n. 11.

The main innate faculty activated in our individual and collective confrontations is the universal instinct of self-preservation. Its characteristics include the innate will to be free and fear to lose freedom; the will to secure or fear to lose one's possessions, territory, its resources, etc. On a higher cultural level, injustice, family honor, intransigent defense or expansion of one's moral, religious, ethical influence are typical causes of major conflicts in life as well as in their literary representations. The stimulative substance in the transposed and perceived clashes can be labeled esthetics of violence, fear, risk, victory, defeat.[13]

Cycles of Mimesis: Voltaire on Shakespeare and Rabelais

Writers' treatment of and readers' responses to conflicts vary from era to era, from culture to culture, from trend to trend; their intra- and extratextual esthetic potential fluctuates according to our cyclically evolving esthetic propensities and vacillating socio-cultural standards. In the Shakespearean tragedies, violent encounters often mark the theatrical peaks while, in the French classical tragedy, duels, murders, mortal accidents, suicides, executions and wars are banished from the scene. Instead, survivors eloquently report such events, drowning them in baroque grandiloquence. While reservedly respecting Shakespeare as a born and prolific poet of rare creative force and sublime imagination, a defender of the then moribund classical tragedy as cultured as Voltaire also found that the Bard neither had the least spark of good taste nor the least knowledge of dramatic rules.[14] His opinion illustrates the cyclic as well as socio-cultural evolution of our individual tastes, inevitably blended with certain ethnic esthetic biases which precondition our spontaneous perceptions and judgments of any stimulative subject. Voltaire's 18th century, typically French, irreverent and at the same time normative "expectation horizon"[15] determined his harsh subjective

13 See Malik's comments on the physiology of perception of and responses to literary mimesis of conflicts, ch. VIII.

14 "Génie plein de force et de fécondité, de naturel et de sublime, sans la moindre étincelle de bon goût et sans la moindre connaissance des règles." *Lettres philosophiques*.

15 Term coined by H.R. Jauss to designate the individual psychological, social, historical, and ethnocultural orientation involved in our perception and potential assessment of art and shaping our individual and collective criteria and biases. See also *LP I*, p. 21, n. 5.

verdict.[16] What Shakespeare wrote to please English tastes of the 16th and early 17th centuries, Voltaire saw from his historically distant and ethno-culturally dissimilar perspective as the vital art of an indisputable genius. His mimesis of human discords, however, was tainted by heavy-handed transpositions of shocking subjects and lack of finesse.

Unless supported by compelling arguments based on textual evidence, such general appraisals are always disputable. Perhaps the gore and cannibalism in *Titus Andronicus* shocked the Frenchman more than other Shakespearean scenes of duels and murders. In this play the Byzantine general, following his victory over the Goths, takes the Queen Tamora, her three sons and her Moorish confidant and lover prisoners. As soon as he brings them to Rome, he gets involved in a power struggle between the Emperor Saturninus and his brother Bassianus (who kidnapped Titus' daughter Lavinia). Saturninus soon falls in love with the state hostage Tamora. During a hunting party, Tamora's sons murder Bassianus, rape Lavinia and cut off her tongue and arms. In addition, they succeed in blaming it on the two sons of Titus. Emperor Saturninus, whom Titus Andronicus endorsed during the power struggle, sentences them to death. After several other treacheries, Titus simulates insanity, kills Tamora's sons and has a *pâté* prepared from their brains. At an imperial reception, Tamora before being killed by Titus savors this hors d'oeuvre. Saturninus then kills Titus. Lucius, Titus' exiled son, returns the favor, killing the Emperor and seizing power. Tamora's lover, who fathered her black child, is sentenced to be dismembered (see Appendix, Shakespeare). Shakespeare drew his bloody intrigues from earlier Elizabethan plays by Thomas Kyd, Christopher Marlowe and George Peele.

Mock Violence in Rabelaisian Utopia

For similar reasons Voltaire condemned Rabelais' work as a heap ("ramas") of silly ("sottises"), medieval crudities and undisciplined livresque erudition. He found in its content only two redeeming qualities: intrepid anticlerical satire and barbaric but original farce. Reluctantly and patronizingly he conceded that any culture should have its buffoon but one was enough and, as for the French literary heritage, Rabelais amply

16 Lanson, *op. cit.*, p. 390, says that his Jesuit teachers shaped his taste while the Libertines shaped his "esprit" (intellect): "Enfant intelligent mais polisson insigne."

filled the ticket.[17] Although Voltaire's generalisations cover both contentual as well as stylistic qualities they particularly apply to the medieval vulgarities and stone-age brutality combined with what posterity considers puerile humor. Yet Voltaire's prescriptions were neither precious nor puritanic. In his best fiction he relied on licence, violence and laughter as much as Rabelais, but the polish and professional discipline of an accomplished *homme de lettres* dismissed any marginally stimulative information and focused on the culminating phases of any conflict he chose to treat. Rabelais' endless epical overstatements blur the transposition, while Voltaire's brevity sharpens it. Thus, although both Rabelais and Voltaire describe wars, individual duels or controversies, their subjects and the effects achieved are miles apart, and so are their respective communities of readers. As many as 25 chapters of *Gargantua* relate the digressive utopian saga of Grandgousier's and Gargantua's protracted war against the belligerent King Picrochole and nine of the ten final chapters of *Pantagruel* cover the hero's fabulous campaign against the Dipsods who invaded the Utopian country and besieged its capital. Rabelais' two chapters on Pantagruel's victory over the Dipsods and three hundred giants and their captain Werewolf,[18] may help to explain why Rabelais' irrepressible epical outbursts struck the impatient 18th century critic and satirist as obsolete and boring drivel. Following the farcical massacre of six hundred and sixty mounted enemies, Pantagruel sends the only surviving prisoner of war to pass a container of spiked euphorbium, a very spicy marmalade-like concoction, to the enemy King Anarche. The prisoner has to report the defeat and warn the invading ruler that he cannot defeat Pantagruel unless he can consume euphorbium without having to drink. Anarche and his men fall in the ingenious trap and taste euphorbium with fatal consequences; none of them can stop drinking. When all are drunk and fall asleep Pantagruel, armed with the mast of his vessel, 237 barrels of white Anjou wine and the cargo of salt stored in a bark attached to his belt, approaches the Dipsod lines. Prior to the attack, he and his warriors drink the wine. Then they spread gun powder in the enemy's camp and start fire. Many Dipsods are roasted to death. Having thus weakened the enemy, Pantagruel neutralizes the Dipsod artillerists by filling their throats with salt. His compelling urge to urinate inflicts the final strategic

17 See comments *LP I*, ch. I, p. 22.

18 *Pantagruel*, Paris, Les Belles Lettres, 1946, ed. J. Plattard, chs. XXVIII–XIX, pp. 136–48.

blow: Pantagruel floods the Dipsod encampment and most of the giants drown in the deluge escaping from his bladder like the waters of the Danube and the Rhône. To save Anarche, the giants carry him from the inundated battlefield just like Aeneas carried his father Anchises from the burning Troy. The parody of ancient heroism continues in Pantagruel's mock-skirmish with Werewolf, captain of 300 mounted giants clad in stone armour. His rival's magic cudgel intimidates Pantagruel, but Panurge's jovial peptalk on David and Goliath and Pantagruel's prayer answered in Latin by the Almighty's voice "Hoc fac et vinces"—go for it and you'll win[19]—encourages him to attack the ferocious enemy. After several suspenseful blows the pious warrior kicks his adversary in the belly, knocks him on his back, grabs his feet and drags him on his "arse" as far as an arrow flies. Pantagruel's triumph is a farcical *imitatio* of Achilles' victory over Hector earlier evoked as a precedential model of literary conflicts.[20] Three centuries after Rabelais' debut, Voltaire made an allowance for the originality of Rabelaisian humor but did not overlook its esthetic limitations. In many similar parodies of ancient poetry and scholastic erudition Rabelais, driven by his unruly *joie de vivre*,[21] rarely attempts to sift his material. His very individual yarn, neither a novel nor a collection of novellas but a *causerie/contaminatio* of loosely composed "fabulous chronicles,"[22] requires less creative discipline than the genres demanding strict topical homogeneity. The medley of scrambled subjects is a strong point in the eyes of friendly critics who "understand" Rabelais; it is a weak point in the eyes of those who, like Voltaire, "misunderstand" him because they invoke classical esthetic standards and because they value judicious trimming of cohesive subjects.

War and Duels in Voltaire's Satire

Voltaire obviously concluded that the esthetic impact of perennial stimuli such as representations of conflicts depended not only on the power of the transposed fights but also on their quantity in a given text. His fictional self-caricature, Pococurante, dryly comments on works which, generation after generation, critics venerate as artistic revelations in spite of their topical monotony and excess.

19 Parody of Emperor Constantin's motto *in hoc signo vinces*.

20 See above comments and n. 5.

21 Pantagruelism, "Fais ce que vouldras."

22 G. Lanson's term. *Contaminatio*, Spitzer's term.

> Candide, en voyant un Homère magnifiquement relié, loua l'illustrissime sur son bon goût: "Voilà, dit-il, un livre qui faisait les délices du grand Pangloss, le meilleur philosophe de l'Allemagne. —Il ne fait pas les miennes, dit froidement Pococurante; on me fit accroire autrefois que j'avais du plaisir en le lisant; mais cette *répétition continuelle de combats qui se ressemblent tous*, ces *dieux qui agissent toujours pour ne rien faire* de décisif, cette *Hélène* qui est le *sujet de la guerre*, et qui *à peine* est une *actrice* de la pièce; cette *Troie* qu'on assiège, et *qu'on ne prend point*: tout cela me causait le plus *mortel ennui*. J'ai demandé quelquefois à des savants s'ils *s'ennuyaient* autant que moi à cette lecture: tous les gens sincères m'ont avoué que *le livre leur tombait des mains*, mais il fallait toujours l'avoir dans sa bibliothèque comme un *monument de l'antiquité*, et comme ces *médailles rouillées* qui ne peuvent être de commerce.[23]

Voltaire's blasé dilettante does not reject conflicts and miracles as ineffective stimuli. He merely finds that their Homeric overabundance bores him. He warns that repetitive accumulation of similar subjects reduces their intensity. Voltaire the fiction writer follows his character's doctrine: he draws from similar stimulative sources as Homer and Rabelais—wars, violent duels, erotic entanglements, licence, their parodies (mock violence), farce—but he treats them sparingly. He favors short, fast moving chapters relating a variety of contrastful subjects.[24] His ironic vision of characters, their climactic actions and of the settings relies on minimal information. He selects all epical details with care and turns to satirical advantage not only all contrasts both stylistic and contentual. He knows that excess of marginal information slows down the narrative's dramatic pace. Voltaire trusts his readers, assumes their impatience and offers more freedom to their imagination than Rabelais' ample mimesis of conflicts. The Dipsod war saga requires nine chapters.[25] Voltaire writes only two paragraphs, about 250 words, to create a sufficiently clear illusion of Candide's participation in the Bulgare-Abare "heroic butchery" conducted according to international law and ending with a *Te Deum*. The military thanksgiving offers the hero an opportunity to desert and see the war's aftermath and his author

23 Ed. cit., ch. XXV, my ital.

24 The stylistic breakdown of the represented contentual macrostimuli into short chapters, is arbitrary and has only marginal bearing on the overall stimulative effect: John Updike's *Rabbit at Rest*, (like Voltaire's *Candide*), confronts typical contemporary issues—drugs, addiction, extortion, aids, swapping partners, Japanese cars, coronary bypass, etc. But all fast moving adventures of Rabbit smoothly fuse in three "macrochapters" entitled "FL," "PA," and "MI."

25 *Pantagruel*, chs. XXIII–XXXI.

to demythify the glory of heroic death without decreasing the esthetic impact of the represented military massacre.[26]

Voltaire restricts the information highlights of Candide's individual fights just as drastically as he does in the cited satire of an international massacre. Following his desertion, an earthquake, a shipwreck (ch. V) and a brutal auto-da-fé (ch. VI), Candide is saved by his first love, Cunégonde (ch. VII). Having lost her family in the war, she earns her living as a courtesan of both the court banker Don Issachar and the great inquisitor (ch. VIII). (The latter had Candide whipped in the mentioned auto-da-fé parade for listening "approvingly" to Pangloss' metaphysical heresy.) By mutual agreement the financier enjoys his privileges on Saturdays, while the inquisitor's *jour fixe* falls on Sunday. As soon as Don Issachar steps into Cunegonde's boudoir and finds his concubine on the sofa in Candide's company he draws his dagger to cut the intruder's throat (only the informative microstimuli are identified in parentheses; ironic effects are not under scrutiny here).

> Cet Issachar était le plus colérique Hébreu qu'on eût vu dans Israël, depuis la captivité en Babylone [1. social, racist satire]. "Quoi! dit-il, chienne de Galiléenne, ce n'est pas assez de monsieur l'inquisiteur? Il faut que ce coquin partage aussi avec moi?" [2. Bedroom farce, religious satire.] En disant cela il tire un long poignard dont il était toujours pourvu [3. physical conflict begins], et, ne croyant pas que son adverse partie eût des armes, [4. digressive racist satire] il se jette sur Candide [5. conflict continues]; mais notre bon Westphalien avait reçu une belle épée, de la vieille...Il tire son épée, quoiqu'il eût les moeurs fort douces [6. digressive ironic information, suspense], et vous étend l'Israélite roide mort sur le carreau [7. conflict culminates and ends], aux pieds de la belle Cunégonde [8. erotic correlate stressed].
>
> "Sainte Vierge! s'écria-t-elle, qu'allons-nous devenir? un homme tué chez moi! Si la justice vient, nous sommes perdus [9. fear of doom]. "Si Pangloss n'avait pas été pendu [10. reference to execution—later it turns out that Pangloss survived], dit Candide, il nous donnerait un bon conseil dans cette extrémité, car c'était un grand philosophe [11. digressive satire of Leibnitzian theory]. A son défaut, consultons la vieille." [12. Ironic choice of an underqualified but perhaps wiser advisor.] Elle était fort prudente, et commençait à dire son avis quand une autre petite porte s'ouvrit. Il était une heure après minuit, c'était le commencement du dimanche. Ce jour appartenait à monseigneur l'inquisiteur. Il entre et voit le fessé [13. new rival; ominous flashback] Candide, l'épée à la main, un mort étendu par terre, Cunégonde effarée, et la vieille donnant des conseils [14. prelate's rendezvous wrecked;

26 Text cited in *LP II*, Appendix, p. 242, illustrates Voltaire's rhetoric and macrorhetoric of war. The same ironic diction conditions the esthetic quality of all his subjects including conflicts.

bedroom farce].

Voici dans ce moment ce qui se passa dans l'âme de Candide et comment il raisonna: "Si ce saint homme appelle du secours, il me fera infailliblement brûler, il pourra en faire autant de Cunégonde; [15. grave risk of the ridiculous encounter] il m'a fait fouetter impitoyablement; il est mon rival; je suis en train de tuer, il n'y a pas à balancer." [16. Candide's flashback of past hostility makes new absurd violence invevitable; his incipient inner conflict cannot be developed; no time for a dialogue comparable to verbal exchanges in Achilles vs. Hector or Pantagruel vs. his adversaries.] Ce raisonnement fut net et rapide; et sans donner le temps à l'inquisiteur de revenir de sa surprise, il le perce d'outre en outre, et le jette à côté du juif. "En voici bien d'une autre, dit Cunégonde; [17. another corpse; ironic recapitulation; second farcical massacre over] il n'y a plus de rémission; nous sommes excommuniés, notre dernière heure est venue! [18. Ironic foresight of *Dies irae*.] Comment avez-vous fait, vous qui êtes né si doux, pour tuer en deux minutes un juif et un prélat? [19. Brief ironic paradoxical digression/suspense.] — "Ma belle demoiselle," répondit Candide, "quand on est amoureux, jaloux et fouetté par l'inquisition, on ne se connaît plus." [20. Ironic post-mortem aphorism of a repressed but always gallant cavalier. The rhymed apostrophe/cliché distantly echoes Goethe's "schönes Fräulein, darf ich wagen Ihnen meine Hand zu tragen" in *Faust*. Candide's melancholy subtone, of course, reminds the reader of the character's continuing romantic tribulations].[27]

The colorful happenings condensed in this brief passage constitute the subject matter of a whole chapter.[28] Its content consists of two picaresque microconflicts (3, 5, 7, 8, 11, 13,) with two new farcical characters indirectly sketched through their actions (1, 3, 4, 11, 13, 14). In spite of its narrative speed Voltaire's inventive mimesis of two duels also covers correlated erotic topics (1, 2, 11, 14), and adds a few side shots of racial and religious satire (1, 2, 4, 9, 10, 11, 12, 18, 19) which further corroborate the density and intensity of an effective macrostimulus. The final aphorism (20) is a subdued hyperbole on the power of true love challenged by influential rakes. The episode's conclusion—some 150 words—prepares the ground for the following chapter: Cunégonde and her maid gather all available cash and jewels, Candide saddles three horses and the trio rushes off through the balmy midnight air to the seaport of Cadix. Voltaire even devotes 14 words to a satirical requiem for Candide's rivals: as soon as the refugees leave the threatened love nest, a squad of vigilantes arrives; they bury the Monsignor in a beautiful church and throw the Jewish corpse on a dung

27 *Candide*, ch. IX. Perhaps a new variation of the reflexive sigh "Hélas!...je l'ai connu, cet amour, ce souverain des coeurs..." See ch. IV.

28 See n. 23: it is the density of information per word that counts.

heap. Like the philandering Inquisitor, the reader has no time to recover from surprise; the brief continuity segment is another example of Voltaire's informational crossfire. If I schematized this satirico-epical passage, like the diagram of the Homeric duel (Table 2), the two successive gradations would form a row of ascendant microstimuli. The peak of each gradation is a manslaughter (7, 17). Voltaire's irony in the final repartee between Cunégonde and her rediscovered beau (19, 20) punctuates the bravado with an anecdotal maxim.

Regicide in *The Heptameron* and *Lorenzaccio*

While Rabelais' war against the Dipsodes is a fantasy, *The Heptameron*, written some 15 years later by Marguerite de Valois[29] draws from her milieu and the history of her time; she claimed that every tale was a true story. Her well known 12th novella[30] fictionalizes the then timely vendetta within the Medici family (1537–47). Today, an assassination of a head of state by his distant relative and an ensuing retaliation would be called "political dynamite," especially if the involved parties were either protégés or opponents of the most influential international leaders: the Florentine Duke Alessandro, who was murdered in 1537, was allegedly an illegitimate son of the Pope[31] and a mulatto waitress; when he assumed power as a very young man he married the 12-year-old illegitimate daughter of the Emperor Charles Quint. Consequently, both the Pope and the Emperor politically and militarily supported Alessandro's despotic rule. On the other hand, the French King François I, brother of Marguerite de Navarre, sided with the Florentine patricians who kept trying to restore the old families' republic. Like them, Alessandro's distant cousin Lorenzino (generally called Lorenzaccio) may have secretly resented the occupation by German imperial troops as well as the Vatican's meddling into Florentine autonomy. Naturally, Marguerite's version of the assassination is not a *reportage* and, for political reasons, she could not spell out all the timely

29 Known also as M. de Navarre, d'Angoulême, d'Alençon; *L'Heptaméron des Nouvelles de très illustre et très excellente Princesse Marguerite de Valois, Royne de Navarre*, published in 1559, ten years after the author's death. The subsequent citations refer to *Oeuvres Choisies Marguerite Navarre*, t. II, ed. H.P. Clive (New York, Appleton-Century-Croft, 1968), pp. 152–60.

30 "Douziesme Nouvelle" entitled "Lorenzaccio" in Classiques Larousse "*Les Conteurs français du XVI siècle*", ed. Jules Hasselmann, p. 53.

31 Either of Lorenzo d'Urbino or his successor Cardinal Giovanni dei Medici, i.e., Clement VII.

and juicy intricacies of the preliterary historical plot. Further, she had most probably written her tale prior to the killing of Lorenzino in Venice (1548) by the spies of Alessandro's successor Cosimo Medici; perhaps she went as far as she could by identifying the duke as the Emperor Charles' Quint son-in-law but fictionalized Lorenzino (then exiled in France) as an anonymous nobleman in the Duke's entourage. The novella starts with the Duke's circumspect *captatio benevolentiae* addressed to his loyal courtier:

> S'il y avoit chose en ce monde, mon amy, que je ne voulsisse faire pour vous, je craindrois à vous declarer ma fantaisye; et encores plus à vous prier m'y estre aydant. Mais je vous porte tant d'amour, que, si j'avois femme, mere ou fille qui peust servir à saulver vostre vie, je les y emploirois plustost que de vous faire laisser mourir en torment.

After this hypocritical ouverture, the Duke demands assurance of blind loyalty in a confidential affair soon to be revealed.[32] In such a position, no courtier can ask questions or even refuse the mysterious favor. Without the slightest hesitation the nobleman replies that he is prepared to undertake anything the Duke wishes. He is, however, terrified when he learns that he should deliver his own sister to the Duke's bed.[33] Polite protests provoke the master's wrath. Biting his nails, the Duke ominously utters: "Since you show no friendship, I know what to do." Fearing the worst the nobleman promises to cooperate. He ponders the issue for a couple of days and decides to murder his master. Without even talking to his sister, the nobleman informs his master that she agrees to meet him in her own bedroom. The nobleman personally leads the Duke to the rendez-vous, undresses him, puts him to bed and tells him that his blushing sister is ready to join him. He leaves the room but only to return armed to kill the lusty tyrant. The naked Duke fights back with nails and teeth; he rolls out of bed and bites his traitor's thumb. To extricate himself from the precarious clinch the nobleman

32 "...et j'estime que l'amour que vous me portez est réciprocque à la mienne; et que si moy, qui suys vostre maistre, vous portois telle affection, que pour le moins ne la sçauriez porter moindre. Parquoy, je vous declaireray un secret,...duquel je n'espere amandement que la mort ou par le service que vous me pouvez faire."

33 Referring to Benedetto Varchi's *Storia fiorentina* (about 1550), Paul Vinogradoff "Medici" (*Encycl. Brit.* 11th ed.) indicates that the lady whom Alessandro courted in this instance, was Leonardo Ginori's wife, aunt of the historical Lorenzaccio. (See nn. 36 and 40).

calls his trusted servant.[34] Marguerite's vision of the fight's culminating moment may strike us today as an early feminist put-down of absurd male bravery.

> Le gentil homme, qui n'estoit trop asseuré, appela son serviteur; lequel, trouvant le duc et son maistre si liez ensemble qu'il ne sçavoit lequel choisir, les tira tous deux par les piedz, au milieu de la place, et avecq son poignard s'essaya à couper la gorge du duc, lequel se defendit jusques ad ce que la perte de son sang le rendit si foible qu'il n'en povoyt plus. Alors le gentil homme et son serviteur le meirent dans son lict, ou à coups de poignart le paracheverent de tuer. Puis tirans le rideau, s'en allerent et enfermerent le corps mort en la chambre.

The Queen of Navarre does not fail to invent a farcical side of the bloodshed in the solitary bedroom. Although it would be farfetched to consider the text as an Homeric *imitatio*, one cannot help hearing an intertextual echo of Hector's humiliation: it is the butler who pulls both combatants by the feet from the narrow "ruelle" between the bed and the wall. Feeling so invincible (after the valet saves his neck), the nobleman can't wait to dispatch the Duke's entire entourage. Marguerite's ironic finale, could be conveniently labelled as an antiheroic decrescendo, or a comical accent reminiscent of Sancho Panza's prudence.

> Et, quand il se veid victorieux de son grand enhemy, par la mort duquel il pensoit mettre en liberté la chose publicque, se pensa que son euvre seroyt imparfaict, s'il n'en faisoit autant à cinq ou six de ceulx qui estoient les prochains du duc. Et, pour en venir à fin, dist à son serviteur, qu'il les allast querir l'un après l'autre, pour en faire comme il avoyt faict au duc. Mais le serviteur, qui n'estoit ne hardy ne fol, luy dist: "Il me semble, monsieur, que vous en avez assez faict pour ceste heure, et que vous ferez mieulx de penser à saulver vostre vie,... Car, si nous demeurions autant à deffaire chascun d'eulx,...le jour descouvriroit plustost nostre entreprinse,... Le gentil homme,...creut son serviteur,...

Like the historical Lorenzino, her hero tricks the guardians of the closed city gates and finds asylum in Venice, Constantinople and later in France. Marguerite's tale makes no allusion to the final showdown in 1548. Should we read it as the Queen's representation of illusory divine justice or a memoir on a regicide which rid "decent society" of a Prince allied with a Pope and an Emperor detested both in Florence and France? Or is it merely an anecdotal affair which could fit in the memoirs of a politically involved Queen recalling a "veritable histoire"?

34 According to Vinogradoff and Varchi, Lorenzino's hired hitman was a "desperado" known as Scoronconcolo (dramatized in Musset's play).

The same conflict, already buried in distant history by the mid 19th century, attracted the artistic attention of George Sand who drafted a play entitled *Conspiracy in 1537*.[35] Later she gave her unpublished manuscript to one of her lovers, Alfred de Musset, who rewrote it, discarding all discrepancies with the history of the murder as related in the above mentioned *Storia fiorentina*. In his version, however, he did not retain the eleven-year-lapse between the 1537 assassination and the delayed vendetta. In addition, his murderer of the Duke is not modeled after the historical Lorenzino but represented as a Romantic guard of political integrity rightly or wrongly attributed to the old Florentine bourgeoisie. To succeed, he infiltrates the inner circle of Alessandro's sycophants and publicly participates in the Duke's ostentatious depravities. This dangerous game provokes the disdain of decent fellow citizens whom he respects but who do not realize that Lorenzaccio is a crypto-republican risking his own life. The murder in Musset's play is not only a result of a personal *collisio officiorum* as represented in *The Heptameron*—loyalty to the prince vs. commitment to one's own blood and family honor—it also is a daring *Sturm und Drang* struggle for political ideals. Like many historical plays or novels, *Lorenzaccio* is an anachronistic transformation of Alessandro's despicable license and his death. Musset's own political sentiments colored his work with excessive Romantic pathos. It was published in 1834 but never put on stage during his short life (1810–57). It was not playable as written in 39 scenes—the production would have required two full evening performances. Further, the proposed cast of 100 actors and 30 different sets did not comply with a normal time frame and budget. A decade after Alfred's death, his older brother Paul condensed the work to facilitate the play's production but, in 1864, the imperial censor killed the project; just as in Marguerite's day, the subject was considered political dynamite. "[T]he discussion on the right to assassinate the sovereign whose crimes call for punishment as well as a murder of a prince by his relative..., would be a spectacle...too dangerous to show the public,"[36] he wrote. In the long run the ban was

35 She drew from Florentine history but her artistic and ideological model was J.C.F. Schiller's *Conspiracy of Fiesco of Genua* (1782–3).

36 Cited in Jacques Nathan's "Notice" *Lorenzaccio*, Classiques Larousse, p. 6, (my transl.) At the time the French censor vetoed the production of *Lorenzaccio*, Dostoevsky was writing *Crime and Punishment* (1866), envisioning the psychology of a self-deceiving assassin. His hero, Raskolnikov, contemplates a "socially excusable" murder and robbery of a parasitic old usurer in order to secure a decent living for his destitute mother. Needless to say, Lorenzaccio's and Raskolnikov's

bound to be broken: times keep changing and writers are like athletes—they want to beat the old records. In addition, their readers, like Bluebeard's wives, must see what is behind the locked door. Finally, 62 years after its publication and long after Alfred, Paul, the imperial censor and the Second Empire were safely put to rest, the Second Republic finally authorized the presentation. Sarah Bernhardt had *Lorenzaccio* adapted and starred in its 1896 première.

Shortly before the overthrow of the Communist dictatorship in Czechoslovakia (1989), a theatre operating in a small château on the outskirts of Prague included *Lorenzaccio* on its repertoire. One may wonder why. Paradoxically, the production of the Romantic freedom play must have been subsidized by the country's corrupt totalitarian regime as was the salary of the whimsical producer/director. The program planners correctly anticipated that the Communist censor would miss the political ambiguities of the play. Besides, they could always argue that Lorenzaccio was a Renaissance precedent of a revolutionary saint such as Lenin who had the Czar and his imperial family massacred as soon as he seized power. At the same time, they must have hoped that the freedom-hungry Prague public would applaud any assassination (real or only mimetic) of any brutal tyrant, historical or contemporary. The producers must have been aware that imaginative theatre goers would immediately find at least some analogies between the Florentine tyrant and the Communist bigwigs crushing their everyday happiness.

The idealistic approval of an old "regicide" in an unsettled French political climate,[37] along with the publicity related to the banning of a controversial subject, naturally increased the play's stimulative potential in Sarah Bernhardt's era. In Czechoslovakia, then (1986) groaning behind the Iron Curtain, the staged overthrow of a despot must have appealed to the public as the next best thing to real sedition.

The remarks on these two historically distant and quite different treatments of the once sensational Florentine murder not only exemplify the genesis and artistic peripeties of an original stimulus derived from a newsworthy act and subsequently transformed into a viable literary macroconflict; the historical distance between its two artistic versions also illustrates the fluctuations of the subject's informative intensity.

---

motives are not comparable. For another politically motivated murder, see below "Terrorist Tchen, Malraux' Communist martyr."

37 Revolution, abolition of monarchy, directorate, Napoleon's Empire, restitution of monarchy, Second Empire, the Commune, second republic.

Obviously the esthetic appeal of Marguerite's novella would have culminated while the actual murder and retaliation were still timely (1537–48). But in 1559, when *The Heptameron* had finally been published, the "très illustre" author was dead and her story was history, not a bombshell. (The rush by Monica Lewinski and by President Clinton's former advisor, George Stephanopoulos to publish their White House sagas in 1999 illustrates the pragmatism of my esthetico-historical argument.) The stimulative subject had to hibernate almost three centuries until George Sand and Musset revitalized, "distorted" and actualized the shocker in the turbulent political and social climate prevailing in their era. As adults, they had witnessed the protracted struggle between the conservative forces of restoration and both the republican (liberal) and newborn socialist movements; they lived through two revolutions—1830 and 1848—and two insurrections—1832 and 1834; a *coup d'état* in 1851 and so on. Musset's contemporaries (who could only read, not see his play) found in it a timely apotheosis of republican virtues opposing the autocratic rule of the pre-revolutionary monarchy or the post-revolutionary empire. When, after 1870, the Third Republic authorized the performance, the spectators who came to see the great actress in the male role of Lorenzaccio, were also eager to see the "controversial" play banned not so long ago by the imperial censor. A century later, this "outdated" French "masterpiece", gained new extra-textual stimulative power in a milieu frustrated by the long lasting Communist oppression.[38]

Executions: Anatole France

Conflicts in life as well as their mimesis may culminate in capital punishment of the criminal or innocent rebel. The tragic intensity of this act may increase if the loss of life is unjust, totally absurd or even sheer murder. The final chapter of Anatole France's early novel *Les Désirs de Jean Servien* (1882) is an adaptation of historical events which occurred at Haro Street during the lawless days of the Parisian *Commune* following the French defeat by Prussia in 1870. The novelist, who obviously did not personally witness the pathetic scene, borrowed and modified the subject from Maxime Du Camp's work entitled *Les*

38 Prévert's surrealistic formula of regicide and John Updike's gallows humor are discussed below in ch. V, "Black Humor".

Convulsions de Paris.[39] Jean Servien is a sensitive dreamer frustrated by unrequited love for an actress and by his inability to earn a living befitting his education and ambitions. In the days of the *Commune*, he is falsely accused of spying for the defeated Versailles Government and taken hostage by the Communards, then released when government soldiers approach. However, he is trapped between "the red pants" and the revolutionary "Lutèce Avengers" commanded by a bloodthirsty canteen keeper who would like to have someone killed especially for her. In his text France mixes melodrama, poetry and a burlesque murder no less absurd than the executions in Sartre's well-known story "Le Mur" discussed below.[40]

> De sa...bouche...sortaient des menaces obscènes, elle agitait un revolver. Les vengeurs de Lutèce, harassés et stupides, regardaient leur prisonnier, pâle contre le mur, et se regardaient entre eux. Elle les menaçait...et les pénétrait de son influence. Ils se formèrent en peloton. "Feu!" cria-t-elle. Jean étendit les bras en avant. Deux ou trois coups de feu partirent. Il entendit les balles s'écraser contre le mur. Il n'était pas touché.
>
> "Feu! feu!" répéta la femme avec une obstination d'enfant colère... On ne faisait que tuer autour d'elle, et on n'avait encore tué personne pour elle. Elle voulait qu'on lui fusillât quelqu'un à la fin! Et elle criait en trépignant: "Feu, feu! feu!"
>
> Les fusils s'armaient de nouveau...mais les Vengeurs de Lutèce manquaient d'entrain; leur chef avait disparu... Ils voulaient bien, tout de même, fusiller ce bourgeois-là, avant d'aller se cacher chacun dans son trou... Un des Vengeurs...vit les fédérés qui lâchaient pied. Il dit, en se mettant l'arme à l'épaule: "F..s le camp, nom de Dieu!"...
>
> Alors la cantinière hurla: "Sacrés c..s! c'est donc moi qui lui ferai son affaire."
>
> Elle se jeta sur Jean Servien, lui cracha au visage...et lui mit le canon du revolver sur la tempe. Alors il sentit que tout était fini et il attendit... [I]l se revit lui-même petit enfant heureux et étonné; il se rappela les châteaux qu'il construisait avec des écorces de platane... Le revolver partit. Jean battit l'air de ses bras et tomba la face en avant. Les hommes l'achevèrent à coups de baïonnette, puis la femme dansa sur le cadavre en poussant des cris de joie.

The specific power of this treatment springs from three gradation-linked microstimulative subjects: France's harmless hero becomes a random victim of a would-be revolutionary mob. He is senselessly lynched rather than executed. His executioner is not even a firing squad but a sadistic

39 Hachette, 1880, vol. I, 429, see Anatole France, *Oeuvres*, Gallimard, Pléiade (1984), ed. Marie-Claire Bancquart, footnote material, p. 1220. A. France acknowledged his debt in his correspondence to Du Camp. See Bancquart's "Notice," p. 1187.

40 Discussed below.

hussy who normally serves soup in a canteen but who, for once, happened to get hold of a revolver. The humanistic and macrostimulative subtext of this mimesis is an early precedent of the plea re-emphasized in France's mature novels—revolutions are outbursts of social folly.[41]

Stendhal

Stendhal's best known novel *Le Rouge et le Noir* also ends with an execution of the plebeian Romantic climber Julien Sorel who is guillotined after firing two shots at his first mistress, Mme de Rênal, at church. Unlike France, Stendhal does not shock his reader with the melodramatic details of Julian's ascent to the scaffold. Instead, in his climactic passage, Julien's pregnant second mistress, Mathilde de la Môle, contacts her lover's friend Fouqué to claim the head of the executed lover. As she is driven in the coach to a grotto where Julien's body will be buried, she holds on her knees the head of her yet unborn child's father. What gives her moral strength during the pathetic journey is the memory of her distant ancestor, Boniface de la Môle, who allegedly was a lover of the licentious Marguerite de Valois (Queen Margot, 1553–1615) and was beheaded like Julien. Marguerite bribed the executioner to give her the head of her beloved and secretly had it buried in a chapel.

> Le souvenir de Boniface de La Môle et de Marguerite de Navarre lui donna sans doute un courage surhumain. Elle allumait plusieurs bougies. Lorsque Fouqué eut la force de la regarder, elle avait placé sur une petite table de marbre, devant elle, la tête de Julien, et la baisait au front.
>
> Mathilde suivit son amant jusqu'au tombeau qu'il s'était choisi. Un grand nombre de prêtres escortait la bière, et à l'insu de tous, seule dans sa voiture drapée, elle porta sur ses genoux la tête de l'homme qu'elle avait tant aimé.

The obvious originality of this harrowing Romantic *topos* is Mathilde's last vaguely necrophiliac kiss as well as her reminiscence of the gruesome historical analogy experienced by her ancestor : a strange and fateful *duplicitas casuum.*

Sartre

The night preceding the early morning execution of three prisoners put on the death list by Spanish fascists is the subject of Jean-Paul

41 *Les Dieux ont soif*, 1912, and *La Révolte des anges,* 1914; see ch. VI, "Anatole France's Olympians".

Sartre's well-known short story *The Wall* (1939). His characters include the Spanish trade unionist Pablo Ibbieta, an American volunteer in the Republican International Brigade, Tom Steinbeck, and Juan, politically uncommitted brother of José Mirbal, an anarchist sought by Franco's regime. The trio is watched by a Belgian doctor who monitors symptoms of the prisoners' physiological and psychological stress, ranging from shortness of breath or sweating to spontaneous urination and mental collapse. At dawn Tom and Juan are shot whereas Pablo is once more interrogated and promised life in exchange for information on the hiding place of his friend Ramon Gris whom he had sheltered prior to his arrest. As his last joke he sends the phalangists to the cemetery saying that they will find Ramon in the grave digger's hut. He "knows" that it is a sheer fantasy. When the search unit returns, Pablo's execution is suspended and he learns that Ramon was killed at the cemetery. A sense of the ultimate absurdity of life overwhelms him and in his agony he bursts out laughing.[42]

The innovative stimulus in this prewar existentialist subject matter is its quasi-scientific analysis of pre-execution agonies experienced by the three political prisoners. The omniscient author cooly dramatizes the degrading physical and psychological manifestations of their growing fears; meanwhile the prison doctor records their "symptoms" as the hour of death approaches. Implicit in this scene is a morbid satire of the fascist contributions to clinical psychiatry. The chain of dramatic absurdities saturating and unifying Sartre's plot allegorizes the major tenets of his existentialist creed. Not even Pablo Ibbieta's militant devotion to the socialist cause—distinguishing his heroic essence from the unworthy vegetation of the non-committed Juan Mirbal—can prevent a fresh outburst of existentialist *Angst*.

Among the many potential intertextual associations emerging spontaneously in the critic's mindscape upon reading Sartre's mimesis of absurdity is the recollection of the Greek *Ananke*-Necessity, whose fateful whims Zeus himself could not avert. A more specific analogy intensifying the stimulative potential of "The Wall" could be, of course, Dostoevsky's sentence and interrupted execution: in 1849, the writer stood on the scaffold, lined up with 19 members of a debating society, kissed the cross and watched the first three condemned men being blindfolded and attached to the poles. Soldiers stood ready to fire; a row of 20 coffins awaited the corpses. Only at that point was the sentence

42 See Appendix, Sartre. Also see ch. VII, "Existentialist fantasies."

commuted to eight years of forced labor. One of the three blindfolded men went mad.[43]

Zikmund Winter

In returning to a memorable text after some time, a reader may discover that its extratextual impact is stronger or weaker depending on the experience over the intervening years.[44] In 1992, I re-read a Czech classic, *Master Kampanus*.[45] The author was an historian who fictionalized the violent and tragic end of Czech political independence after the battle at White Mountain near Prague in 1620. I first read the novel as a teen-ager during the brief period when the country's lost freedom was restored (1918–1939). In that happy era, it evoked the gloomiest stage of Czech history. After having experienced a number of painful clashes which radically transformed Central Europe, and having extended my academic background, I read *Master Kampanus* with an eye for timely stimulative analogies of which, naturally, Winter could not have been aware before World War I when he wrote the novel.

Master Kampanus was awarded a Czech literary prize in 1912, but, as *bohemica non leguntur*,[46] it was not predestined to stimulate the broad community of international readers. When writing this chapter in 1992, I glanced at the bibliophile edition from my father's library and suddenly I was hooked: I read it in one blow. The old stimulations of violent political conflict, the mimesis of tragic historical events were still there, but more recent experiences heightened them: the humiliation of Munich, the years (1939–45) spent in the Nazi-occupied Protectorat Böhmen und Mähren, the shaky liberation and the repressive Communist regime of 1948–89. Having also witnessed, both in my old home and from my new home, the desperate political fence-sitting; silent, melancholy shame; minimal preventive collaboration or worse, I found Winter's representation of the Czech Calvary and of the Renaissance Rector's moral conflict timely and esthetically persuasive. The panorama of the battle, the endless *Dies irae*, massive confiscations of Czech properties

43 See Laurence Irving's "Introduction" to *Crime and Punishment*, transl. Constance Garnett (London: Dent, New York: Dutton, 1911), pp. v–vii, citing Sonia Kovalevski's *Reminiscences*.

44 See comments on fluctuating extratextual intensity of comical stimuli, ch. V, "Quality of humor."

45 Zikmund Winter, *Mister Kampanus*, Prague, Otto, 1911.

46 The Czech writings are not read.

transferred along with nobility patents to foreign mercenaries, execution or exile of Czech elite, the Jesuit triumph over the Liberal Hussite university form the epical *Requiem* addressed to the posterity of those who survived but were scarred by the Apocalypse. *Master Kampanus* and many other historical novels[47] boosted Czech nationalism and the drive for autonomy which helped dismember the moribund Hapsburg monarchy in 1918. The novel urgently told the turn-of-the century Czech readers what not to do, if they should ever again live as a free nation. During the 1948–89 dictatorship, it became timely and regained its pre-World War I intensity. A rediscovery of the novel's spell by a solitary reader like me illustrates the instability as well as the dynamism of extratextual perception, triggering unpredictable valuatory or hermeneutic responses to the intratextual stimuli stabilized long ago.

Its text relates the complex tragedy through the eyes of a forgotten Czech humanist, rector of the then Hussite Charles University. This neo-Virgilian poet and classical scholar witnesses the uprising of Protestant Czech leaders against the Catholic Hapsburg Emperor. He watches them throw the Imperial governors from the windows of the Prague Castle.[48] The "defenestration" marking the beginning of the Thirty Years War brought about a fatal retaliation: the Imperial mercenary troops under Duke Maximilian of Bavaria crushed the Czech and allied forces, occupied Prague and a special court presided over by Duke Liechtenstein condemned the Czech leaders to death. From the spire of the Tyne cathedral the rector watches the execution of 27 patriots who had defended political and religious freedom against the Austrian Catholic autocracy. In some instances, prior to ultimate decapitations or hanging, the rebels' bodies are quartered. When Dr. Jessenius, former university rector[49] is brought to the scaffold, the excutioner cuts out his tongue and

47 E.g., by Alois Jirásek.

48 The defenestrated lieutenants fell on a manure heap, found shelter in the palace of a Catholic aristocrat and were whisked expeditiously to the Imperial court in Vienna. The rebels immediately elected a Protestant King—Falzgraf Friedrich, son-in-law of the King of England. Winter's fiction does not substantially deviate from historical sources. In spite of Czech hopes, the English monarch offered no help to his son-in-law (who was also the head of the continental Protestant League).

49 Ironically, a pioneer of modern anatomy who, following his term as rector of the university, served as a politically engaged member of the university board (*defensor*). A.M. Ripellino (*Magic Prague*, transl. D.N. Marinelli, ed. M.H. Heim, Berkeley, L.A., U. of California Press, 1994, pp. 153–8) recapitulates the legendary details of the grusome show of power.

only then slowly proceeds with his decapitiaton. This frightful spectacle, the long-lasting terror and the radical anti-reformation drive undermines Kampanus' moral courage. To save what can be saved he collaborates with the Jesuits, who take over Charles University, and converts to Catholicism. He is torn by a traumatic inner conflict—should he betray his patriotic Hussite liberalism and ingratiate himself to the militant Jesuit establishment? What is there after all to be saved? When Kampanus and his colleagues are fired, when expropriated patriots are forced into exile, when the Jesuits take total control of his *alma mater*, the heartbroken ex-rector takes rat poison. The Jesuits bury him with modest pomp as an exemplary convert and loyal subject of the victorious Catholic Majesty.

One digressive association accompanying my deliberation on the qualities of the re-read patriotic prose was intertextual. I kept recalling a stanza of a half-forgotten Czech lyrical poem by Viktor Dyk (1877–1931). The quatrain which so urgently entered my thoughts in connection with *Master Kampanus* alludes to a solitary reader sitting late at night above a book read "ages ago"; its "flamboyant language" which continues holding "you", the overwhelmed reader, under its profound spell: "A single line has seared your soul; / All night its fiery language burned. / Book in hand you sit transfixed, / the final page long since turned."[50] This esthetic echo could be nothing else than my silent tribute to the powerful art of Zikmund Winter, doubly confirming the proverbial cliché—*pro captu lectoris habent sua fata libelli*.[51]

Terrorist Tchen: Malraux' Communist Martyr

The turbulent history of the twentieth century has transformed the literary representation as well as perception of violent conflicts: the 1914 assassination of Archduke Ferdinand at Sarajevo; unprecedented massacres on European battlefields, the Bolshevik slaughter of the Russian Czar's family, Stalin's purges, Al Capone's shoot-outs, Nazi terror; the brutalities of the Second World War, Katyn, Hiroshima, the Kennedy assassinations, global terrorism, "ethnic cleansing", etc. have increased the arsenal of conflicts art can imitate in its search for

50 Today I remember neither the title of the collection nor that of the poem. The once memorized stanza: "Jediná stránka tebe chytne / Promluví řečí plamennou / Dlouho do noci pak sedíš / Nad knihou dávno dočtenou." Versified by Louise Bresky.

51 According to the reader's sensibilities, books have their own destinies. Attributed to Terentius Maurus, approximately 2nd century A.D., (l. 1286).

originality and the highest intensity. Increasingly cinematic violence and graphic TV images of actual violence seem to have heightened our appetite for explicit representations of such conflicts. Twentieth century censors in democratic countries seldom interfere with either verbal or audiovisual transpositions of gruesome acts unless the mimesis is obscene or perverse.

André Malraux, winner of the 1932 Prix Goncourt, relates in *La Condition humaine* the bloody power struggles between capitalist and Marxist forces shaping post-feudal China into a cruel modern colossus. The novel exploits espionage violence, spectacular terrorist attacks on police headquarters, an attempt on Chiang Kai-Shek's life and other highlights of the brutal 1927 uprising in Shanghai. This is followed by sadistic executions of the "victorious" Communist rebels by their own temporary allies fighting under the banners of Kuomintang. The fictional, serialized reportage turns Chinese civil war into exotic nascent mythology. This narrative frame lends an illusory authenticity to all characters and their actions. Obviously, in a novel echoing contemporary events some of Malraux' secondary characters could not be totally "fictionalized" (e.g., Chiang Kai-shek). On the other hand, his protagonist, the intellectual Kyo Gisors, son of a European professor of sociology in Peking and a Japanese mother, is only vaguely modelled after the prominent Communist leader Chou-En-Laï (Chou, unlike Malraux' tragic character, was not Eurasian but Chinese and had survived the bloody revolution described in the novel). Whether historical, semifictional or invented, all Malraux' characters interact in a convincing literary replica of current political happenings which he, often ironically, observed. As a young, then *engagé*, writer he mythified the tragic and absurd destinies of dedicated terrorists fighting for Communist China. The text opens with a thrilling murder of a sleeping arms dealer who has in his possession the bill of lading for an arms shipment sold to the shaky Chinese regime. The Communist revolutionaries, who need more arms, instruct a terrorist novice Tchen (Professor Gisors' former student) to kill the agent and steal the transaction document. It will enable the party to intercept the shipment destined for the government the Communists hope to overthrow. Tchen, armed with a dagger and a razor, steals into the agent's hotel room. More of a romantic idealist than a cold-blooded assassin, he is torn between partisan discipline and human sentiment. He is determined to carry out the party's order but cannot execute it without a moral shake-up. His suppressed respect for human life clashes with his dogmatic loyalty to the rebel cause.

> Tchen tenterait-il de lever la moustiquaire? Frapperait-il au travers? L'angoisse lui tordait l'estomac; il connaissait sa propre fermeté, mais n'était capable en cet instant que d'y songer avec hébétude, fasciné par ce tas de mousseline blanche qui tombait du plafond sur un corps moins visible qu'une ombre, et d'où sortait seulement ce pied...vivant quand même—de la chair d'homme.[52]

Malraux' suspenseful description is much more detailed than the prelude to the stabbing of the Florentine duke in *The Heptameron* novella or than the assassination scene in *Lorenzaccio*. The reader "sees" the nocturnal urban setting, and "hears" the horns of the cars passing in front of the hotel. Malraux reveals his character's worries: is he being followed, Tchen wonders. He is not the expeditious butler of *The Heptameron* and his reluctance to kill the unknown sleeper keeps growing.

> Tchen découvrait en lui, jusqu'à la nausée, non le combattant qu'il attendait, mais un sacrificateur. Et pas seulement aux dieux qu'il avait choisis: sous son sacrifice à la révolution grouillait un monde de profondeurs auprès de quoi cette nuit écrasée d'angoisse n'était que clarté. 'Assassiner n'est pas seulement tuer...'

After this contemplation Tchen starts deliberating whether he should kill with the dagger or a razor. The dagger might be more compatible with the code of honor of a respectable commando. He feels an idiosyncratic resentment of the razor, although he thinks that it may be more effective. Trying to find his target in the darkness, the tense spy apprentice plants the dagger in his own left forearm. (A comical blunder worthy of Buster Keaton: it breaks, yet paradoxically heightens the grim suspense). As in a trance Tchen once more examines the sleeping victim:

> ...c'était bien l'homme qu'il avait vu, deux heures plus tôt, en pleine lumière. Le pied, qui touchait presque le pantalon de Tchen, tourna soudain comme une clef,... Peut-être le dormeur sentait-il une présence, mais pas assez pour s'eveiller... Tchen frissonna: un insecte courait sur sa peau. Non; c'était le sang de son bras qui coulait goutte à goutte. [Deadpan black farce continues.] Et toujours cette sensation de mal de mer.
>
> Un seul geste, et l'homme serait mort. Le tuer n'était rien: c'était le toucher qui était impossible. Et il fallait frapper avec précision.

As incredible as it may be, the self-inflicted wound serves as an antidote against the assassin's lethargy. Hastily he ponders the technicalities of

52 This and the six subsequent quotations cite André Malraux, *Romans, La Condition humaine* (Paris: Gallimard, Pléiade, 1947), pp. 181-3 and 353-5.

the brief death blow which would snuff the victim's life with professional integrity; he weighs the advantages and disadvantages of vertical or horizontal swings. A sudden touch of deadly farce prolongs the suspense—the sleeper snores. Finally Tchen strikes so hard that the blade would pass through a board.

> D'un coup à traverser une planche [literal overkill], Tchen l'arrêta dans un bruit de mousseline déchirée, mêlé à un choc sourd. Sensible jusqu'au bout de la lame, il sentit le corps rebondir vers lui, ...les jambes revenaient ensemble vers la poitrine, comme attachées [morbid, clinically farcical detail]; elles se détendirent d'un coup. Il eût fallu frapper de nouveau, mais comment retirer le poignard?

Feeling like an amateur, Tchen is not sure how well he killed the arms dealer and, for a long time, he holds the corps pinned to the bed with his dagger. He is unable to let go the handle until a spasm in his arm muscles allows him to open his clenched fist. All reflexes of the gradually collapsing body are described with a somewhat perverse naturalistic precision. A cat climbing on the balcony is the only witness of the murder. Once more Tchen overreacts by opening his razor but the animal runs away. Only then he calms down, steals the bill of lading, vanishes in the street, flags a taxi and joins the conspirators who await him at the "headquarters" disguised as a drab record shop.

The historical events Malraux transposes to open his teleological discourse on contemporary life strikingly differs from subject matter treated by the preceding generation of authors also known for their mimesis of the human condition, such as André Gide, Romain Rolland, Marcel Proust, Thomas Mann, John Galsworthy, Roger Martin du Gard, Jules Romains, Sinclair Lewis. His material rather foreshadows the content of spy thrillers mainly developed only after World War II.[53]

The yarn relating a Chinese terrorist's debut was in 1933 an original macrostimulus of high intensity. It led his readers into an exotic bloody plot and disclosed, though not fully, the meaning of the novel's abstract title. Malraux broadens the connotation of the human condition in the dialog which follows the transposition of the arms dealer murder. After his criminal act the traumatized killer seeks moral support at the home of his Marxist mentor, Gisors, senior. Like the professor's (fictitious) son Kyo, Tchen is a Eurasian. During his childhood, a Protestant minister

53 E.g., John le Carré's *The Spy Who Came In from the Cold*, *Tinker Tailor, Soldier Spy*, etc. Unlike Tchen, Le Carré's cerebral and cynical heroes contemplate neither Communist nor democratic "sainthood."

showed him the path of Christian self-sacrifice and the pathos of sin and damnation. The subsequent Marxist indoctrination weakened his Christian faith but neither his spontaneous human compassion nor his heroic disposition to live and die for a worthy social cause. In his discussion with the old Gisors, Tchen confesses that his first murder shook him up and haunts him with an urgent premonition of tragic fate—"fatalité". "I will soon be killed" he says, foreshadowing the peak of Malraux' epic. Against the pragmatic wishes of Moscow, Tchen, determined to overcome the traumatic malaise which followed his first murder, decides to kill the Communists' ally, Chiang-Kai shek. He fears that that the better equippped Kuomintang might overpower the forces of the hostile "government" (i.e., generals controlling major parts of China such as Tchang-Tso-Lin and Wou-Pei-Fou) but also their pragmatic Communist fellow fighters. Needless to say Chiang-Kai-shek is not fooled by the strategy of his ally who hopes to crush the Kuomintang as soon as Communist military strength allows.

On their own initiative, Tchen and his conspirators trail the nationalist leader during the Shanghai uprising. They monitor the moves and routine schedules of the general's Ford. However, they are not fully informed about the last minute precautionary measures taken by Chiang-Kai-shek's entourage. The message that the leader will not be in his usual car does not reach Tchen as he waits in ambush for the approaching motorcade. Recognizing the official Ford with two bodyguards standing on the running boards Tchen, swinging the bomb above his head throws himself against the car hood. Malraux' ironic obituary canonizes Tchen's martyrdom—however futile—while at the same time illustrates the tragic absurdity of the "condition humaine."

Relating Tchen's final act, Malraux grants his Communist revolutionary a faith in the metaphysical merit of political self-sacrifice. To be heroic and even sacred, terrorism must become a "mystique," a religion. It cannot be only a political party, which ultimately motivates its militants, it has to be an ideal urgent enough to "faire renaître les martyrs." With such fleeting sentiments, the terrorist observes the approaching American car. "Il prit sa bombe par l'anse comme une bouteille de lait. L'auto du général était à cinq mètres, énorme. Il courut vers elle avec une *joie d'extatique*, se jeta dessus, les yeux fermés…"

In spite of the lethal explosion and before ascending to mystical Marxist heights, the…neomartyr regains consciousness, clutching a fragment of the car hood in his hand. Overwhelmed by unbearable pain, he tries to grasp the revolver in his pocket but his hand finds neither pocket nor pants. Where the pocket was, he feels only a mushy mass of bleeding flesh. The second revolver is in his shirt pocket; he manages to pull it out and release the safety catch.

> Il ouvrit enfin les yeux... Un policier était tout près. Tchen voulut demander si Chang-Kaï-Shek était mort, mais il voulait cela dans un autre monde; dans ce monde-ci, cette mort même lui était indifférente. De toute sa force, le policier le retourna d'un coup de pied dans les côtes... Il allait s'évanouir ou mourir. Il...parvint à introduire dans sa bouche le canon du revolver... Un furieux coup de talon d'un autre policier crispa tous ses muscles: il tira sans s'en apercevoir.

Malraux' research in Oriental archeology and his political contacts made him acquainted with the Far East and the then ongoing Chinese revolution.[54] In the early thirties, his mimeis of this monumental conflict and of the new breed of Chinese radicals ranging from academic ideologists to terrorists, was timely and prophetic. His conspirators were both idealists and brainwashed puppets controlled and sacrificed by anonymous apparatchiks pulling the strings in the distant Communist International. Malraux' Tchen, who yearned for Marxist martyrdom, must have struck pre-war readers as a naive victim of ruthless, doctrinaire demagogues. In the post-cold war climate he stimulates us as a literary precedent of suicide bombers hallowed by zealots and terrorists of all colors and condemned by advocates of law and order.

In dramatizing a modern exotic protagonist such as Tchen, Malraux adds a new portrait to the gallery of killers and assassins depicted by Malraux' 19th and 20th century predecessors to stimulate their readers. Just a few comparative glances in this gallery will testify to his originality. Salient examples of violent fiction produced during that era include, for instance, Prosper Mérimée's 1829 mimesis of the black chieftain Tamango, biting the jugular of the slave trader Ledoux; Dostoevsky's detailed 1866 profile of the indebted student Rodyon Raskolnikov who, following a multipartite inner conflict, murders an old parasitic pawnbroker Alyona Ivanovna and her sister; Zola's naturalistic clash between Etienne Lantier and his vulgar rival in love, Chaval in the flooded mine; Wilde's whimsical 1891 sketch of Lord Arthur Saville,

54 It started in 1911 when republican forces overthrew the Manchu dynasty and Sun-Yat-sen organized the Kuomintang party; its second phase began in 1928 when under Chiang-Kai-shek's leadership Kuomintang defeated the ruling war lords. Prior to this victory he brutally supressed his Communist allies. Only after World War II, with the Soviet support, Mao-Tse-tung seized power in 1949.

who drowns the palm reader who predicts he must murder before he can marry; Gide's 1914 apostle of *acte gratuit*, Lafcadio Wluiki, who "without any motive," throws his victim from the speeding train.[55] None of these killers served as a model for Malraux' revolutionary; his story on Tchen's terrorist undertakings undeniably extends the range of effective subject matter drawn from modern political violence and its absurd tragedies. In the shadow of the 2001 New York World Trade Center bombings, *La Condition humaine* gains new power by illuminating the pseudomystical essence of the political/religious terrorism now threatening civilized secular cultures.

Psychological Conflicts: Biblical and Ancient

My earlier comments on *Master Kampanus*—a novel buried now in Czech literary history, just as the historical events treated in its text are now buried in the 17th century history of Central Europe—make clear that the discussed macro-conflicts include not only violent encounters between the Czech nobility and the Hapsburg Catholic empire and the non-violent political clash between the Hussite and Jesuit intellectuals but also the learned Master Kampanus' crisis of conscience. This conflict culminates with his suicide, which also marks the novel's epical climax.

The first phase of any inner conflict is a character's weighing and prioritizing one of his/her two mutually opposed duties or beliefs. In the second phase the character ends the agonizing deliberation with an irrevocable choice. Malraux' terrorist Tchen balances the merits of political commitment against individual moral imperatives and ultimately subordinates his personal life to the goals of a revolutionary movement. The representation of Tchen's dilemma supports the overall dramatic intensity of Malraux' violent macroconflicts.

Such inner conflicts fought in the heart—conflicts which tradition labels as *collisiones officiorum*,[56]—do not stimulate the same instincts as

55 Re Tamango killing Ledoux, see cit. and comments, *LP I*, pp. 149–51. Both *Tamango* and *Lord Arthur Saville's Crime* are discussed below in ch. V, "Irony of Fate" and Zola's *Germinal* on Appendix. A mini-anthology of "Murderers" is ch. IV in the *Oxford Book of Villains*, ed. John Mortimer, Oxford Univ. Press, 1993.

56 See Hegel (op. cit. n. 10,) p. 113. "The *collision* arises…in an act of *violation*, which is unable to retain its character as such, but is compelled to find a new principle of unity; it is a change in the previously existent condition of harmony, a change which is still in process. The collision *is*, however, *not an action*, and is to be taken simply as *stimulus to action* to all that characterizes the situation. And this is true, although

those aroused by representations of violence, but due to their intensive polarity and to their triumphant or fatal outcomes, I treat them here as an autonomous topic belonging, nevertheless, in the broad category of conflicts. As they have to be epically or dramatically developed they usually offer a macrostimulative effect.[57] Like physical confrontations our psychological conflicts are seen here as acute contrasts between the unavoidable and fatal choices the characters have to make. Like violence and dramatic feuds they too lead to "victories and defeats."

Among the obvious biblical and mythological precedents of stimulative subjects categorizable as inner conflicts are Abraham's willingness to sacrifice to Jehovah the life of his own son Isaac and Antigone's attempt to bury her brother Polynices and thus violate the interdict of her uncle Creon. Abraham, like Eve and Adam before him, directly communicates with the Lord; in his divine wisdom Jehovah tests Abraham's faith and fear of God in a manner which strikes modern posterity not only as absurd but plain sadistic. The trusted patriarch should burn his son as an offering inexplicably worthy of the revered jealous God: "And he said, take now thy son, thine only *son* Isaac, whom thou lovest, and get thee into the land of Mö-ri´åh; and offer him there for a burnt offering upon one of the mountains which I will tell thee of."[58]

Without a single word of protest the centenarian saddles his ass and puts a load of firewood "upon Isaac his son" (to be burnt) and the two set out for the Moriah highlands. During the journey Isaac is unaware of Jehovah's and Abraham's deal. Only when God's obedient servant takes "knife to slay his son" before the ritual cremation, the Lord's angelic messenger tells Abraham to "cool it" (literally). Although the scriptures do not allude to any inner conflict or shock affecting Jehovah's steadfast

---

the contradiction in which the collision is enclosed may be the result of previous action. As an example of this we may cite the trilogies of the ancients, which carry forward the main theme by presenting at the close of one drama the collision which forms the stimulative impulse of the next, which is carried out by the third." The Hegelian "collision," "an *act* of violation" which "is however, not an *action*" (my italics) is foggy. One could argue that inner conflicts are suspenseful moral preludes to external conflicts.

57 However, e.g., Candide's inner conflict whether to kill or not to kill the inquisitor (see previous discussion on Voltaire's conflicts) is microstimulative. Often the degree of stimulation inner conflicts offer depends on the intensity of the reader's empathy with the character experiencing the conflict as well as on the perceivable authenticity or artificiality of the represented dilemma.

58 *Genesis*, XXII, 2–17.

devotee, the modern interpreters of this *topos*, however, suggest that the god-fearing Abraham must have experienced a replica of the existentialist Kierkegaardien *Angst* (*angoisse*) and a deep sense of absurdity over his own staunch loyalty to his maker. Hegel distinguishes two types of inner conflict in Greek tragedy—"the dilemma of moral responsibility incurred for the character's deeds committed", however, "under the directing providence of the gods'". An example of the first type would be Agamemnon's sacrifice of his daughter Iphigenia to Artemis, demanded in exchange for favorable winds awaited by the Greek fleet ready to sail against Troy.[59] Antigone's inner conflict in Sophocles' tragedy represents another prototype "dealing with the opposition between ethical life in its social universality and the family as the natural ground of moral relations."[60] The tragic subject is the heroine's attempt to bury her older brother Polynices who was killed while fighting to seize power in Thebes dominated by Eteocles, his younger brother. However, the fallen aggressor had killed Eteocles. His successor Creon (Polynices', Eteocles' and Antigone's uncle) rules that Polynices shall remain unburied. In vain, Antigone invokes divine laws and disobeys Creon's order. For this she is sentenced to death and, to avoid execution, commits suicide. Her fiancé, Creon's own son, kills himself. Creon's wife, learning about her son's suicide stabs herself to death. The crushed Creon finally deplores the cruelty of the law he declared without making any allowance for compassion and mercy.

The anecdotal plot of "The Matron of Ephesus" exemplifies comical, short-lived inner conflicts. The tale relates the dilemma of a young widow who decides never to leave her deceased husband and to die at his side in his Greek-style sepulchre. This burial ground is located near the site where several thieves have been crucified. To prevent relatives from burying their remains, a soldier guards the bodies. When he hears loud laments coming from underground, the mystified soldier descends into the vault to find the charming mourner. Not only does he persuade the widow to stay alive, he even manages to seduce her. At the end of their sepulchral tryst, the lovers discover that one of the thieves has been removed from the cross by his relatives. Fearing her new lover might be court martialed or even executed, the widow suggests they replace the dead criminal with the remains of her husband. "Better to hang up a dead

59 Euripides, *Iphigenia in Aulis* (Agamemnon's dilemma is a Greek analogy of Abraham's Hebraic collision).

60 Hegel, see n. 10, "Introduction," p. xxv referring to Hegel's *Fine Arts* IV, p. 318–19.

body than to kill a living man," says the Matron of Ephesus.[61] Imitators of this memorable plot include La Fontaine and Voltaire.

Inner Conflict: Medieval and Classical

As we see, the inner conflicts in literature are not always tragic but, as suggested, they are often related to violent actions: in *La Chanson de Roland* the lives of the knights forming the rear-guard at Roncevaux in the Pyrenees (778) could have been saved, had Roland blown his horn *olifant* in time to call for help of Charlemagne's troops. However, the intrepid rear-guard commander rejected this signal fearing that his peers would judge it cowardly. He prefers to die.

The early medieval poet Aurelius Prudentius Clemens saw the human soul as a battleground of Christian virtues and pagan vices. He allegorized our noble and sinful propensities and pitted one against the other in his *Psychomachia* (4–5th century A.D.). Its second part, some 915 hexameters, invents conflict between human Faith and Idolatry, between sensuality and sobriety, and so on. The critics[62] tend to dismiss the text as a poor work of art but cautiously credit Prudentius for "improving" Plautus' and Virgil's mimesis of our moral qualities.

The inner conflict of Rabelais' Panurge has little in common with a tragic *collisio officiorum.* His mental struggle is nothing but trivial indecision; his desire to get married constantly clashes with his pessimistic vision of conjugal bliss. This never-ending deliberation of the pros and cons of matrimony inspires Pantagruel's and Panurge's pilgrimage to hear the oracle of the divine bottle.

The French classics considerably enriched the esthetics of grave moral conflicts. They imitate not only the mythological and ancient precedents but also draw from Christian and chivalrous sources. In Corneille's best known tragi-comedy *Le Cid* (1636), Don Rodrigue and Chimène, who love one another, experience tragic inner conflicts: Chimène's father Don Gomas politically humiliates her lover's father, Don Diègue. The family "honor" compels the reluctant son to seek satisfaction from his prospective father-in-law and ultimately to kill him in a "socially unavoidable" duel. Chimène's loyalty to her father's memory prevents her from marrying (at least without delay) the man

61 Gaius (Titus?) Petronius Arbiter (approx. 20–66 A.D.) *Satirae.*

62 E.g., see comments in C.S. Lewis, *The Allegory of Love* (New York: Oxford University Press, 1958), p. 66, q.s.; also Laffont-Bompiani *Dictionnaire des Oeuvres*, vol. IV, *Psychomachie.*

whom she continues to love.[63]

The 1677 appearance of *Phèdre* marks the peak of Racine's art. At this point the tragedian is named Royal Historiographer and gives up his dramatic writing. His version of *Phèdre* owes more to Seneca's (65 A.D.) *Phaedra* than to Euripides' *Hippolytus, the Wreath Bearer* (429 B.C.). Phedre commits suicide because of her fatal incestuous love for her stepson Hippolyte. In his turn Hipppolyte becomes a tragic victim of circumstances. Because he is not willing to accuse his scheming stepmother, he provokes the curse of his father Theseus, a curse which causes his tragic death.[64]

Literary historians consider Madame de La Fayette (1634–93) as a forerunner of the modern psychological novel. Her *La Princesse de Clèves* (completed with some assistance from the Duke de La Rochefoucauld in 1678) prepared the ground for the 18th and 19th century masters of psychological genres, ranging from Richardson, abbé A.-F. Prévost and Rousseau to Dostoyevsky, Gide and Proust.

Sacrifice of a Patriotic Prostitute

In my comment on macrorhetoric, I discuss several texts whose specific content level can be seen as an allegorical image hiding a universal meaning. Maupassant's "Boule de Suif"[65] exemplifies such texts. My stylistic analysis of his story marginally touches on the tragic inner conflict of the patriotic prostitute, the heroine of the story. While she travels in the company of several countrymen from Rouen, occupied in 1870 by the Prussian army, to the unoccupied Le Havre, their diligence is detained at Tôtes by a German officer controlling traffic into unoccupied zones. He informs them that he will not let them through his check point unless Boule de Suif appeases his erotic longing. Such a *quid pro quo* clashes with her national pride: she left Rouen precisely to avoid any contact with the German invaders. Her conflict is polyvalent—national honor vs. venal collaboration; moral integrity vs. despicable compromise; it also has tragicomic and libertine accents. All her fellow travellers insist that this kind of sacrifice is nothing new for her. They claim she owes it to them, her French compatriots, who want to escape from occupied France as fast as they can.

When Flaubert wrote Maupassant "ce petit conte *restera* soyez-en

63 See discussion on content and form *LP I*, pp. 70–1.

64 See comments and citations in *LP II*, pp. 152–54.

65 See *LP II*, Appendix, pp. 232–34 and comments, ch. IV, "Allegory" pp. 115–18.

sûr...elle est charmante votre fille," he admired Maupassant's esthetic development of the character's inner conflict. His prognosis was correct: modern readers feel the intensity of Boule de Suif's pathetic dilemma as acutely as the readers in 1880 who remembered the defeat at Sedan (1870). It has retained its timeliness during the two world wars and it may have seemed very convincing to the readers who witnessed various methods of collaboration behind the vanished Iron Curtain. Today, it may provoke (stimulative) empathy of modern feminists fighting all forms of sexual harassment.

White Man's Burden French Style

In the same discourse on the art of allegory I allude to typical existentialist characters whose inner conflicts and resulting actions usually reflect the author's *engagé* humanism. The inner conflict of the French-African teacher Daru is one of the main contentual stimuli in the well-known anthology piece "L'Hôte",[66] Camus' last prose published before his death in 1960. Its subject matter is drawn from a then rapidly developing political crisis which lead to the termination of the French colonial rule in North Africa. This loss of influence divided the French public, embittered the French colonial *pieds noirs* and, in the early sixties, led to terrorist attempts by the Secret Army Organization. As a result of the protracted national inner conflict, the SAO tried to assassinate Gen. Charles de Gaulle, overthrow his regime by a *coup* and renew French military dominance in Algeria. Several high-ranking officers were arrested, one kidnapped from Germany where he was hiding, and Lieutenant-Colonel J.-M. Bastien Thiery was executed in 1963.[67] I allude to this political turbulence, triggered by the Arab independence movement and decline of French influence in North Africa, to stress how timely and newsworthy any discussion on French colonial power was in the late fifties. At that time, Camus' fiction, set in Algeria and describing the tragic dilemma of a French educator, was bound to arouse the interest of French and Algerian intelligentsia.

The dramatic episode unfolds during the political unrest in the vast region where Daru works as a teacher/principal in a primitive one-room

66 *L'Exil et le royaume*, Paris: Gallimard 1957. See résumé of "L'Hôte" in *LP II*, ch. IV, "Macrorhetoric", pp. 135–36 and *LP II*, Appendix, pp. 222–23. *Le Premier Homme* (Paris: Gallimard) was published posthumously in 1994.

67 This revolt inspired Frederick Forsyth's 1971 bestseller *The Day of the Jackal* and its film version.

school built on a solitary arid plateau. Because of this emergency, the colonial gendarmerie has to discharge military duties and the teacher is deputized to replace the busy gendarmes and to deliver an arrested Arab murderer to a colonial jail. He anticipates that the Arabs will kill him if he obeys and the government will punish him if he does not. The high literary intensity of Daru's predicament springs from the then ongoing agitated debates, political tension, the exotic subject matter and the earlier identified poetic ambiguities, which invite at least two additional levels of allegorical interpretation. All of these further enhance both the intra- and extratextual esthetic potential particularly in the eyes of readers curious about the political implications of Camus' content.

The time spans during which Boule de Suif and Daru encounter and solve their respective moral challenges is comparable to the 24-hour unity of time customary in classical tragedy.[68] The length and the reading time of the two transpositions differs though not significantly. In *Boule de Suif*, which has some 14,000 words, the author devotes roughly 5,700 words to the stubborn refusal of the heroine to comply with the German officer's condition, to her countrymen's pressure and to her lamentable capitulation—"l'amour sacré de la patrie..." In "L'Hôte" (about 4,500 words) some 3,000 words dramatically outline Daru's collision between his new unprecedented civic duty on one side and his individual moral and professional standards on the other (Table 3 below, 1–5). The identification of the dramatic stages projects both the density and growing intensity of the stimulative gradation. Almost word by word, line by line, Camus implicitly increases Daru's stress which culminates at the very end (10–14). Tragically, his decency will never be rewarded. Camus does not spell out Daru's ultimate destiny, he merely foreshadows it. He leaves it to the reader to guess when, how and if the natives will fulfil the warnings which Daru finds jotted on the school's blackboard after his return. Table 3 traces the intratextual build-up of the dilemma as well as the correlated extratextual stimulation potentially experienced by qualified readers.

As illustrated, the fictional characters' inner conflicts spring from their double loyalties, or opposed, for example, political or erotic bonds. In other cases, they are epical or dramatic correlates of collective defeats affecting an entire group, of violent threats, blackmail. Romeo and Juliet conceal their love and die because of the families' inexorable rivalry. Tchen's moral reluctance to commit terrorist crimes is weaker than his

68 In major epical works, the duration of growing conflicts may be longer.

devotion to the communist cause. Its reward is tragic. Master Kampanus' fear, shameful collaboration and suicide are consequences of the Hussite defeat by the Catholic Hapsburgs. Daru's Sisyphian humanism meshes neither with the orders of colonial administration nor with the Arab tribal vendetta. He stands alone while absurd collective forces crush him.

TABLE 3

	The Phases of Daru's Inner Conflict	Intensity
1	Gendarme Balducci tells Daru (dismal order): ..."tu livreras le camarade à Tinguit" "Ce sont les ordres" (of distant government) "Nous sommes tous mobilisés"	
2	"Il [prisonnier] est contre nous?" "Je ne crois pas"	
3	"Pourquoi a-t-il tué?"... "L'un devait du grain à l'autre." (Non-political tribal crime)	
4	...tu es armé? Il [gendarme] tirait...son revolver et le posait sur le bureau. (Your life threatened)	
5	...Balducci, tout cela me dégoûte. (Am I mobilized or only a policeman ?)	
6	C'est un ordre. Tu vas me signer le papier	
7	Il signa...il...fourra [le revolver] dans sa poche	
8	Dans un moment le revolver le heurta...[Daru] mit le revolver dans le tiroir. (Risky decision)	
9	Account of suspenseful night—e.g., Arab leaves the room but does not escape. He urinates in front of the school house and returns to his folding bed. Daru hopes in vain that the Arab will solve his own as well as Daru's inner conflicts	Suspense grows
10	The two men's journey to the jail	Suspense continues
11	Daru offers Arab money and shows him the way either to jail or to freedom	
12	Unexpectedly Arab proceeds toward the jail	
13	Daru's anxiety grows	
14	Daru reads the fatal warning on the blackboard	

Rutherford's Thesaurus of Russian Atrocities

Among recent bestsellers offered to the post-cold war public is Edward Rutherford's *Russka*.[69] The abhorrent massacres, diverse social and personal hostilities and the contrastful torments which the author

69 New York: Ivy Books, Ballantine/Random, 1992.

condenses in 900 pages reconfirm that barbaric violence stimulates modern readers just as much as it once stimulated Homeric patrons. Its density and variety make this epos a thesaurus of Russian and Asiatic atrocities. Rutherford's distinct genre can be characterized as a nostalgic variation of a livresque family saga or *roman fleuve* in which amply footnoted key moments of Russian history serve as backdrop for the melodramatic chronicle extending from 180 A.D. to 1992. His fictional characters are members of three interacting families, peasant, merchant and aristocratic, whose bloodlines survive for almost two millennia in two villages both named Russka. Their origins go back to Scythian and Macedonian horsemen, Greeks, early migrant Slavs, Subaltaic Fins; following their conversion they mix with the victorious Tatars, Vikings, Turks; Kossacks, Poles, Jews, Ukrainians, Lithuanians intermarry with Russians. Such a millennial melting pot implies not only dialectic assimilation but also centuries of atavistic ethnic and religious discords. Rutherford's protagonists witness or participate in historical conquests as both conquerors and conquered. Never ending invasions, wars, terror, revolts, repression, slavery, pogroms, epidemics, rapes, adultery, incest, executions twist the souls and haunt the memories of the vital but chronically beleaguered survivors. The transpositions of their destinies offer Western readers a striking mosaic of historic, often exotic personal and political conflicts unfolding in distant, never seen settings.

The Tatar

This medieval melodrama evokes a Russian child's trauma. In December 1237, a Mongolian officer Mengu (25 years later known as Peter the Tatar) participates in the violent conquest and destruction of (southern) Russka during which, (to avoid any blame from his commanders,) he reluctantly kills a peasant mother in front of her seven year-old daughter Yanka. His troops also burn the church sheltering the villagers. After his brief cavalry career he becomes a rich *baskuk*, (tax collector), and, in 1262, following his conversion to Nestorian Christianity,[70] he visits the northern village built and named Russka by the survivors of the 1237 massacre in the original Russka on the southern steppe. There the penitent convert plans to build and endow a monastery. While examining its future site he leans his bow and arrow against a tree, unaware that a peasant woman watches him. She is the adult Yanka

70 See ch. VII, n. 26.

married now to a Mordvinian pagan. Recognizing the scarred face of the Tatar who killed her mother, she seizes the bow and arrow and kills Mengu. Her husband cuts his body into pieces small enough to drop into a hollow bee-inhabited tree in the woods and then buries the identifiable head under the threshold of his feudal lord's home. From that moment on, a series of dreadful misfortunes afflicts the accursed lord.

Ivan

Rutherford's portrait of the demonic sovereign somewhat evokes the fragile bond between Lorenzaccio and Duke Alessandro but its tragic follow-up differs. The 16-year-old cavalry man, Boris Bobrov of Russka, swears a lifelong allegiance to the young Tsar Ivan whom he first meets on the shore of the Volga during a glorious campaign. Neither of them ever forgets the pledge. Later in his life, the *boyar* is admitted among Ivan's black shirt insiders called "Oprichniki." They spy on and terrorize everybody even faintly suspect of lukewarm respect for the paranoid Tsar. In 1567 Ivan casually accuses Boris' father-in-law Dimitri Ivanov of being friendly with the gentry unsympathetic to his rule. Boris listens silently knowing that any defence of his relative would compromise him. Shortly after, the old man is secretly murdered along with 3000 other noblemen in the Kremlin armory where the Oprichniks prepare "a huge frying pan underneath which [is] fire. In this they [fry] him."[71]

This mass liquidation of alleged aristocratic dissenters is far from the climax of Ivan's terrible tale. Next comes the spurious Church: Ivan orders the murder of St. Philip, metropolitan of the Russian Church, for declaring the Oprichina "un-Christian" and witholding his blessing of the Tsar. He then launches an "anti-heretic" purge to crush any spiritual opposition to his will. During this reform the Tsar and his sinister entourage come looking for clandestine heretics in Bobrov's domain. There, Ivan forces his own Oprichnik to accuse the Russka priest of heresy. The victim is roped to a bear in the hopes that the animal will tear him to pieces; when the bear fails, the black-shirts beat the clergyman to death. As he watches the bloodbath, the drunken Tsar makes Boris confess that he accused the priest because he suspected him of seducing his wife and fathering his baby son Feodor. Infuriated , Ivan goes to Boris' residence in the middle of the night, takes the sleeping Feodor

71 Ibid., p. 309. Again associatively, the reader may consider such sadism as a precedent of Stalinist purges, Katyn, etc. Three centuries later, black shirts still evoke not only Italian Fascists and the German SS but all uniformed oppressors.

from his mother, ascends the Russka observation tower and throws the child down onto the icy ground in front of his agonizing mother. Rutherford's final stroke in this double portrait of the insane Tsar and his desperate Oprichnik depicts the ultimate imperial atrocity (1580): "Ivan, in a fit of anger, killed his own son," Crown Prince Ivan.[72] The Oedipus myth perverted *à la Russe*.

Intensified Conflicts

Both my illustrations of fictitious conflicts and my valuatory readings stress that in both life and art their observable epical and dramatic gradations and culminations are their key qualitative attributes. I also maintain that these gradations are topical and endogeneous and not stylistic and/or exogeneous.

Authors first choose their conflict, then stylize it. The characteristic build-up of dramatic events linking, for example, the romantic beginning and stunning end of Helena's and Paris' elopement , which escalates into a bloody, l0-year war, is clearly an epical, not a stylistic gradation. Skillful writers spontaneously support any stimulative information with their rhetoric. But in such fusions of topical and stylistic highs and lows, it is, above all, the unity and cohesion of epical steps leading to the conflict's peak and their endogeneous gradation which make battles, struggles and rivalries primary stimulative material in all epical and dramatic genres. Their integral duration and suspense also influence their stimulative potential. Even the episodic confrontations, like Candide's two duels (see above), have their contrastful low openings and dramatic peaks: one after the other, Cunegonde's elderly suitors are killed in the boudoir where Candide finally begins enjoying her intimate attentions; one after the other, they attack him and in self-defense he manages to kill them both. The love nest suddenly becomes a morgue. Writers have always known that we readers crave such exciting encounters and that many of us would stop reading if we could not find some extratextual merit in the combination of their intratextual subjects and style. On one side, the author's creative choices form a chain of free intratextual, esthetically adapted information; on the other side, these choices are subject to extratextual scrutiny by publishers, critics and readers. Once writers comply with reader expectations, their absolute freedom to choose subject matter shrinks. The conventional valuatory norms of

72 Ibid., p. 339.

quality demand conflicts which are (1) surprising (not dull), (2) original (fresh, timely, not stale), (3) contrastful (not monotonous) and (4) fast-moving (not stagnant). Though merely conventional and optional, these prescriptions are never quite ignored whether for artistic or commercial reasons. The public interest in recent political conflicts, crimes or scandals also primes the readers' taste for the transposition of such events or the invention of analogical intrigues and plots. Trying to maximize esthetic impact of any conflict they treat, writers often achieve it by various stylistic means. The non-stylistic practices designed to boost the stimulative power of represented conflicts can be exemplified and generally outlined rather than exhaustively enumerated.

While we unmistakably notice the calculated highs and lows of topical intensities in the texts under scrutiny, we cannot convincingly quantify them. This, however, does not invalidate normative criteria applicable to intensity of content. As I progressively identify and compare the successive contentual stimuli, I speculate that the impact of content grows, for example, due to a judicious selection and transposition of truly original (often unprecedented, contemporary, newsworthy) material and its most striking details. The murder of Duke Alessandro was fresh when Marguerite de Navarre represented it in her *Heptameron*; so was the Chinese revolution when Malraux fictionalized it in *La Condition humaine*. Musset's *Lorenzaccio,* staging a political attentate against a forgotten Renaissance tyrant appealed to 20th century spectators suffering under Communist dictatorship. The excess of transposed dramatic subjects in the lengthy first version (1834), which would have required two full evenings to reach its stirring climax, defied both dramatic discipline and audience attention span. The slow pace of such an interminable drama proved forbidding; the play was never produced in its original form.

Rutherford's bookish resurrection of the Tatar invasion and Ivan's despotism provokes the interest of post cold-war occidental readers who, without wading through centuries of Russian history, are still eager to catch a few artistically unified glimpses of rulers and martyrs fatefully born in the autocratic land first known as Holy Russia, then as the Union of Soviet Socialist Republics and finally christened by President Reagan as the "Evil Empire." The analogies between the Tsars and the Soviet dictators and the contrasts between Russian and Western cultures induce long-lasting, mainly humanistic contemplations among readers who finish Rutherford's epic marathon.

The Homeric integration of heroic violence with divine (supernatural) intervention; the Rabelaisian assemblage of crude brutality, farcical, utopian and fabulous stimuli; Marguerite's farcical vision of the murder; the Voltairean mix of violence, libertinage and satire; or Malraux' blend of terrorism and psychological trauma experienced by an "exotic hero" all demonstrate the common practice of twinning or combining several heterogeneous stimuli to enhance overall macrostimulative effects.[73] In various psychological genres, such as *Les Liaisons dangereuses* by Choderlos de Laclos, inner conflicts are often amalgamated with macrostimulative erotic affinities, intrigues, passions, treasons and secret torments. Some of such combined stimuli are addressed in the comments on the power of erotic subplots.[74] Voltaire's and Rabelais' texts further show stimulative advantages and drawbacks of an effective or ineffective adjustment of the narratological focus. This act can be defined as the art of restricting and climactically arranging the material—in this case the consecutive peaks of conflict and its stimulative details—to a coherent minimum. The reader's surprise depends first on the quality and prestylistic condensation (quantity) of stimulative content; thereafter on stylistic economy. Both the topical quantity and stylistic concision either accelerate or retard the narrative tempo.[75]

73 Ch. III, p. 59, n. 73. Quotations of *Germinal* and comments (Appendix, "Zola") demonstrate the technique of boosting macrostimulative impact by integrating several heterogeneous conflicts and other stimulative subjects. In subsequent chapters I examine macrostimulative plots/conflicts esthetically amalgamated with other stimuli. For example, Mérimée's treatment of 19th century slave traffic and a bloody mutiny is discussed in ch. V, "Grave Irony." Also see above n. 31, etc.

74 Ch. IV; among the well-known texts are for example, the medieval romance on Tristan and Iseut by Thomas, Beroul, Gottfried von Strassbourg, etc., Shakespeare's *Romeo and Juliet*, Madame La Fayette's *La Princesse de Clèves*, Richardson's *Clarissa*. Rousseau's *Julie ou la Nouvelle Héloïse*, Abbé Prévost's *Manon Lescaut*, Diderot's *La Religieuse*, Jane Austen's *Pride and Prejudice*. Flaubert's *Mme Bovary*, Tolstoy's *Anna Karenina*, Gide's *Les Faux-monnayeurs*, *La Porte étroite*, *La Symphonie pastorale*, Nabokov's *Lolita* with its ridiculous yet pathetic inner conflict of a pedophile. Malamud's *The Tenants* and Updike's *S.*, *Brazil* and the 1992 *Memoirs of the Ford Administration* effectively develop original inner conflicts of modern Americans, including those of Lincoln's predecessor, President James Buchanan.

75 In the context of *LP II*, ch. I, p. 10, I designate the preliminary selection and pruning of the subject as the first (negative) stylistic act. In fact, it falls in the "grey" creative domain where the choice of specific subjects intentionally or inadvertently concurs

"Gut" Reactions

These normative guidelines, which spring both from long empirical practice as well as from humanistic erudition, are likely to be invoked by esthetically oriented critics and publishers. The precedents of all criteria applicable to the mimesis of epical or dramatic clashes must be our vaguest atavistic recollections of prehuman fights for food, territorial defense, revolts of strong young males against aging leaders, competitions for females. Their mythological analogies include ethnic power struggles, kidnapping of enemy women, dynastic hostilities. All these precedents sheltered in our subconscious—our "gut" instincts along with personal experience and the constantly changing degree of cultivation—determine our spontaneous responses to any mimesis of conflicts. The reactions of any reader, whether literary amateur or professional critic, are further individualized by early home reading preceding or paralleling the first formal introduction to the classics at school. Before graduating to Virgil, Homer, Rabelais or Voltaire, I savored the ingenious ruses of the little Poucet (echoing Odysseus in Cyclops' cave or David resisting Goliath.) I enjoyed the courage and cunning of Janošík (the Slovak Robin Hood) in his brave fight against the feudal cruelty and exploitation of the serfs. My discovery of the ancient classics at school was mixed with extracurricular reading of *Robinson Crusoe* (1719), *The Three Musketeers* (1844), *Treasure Island* (1887), *White Fang* (1906) and so on. To enjoy them, I did not have to learn how to conjugate Greek verbs in aorist or get the occasional "F" for mistranslating a tricky Virgilian hexamater. The conflicts in Defoe, Dumas, Stevenson or Jack London—even in translation—required no footnotes, no dictionaries. As a "qualified" reader, I nostalgically recall the puerile delight triggered by Crusoe's gunning down from ambush the cannibals who had hoped to barbeque the enslaved Friday for a victory picnic on the beach. Or the veteran baroque security men and their apprentice d'Artagnan ever-ready to cross swords with the cocky henchmen of Cardinal Richelieu; or the shoot-outs between Jim Hawkins' team of respectable treasure hunters and the mutinous crew of pirates led by the one-legged charmer John Silver; or the fearless fights of the brave half-wolf and his master against the "bad guys" of the North. Such stories once primed an innocent but often bloodthirsty "expectation

---

with the pregraphical and prestylistic planning of the global mimesis, i.e., its main sequences.

horizon." Today, our qualitative appraisals of fictional clashes are inevitably affected by the excitement and pleasure of battles which thrilled us long before we learned to categorize them as "macroconflicts."

* * *

IV

EROTIC JOYS AND SINS

"...coeamus!...coeamus."
"Truly, sex was God's cosmic joke."[1]

Incompatible Creationist Mythologies: Gaia and Eros. Jehovah's Single-handed Genesis. Christianity and Sinful Sex. Mimesis of Sensual Love: Erotic Micro- and Macrostimuli. Religious, Ethnic, Statistical Biases in Erotic Polyculture. Barthes' "Erotic Codes." Scholarly Concepts; Bataille's Anthropological Speculations. The Menads. "The Right Chemistry": The Role of Amphetamines. History: Ovid's *Art of Loving*. Saint Virgins in *Legenda aurea*. Neopagan Nostalgia—*Fin Amor*, *Romance of the Rose*. From Rabelais to Montaigne and Ronsard. Theophile de Viau's and Malherbe's Pornography. Baroque Restraint. La Fontaine's *Libertinage*. The Gallant Eighteenth Century. Peyrefitte's Debt to Voltaire. Sadean Erotica. Flaubert's and Baudelaire's "Corruption of Public Mores." Maldoror's First True Love. Pioneers of Relaxed Erotic Mimesis: from *Corydon* to *Lolita*. Bataille's Psychotherapy: Art or Pornography? Updike's Neopagan Christians and Jews. Erotic Mores and their Mimesis Deregulated.

Incompatible Creationist Mythologies: Gaia and Eros

The bas-relief on a baroque Prague palace depicts a rotating globe whose axis is discreetly anchored in the vagina of a reclining Aphrodite.

1 Ovid *Metamorphoses III* ("Narcissus and Echo"), l. 392 and Tom Wolfe, *A Man in Full* (Toronto, Bantam Bks, 1998), p. 392. In this chapter I draw from my previous publications: *The Art of A. F.*, ch. VII "Eroticism and Gauloiserie"; *Cathedral or Symphony*, ch. IV, "[L]ove and friendships," pp. 58–62. "The Civilized Eros", *Laurentian Univ. Review II*, No. 2, 1969, pp. 4–17. "Erotic Culture in France: Pagan or Christian?", *Humanities Association of Canada Newsletter*, XI, No. 2, March 1983 pp. 31–41; "Eros—Maupassant's Only God", *Eroticism in French Literature, French Literature Series*, X, 1983, Univ. of South Carolina, hereafter *Eroticism in French Literature*.

It tells everybody who glances upward that everything on our planet turns around love making. Our birth, carnal joy, the resurrection of our mortal flesh, all start with copulation. Without the vital coition of macrocosmic powers, Life and Mankind would have never been created: this at least is the assumption of Hesiod's mythological poem *Theogony* (approx. 7th century B.C.). Goddess Gaia Earth and the nebulous Eros/Love,[2] spontaneously evolved from primordial Chaos. Having no mate, Gaia begot Uranos and the two began building a home for their forthcoming family—mountains, sky, sea, the hellish *Tartaros*. After this initial creation, they engendered (using the method bequeathed to mankind) the second generation of gods. Among their children was the prolific couple Cronus and Rhea, whose union gave life to Zeus and his sister and spouse Hera. Like his ancestors, Zeus had incestuous[3] marriages and affairs: the first with his second cousin Oceanide Metis. He made her pregnant and then swallowed her. The already conceived Athena sprang from her father's head. Throughout his immortality he was a restless and relentless womanizer. He had three divine children with Hera and fathered Apollo and Artemis with Leto, Dionysus with Semele, Hermes with Maia, Aphrodite with Dione,[4] Epaphus with Jo, Perseus with Danae. Among his numerous mistresses was, for example, Leda, Spartan Queen, whom he seduced when she was incarnated in the body of a swan and their two sets of twins were born from two eggs. Mischievously, he paraded as his very own great-grandson Amphitryon to seduce his chaste wife Alkmene who then gave life to the intrepid Hercules. Homer reports that Hera was jealous of her husband and bitterly resented his affairs.[5] Zeus also had a homosexual crush on Ganymedes, his Olympian waiter.

Drawing from abundant and often discrepant myths known to him, Hesiod sums up traditions crediting the immortal Olympians with

2 According to other myths, Eros (Lat. Amor) is the son of Aphrodite and her adulterous lover Ares, god of war. Annemarie and Werner Leibbrand, *Formen des Eros, Kultur* u. *Geistesgeschichte der Liebe*, vol. I, Freiburg/Munich, K. Alber, 1972 (hereafter Leibbrand) cover in detail the Greco-Roman, Judaic, Christian and Islamic erotic traditions.

3 Let us fairly recognize that the Olympian dynasty did not offer other options to its mating children.

4 Another myth suggests that Aphrodite *Anadyomene* emerged from the foam created when the castrated Uranos' testicles fell into the sea. See Leibbrand citing Hesiod pp. 42.

5 See ch. V, Homeric laughter.

the creation of mortals. He says next to nothing about their procreation techniques or about the specific obstetrics related to the birth of humans. Generally he relies on mythological testimonies of human existence when, during Kronos' cosmic tenure, gods began intermingling with their mortal lookalikes. The marriages and affairs between gods and humans gave life to demigods and to mortal heroes. The early heroic period was followed by golden, silver, bronze and iron ages. During this pre-Darwinian evolution, the paradisiac status of humans was continually downgraded. Ovid, inspired by the same myths some seven centuries after the completion of *Theogony*, tentatively attributed the creation of the human race to Prometheus.

> Then man was born; either the creator of the universe, originator of a better world, fashioned him from divine seed or earth, recently formed and separated from the lofty aether, retained seeds...and was mixed with rain water by Prometheus...and fashioned by him into the likeness of the gods who control all.[6]

In the mid 19th century the young Anatole France still found merits in Hesiod's poetry. He managed to reconcile his positivist skepticism with the Greek concept of diverse cosmic forces. "Eros...who relentlessly recreates the world...is the father of our life and destiny... Fateful love and its cruel struggles animate the universe."[7]

Jehovah's Single-handed Genesis

Judeo-Christian and Greek mythologies have one main feature in common. Like the Greek gods, Jehovah fashioned humans in his own image; unlike them, he did it single-handed. Chapters I and II of *Genesis* offer two contradictory versions of humankind's origin. The first version (*Genesis* I, 26, 27) states that "God said, Let *us* make *man* in *our* image...*[pluralis maiesteticus*] So God created *man*[8] in *His* [third person-singular masc.] own image, in the image of God created *he him*

6 M.P.O. Morford and R.J. Lenardon, *Classical Mythology:* New York, London, 1977), pp. 40–1, citing *Metamorphoses 1.* 78–83. Let us add that Prometheus is Deukalion's father and grandfather of Hellen, ancestor of the Hellenic people. After the deluge, the survivors Deukalion and his wife Pyrrha reproduced the drowned population by throwing stones behind their backs: Deukalion's stones miraculously became sons; Pyrrha's, daughters. The skeptical Greeks were free to believe or doubt it.

7 *O.C.* I, *Poèmes dorés* (Paris: Calmann-Lévy, 1925–35), p. 132, my transl.

8 The 1613 Czech *Kralická Bible*, translated from Hebrew and Greek texts by then prominent scholars, refers to "človek"/human being," not to "man".

[both masculine]; *male and female* created *he them.*" (Provided this information is correct, the biblical God was hermaphroditic but could not have greatly differed from Olympian gods whom ancient sculptors used to represent in the human male and female image. On the other hand, unlike Greek mortals, the Hebrew forefather was not born but created by "him...God" without any spousal interaction.) The second chapter, however, implies that the author of *Genesis* may have forgotten that, in the first chapter, God already had created them—"male and female"—in *his* image: *He* felt sorry for the lonely Adam and decided to create "a help meet" for him. In this final creative stage he transformed Adam's rib into a nubile Eve. What happened to the female created in the first chapter, the author of the second chapter fails to clarify.[9] The Creator did not offer any sex education, but the biblical couple discovered on their own the method of regeneration to which Adam must have been introduced during his first marriage. Although neither as aggressive as the Greek Zeus nor as fertile as Heracles[10], Adam's and Eve's descendant and Jehovaḥ's favorite "son" Abraham set high standards in populating Israël. He had several wives and concubines—some pertaining to his class, others servants or foreigners. He was sexually active until his death at the age of 179 years.

Christianity and Sinful Sex

His legendary vigor did not please Christian Church Fathers, who grudgingly conceded that nobody can extend either terrestrial or eternal life without the "unchaste" act of love, but proscribed carnal lust as a sin worthy of Hell. "*Femina ianua diaboli*—Woman is the Devil's gateway...a temple built over a sewer," claims Tertulian. Examining the Christian reprobation of the second sex, Simone de Beauvoir indicates the reasons which led the Ephesus and Lateran Councils to accept the dogma of immaculate conception: "All Christian literature strives to enhance the disgust that man can feel for woman...St. Augustine called attention with horror to the obscene commingling of the sexual and

9 *Genesis* ch. II, 18 and 21–5. Did Adam's first wife, Lilith, fly away from him to become a demon, as reported in rabinical literature? See, e.g., A. France's livresque "La Fille de Lilith," *O.C.* IV, *Balthasar*, pp. 123–48.

10 In a single night H. impregnated 49 daughters of king Thespius, the 50th turned down what appears to be a mythical sexual harassment.

excretory organs... We are born between feces and urine."[11] The patristic view of physical love seems to haunt Christianity even today: Boris Pasternak's hero, Doctor Zhivago, with benevolent heresy, reinterprets the dogma of immaculate conception: "[E]very conception is immaculate...this dogma concerning the Mother of God expresses the idea of all motherhood".[12] On the other hand, Thomas Mann's modern Faust, Adrian Leverkühn, half facetiously, half seriously sheds doubt even on the moral legitimacy of holy matrimony. Reflecting on his sister Ursula's wedding and on her future husband, this young theologian says:

> He [the husband] could...desire her, covet her as a Christian wife, as we theologians say...with justified pride and swindling the Devil out of the carnal concomitant and making a sacrament of it, the sacrament of Christian marriage. Very droll...this turning the natural and sinful into the sacrosanct just by putting in the word Christian—by which it is not fundamentally altered. But one has to admit that the domestication of sex, which is evil by nature, into Christian marriage was a clever makeshift.

Adrian finds no logic in the Christian blessing formula—"And they twain shall be one flesh"—which tries to conjure away marital sensuality, lust and sin. The young theologian reasons that "lust is certainly only in flesh of two different kinds, not in one." Consequently he finds the premise that man and woman "are to be one flesh...soothing but nonsensical."[13]

As the Christian doctrine evolved, Tertulian ascetic abstinence and St Augustine's pristine antisexualism were officially espoused only by the monks and nuns; secular clergy had to live in celibacy only after the 12th century. Many descendants of the converted pagans, however, found the sexual interdicts unnatural and their instincts resented ecclesiastic regulation of normal physiological functions. Many medieval poems show that the ascetic creed could neither eradicate the "pagan" taste for carnal bliss nor weed out the unorthodox ambivalence discernible in secular treatments of erotic subjects. Yet, in the days when the spiritual and secular power of the Church culminated, it was risky to challenge any dogma; hence unofficial protests were limited to passive resistance, subdued hints in poetry and to the racy but tolerated *fabliaux*

11 Citations and comment in *The Second Sex*, transl. by H.M. Parshley (New York: A.A. Knopf, 1957), p. 167. For the Church Fathers' erotic outlook see Leibbrand.

12 *Doctor Zhivago*, transl. Max Hayward and Mavia Herari (London: Collins/Harville, 1958), p. 255.

13 *Doctor Faustus*, transl. H.T. Lowe-Porter (London: Secker/Warburg, 1979), p. 253.

of the jugglers and minstrels. Their erotic genres not only confirm that, in literature, the victory of Christianity over paganism is precarious but that the conflict between the two cults has never been settled. Viewing our occidental erotic culture as a protracted truce between incompatible pagan and Christian traditions, Anatole France summed up the contradictions of their fragile coexistence by saying that Christianity has done a great deal for love by making it a sin.[14] The modern pagan not only talks as a wise man whose Christian upbringing taught him that forbidden fruit tastes better than the authorized low-calory (procreation only) erotic diet; he also mocks the theology which seeks to tame an irrepressible instinct. Above all, France talks as an experienced artist. Without having the opportunity to read Lévi-Strauss, George Bataille or Michel Foucault, he certainly knows that pagan society also condemns illicit sexual transgressions—kidnapping and rape of women, incest, adultery—but except for the mainly eugenic tribal interdicts and rites,[15] pagan sex is blissful primordial energy. It is the only cosmic shield against death, a blessed dynamism performing in discreet seclusion but *ad maiorem Dei, scilicet deorum Amoris, Veneris, Priapique, gloriam* what comes as naturally as eating, drinking or breathing.[16] But what a *coup* it is to link this everyday activity with a sin of the flesh and let the Devil manipulate it. The artistic benefit of so vilifying an overly exhausted subject is immense. Over the centuries of Christian indoctrination, Christian writers and readers have become conditioned by the official cult of chastity, even if their speculative vigor or natural inclinations gradually have emancipated them from excessive dogmatic constraints. Willy-nilly our imagination retains a residue of guilt for sins condemned by our fathers' official creed and going far beyond the pagan socio-cultural interdicts. As long as our erotic culture is at least partially

14 *O.C.*, IX, *Le Jardin d'Epicure*, p. 399. See Leibbrand, ch. X, "Die nachpaulinische Zeit bis Augustin." See also Michel Foucault, *The History of Sexuality*, transl. Robert Hurley (New York: Random House, 1978), p. 9: "It is...legitimate to ask why sex was associated with sin for such a long time... [and] why we burden ourselves today with so much guilt for having once made sex a sin." (Hereafter Foucault).

15 See George Bataille, *L'Histoire de l'érotisme* (*Oeuvres Complètes*, VIII, Paris, Gallimard, 1976; hereafter Bataille, *O.C.)* Foucault's French original of *Histoire de sexualité* was also published by Gallimard in 1976.)

16 Pagan love also has its tragic side: Death/Thanatos often trails Eros. *Post coitum omne animal triste*, says an anonymous sage. Also see Leibbrand, p. 214, Foucault, "Right of Death and Power over Life," pp. 135–59 and Appendix, A. France.

Christian, lust both in life and art will always provoke at least a shiver of sin.[17] Such a fresh esthetic spice is precious. This associative shiver is precisely the new and original dimension Christianity introduced in our esthetic responses to erotic information. Probably it even invigorated the ancient mimesis of sensual love. It created a controversy where none had existed before. The rigorous religion scared the flock of converted womanizers but enhanced their thrill once they began reading *Ars amatoria*.

Mimesis of Sensual Love: Erotic Micro- and Macrostimuli

Like other types of stimulative material, erotic features can be classified as micro- and macrostimuli—each with its variable excitive potential addressed to readers whose individual responses reflect their inborn erotic make-up, cultural background and acquired outlook. In this study, erotic stimulus is any transposition of an erotic subject—real or imagined—integrated in the text to activate the reader's erotic awareness, fantasy or instinct. Most references to sexual organs, sensual longing, scheming, love-making, nudity are characteristic erotic features. Like other contentual stimuli they often overlap with heterogeneous stimulative subjects. Authors combining, for example, erotic, comical or bizarre features, simultaneously provoke several innate faculties of their readers—their sexual instinct, curiosity and laughter. Erotic microstimuli are minor single references introduced in the text to increase its overall impact. Macrostimuli are complex extended representations of erotic actions and/or of erotically motivated characters involved in a major erotic plot or subplot. Long gradations and/or cohesive condensations of erotic microstimuli often create macrostimulative effects. For example, the jubilating father and mourning widower Gargantua laments the death of his wife Badabec, after her giving birth to their herculean son Pantagruel. In his *oraison funèbre* he addresses the deceased "mamye, mon petit con," a diminutive which, however, Rabelais immediately rectifies: "toutefois elle en avait bien trois arpents." In such a context, the synecdoche "my little cunt" is an obvious erotic microstimulus, in spite

17 Bataille (*O.C.* VIII, p. 20) alludes to the absence of the sentiment of sin in J.-P. Sartre's thought, i.e., "the necessity of the interdict". Unlike Bataille, I distinguish between the Christian *sin* and pagan *transgressions* or *interdicts*. This chapter's frame of reference is eroticism in Occidental culture. Erotic outlooks in other cultures and their literatures, e.g., Islamic or Oriental cannot be covered in this study.

of its phenomenal size outlined in the comical and antithetic hyperbole, "three acres." On the other hand, the Duke de Blangis' detailed character sketch in *120 Days of Sodom* (discussed below) is macrostimulative.

It is easier to document and approximate the power of erotic features than the impact produced by other types of contentual stimuli. This is so because our individual (physiological) as well as social (legal) reactions to erotica are at least marginally indicative of high or low impact. Literary references to physical love, like spontaneous sexual fantasies, may activate the reader's imagination as well as flesh.[18] On the social level we can consider positive or negative publicity, anonymity of authors, delayed publication of completed works, involvement of foreign publishers and, above all, criminal bans of erotically intensive books as characteristic symptoms of their provocative potential. In such instances, authors and their publishers face charges of violating the legal limits of erotic explicitness or of spreading obscenity, offending decent society and of corrupting young readers. Combining erotica with satire of the Church or of the secular establishment used to be seen as an aggravating circumstance. Prior to the now common separation of Church and State, (most often) celibate clerics and secular censors had jointly drawn the line between permissible and prohibited content and defined appropriate penalties for the nuisance caused by scurrilous subjects. Due to the cycles of generational attitudes ranging from the decadent taste for licence (e.g., during Tiberius' rule) to the rigid puritanism of the Inquisition or of the witch hunters, these criteria constantly fluctuate. The medieval cult of sexual ascetism follows ancient hedonism and precedes the Renaissance rediscovery of pagan beauty radiating from the nude, fit bodies of Greco-Roman goddesses, gods, athletes.

Religious, Ethnic, Statistical Biases in Erotic Polyculture

As the information revolution, technology and population explosion

18 See Malik's comments. Also see S.T. Kellman ("The Sadist Reader" *Eroticism in French Literature*, pp. 26, 31, nn. 4–6 discusses human responses to erotic art: Robert H. Loiselle and Sandra Mollenauer, "Galvanic Skin Response to Sexual Stimuli in a Female Population," *Journal of General Psychology*, vol. LXXIII No. 2 (1965), pp. 273–8. Brian T. Jordan and Joel R. Butler, "GSR As a Measure of the Sexual Component in Hysteria," *Journal of Psychology*, vol. LXVII No. 2 (November, 1967), pp. 211–9. L. Levi, "Sympatho-Adrennomedullary Activity, Diuresis, and Emotional Reactions during Visual Sexual Stimulation in Human Females and Males," *Psychosomatic Medicine*, vol. XXXI No. 3 (1969), pp. 251–68.

are closing gaps among the previously isolated races and their ramified erotic cultures, the ambiguous occidental tradition turns back to pre-Christian sinless sex. But while becoming increasingly secular and while gravitating toward sexual freedom anchored in "equality of males and females sharing the enjoyment of orgasm within a meaningful sexual union",[19] our erotic polyculture still offers no universally acceptable erotic conventions to men and women of all ethnic and racial origins or of various religious and political convictions. In the Occident, orthodox Vatican sex regulators still condemn, for example, contraceptive methods as a sinful interference with divine will. On the other hand, secular educators, in the effort to limit the number of precocious pregnancies, install condom dispensers in secondary schools; overpopulated Communist China imposes a punitive tax on parents of more than two children. Countries such as the United States and Ireland are politically divided on the issue of a woman's free choice to terminate an unplanned pregnancy. In Asia and Africa, Islamic patriarchal polygamy or forced marriages contracted by parents on behalf of their under-age children appear cruel to Occidentals. And even within homogeneous social groups, our individual spontaneous reactions to erotic experience as well as to the transposition of erotic subjects are rarely identical. Our biases range from dogmatic to skeptical, from frigid to carnal, from phlegmatic to passionate, from balanced to perverse...Male and female responses differ. Some of us rationalize that, if pills, condoms and sex education cannot halt the planet's disastrous overpopulation, then nuclear power and AIDS will. Religious fundamentalists dismiss the fears of overcrowding and polluting the Earth as unsubstantiated. In any era, some people are sexually promiscuous, others are monogamous. Some find no guilt in sexual promiscuity, others confess to masturbation or premarital sex as sins grave enough to call for some penitence but hopefully deserving divine pardon.[20] A polygamist, still sheltering a harem in his residence, probably has different erotic expectations both in life and in fiction than a gay movie director in Rome or an illiterate inhabitant of tropical forests. Our ethnic and religious backgrounds condition our erotic behavior. For example, the British satirist of Hungarian descent George Mikes facetiously divides Europeans into two major categories: "Continentals [who] have a sex life and the English

19 See J.F. Revel's "Les succès du moi, Préface" to *120 Journées de Sodome* by D.A.F. Sade, vol. I (*O.C.* XXVI, Paris, J.-J. Pauvert, 1967), p. xvi, my transl.

20 See below comments on Updike's mimesis of sex.

[who] have hot water bottles."[21] Mikes' apodictic one-liner is quotable rather than convincingly researched. It keeps alive a lighthearted myth spread by continental males like Mikes and possibly supported by French sociologists such as Edith Cresson; prior to becoming the first French woman Prime Minister Ms. Cresson concluded that "Anglo-saxon men are not interested in women" and that 25% of them are homosexual. A 1992 British survey claims to have discredited her French statistics.[22] Mikes' or even Cresson's research keeps revitalizing ethnic legends on expert Latin (or perhaps Hungarian?) lovers such as Don Juan[23] or Casanova. Military clashes may encourage male collectives to adopt biased views on foreign women: a subcultural ballad sung at Czech beer parties, evoking the heroism of the infantrymen fighting during the bloody Austro-Hungarian annexation of Bosnia-Herzegovina in 1878, relates what the racist and politically incorrect Czech machos discovered on the battlefield. "Over behind the bush", they saw "hidden Mohammedans...repulsive pagans" clad in "frazzled dirty shirts" and "no pants." One stanza suddenly digresses from the infantry to glance at "these Turkish females," and characterizes them as tarts (sows) whom our "Emperor Lord" (salute) dislikes seeing in his "family" (salute).[24] Mikes' ethnic aphorism, Ms. Cresson's demeaning statistics and British denial, along with the Czech beer song, show how ethnicity affects one's erotic outlook. The same informative bits of erotic content transposed as journalistic, sociological or folkloric subject matter (or coloring my scholarly discourse) exemplify minimal informative quanta which, if transposed in a literary context, would become erotic microstimuli.

Barthes' "Erotic Codes"

Although not inspired by Roland Barthes' approach to eroticism, my

21 Cited by Michael Brunton, *Time Magazine*. "Sex please. We are British", Sept. 28, 1992, p. 76. He covers the "educational" explicit video tapes marketed in Britain. The headline parodies the bedroom farce "*No Sex Please—We Are British*."

22 *Time Magazine*, Dec. 14, 1992: "It's a Draw," p. 39. Cresson seems to concur with Simone de Beauvoir who (à propos of Gantillon's *Maya*) comments that Anglo-Saxons "regard the flesh as more or less abominable." (*The Second Sex*, p. 194).

23 "...great violator of the rules of marriage-stealer of wives, seducer of virgins..." Foucault, p. 39.

24 Each time the words "infantry," "Lord Emperor" or "his family" are uttered, the singers get up, lift the beer mug with the left hand and salute with the right. The "esthetic" backbone of this folkloric levity is the semi-automatist rudimentary rhyming: Turkish women/Turkyňe...sows/*sviňe*...family/*rodiňe*, etc.

isolation of erotic stimuli is somewhat comparable to his segmentation of literary content. In his hermeneutic tryptych on the "logothètes," *Sade, Fourier, Loyola*, Barthes identifies what he calls an "erotic code." This theoretical term designates a composite of several units "thoroughly determined and identified by Sade himself." The code's minimal "unit" is "la posture," an erotic position of the body. Combination of positions constitutes an "opération" requiring several characters; the sum of their simultaneous positions forms a "figure" whereas the progressive succession of positions Barthes dubs an "épisode"; finally, a developed sequence of integrated *opérations* forms the ultimate "unit" of the "erotic grammar"—"la scène" or "la séance".[25] I appreciate Barthes' methodical *semiotic break-down* of Sade's erotic information even though his "erotic codes" have nothing in common with my esthetic (stylistic or contentual) micro- and macrostimuli. From my valuatory perspective, the discernible minor or major quanta of erotic information in esthetically categorizable micro- and macrostimulative erotic content are not elements in an abstract "erotic grammar" of a single author—they apply to any type of erotic discourse. Their variety forms a distinct domain of more or less stimulative subjects which potentially prompt delectation, shock, valuatory reaction and so on. I do not find Barthes' abstract units particularly "erotic." Signifiers such as the "vit, engin, con, foutre, décharger, branler, sperme, gomèche, clitoris," etc. "codify" and signify the specific erotic substance in Sade's pornographic "structure" more than the indefinite "postures, figures, opérations." Separated from their unmistakably erotic qualifiers such signifiers could allude to non-erotic, e.g., diplomatic or choreographical projects or to religious rituals. Barthes' "units" do not *eo ipso* eroticize Sade's context; they are eroticized only when they are linked with irrefutably erotic referents.[26]

Scholarly Concepts; Bataille's Anthropological Speculations

To define eroticism as an evolving critical concept, Edouard Morot-

25 Paris: Seuil, 1971, pp. 33–4. This study claims that these "logothètes" adopted analogical semiotic techniques to articulate their heterogeneous creeds. My quotations reflect Barthes' French terminology. The proairetic, hermeneutic, cultural and connotative codes and the code-like symbolic field (see comments on *S/Z* in *LP I*, ch. I, n. 1) have no place *in Sade, Fourier, Loyola*.

26 Beatrice Fink divides Sade's erotic vocabulary into "authorized" euphemisms, "prohibited" vulgar "lexies" and scientific and technical terminology ("La Langue de Sade", *Eroticism in French Literature*, pp. 103–12).

Sir[27] explores the modern connotations and definitions of the term in respectable encyclopedias of this and previous centuries. He cites a 1870 tautology describing it as "sensual love" and to exemplify the then current use, the dictionary cites Proudhon's Victorian maxim (echoing the Ronsardian "beau péché,") "[L]'amour des enfants achève de *purger* de tout érotisme l'affection conjugale." A more recent lexicon describes it as a tendency toward sensual, sexual love; used metonymically it is the manner of manifesting, expressing and satisfying such a taste. It refers to the Marquis de Sade and to Austrian Leopold Sacher-Masoch[28] as apostles preaching innovative shocks ranging from sexual brutality to sexual penitence and self-torture. Finally, the *Grande Encyclopédie Larousse* (1976 ed.) interprets the concept analogically, while adding a modern *aficionado*—Georges Bataille—to the two inveterate prophets of eroticism. Morot-Sir seems to imply that no broad discussion on erotic subjects can ignore radical ideologies such as Sade's libertine creed[29] or the modern blasphemous "agnose" first reflected in Bataille's pornographic fiction *Histoire de l'oeil* (1928) and later outlined in his interdisciplinary anthropological and socio-cultural essays forming *L'Histoire de l'érotisme*.[30] In it he traces the evolutionary transition from animal to human, and examines such topics as incest, interdicts, death, marriage, orgy, etc. His reflections complement the earlier works of scholars such as J.G. Frazer (1854–1941) or Lévy-Strauss. "In essence, eroticism is humankind's sexual activity as opposed to that of animals," Bataille states,[31] speculating further that our human erotic impulses crystalized when we ceased to be animals. "For Bataille the erotic is specifically the point of tension between animal body and the civilized body."[32] Bataille sees the elevation above the prehuman animal level as a "negation of nature." We humans revolt against our cosmically defined condition ("condition proposée").[33] This anthropological hypothesis makes one wonder how could the (pre-human) animals ever "revolt" and

27 "Erotisme et poésie dans l'oeuvre de Georges Bataille," *Eroticism in French Literature*, pp. 123–137.

28 Author of *Tales of Galicia* (*Galizische Geschichten*) 1876. Also see, e.g., Sacha Nacht, *Le Masochisme* (Paris: La Petite Bibliothèque, Payot, 1965).

29 See below comments on the *Cent-vingt journées de Sodome*.

30 *O.C.* I and VIII.

31 Ibid., vol VIII, p. 23, my transl.

32 Paul Smith, "Bataille's Erotic Writings and the Return of the Subject," *Eroticism in French Literature*, p. 48.

33 *O.C.*, VIII, p. 66.

become civilized without an effective Promethean intervention or (if there had been no Prometheus) without an inborn genetic faculty to evolve without any revolt, beyond the animal level of the preordained "condition proposée." "Proposée" by whom, why and when and for how long? Could a series of accelerated evolutionary leaps have sprung from the timetable determined by the primary discharge of cosmic energy? Archeologist Bataille does not and cannot elaborate. Like Barthes' theoretical arguments, Bataille's hypothetic commentaries, including a number of *ad hoc* "definitions"[34] covering human erotic involvements, never address the artistic *mimesis* of erotic acts and the esthetic intensity it may generate. In addition, their interdisciplinary theoretism glosses over the esthetically relevant correlate of human (and possibly also animal)[35] erotic love—the progressive escalation of pleasure represented in the texts describing erotic interaction ranging from first eye contact to ejaculation, orgasm, from promiscuity to erotic loyalty beyond the grave possibly still existing in many marriages.

The Menads

Under the general subheading "l'objet du désir a le sens de la jouissance dans l'instant,"[36] Bataille suggests that "fulgurating" pleasure is provoked by the Dionysiac Menads (Bacchantes, Euripides' Bakchai—mythical incarnations of the prostitutes) running wildly through the night. Sociological as well as literary dissertations could be written to support or reject Bataille's personal opinion: Manon Lescaut, Juliette (Sade's counterpoint to Rousseau's Julie), Laclos' Marquise Merteuil, *La dame aux camélias*, Zola's Nana, Maupassant's Boule de Suif, or Madame Tellier's employees,[37] Colette's Claudine, Gigi, even Sartre's *Putain respectueuse* all are modern descendants of the ancient

34 E.g., "L'érotisme, c'est essentiellement, dès le premier pas, le scandale du 'renversement des alliances'", Ibid., p. 65.

35 For example, in Tom Wolfe's Wolfe's *A Man in Full* (cit. above, n.1), ch. X, "The Breeding Barn," pp. 298–310, relates the mating of a three-million-dollar stud "First Draw" with a mare thoroughly strapped in the barn's narrow enclosure. The volcanic outburst of the stallion's lust becomes an unforgettable erotic show presented by the macho tycoon Charlie Croker to a few shocked plutocrats invited to his plantation near Atlanta. For a comic treatment of canine and bovine mating, see ch. V, "Literary Anecdote and its comic frame in *The Grapes of Wrath*" and nn. 30, 31.

36 Ibid., p. 24.

37 See *LP II*, ch. III, IV and Appendix, pp. 232–34 and *LP III*, ch. V, "Sublime Irony".

Menads. Durell's heroine Clea concurs with Bataille in commenting on another character: "The true whore is man's real darling—like Justine; she alone has the capacity to wound men. But [she] is only a shallow reproduction of the great *Hetairae* of the past...Lais, Charis and the rest..."[38] In one of the erotic vignettes by Anaïs Nin, her fictionalized painter confesses: "I like a whore best of all because I feel she never clings to me...The only woman who ever gave me the same pleasure was a woman...who gave herself like a whore..."[39] The critic seeking an analogy of Bataille's vision of voluptuous ecstasy in modern texts may remember the seduction scene in A. France's short story "Le Saint Satyre." Its hero, the Franciscan abbot Mino whose monastery is on the site of an ancient pagan temple, has nocturnal visions of satyrs chasing the nymphs,[40] who, throughout their mythological existence live for nothing else than recurrent libido.

One can nevertheless argue that Bataille's narrow and prevalently male concept of pleasure inspired by the Menads' abandon makes no allowance for other kinds of erotic longing and joy such as the bonds between Orpheus and Euridice, Philemon and Baucis, Tristan and Isolde, Romeo and Juliet or the representations of sincere love by J.-J. Rousseau, Jane Austen, Charles Dickens, Victor Hugo. The author of *Les Misérables* idealizes the erotic bond as a rendezvous with God: "Cosette the sun for Marius and Marius the whole world for Cosette...Each must be religion to the other. We all have our own way of worshipping God, but the best of all, heaven knows, is to love one's wife."[41] Like Hugo, few authors representing erotic reality limit themselves to transpositions of erotica marketed on the street or in the *demi-monde*. Foucault identifies the links between erotic drives and our vital environments—political, social, religious, economic. Erotic power competes and interacts with other universal forces involved in the global dynamism of life. Our attempts to understand, to exploit and regulate the erotic *perpetuum mobile* characterizes both the history of life as well as the spectrum of its powerful and banal artistic transpositions.

38 Lawrence Durell *Alexandria Quartet, Justine*, New York: Pocket Bks. 1957, p. 71. See de Beauvoir's "Prostitutes and Hetairas" in *The Second Sex*, pp. 555–74 and many other references.

39 *Little Birds*, "The Queen", (New York, London: Harcourt Brace Jovanovich, 1979), pp. 93–94.

40 *O.C.*, X, pp. 17, 18. See *The Art of Anatole France*, pp. 149–53, and *LP II*, ch. V, pp. 61–4.

41 *Les Misérables*, transl. Norman Denny, Penguin Books, vol. II. p. 443.

"The Right Chemistry": The Role of Amphetamines

A recent résumé of modern research entitled "The Right Chemistry"[42] is more specific than Bataille's or Foucault's studies in claiming that "4 million years ago" romantic love evolved when human ancestors, "*graduated* from scuffling around on all fours to walking on two legs," displayed their genitals and "began to *enjoy* face to face couplings." This new style of romance served the evolutionary program of initiating "long term [about 4 years] partnership...essential to *child rearing*." Unlike Bataille, the scholars covered in Touflexis' synopsis do not refer to any revolt other than evolutionary refinement (spontaneous or projected by the unidentified cosmic energy preconditioning the speed of the transformative process.) Neither do they speculate about a premythical conflict not stored in prehuman beings' memory but vaguely preserved in their descendants' atavistic instincts. They rather seek the chemicals which pull individual males and females toward one another and ultimately initiate their intercourse. Biochemists have identified the phenylethylamine and neurochemicals dopamine and norepinephrine, all natural amphetamines, as organic agents initiating our physical attraction, euphoria and elation; endorphins flood the brain to create attachment, calm and sense of security; ultimately oxytocin triggers satisfaction and attachment during love making. Have they finally found the ingredients of Hesiod's erotic glue? Are they the cosmic fuel propelling *das ewig Weibliche*? In any case, like an erotic radar, these organic chemicals help us detect our compatible partners. They monitor our preliminary stage of sex for sex, intimate love for love's sake, a stage which either precedes or is implied by the cosmically planned reproductive process. The mimesis of our erotic impulses, pursuits, fantasies constitute a characteristic domain of micro- and macrostimuli to which we esthetically motivated readers respond according to the potential impact which a given stimulus may have on our individual sexual drive, experience, wisdom...[43]

42 By Anastasia Touflexis, reported by Hannah Bloch and Sally B. Donnelly in *Time* 15, 1993, pp. 39–41, (my ital.) A valuable research devoted to evolution of erotic instinct is Robert's Wright's *The Moral Animal: Evolutionary Psychology and Everyday Life*, Pantheon, 1994. Substantial excerpts ("Our Cheating Hearts") were published in *Time* August 15, 1994, pp. 29–36.

43 See ch. VIII, "Perception and neurological reaction to erotic information."

Ovid's *Art of Loving*

A cursory comparison of two representative texts immediately shows the gap between ancient erotic hedonism and Christian carnal sins. Perhaps the best known handbook of Roman sex education is Ovid's didactic *Art of Loving—Ars amatoria.* It advises men and women, single, married, virtuous novices as well as adulterous roués how to achieve and extend the joys of courting, seducing and love-making. This poetic triptych takes a form of versified lessons in erotic strategy. They range from sartorial and cosmetic tips or from masculine and feminine ruses to optimal intercourse positions suited to women's specific anatomical assets such as their height, short figure, comely face or seductive backside. The poet invokes mythological precedents to illustrate his lessons. For example, Andromache, Hector's wife was tall, thus she could not "ride on his horse". Along with other erotic poems such as *Remedia amoris*, the work reflects relaxed, everyday sex in Rome during the earliest years of the Christian era; it is neither libertine in spirit nor lubricious in details. Nevertheless, the aging Emperor Augustus deemed it rather scandalous: in his eyes Ovid's poetry may have inspired the erotic licence of his granddaughter Julia. Influenced by his scheming wife Livia (supporting the dynastic interests of the young Tiberius) the Emperor banished Julia and her lover for their alleged neglect of imperial dignity. At this occasion he also punished the sybaritic poet, not exclusively for his popular erotica but for his probable awareness of Livia's intrigues. In an intercepted letter Ovid warned a friend against the risk of seductions in the imperial inner circle. With regard to this delict and due to Livia's clout, the authorship of *Ars amatoria* became an aggravating circumstance.

Saint Virgins in *Legenda aurea*

One thousand years later, the Christian cult of chastity culminates in the hagiography. The clergymen exalting the ascetism and miracles of medieval saints do not oust erotic temptation from their epical repertoire. The author of the *Legenda aurea*, Archbishop Jacques Voragine (1230–98), does not ignore Eros, he simply makes him a Devil. His heroines, Euphemie, Justine, Catherine and Marguerite, protect their virginity against pagan lechers such as the emperor Maxentius, the devil disguised as an innocent Christian virgin, the satanic lover Cyprien magically metamorphosed into a bird. St. Marguerite even defends her virtue against her charming husband and saves her virginity for greater things than a happy family life. In these hagiographical melodramas the omnipresent protectors of female ascetics include the sign of the cross and a variety of miraculous divine interventions. The following fragments of the legend of "Sainte Justine, vierge" shows how the Genoese Archbishop blends devilish temptations with miracles. St. Justine, converted daughter of a pagan priest, resists all eager efforts of the young satanist Cyprien to seduce her. "Il s'éprit d'un amour brûlant pour la vierge Justine, et il eut recours à la magie afin de la posséder soit pour lui, soit pour un homme nommé Acladius, qui s'était également épris d'amour pour elle." To seduce her he consults his friendly devil:

> "J'aime une vierge du nombre des Galiléens; peux-tu faire que je l'aie et accomplisse avec elle ma volonté?" Le démon lui dit: "Moi qui ai pu chasser l'homme du paradis, qui ai amené Caïn à tuer son frère, qui ai fait crucifier J.-C. par les juifs,...je ne pourrais donc pas faire que tu aies une jeune fille...?"

But the vigilant convert is not an easy mark: making the sign of the cross she chases away Satan's understudy. Not discouraged by her steadfast virtue, Cyprien solicits the aid of the sophisticated prince of Darkness who transfigures himself into an innocent maiden and shrewdly seeks Justine's moral counsel:

> Je viens vous trouver, parce que je désire vivre avec vous dans la chasteté: néanmoins, dites-moi,..., quelle sera la récompense de notre combat?" Cette sainte vierge, lui répondit: "la récompense sera grande et le labeur bien petit." Le démon lui dit: "Qu'est-ce donc que ce commandement de Dieu:...multipliez et remplissez la terre? Je crains...que si nous restons dans la virginité, nous ne rendions vaine la parole de Dieu... Alors le coeur de Justine commença à...être enflammé...de la concupiscence... Mais cette sainte vierge revenue à elle,...se munit aussitôt du signe de la croix, puis soufflant sur le diable, elle fit fondre comme cire[.][44]

Seeing the Devil's impotence, Cyprien loses his confidence in him. He himself learns how to use the sign of the cross to chase away the devils and gets baptized. He never consummates his love for Justine and, following the death of the bishop who converted him, the penitent sinner inherits the bishopric.

44 Jacques de Voragine, *La Légende dorée*, II, trans. J.-B.M. Rose (Paris: Garnier-Flammarion, 1967), p. 223. Today, such a passage may offer higher stimulative intensity to readers who, ironically, see St. Justine as a pioneer of the Vatican's politics designed to prevent overpopulation.

Neopagan Nostalgia—*Fin Amor, Romance of the Rose*

In the days when similar legends were written, the church exercised considerable political clout and any doctrinal dissent became a risky gamble with heresy. Yet, paradoxically, the then-common genres, *geste*, *romance* and *fabliau*, ignore the patristic views. Commenting on the heroines of the *gestes*, Léon Gautier suggests that Christian upbringing did not subdue their barbaric erotic verve: "The young maidens of our distant past show nothing of that charming chastity which distinguishes Christian women. Seeing the first lad they shamelessly beg him to relieve their brutish appetites." As an example of such carnal *élan*, the historian mentions Princess Bellisende, daughter of the legendary defender of the faith, Charlemagne. Without beating around the bush she seduces the politically astute Amile, who is seneschal (imperial steward) at her father's court: "Grant me a night in your bed and I shall offer you my body".[45] Like Bellisende the bards of *fin amor* seem to pay little attention to the prejudices of the church fathers. They place the unimpeachable lady on a pedestal and worship her as a saint rather than as a "temple built over the sewer." This pious reverence, however, cannot discourage troubadour Guillaume IX de Poitiers from contemplating a happy adultery. Naturally the *bagatelle* will not be confessed, for in the *fin amor* creed, the total discretion of a gentleman is always guaranteed: "If my lady grants me her love I shall take it and show my gratitude. I'll conceal my happiness..."[46]

Thomas and Béroul's dramatization of Yseult's and Tristan's fateful love is transgressive only inasmuch it is adulterous but even so, neither Tristan nor Yseult are cruelly punished by Iseult's noble husband. Both the Christian as well as the pagan establishment generally frown at any royal *ménage à trois*. The adultery between Lancelot and Guinevere as told by Chrétien de Troyes (approx. 1170) implies no condemnation of the erotic act whatsoever. Having encouraged Lancelot to break out the window grill, the Queen receives him in her bed without the slightest Christian scruple: "...[E]t la Reine...l'embrasse, / étroit sur son sein elle l'enlace / et l'attire près d'elle en son lit / et lui fait le plus bel accueil / que jamais faire elle lui pût,..." Following this rendez-vous the Queen is not sin-ridden, on the contrary, what prevails is a souvenir of a fine joy forever: "[I]l leur arriva sans mentir / une joie et une merveille / telle que

45 Cited by André Berry, *L'Amour en France*, I (Paris: La Table Ronde, 1962), p. 29, my transl.

46 Ibid., p. 33, my transl.

jamais sa pareille / ne fut entendue ni connue…"[47]

The *Romance of the Rose*, written one century later, drops the Christian doctrine of sinful sex, preventively wraps it in symbolic but not too cryptic rhetoric and cynically rediscovers *Ars Amatoria* and the ancient naturalism. A bourgeois prehumanist, Guillaume de Lorris (about 1230), starts and after him author Jean de Meung finishes the allegory around 1277. Without alluding to any specific cases of *imitatio*, Lanson emphasizes the two poets' debt to Ovid. Their work's final chapter, entitled "Venus' Conflagration and Winning of the Rose," gives a medieval twist to a Greek myth about the gynophobic King of Cyprus and the sculptor Pygmalion. Paradoxically, the royal dilettante falls in love with his own marble statue of a young woman and prays to Aphrodite to give it life. The goddess responds to his plea, changing the marble into Galatea whom the confirmed bachelor marries. Modern readers could diagnose Jean de Meung's Christian Pygmalion as a typical sexually repressed lover; in his dream, the character does not meet the Holy Virgin but Venus. He swears to "flee into banishment" if, from then on, he does not "avoid chastity". After his vow, he sounds the allegorized rose with his "staff. " Regretfully, an *ejaculatio precox* puts an end to his break through the "narrowish" entry:

> …[B]etween the two fair pillars, for I was very hungry to worship the lovely, adorable sanctuary… I partly raised the curtain…and then, to enter the sheath safely, wished to put my staff into the aperture, with the sack hanging behind. Indeed I thought that I could shoot it in at the first try, but it came back out. I replaced it, but to no avail; it still recoiled…[Because] there was a paling in front… I had to assail it vigorously, throw myself against it often, often fail…I broke down the paling with my staff and gained a place in the aperture…[b]ut I hadn't the power to go on.[48]

This passage evokes one of Ovid's tips to lovers who wait too long for the consummation of their great true love: to cool their lust in the arms of any *ad hoc* mistress willing to oblige. Jean de Meung probably read the Ovidian topos and asumed that a little gauloiserie would enhance his readers' stimulation. Thus, his medieval Pygmalion learns the Ovidian lesson the hard way.

In view of contradictions between the first 4,058 lines first written by Guillaume de Lorris and some 17,000 lines added by Jean de Meung and

47 Ibid., p. 42.

48 *Romance of the Rose*, transl. Charles Dahlberg (Princeton University Press, 1971), pp. 344, 352. Dahlberg also comments on the work's critics, pp. 1–27.

in view of a number of both older and up-to-date interpretations, any overly general statement may appear to be a simplification. Yet the opinions of scholars such as Gaston Paris or Gustave Lanson are not less valid today than they were at the beginning of the past century. They agree that the text celebrates the advent of Amor and Venus and reflects Jean de Meung's debt to Ovid's *Ars amatoria* or to Lucretius' *De rerum natura*. We may add that, if the two Medieval authors had been acquainted with patristic tracts on carnal love such as Tertulian's *Ad uxorem* or *De exhortatione castitatis*, they offered no support to his anti-erotic doctrine. Pygmalion's undertaking may lack the *fabliau*'s *gaulois* licence but, like the *fabliau*, it challenges the Christian repudiation of the flesh and its natural joys; like the *fabliau* it foreshadows Boccaccio's *Decameron* (1350–55), Rabelais' *joie de vivre* and the hedonism of Ronsard.

From Rabelais to Montaigne and Ronsard

The wave of the Renaissance, spreading from Italy across the Alps ultimately weakens the doctrinal obsession with erotic "sins" much more severely than did the medieval authors. The new *Weltanschauung* neutralizing ecclesiastic abhorrence of erotic activities came from many causes, political, economical, social. Chiefly, however, the secular return to Venus, Amor, Priapus and Bacchus, seems to be the most visible memento of neo-pagan teleology. The sculptors and painters discovering the naked beauty of Greek and Roman gods, the writers imitating ancient poetry, pay no attention to doctrinal proscription of natural drives. Renaissance art contributes to the emancipation of human thought and behaviour just as much as the effects of papal decadence, the growth of cities, the discovery of the New World, or Lutheran abolition of clerical celibacy. Like the *Romance of the Rose*, most major authors dismiss asceticism and excessive chastity as moral tenets.

Rabelais' vision of the antigothic life style in "L'Abbaye de Thélème" endorses the triumphs of natural instincts. There is no place for the sins of the flesh in his naturalistic imperative "Trinc." Rabelais' third book, in which Panurge endlessly meditates on whether or not to get married, satirically projects cuckoldry as an integral part of any normal marriage.[49] In this respect Rabelais is a whimsical harbinger of

49 *Gargantua*, ed. Jean Plattard (Paris: Société des Belles Lettres, 1948), ch. LVIII; *Le Cinquième Livre*, ch. XIV, p. 167; *Le Tiers Livre*, chs. IX, XVI, XXIV, XXXV.

Montaigne's serious reflections on love and marriage. The essayist's erotic outlook is genuinely anti-Christian and far behind or far ahead of his time. Like Rabelais, Montaigne cannot associate any healthy impulse of the flesh or mind with sin and evil. He too resents asceticism. For him the quest of pleasure is natural and in harmony with the principals of cosmic creation. As a Christian he has difficulty digesting the dogma of immaculate conception.[50] Taking into account a typical marriage in his social strata, he advocates toleration not only of generally accepted male adultery but also of discreet feminine adultery. He reasons that conventional marriage is rarely inspired by love. Many legitimate family and economic interests as well as the interests of future posterity cannot and should not be subordinated merely to the strong erotic impulse of young lovers. Often, young women get married to old husbands who soon become impotent. And if the husbands have any vigor left, they will more likely, display it in their extramarital affairs. Thus, Montaigne claims, society should not ostracize women seeking erotic satisfaction just as men do. With some sympathy Montaigne evokes the civilized habit of Roman husbands who, trying to spare their wives the embarrassment of being caught *in flagranti*, used to send messengers home to announce their return from longer trips.

Les cent nouvelles nouvelles (1460), Bonaventure des Périers' *Nouvelles récréations et joyeux devis* and *The Heptameron* by Marguerite de Navarre[51] all exude sympathy for unrepressed physical love hardly ever punctuated by feelings of excessive guilt. Des Périers' anecdote about three pregnant brides documents the stimulative potential of a subject such as premarital sex with its *ad hoc* solutions. Three daughters of a licentious widower get pregnant out of wedlock at about the same time. The father arranges a triple wedding to three brothers from a respectable family who, however, put a high premium on virginity. He promises a generous reward to the daughter who, during her wedding

50 *Les Essais de Michel Montaigne*, ed. P. Villey, pref. V.-L. Saulnier (Paris: Presses Universitaires de France, 1965), p. 421. "[I]l estoit tenu pour certain à Athènes que Ariston, ayant voulu jouïr de la belle Perictione, n'avoit sceu; et fut averti en songe par le Dieu Appollo de la laisser impollue et intacte jusqu'à ce qu'elle fut accouchée: c'estoient le pere et la mere de Platon. Combien y a il, es histoires, de pareils cocuages procurez par les Dieus contre les pauvres humains? et des maris injurieusement descriez en faveur des enfants?" See further pp. 864–65 and 869.

51 Des Périers died approx. 1544, Marguerite in 1549; their works were published posthumously in 1558 and 1559. The 12th novella of *The Heptameron* is discussed above in ch. III.

night, most successfully soothes the bridegroom's annoyance. Each of the three daughters downgrades the gravity of her premarital fornication and consummates her marriage with such ease and true Boccaccian *ingenio* that, in the morning the happy father does not know which of the three brides should get the prize. Perhaps inspired by the parable of the three rings, Des Périers suggests that all three deserve their father's recognition.

> Les litz se font, les trois pucelles se couchent, et les maris après. Celuy de la plus grande, en la mignardant, luy met la main sus le ventre et par tout, qui trouva incontinent qu'il estoit un petit ridé par le bas, qui luy fit souvenir qu'on la lui avoit belle baillée. "O ho! dit il, les oyseaux s'en sont allez." La damoiselle luy respond tout contant: "Tenez vous au nid." Et une. Le mary de la seconde, en la maniant, trouva que le ventre estoit un peu rond. "Comment! dit il, la grange est pleine? - Battez à la porte," luy respondit elle. Et deux. Le mary de la tierce, en jouant les jeux, cogneut incontinent qu'il n'estoit par le fol. "Le chemin est battu," dit il. La jeune fille luy dit: "Vous ne vous en esgarerez pas si tost." Et trois.[52]

In the second half of the 16th century even the *poeta laureatus* Pierre Ronsard (1524–85) entertains his distinguished male and female readers with metaphorical hyperboles immortalizing his mistress' and his own genitals. With all its polish his rhetoric is not much subtler than Jean de Meung's "staff, seamless leather bag, sanctuary" or "narrow entry." (Saying this let us, nevertheless, give Ronsard some credit: unless his erotic discourse is not sheer bragging, his firm "lance" must be superior to the stuff of which Pygmalion's staff is made!) "Lance au bout d'or, qui sais et poindre et oindre, / De qui jamais la roideur ne défaut"...His eulogy of unveiled feminine anatomy somewhat rectifies the macho's "jamais": even the spurious lance with the golden tip can be "tamed": "Je te salue, " merveillette fente, / Qui vivement entre ces flancs reluis; / Je te salue, " bienheureux pertuis, /...O petit trou, trou mignard, trou velu, / D'un poil folet mollement crespelu, / Qui à ton gré domptes les plus rebelles. . ." In the sonnet beginning "Maîtresse, à tous les coups vous m'alléguez Saint Pol," Ronsard admits that his seduction attempts may clash with the apostolic principals, "Je sais que je commets envers vous une faute"—but who can blame his urgent desires provoked by excess of feminine beauty: "Ou bien ne soyez plus si gentille et si belle, / Ou bien je ne saurais (tant que vous serez telle) / M'engarder de vouloir faire si

52 Bonaventure Des Périers, *Nouvelles Récréations et Joyeux Devis*, 1, ed. Louis Latour (Paris: Librairie de Bibliophiles, 1874), pp. 33–4.

beau péché."[53] His banal apology of "charming sins" affirms the continued aversion to Christian sexual puritanism.

Théophile de Viau's and Malherbe's Pornography

The poets who followed Ronsard were even less puritanic. A lascivious epigram by Théophile de Viau (1590–1626) not only alludes to the intimate priorities of his fictionalized mistress, it unmistakably forebodes the advent of libertine materialism. "Mes couilles, quand mon vit se dresse, / Gros comme un membre de mulet, / Plaisent aux doigts de ma maîtresse / Plus que deux grains de chapelet."[54]

During the same period even the anointed founder of classical prosody François Malherbe (1555–1628) combines prosodic austerity with carnal licence. In one of his sonnets he confides that his first morning thought goes to his nymph's womb and her vital *mons veneris* overgrown with blond hair. "Sitôt que le sommeil, au matin, m'a quitté, / Le premier souvenir est du con de Nérée, / De qui la motte ferme et la barbe dorée / Esgale ma fortune à l'immortalité." This sweet recollection activates his responsive flesh: "Mon vit, dont le plaisir est la félicité, / S'allonge incontinent à si douce curée, / Et d'une échine roide, au combat préparée, / Montre que sa colère est à l'extrémité." At dinner time the lusty sonneteer cannot even let his lady top off their entrée with dessert—he has another last course in mind:

"Là! Là! pour dessert, troussez-moi cette cotte
Vite, chemise et tout, qu'il n'y demeure rien
—. . . . .
Ma belle, baisez-moi, c'est à vous de tout faire—
Ma foy, cela vous gâte au milieu du repas...
— Belle, vous dites vrai, mais se pourrait-il faire
De voir un si beau con et ne le foutre pas?[55]

One can speculate that, had Tertulian been given the opportunity to read Montaigne's advice to married women, Malherbe's love confessions or Viau's version of an erotic rosary, he would have summoned the exorcist. As it turned out, the Renaissance slowly but surely

53 *La poésie érotique*, ed. Georges Pillement (Bordeaux: R. Deforges, 1970), pp. 24–25.

54 *La poésie érotique*, ed. Marcel Béalu (Paris: Seghers, 1971), pp. 46–8. The substantial bulk of de Viau's pornography is concentrated in the *Parnasse satyrique*. See Appendix.

55 Ibid., pp. 87–8.

compromised forever the patristic approach to sex. In the long run, in spite of the active Inquisition, later attempts to discredit sacerdotally unauthorized lust only helped increase French anticlericalism. Obviously, major social attitudinal mutations do not occur overnight; the fanatic defenders of crumbling ideologies keep trying to enforce doctrinal taboos long after they have become obsolete. This is why Father Garasse accused the young de Viau of atheism and had him sentenced to be burnt alive. At the same time the incident reveals the cracks fast appearing in the monolithic power of the Catholic establishment: the sentenced heretic suspected of being the editor of the clandestine and popular racy publication *Parnasse satirique* (1622) was helped to escape from his death cell and find protection on the domain of the Duke de Montmorency.[56] De Viau's risky brush with ecclesiastic censorship characterizes the revival of conservative clerical power after the assassination of Henry IV (1610).

Baroque Restraint

Richelieu's era slowed down the progress of erotic emancipation sought by the lay community and its writers. Renaissance candor was subdued by the fashionably chaste temperance which, on the surface, changed the trappings of sensual art. Pagan nudity had run its cycle. The nymphs and satyrs were draped in brocades befitting the baroque pomp of the royal courts and the ostentatious saintliness of the *Ecclesia triumphans*. Humanists and theologians, Pascal, Bossuet, Bourdalou and even the cerebral Descartes, tried to prove the existence of God and revitalize the Christian heritage. Poets, their critics and their patrons exchanged views in the plush *salons* run by cultivated forerunners of feminism. Their prudery and refined manners were direct opposites of the relaxed candor in Marguerite de Navarre's *Heptameron*. Rabelais was condemned, though not on the grounds of erotic emancipation but rather for his semantic redundance and plebeian gusto. The baroque passion for noble monuments of royal and divine majesty wrapped feminine bodies in impressive wigs and impenetrable crinolines reinforced by the overwhelming baroque underwear which certainly inhibited spontaneous rapprochement between the sexes.

First came *préciosité*; Madeleine de Scudéry (1607–1701) drew *La Carte du Tendre*. The restrained classical *bon goût* alluded to erotic

56 See Appendix, de Viau.

vibrations in general civilized periphrases, euphemisms and metaphors. Madame Marie Madeleine de La Fayette (1634–93), an authentic pioneer of feminism, wrote the first French psychological novel, *La Princesse de Clèves* (1678), fictionalizing the misery of a conjugal triangle.[57] But even this short era of external erotic reserve had its counterpoints: Molière and Gassendi's Epicurean hedonism, the libertines' atheistic materialism, La Rochefoucauld's skepticism, Jean de La Fontaine's pagan naturalism.[58]

La Fontaine's *Libertinage*

After Richelieu's era, during the reign of Louis XIV, La Fontaine's clash with censorship no longer threatened his life. His *Fables* were unreservedly admired and ultimately paved the poet's path to the *Academy*. But the whole edition of the fourth volume of his love stories[59] (published without official permit) was seized by the police. While the first three volumes imitated mostly Boccaccio, Ariosto, Macchiavelli's *Mandragora* or Petronius' "Matron of Ephesus", the unauthorized sequence entitled *Nouveaux Contes* (1674) appeared to be more licentious than the earlier collections; it drew from the *Cent nouvelles nouvelles* (approx. 1460) and the "scandalous" *Parlatorio delle monache* and from the *Nouveau parloir des nonains*.[60] The poet, who was a *protégé* of the influential mistress of Louis XIV, the libertine Madame de Montespan,[61] risked neither arrest nor jail, but the confiscation of his poetic levity as well as the hostility of Colbert was serious enough to delay for 10 years his admission to the Academy. In addition, as a moribund academician the poet was haunted by tenacious clergymen

57 See *LP II*, Appendix, La Fayette, and ch. III, "Psychological conflicts."

58 Herbert De Ley, ("'Dans les reigles du plaisir...' Transformation of sexual knowledge in 17th century France," *Eroticism in French Literature*, pp. 10–20) points out that sex education was rudimentary during the classical era. The main guides were Ovid's *Ars amatoria* (published in 36 editions prior to 1610) and Aretino's *Ragionamenti*. Only Miliot's *Escole de filles* and Charles Sorel's *Histoire comique de Francion* modestly enriched erotic information and its vocabulary.

59 *Contes et Nouvelles en vers de M. La Fontaine*, 1664, 66, 67, 74, 85. See Appendix.

60 See Antoine Adam, *Histoire de la littérature française au XVIIe siècle*, "La Fontaine—Contes", p. 29. *The Decameron* was, of course, on the *Index librorum prohibitorum*.

61 She allegedly used to invoke Satan to secure the fidelity of the King. See Montague Summers, *The History of Witchcraft and Demonology*, New York, University Books, 1956, p. 160 and n. 158. See also comments *on Là-bas* and citations, *LP II*, pp. 205–7.

until he recanted his sinful erotica—somewhat like Boccaccio, who abjured *The Decameron* on his deathbed (1375). The young priest Father Poucet threatened La Fontaine that the Church would refuse to bury him in sacred ground, embarrass his survivors and tarnish his memory.

The Gallant XVIIIth Century

The rationalistic, anticlerical as well as licentious 18th century undermined the antisexual moralism of the Church while the Revolution put an end to its political clout. The ecclesiastic harassment which La Fontaine experienced for the satirical mockery of lecherous monks and nuns would have been gentler a century later. Voltaire's (1694–1778) and Goethe's (1749–1832) generations had no place for the pompous courtship of the Louis XIV era; they started to discover intimate sensual spontaneity uniting loving souls. The first and the last stanzas of Voltaire's *épître* entitled "Les Vous et les Tu" (1730) resurrects discreet souvenirs of rococo romance:

Philis, qu'est devenu ce temps
Ou, dans un fiacre promenée,
sans laquais, sans ajustements,
De tes grâces seules ornée,
Contente d'un mauvais soupé
Que tu changeais en ambroisie,
Tu te livrais, dans ta folie,
A l'amant heureux et trompé
qui t'avait consacré sa vie?
. . . .
Ah, Madame, que votre vie,
D'honneurs aujourd'hui si remplie,
Diffère de ces doux instants!
Ce large suisse à cheveux blancs,
Qui ment sans cesse à votre porte…

The ironic melancholy and understated candor of the betrayed yet happy cavalier, who contemplates, twenty years later, the transformation of the once warmhearted "tu" Philis into the status conscious "vous" Madame.[62]

Undoubtedly familiar with Samuel Richardson's melodramatic saga *Clarissa* (1748)[63] and abbé A.-F. Prévost's *Manon Lescaut* (1753), Voltaire projected his erotic material as a licentious satire of naïve illusions. Prudently, he published *Candide*'s first edition (1759) as an opus by the mysterious doctor Ralph translated from German. Neither the name of author, publisher or place of original publication figure on

62 In one of his lectures Leo Spitzer discussed the suggestive analogies between the ornamental rococo curves and Voltaire's gallant antitheses.

63 Its erotic climax is the rape of the heroine drugged by the libertine Lovelace; Clarissa's cousin kills Lovelace in a duel. She dies in a London hospice. Masterpiece Theatre resurrected it in an impressive TV series.

the title page of the slender volume which appeared outside France in Geneva. All Voltaire's characters pay a high price for their sensual longing: his prophet of optimism Pangloss becomes a victim of syphilis; his disciple Candide remembers that all his tender love had ever earned him were two kicks in his ass. Cunégonde, once drawn to Candide and willing to study with him the laws of "physique experimentale," loses her lover and is many times raped and disemboweled by brutal soldiers before she can start her free research. She survives only because the lusty males find her an attractive enough concubine, etc., etc.

As the author and publisher expected, not all readers greeted the philosopher's libertinage with enthusiasm. Although it faced no Jesuit curse in the bastion of Calvinism, it stirred up the indignation of virtuous Swiss Protestants. One month following the publication, the Geneva Council ordered the destruction of the book. The suspect flatly denied his authorship, saying that he had finally read this "student joke" and that he had more important things to do than write such a "connerie".[64]

Peyrefitte's Debt to Voltaire

In the previous volume Pangloss' macrostimulative mischief on the "genealogy" of his syphilis is broken down to stylistic and contentual microstimuli.[65] The once controversial anecdote is today an integral part of our literary tradition and read in the lycées or university courses. Like any true topos it has become an old chestnut while still retaining a great deal of its stimulative potential. Roger Peyrefitte must have thought so when he decided to revitalize it in his satire of French decadence entitled *Des Français*. His novel is a sequence of cynical *causeries* loosely structured like Voltaire's *roman philosophique* or perhaps like A. France's *L'Histoire contemporaine*. The targets of his wit range from de Gaulle to sex shops. While following the tradition of Voltaire, Montesquieu or Anatole France, Peyrefitte is not their epigone. Like them, he is a born mocker with a sharp pen. But he could not resist the temptation of offering an explicit gay "perversion" of Voltaire's joke.

A comparison of the precedent with the borrowing enables us to establish the scope of Peyrefitte's debt to Voltaire as well as the scope of his originality. When asked how love—"cette belle cause"—could have lead to such an abominable result, the incurable optimist and syphilitic

64 See ed. R. Groos, Pléiade edition of Voltaire's work, vol. *Notes*, p. 676.

65 *LP II*, ch. III, pp. 73–77 and tables IV and V, pp. 77–80. The text is reproduced below to facilitate the comparison with Peyrefitte's *imitatio*.

Pangloss replies:

> "O mon cher Candide! vous avez connu Paquette, cette jolie suivante de notre auguste baronne: j'ai goûté dans ses bras les délices du paradis, qui ont produit ces tourments d'enfer dont vous me voyez dévoré;...Paquette tenait ce présent d'un cordelier très savant qui avait remonté à la source, car il l'avait eue d'une vieille comtesse, qui l'avait reçus d'un capitaine de cavalerie, qui la devait à une marquise, qui la tenait d'un page, qui l'avait reçue d'un jésuite qui, étant novice, l'avait eue en droite ligne d'un des compagnons de Christophe Colomb. Pour moi, je ne la donnerai à personne, car je me meurs."
>
> "O Pangloss!" s'écria Candide, "voilà une étrange généalogie! n'est-ce pas le diable qui en fut la souche?"[66]

No women have a role in Peyrefitte's modern echo of this classical gauloiserie. One of his main observers of French life is Francis Grandville, *licencié ès lettres* (*mention très bien*). Francis is a hippy who left his well-to-do family to live with Maria Dolores, a young anarchist. Among the friends of the young couple is a medical student, "Jeannot le carabin," an anarchist for whom homosexuality is a badge of his revolt. The three friends attend the swinging abbé de Fatto's jazz rally organized in the Saint-Germain-des-Prés church by the enlightened Parisian hierarchy. The goal of this jazz crusade is to attract French youth, if not to orthodox Christianity, at least to a church. During the concert the anarchist reveals to Francis the main goal of his visit: "Je ne suis pas venu pour prier ou pour danser...Il paraît qu'on baise dans les couloirs...On vient d'y casser les lampes. Je vais y chercher un pot à casser". A few days later, discussing with Francis and Maria the happening in the church, Jeannot sums up his activities in the house of God in the following epilogue: "Vous ne me reprendrez plus à faire l'amour dans une église, dit Jeannot. J'y ai attrapé la chaude-pisse." In the dialogue which follows this confession, Jeannot hints that the punishment of his blasphemy by the Christian God was excessive: wasn't his little adventure a peak of discretion? Hadn't he had sex with a "noir, dans le noir"? "Ah! le cochon!" Jeannot remembers his anonymous African lover. When his friends reprove his fit of racism Jeannot argues:

> — Il m'a certainement rendu un cadeau de la civilisation blanche,... Ce doit être pour ma formation de toubib [doc, army doctor] que je me suis fait poivrer de toutes les manières... J'ai attrapé avec un jaune l'urétrite à gonocoque, avec un Philippin l'urétrite à colibacille, avec un Hindou l'urétrite à spirochète... [J]e m'étais juré de ne plus entrer dans des trous que je ne connaissais pas. Ayant pratiqué le coït interfémoral avec un Nord-Africain, ce

66 *Voltaire Romans et Contes*, ed. R. Groos (Paris: NRF, Pleiade), p. 157.

> me fut l'occasion de découvrir l'urétrite à staphylocoque,... Il ne me manque désormais que l'urétrite traînante, pour...passer à la vérole.
>
> — J'ai l'impression que tu n'as pas la main heureuse," dit Maria Dolores.
>
> — Les couples comme vous ne savent pas à quoi ils échappent, dit Jeannot. C'est le revers de l'homosexualité d'être insatiable et, par conséquent, à la merci de tous les revers."[67]

The differences between the 18th and 20th century anecdotes testify to the adequate originality of Peyrefitte's *imitatio rerum*, but his content and style also ascertain his literary debt: both texts treat the risks of promiscuity; the rhetorical backbone in both versions is the extended enumeration-climax punctuated by a double *pointe* ("je ne la donnerai à personne, car je me meurs"/"passer à la vérole;" "étrange généalogie" / "à la merci de tous les revers"). Both contain mischievous puns ("novice," "revers".) On the other hand, the two treatments differ a great deal: Pangloss is hetero-, Jeannot is a homosexual. Pangloss is one of several lovers who all have one thing in common—syphilis. Jeannot is the exclusive owner of a collection of rare types of gonorrhoea and uretritis. Pangloss is incurable but a stubborn optimist. Jeannot will be cured ("...tout cela se guérit") but he is a cynic. Pangloss is one of the main characters, Jeannot is one of the many *Des Français*. Voltaire's insinuating euphemisms and hyperboles provoke the reader's imagination. Peyrefitte's treatment of the farce esthetically relies on the clinical diagnosis accurately identifying the range of exotic infections (urétrite à gonocoque, à spirochète; Philippin, Hindou). Stylistically it exploits the contrast between the slang ("chaude-pisse," "se faire poivrer") and *savant* diction ("coït interfémoral").

In spite of its originality Peyrefitte's *imitatio* is less tightly written than Voltaire's text. Consequently, the esthetic density of the latter is higher. The esthetic contrasts (Paquette, monk, old countess, etc.) and the switch from hetero- to homosexual adventure (page, Jésuit, etc.) are more unexpected than those Peyrefitte managed to condense in his text. The passages framing the respective punch-lines do not reach the same esthetic intensity. The ironic *mot juste*, "une étrange généalogie", is a brighter stylistic spark than the understatement, "tu n'as pas la main heureuse".

Peyrefitte's maxim, "...c'est le revers de l'homosexualité...d'être à la merci de tous les revers", would be more credible in Voltaire's text: in Jeannot's mixture of slang and medical semantics, the aphorism is too

67 *Des Français* (Paris: Flammarion, 1970), pp. 116–17.

precious to be esthetically convincing. The main strength of Voltaire's version is its definite satirical focus: as soon as Pangloss identifies the source of his predicament, true to his doctrine, he interprets it as the finest evolution in the best of all possible worlds: without syphilis we would enjoy neither chocolate nor cochineal. There is no such satirical development in *Des Français*. Jeannot knows that medical science will cure him. His account turns out to be an introduction to statistics on venereal diseases among French homosexuals.

This comparison not only shows the difficulty of imitating an inimitable classical model, it also acknowledges higher stimulative impact of Voltaire's "old chestnut". Even the fact that Voltaire challenged the censors of his day while none was shocked by Peyrefitte's "licence" illustrates two different levels of provocation experienced by the two authors' contemporaries.

Shortly after *Candide*'s publication, Denis Diderot (1713–84) completed his *La Religieuse*. It was published only in 1796, long after his death. Throughout his whole life the erudite and courageous editor of the *Encyclopedia* was watched by French censors. Only the revolutionary and post-revolutionary regimes were ready to sanction the unprecedented candor of his novel.[68]

Sadean Erotica

The humanistic messages found in pre-Revolutionary transpositions of erotic subjects spring from preromantic idealism. They reflect the revolutionary tenets pleading for the emancipation of sex life from ecclesiastic prescriptions and restrictive social conventions. Whether satirical (*Candide*), crusading (*La Religieuse*), melodramatic (*Clarissa*, *Manon Lescaut*), tragic (*The Suffering of the Young Werther*), psychological (*Elective Affinities*, *Julie ou la Nouvelle Héloise*) or autobiographical (*Les Confessions*), the heroines and heroes of these texts variously confront outdated prejudices and dream of freer erotic choices, based on equality and spontaneous intimacy, not subjugation.

On the other hand revolutionary brutality, terror, anarchy, low instincts and corruption also have their parallels in 18th century literature: in the libertine pornography of Marquis D.A.F. de Sade, the ever controversial "lumière noire".[69]

68 See above ch. II, "Recurrent Characters" and Appendix, Diderot.

69 Béatrice Didier, préface, "Sade aujourd'hui," *Justine*, Livre de Poche, 1973, p. ix–xxxi.

Many of his contemporaries, including Napoléon Bonaparte, considered him a criminal or a derailed psychopath who, according to the Emperor, should not have been allowed to publish even during the lawless revolutionary spell. This descendant of an old aristocratic family was jailed at Vincennes in 1777 following his brutal sodomist orgy in Marseille. During this adventure he and his butler abused four prostitutes and allegedly offered some of them pills spiked with an aphrodisiac. The women, who suffered severe vomiting spasms and were forced to participate in sodomy (which, at that time constituted a capital crime,) accused the Marquis of trying to poison them. Seven years later, he was transferred to the Bastille where he completed several of his libertine "classics." *Justine ou les malheurs de la vertu*, written in 1787, appeared in 1791 in Holland without the author's name. It was followed by *L'Histoire de Juliette ou les prospérités du vice* in 1797. Both publications were confiscated in France during Napoléon's consulate in 1801. Although De Sade denied his authorship, he was rearrested, this time for his criminal mimesis of depravity and later transferred from the prison to the insane asylum at Charenton.[70] Among the 30 volumes of his *Collected Works* the two mentioned novels may be the best known monuments of Sade's antihumanism but *Les Cent vingt Journées de Sodome* probably contains the richest arsenal of sadist topics.[71]

J.J. Revel's "Note" in this critical edition[72] sums up the bizarre destiny of the manuscript which the prisoner completed in the Bastille in 1785, pasted into a twelve-meter-long strip rolled up and, with the help of his visiting wife, had smuggled out of prison. Following his release from jail, Mme de Sade, however, never returned the blighted *chef d'oeuvre* to her husband. Throughout the 19th century the manuscript was allegedly "traced" to several private collectors. Only in 1904 it surfaced in Berlin, where the pioneer of modern sexology, Dr. Iwan Bloch, published it under the pseudonym of Eugen Dühren. This edition consisted of 185 copies and designated as publisher the Parisian Club of Bibliophiles. The first French edition appeared in 1929, through the

70 These historical comments draw from Raymond Jean, *Un portrait de Sade*, Actes Sud, 1989, n.p., pp. 106–28, 306.

71 D.A.F. de Sade, *Oeuvres complètes* (Paris, Jean-Jacques Pauvert, 1967), vols. XXVI–IX. On the other hand, *La Philosophie dans le boudoir* (1795, London) appears to be Sade's most "systematic" exposé of his voluptuary bestialism. In it, his fictitious libertines preach and/or indulge in greed, theft, murder, incest, sodomy and pedophilia.

72 Ibid, vol. XXVI, pp. xix, xx.

initiative of Maurice Heine, who acquired the manuscript in Germany. His publishing adventure, however, turned sour when he ran out of funds and was unable to finance the production of the last volume. After World War II a clandestine edition appeared.[73] So far, only the 1967 orthographically modernized *Collected Works* in 30 volumes draw from the original manuscript and form the works' ultimate edition including the blasphemous *120 Journées de Sodome*. These publishing peripeties and the manuscript's century-long storage in the "underground" affirm the high risk of publishing Sade's explosive erotica and also serve as an indirect criterion of their outrageous vitality. Because of many pornographic passages and the correlated legal obstacles to the publication, any critic and/or publisher of the Sade brand of art should ask and answer two questions—1. are the most provocative volumes of the Marquis' production psychopathic scatology? and 2. can we classify at least some of them as erotically intensive literary art? After long deliberations I tend to answer both questions affirmatively.[74] The objections that art and scatology are mutually exclusive or that art can represent corruptive licence but not preach it at the same time, strike me as dogmatic premises rather than irrefutable arguments. Such opinions, however, may have some merit, especially if one narrows down a broad concept of literary art to the literal meaning of the traditional labels such as *humaniores litterae* or *belles lettres*. Even if taken only semi-seriously, Sade's brutal erotomania is dehumanizing and his stimulative fantasies are consistently repulsive. Yet such a grave inflexible verdict should not discourage us from reading his salacious farce as a morbidly unique work, written by a stylistically talented lunatic in the grim isolation of his prison cell. His sophisticated crackpot delight in sexual often criminal eccentricities helped to create a *sordide* counterpoint to *Candide* as well as to Rousseau's idealistic assumption that all of us are

73 It declares Brussels as place of publication and, according to Revel, it is full of errors.

74 Béatrice Didier, ed. *Justine ou les malheurs de la vertu*, (Livre de Poche, 1973), "Sade aujourd'hui," pp. ix–x. "Le XX siècle est le lieu d'une apothéose ambigüe". Without being an "apotheosis" my balance sheet of positive and negative qualities will too be ambiguous. I concur with Paul Goodman's dictum, "[t]he question is not whether pornography but the quality of pornography" (i.e., artistic quality). Cited in *A Susan Sontag Reader*, "The pornographic Imagination," (New York: Vintage Bks, Random, 1982), p. 233.

born good.[75] Although the 19th century imitates his antihumanism, for instance, in *Ubu roi*'s moronic pataphysics (1888–94),[76] only in the liberal climate of the 20th century is Sade freely read and decriminalized as a victim of socio-cultural discrimination. While decadent works generally revolt against current legal standards and literary tradition, they form an integral stage of that same tradition and along with other factors, initiate recurring cycles from positive to negative esthetic qualities.

To illustrate the global impact of Sade's iconoclastic pornography, hyperbolic irony and pleonastic *élan*, let us start with a macrostimulative portrait of one of Sade's misanthropic "Sordides." Preparing the ground for his fictional four-month sodomist "workshop" moderated at Silling by the fictitious Duke de Blangis, the Bastille's writer-in-residence introduces a foursome of egotistic and merciless debauchers all indulging in criminal depravities, such as rape, robbery, incestual sodomy, sexual torture, relentless sexual abuse of juveniles, blackmail, insidious framing or murdering abused victims. Can modern readers find in de Sade's characters a satire of historical monsters such as the Roman Emperor Tiberius,[77] or the legendary Bluebeard? Or in hindsight, can we not see in de Blangis a parody of a pre-Nietzchean sex-obsessed *Übermensch*, just as the Prague public recognized in Ubu roi (1896) a model of the 1980 Communist nomenklatura?[78] No matter how one answers such hermeneutic questions, one conclusion seems to be unavoidable—no mythology or fairy tale has ever created an archtype as cynical as de Sade's bestial villain: "Le duc de Blangis, maître à dix-huit ans d'une fortune déjà immense...éprouva tous les inconvénients qui naissent en foule autour d'un jeune homme riche...et qui n'a rien à se refuser; presque toujours dans un tel cas la mesure des forces devient celle des vices..."[79] Besides immense wealth, unpredictable Nature gave Sade's antihero a rare physical verve combined with criminal instincts.

75 Another counterpoint is Justine "affublée d'un prénom signifiant, comme Candide" (see Anne Lacombe "Les Infortunes de la vertu, le Conte et la Philosophie" *L'Esprit Créateur, Le Marquis de Sade*, issue vol. XV, No. 4, 1975, p. 426). Alice M. Laborde in "Sade: l'érotisme démystifié" in the same issue, pp. 438–429, discusses Sade's debts to "the sublime Rousseau" (whom he aspired to equal or trump—*à rebours*—Julie/Juliette).

76 See Appendix, Alfred Jarry.

77 As Tacitus, Pliny, Suetonius portrayed him or as Robert Graves fictionalized him in *I Claudius* (1934).

78 See *LP II*, Ch. II, "Semantics" p. 43 and n. 57.

79 *120 Journées*, ed. cit., pp. 18–9.

> Né faux, dur, impérieux, barbare, égoïste, également prodigue pour ses plaisirs et avare quand il s'agissait d'être utile, menteur, gourmand, ivrogne, poltron, sodomite, incestueux, meurtrier, incendiaire, voleur, pas une seule vertu ne compensait autant de vices. Que dis-je! non seulement il n'en révérait aucune, mais elles lui étaient toutes en horreur, et l'on lui entendait dire souvent qu'un homme, pour être véritablement heureux dans ce monde, devait non seulement se livrer à tous les vices, mais ne se permettre jamais une vertu...

If there is any invisible cosmic fuel activating our exploits, it cannot be a god. God cannot even be dead: such a religious chimera had never existed and any moral scruple is a revolting absurdity.

> A vingt-trois ans, il fit partie avec trois de ses compagnons de vice...d'aller arrêter un carrosse...de violer...les hommes et les femmes, de les assassiner après, de s'emparer de l'argent dont ils n'avaient assurément aucun besoin, et de se trouver tous trois la même nuit au bal de l'Opéra afin de prouver l'alibi...personne n'osa le soupçonner.[80]

Unlike the fairy-tale Bluebeard, he does not hide the bodies in a secret chamber. When he gets tired of his wife, who perhaps used to be his late father's own mistress, the Duke wastes no time in making her meet his late mother, sister and all his other victims. Thus he is free to marry the wealthy but discredited mistress of his brother. She does not live too long either, nor does his third wife: "On disait dans le monde que c'était l'immensité de sa construction qui tuait ainsi toutes ses femmes, et...le duc laissait germer une opinion qui voilait la vérité.[81] This sardonically ambiguous rumor confirms that, indeed, it could have been his "immense anatomy" which killed his wives one after the other: was the fatal *corpus delicti* the libertine's monumental and ever-erect phallus?

> Ce colosse effrayant donnait en effet l'idée d'Hercule ou d'un centaure: le duc avait...des membres d'une force et d'une énergie,...des nerfs d'une élasticité, joignez à cela...un tempérament de fer, une force de cheval, et le membre d'un véritable mulet, étonnamment velu, doué de la faculté de perdre son sperme aussi souvent qu'il le voulait dans un jour, même à l'Age de cinquante ans qu'il avait alors, une érection presque continuelle dans ce membre dont la taille était de huit pouces juste de pourtour sur douze de long, et vous aurez le portrait du duc de Blangis... [82]

What are the original epical actions of Sade's characters, such as the duke, his brother, bishop de **, Juliette, her crooked lover, Noirceuil, or a crowd of corrupt go-betweens, whores and profligate nuns whom

80 Ibid., pp. 23–4.
81 Ibid., p. 24.
82 Ibid., p. 25.

Justine, the virtuous sister of Juliette,[83] meets during her endless and vain attempts to find a single decent being on Earth? As their only ambition is abnormal malevolent sex, topical monotony prevails.[84] There are no other plots to speak of than one typically sadist adventure after another. The recurrence of a single epical formula (Barthes' mutable "erotic code") is occasionally interrupted by digressive and contrastful livresque bizarreries or salacious anecdotes related by various artificial characters.

The daily erotic programs scheduled for each of the 120 days of sodomist holidays do not greatly differ. The Silling pilgrims pursue a relentless pattern of sexual aberration for the four full months. When the expedition's leaders become exhausted they have refreshments and listen to scurrilous reminiscences told by their sexual slaves of varying ranks. When, however, the appetites of the sodomite brass dictate, even the meals may be combined with unscheduled perversions.

The fifth day of the libertine seminar opens, as scheduled, with a masturbation lesson offered to the seraglio of eight juvenile girls by one of the project's senior sponsors, president Curval. The instructor of the novice class can barely resist the digital finesse of the fast learning nymphets. "Ce fut Curval qui ce matin-là fut se prêter aux masturbations de l'école, et comme les jeunes filles commençaient à faire des progrès, il eut beaucoup de peine à résister aux secousses multipliées, aux postures lubriques et variées de ces huit charmantes petites filles."[85] Another highlight on that day's agenda is the admission of the boy lovers to the dining room table reserved for the distinguished foursome. During their lunch, the Bishop de..., duke de Blangis' brother, plays first fiddle but his noble colleagues are good sports and know how to add zest to the Monsignor's improvisation.

> L'évêque très en train ce jour-là ne cessa de baiser Céladon presque tout le temps du repas, et comme cet enfant devait être du quadrille servant le café, il sortit un peu avant le dessert. Quand Monseigneur, qui venait de s'en échauffer la tête, le revit tout nu dans le salon d'à-côté, il n'y tint plus.
>
> — Sacredieu, dit-il tout en feu, puisque je ne peux pas l'enculer, au moins lui ferai-je ce que Curval a fait hier à son bardache.
>
> Et saisissant le petit bonhomme, il le coucha sur le ventre en disant cela,

83 *Justine ou le malheurs de la vertu, O.C.* II, III.

84 "...[C]onflict is lacking,...and progress...denied by the compulsion to repeat the same ritual over and over again." Michael Riffaterre, "Sade or Texte as Phantasy," *Diacritics*, Fall 1972, p. 2, cited in "Diderot et Sade: Afffinités et divergences," by Jeny H. Batley and Otis E. Fellows, *L'Esprit créateur, Sade*, p. 456.

85 120 Journées, *O.C.* XXVI, p. 221.

> lui glissa son vit dans les cuisses. Le libertin était aux nues, le poil de son vit frottait le trou mignon qu'il aurait bien voulu perforer;...

The duke, enjoying the impromptu, joins in on his brother's "opération": "...pour l'exciter du spectacle de son libertinage, [le duc] se plaça devant lui en gamahuchant le trou du cul de Cupidon, le second des garçons qui servait le café ce jour-là." The other two convives also wish to stir up the clergyman's ecstasy: "Curval vint sous ses yeux se faire branler par Michette, et Durcet lui offrit les fesses écartées de Rosette."[86] At this point, the fifth day's program is far from being over.

Similar but more rigidly structured lesbian rituals (Barthes' *mot juste* would be "épisodes") characterize the daily routine in the convent where the fast learning heroine of *Histoire de Juliette ou les prospérités du vice* becomes a favorite playmate of the abbesse Delbène. This Mother Superior keeps in unusually intimate touch with her pious flock, spending many happy hours in the company of the thoroughly screened and trained sisters.

> "A cause des goûts de Volmar, il faut que tu lui enfonces ta langue dans le cul, pendant que, courbée sur toi, la friponne te gamahuchera... Pour Sainte-Elme, poursuivit la supérieure, sait-tu ce que j'en ferais? Je m'arrangerais de manière à pouvoir lui sucer à la fois le cul et le con, pendant qu'elle te le rendrait... Et quant à moi, commande, ma mie, je suis à tes ordres. » Échauffée de ce que j'avais vu faire à Volmar, "[j]e veux t'enculer, dis-je, avec ce godemiché." Fais, ma bonne, fais," me répond...Delbène..."voilà mon cul, je te le livre."

Maintaining a sisterly didactic tone common in the upper-crust convent retreat, Sade's young heroine knows how to choreograph the specific details of the group's intimate leisure time and please her demanding superior:

> "Eh bien! dis-je en sodomisant mon institutrice...Chère Volmar,...que ton clitoris rende à mon cul ce que je fais à celui de Delbène; tu ne saurais à quel point mon tempérament s'irrite de cette manière de jouir. De chacune de mes mains, je voudrais branler Élisabeth et Sainte-Elme, pendant que je sucerais le con de Flavie."[87]

To infuse suspenseful contrasts into the tedious scenarios of the *120 journées* or Juliette's phenomenal but dull ascent to the peaks of erotic crime, the pornographer digresses and comments on exotic cultural, religious and social conventions deviating from occidental marriage.

86 Ibid.
87 *O.C.* XIX, ed. A. Pierre de Mandiargues, p. 44.

> On voit une pagode à Cambaye, lieu de pèlerinage où toutes les femmes se rendent avec la plus grande dévotion; là, elles se prostituent publiquement, sans que leurs maris y trouvent à redire. Celles qui ont amassé une certaine fortune à ce métier achètent,...de jeunes esclaves...qu'elles mènent ensuite à la pagode pour se prostituer à leur exemple...

Elsewhere the officating cleric "preconsummates" the marriage to prepare the ground for the wedding night. "Les prêtres de Cumane ravissent la fleur des jeunes mariées: l'époux n'en voudrait pas sans cette cérémonie préalable. Ce précieux bijou n'est donc qu'un préjugé national, ainsi que tant d'autres choses sur lesquelles nous ne voulons jamais ouvrir les yeux." In other countries brides lacking stamina are advised to limit the number of invited guests to minimum:

> Aux îles Baléares, le mari est le dernier qui jouisse de sa femme: tous les parents, tous les amis le précèdent dans cette cérémonie; il passerait pour un homme fort malhonnête, s'il s'opposait à cette prérogative. Cette même coutume s'observait en Islande, et chez les Nazaméens, peuple de l'Égypte: après le festin, l'épouse nue allait se prostituer à tous les convives et recevait un présent de chacun.[88]

Sade also crusades for the feudal (regretfully discontinued) *ius primae noctis*.[89] Entering for the first time Sade's gallery of sodomizing, masturbating, senile rapists, sperm eating ga-gas, bishops, coprophagous presidents, brutal pedophiles, lesbian abbesses, perverse monks, professional male and female *fouteurs*, the overwhelmed critic's first wish may hardly be to evaluate the esthetic impact of these insane fantasies. A seasoned reader may first shake his head, then laugh but at the same time wonder, if what he/she has read is a laughing matter. I confess that my humanistic distaste for the psychopath's subject matter parallels my appreciation of his stylistic gusto, his sardonic semantic shocks, precious sly inuendoes, the ridiculous always lucid "preproustian" syntactic ramifications, all subordinated to the libertine's malevolence and his black humor.[90] Like Barthes I perceive the high intensity of Sade's *parole libertine* which, however, I prefer to call just Sade's stylistic skill.[91] Where the semiotist claims to observe a fusion or confusion of syntactic effects "phrase (oratoire)" with the perverse

88 Ibid., p. 118.
89 "Combien de temps la féodalité usa-t-elle de ce droit...particulièrement en Écosse? Ce sont donc des préjugés que la pudeur...que l'adultère...." Ibid., p. 118–9.
90 Lautréamont's parody of Homeric style creates a somewhat analogical stylistic effect.
91 See comments above, "Barthes' erotic codes" and n. 27.

subject matter—"figure érotique", I see a strong contrast between the stylistic culture and salacious content. Therefore I find it difficult to accept Barthes' sophistry equating the grammatical and epical subjects of Sade's warped erotica, sophistry ultimately leading Barthes to his esthetic dissolution of content; "interdisciplinarily" he speculates but fails to prove that Sade's "parole" and his sick subject matter springing from his sick fantasy—"l'énergie du vice"—*may* somehow jointly constitute the libertine "imagination" which Barthes arbitrarily but only "presque" claims to be "the Sadean word for the language". These reflections further lead Barthes to a mixed semiotic as well as impressionistic value judgement implying that Sade's syntax and rhetoric not only are effective artistic qualities but that they successfully convert Sade's "criminal network" into a "marvellous tree."[92] While concurring with Barthes' appraisal of style, as humantist, I am not willing to rehabilitate Sade's content on account of his amusing rhetoric.

As a modern friendly critic, Barthes seems to dismiss the long silence of several generations of critics and writers who disregard Sade's legacy. Were all of them blind to his brand of originality? Just "bourgeois," as Didier says? Although ostracized, first by his social milieu for his criminal record and later by posterity[93] for the psychopathic propaganda preached *ad nauseam* by the imaginary male and female debauchers represented in his fiction, Sade's literary influence has been growing. His deviant Bluebeards and Messalinas herald the Romantic revolt of instincts against classical Apollonian sobriety and inspire the quest for bizarre shock omnipresent in Baudelairean poetry. (However, Sade's agnosticism would have no place for Baudelaire's platonic preoccupation with the absolutes and his masochistic fascination with sin and guilt.) As suggested earlier, the Sadean characters, who recognize no ethical standards and no law above them foreshadow especially the

92 *Sade, Fourier, Loyola*, pp. 36–7. Seule cette parole est libre, inventée, *se confondant entièrement* avec l'énergie du vice… C'est que la parole se confond entièrement avec la marque avouée du libertin, qui est (dans le vocabulaire de Sade): *l'imagination*: on dirait *presque* qu'*imagination* est le mot sadien pour *langage*… On comprend…sur quoi repose…toute la combinatoire érotique de Sade: *son origine et sa sanction* sont *d'ordre rhétorique*. Les deux codes, en effet, celui de la phrase (*oratoire*) et celui de la figure (*érotique*) *se realient sans cesse*, forment une même ligne… C'est la phrase (ses raccourcis, ses corrélations internes, ses figures, son cheminement souverain) qui *libère les surprises de la combination érotique* et *convertit le réseau du crime en arbre merveilleux*. (My ital.)

93 Familiar with his gradually accessible publications.

"amoral" individualism of *Übermensch.* Victor Hugo's Romantic manifesto ("Préface de *Cromwell*) pays no attention whatsoever to Sade's pre-Romantic pioneering. Didier points out that the "bourgeois" century—Chateaubriand, Lamartine, Baudelaire and Flaubert—owed a great deal to Sade but they would have never admitted it: "Il faut être un peu fou comme Petrus Borel pour intégrer dans un roman paru en 1839, *Madame Putiphar*, un éloge du marquis."[94] Only Freudian hermeneutics and the Surrealist cult of the subconcious began rehabilitating Sade's fantasies as valuable evidence of irrational repressed creative energy seething under the artist's deceptive façade. Today, it is unlikely that many future critics will deny Sade a niche in literary history. But just as he had been transferred from jail to jail or from the jail to insane asylum during his life time, posterity, unable to reach any consensus, might go on shuffling his antihumantist legacy from one niche to another.

Influenced by Barthes, Didier credits him with his creation of a "new language"; this is not accurate: he simply indulged in the vulgar semantics which Rabelais, Malherbe and Théophile de Viau had used more sparingly. Although fully aware of Sade's weak points—repetition, excess, monotony—Didier not only finds them excusable but even original. The tedious repetitions suitably echo "le temps carcéral de la répétition sans issue". Further, the accumulations of more or less identical topical variations do not betray a lack of invention but the author's "pedagogical leanings" [sic.] His redundant ballast allegedly educates the reader.[95] In no case can her possible reservations compromise Sade's prometheism. Implicitly comparing Sade with Montesquieu, Voltaire, Diderot, Helvetius and Rousseau, Didier exaggerates when she proclaims the Marquis to be "the most enlightening lighthouse in the century of the *Lumières*."[96]

The illustrative citations and the tone of my critical comments on Sade's characters and their actions make clear that I share neither Barthes' nor Didier's scholarly enthusiasm. Through his texts I perceive Sade as talented artist/psychopath whose admirable rhetorical talent and perverse disposition produced original but morbidly degrading sex farce powerful enough to influence in varying degrees prominent pioneers of

94 "Sade aujourd'hui," p.x. In 1833 Borel (the lycanthrope) authored Champavert (wolf head), *Contes immoraux*.

95 Ibid., p. xv, "recherche systématique de l'excès." Didier gives a new twist to the proverbial *repetitio mater studiorum*.

96 Ibid., p. ix, "le...phare...le plus éclairant de ce Siècle de Lumières."

experimental black genres including the Monty Python satirists. What also attracts both modern readers and artists are the high levels of explicit shock and abrasive candor ironically defying the legal restrictions applicable to erotic literature. Saying this, I also hope that the tradition of *humaniores litterae*, in finding a proper niche for Sade's sick originality, will not become blind to his lunatic cult of obscene evil, as devilishly comical as it may be. His unique burlesque of human corruption deserves to be recognized as such and identified as an artistic antipole of everything that is charming, serene and joyous in our life and art rather than as a "marvelous tree" or as the "brightest lighthouse" of French Enlightenment.

Flaubert's and Baudelaire's "Corruption of Public Mores"

Among the 19th century writers notorious for their then provocative treatment of erotica are Flaubert, Baudelaire and Lautréamont/Ducasse. The first two were charged in 1857 with offense of public and religious morals. The Imperial Court dismissed the incrimination of certain erotic passages in *Mme Bovary*[97] but it banned several poems included in *Les Fleurs du mal*; the poet was sentenced to pay a 300 Ffrs fine.[98] Both trials were preceded by press polemics which document the full range of public response from condemnation to approval. As always, the liberal public defended the artists and the conservative right wing demanded their scalps. An anonymous review exemplifies the indignation of the Roman Catholic lobby. Its final arguments, however, reluctantly recognize that the days of flagellating poets are over:

> Je vous parlais récemment de *Madame Bovary*, ce scandaleux succès, qui est à la fois une ignominie littéraire, une calamité morale et un symptome social. Ce hideux roman de *Madame Bovary* est une lecture de piété en comparaison d'un volume de poésies qui vient de paraître ces jours-ci, sous le titre de *Fleurs du mal*... Rien ne peut vous donner une idée du tissu d'infamies et de saletés que renferme ce volume...les citations mêmes ne sont pas possibles à une plume honnête. C'est par là et par un sentiment de dégoût, plus fort que tout le reste,

97 See *LP II*, ch. VI and Appendix, Flaubert, pp. 223–4.

98 The publisher was also fined 100 Ffrs. At that time, e.g., a new copy of *Madame Bovary* in two volumes was selling for one franc. Following the Education Department intervention, Baudelaire's fine was gradually reduced to 100 Ffrs. The sum was ultimately paid by the Imperial Princess, patroness of French poets. I mention this to illustrate a French way of rehabilitating controversial poetry.

que M. *Baudelaire échappera au fouet* des gens qui se respectent...[99]

On the other hand, the public prosecution kept a low profile. In his rather prudent indictment Mr. Pinard, "substitute" of the Imperial Prosecutor, argued with professional restraint. Perhaps, after the Crown's unsuccessful attempt to convict Flaubert, he may have anticipated a 50/50 or slightly better chance of convicting Baudelaire. He had to claim that, from the point of view of legal standards he was assigned to invoke, the poet had violated the *then current* social and legal limits. He argued that the dismissal of his charges would encourage everybody to believe that Baudelaire's work complies with desirable moral conventions. To avoid such a misunderstanding he proposed the suppression of specific "condemnable" poems. He charged that the following offensive passages could increase the weak and corruptible readers' "taste for lascivious frivolities" without drawing their attention to other poems' redeeming didactic merits which he gladly recognized:

> La femme nue, essayant des poses devant l'amant fasciné (pièce 20) — La Mégère libertine qui verse trop de flammes et qu'on ne peut, comme le Styx, embrasser neuf fois (pièce 24, *Non satiata*), [sic]); — *La Vierge folle*, dont la jupe et la gorge aigüe aux bouts charmants versent le *Léthé* (pièce 30); — *La Femme trop gaie*, dont l'amant châtie la chair joyeuse, en lui ouvrant des lèvres nouvelles (pièce 39); — *Le beau Navire*, où la femme est décrite avec la gorge triomphante, provocante, bouclier armé de pointes roses, tandis que les jambes, sous les volants qu'elles chassent, tourmentent les désirs et les agacent (pièce 48); — *La Mendiante rousse*, dont les noeuds mal attachés dévoilent le sein tout nouvelet, et dont les bras, pour la déshabiller, se font prier, en chassant les doigts lutins (pièce 65); — *Lesbos*, où les filles aux yeux doux, de leurs corps amoureuses, caressent les fruits mûrs de leur nubilité (pièce 80); — *les Femmes damnées* ou *les Tribales* (pièces 81 et 82); — *les Métamorphoses*, ou la *Femme Vampire* étouffant un homme en ses bras veloutés, abandonnant aux morsures son buste sur les matelas qui se pâment d'émoi, au point que les anges impuissants se damneraient pour elle (pièce 87).

Naturally, Pinard could not limit his arguments to a short list of offensive lines. As one of several specific samples of Baudelaire's transgressive poetry he singled out three quatrains of the poem 39 indicted in the above summation. He solicited the court's reaction to the fictitious lover's luring of his "maîtresse."

1. Ainsi je voudrais une nuit, / Quand l'heure des voluptés sonne, / Sur les

99 *Journal de Bruxelles*, July 15 1857, cited in the Classiques Larousse (1973) edition of *Les Fleurs du mal* (my italics). The subsequent quotations draw from the same edition, pp. 86–103.

trésors de ta personne, / Comme un lâche, ramper sans bruit,
2. Pour châtier ta chair joyeuse, / Pour meurtrir ton sein pardonné, / Et faire à ton flanc étonné / Une blessure large et creuse,
3. Et, vertigineuse douceur! / A travers ces lèvres nouvelles, / Plus éclatantes et plus belles, / T'infuser mon venin, *ma soeur*! [My italics.]

Pinard's reading either overlooks the apostrophized "ma soeur" or deliberately grants it the benefit of legal doubt by interpreting the final accented word and the shocking pointe "soeur" as a metaphor of "maîtresse." Thus he inadvertently or intentionally ignores Baudelaire's obvious incestuous implication which, no doubt, would aggravate the legal transgression just as it increases the degree of the calculated esthetic shock. May we speculate that Pinard knew what he read, but perhaps wanted to neutralize the effect of esthetically but not legally irrelevant objection that the poet had no sister, that "soeur" just has to rhyme with "douceur" and that he, the prosecutor, is just haunted by fantasies of criminal taboos where there are none? Or perhaps, was he more liberal than he had to appear when, *ex officio*, he had to prosecute a book of poetry? Out of some fifteen inculpated entries only six poems were ultimately purged[100] from the first edition by the Justice Ch. Camusat. For example, the heavy dose of erotic farce and fantasy in *Sed non satiata* (24) escaped the censor's guillotine. In hindsight, we may wonder what would have happened if the 1857 prosecution had quoted and the Justice Camusat had read my 1989 stylistic and thematic exegesis.[101]

Maldoror's First True Love

The trimestrially published 1869 *Bulletin* (No 7) of books printed abroad and prohibited in France lists *Les Chants de Maldoror* by Lautréamont/Isidore Ducasse published in Belgium.[102] This author's debt to Sade's libertine teleology far exceeds that of Flaubert or Baudelaire. Among Maldoror's best known sadistic adventures is the souvenir of his first true love: standing on a cliff, the hero is pleased to observe the destruction of a ship in the stormy ocean. The desperate passengers and

100 "Les Bijoux" (20, see Appendix) "Léthé" (30), "À celle qui est trop gaie" (39), cited above, "Lesbos" (80), "Les femmes damnées" (81), and "Les Métamorphoses du Vampire" (87).

101 *LP II*, pp. 102–10 and Tables VI and VII. The judge paid no attention to Pinard's charges that several non-erotic poems treating biblical topics, such as "Les Litanies de Satan" (92), are also offensive to religious morals.

102 Marcelin Pleynet, *Lautréamont par lui-même*, p. 36.

crew surrender the shipwreck and swim in the rough waves battering the inaccessible rocky shore. Maldoror shoots one of them because he is too close to the shore and thus could survive the spectacular catastrophe. However, no further murderous intervention on Maldoror's part will be needed—a school of voracious sharks entertains the spectator by converting the swimmers into a "bloody omelette." Several sharks start fighting over the leftovers when, suddenly, a terrifying female shark puts an end to their gruesome tussle and dominates the bloody dining room. Filled with admiration, Maldoror recognizes in her a being like himself, dives into the waves and consummates his first true love with the slippery monster. Had Sade the chance to read this lurid burlesque, which topped even his own twisted fantasies, he might well have been proud, even jealous of his posthumous disciple."[103]

Pioneers of Relaxed Erotic Mimesis: from *Corydon* to *Lolita*

Following the return to the republican regime, transgressions such as Baudelaire's "Bijoux" or "A celle qui est trop gaie," would no longer be prosecuted. Baudelaire's trial deserves to be remembered as one of the milestones in the history of artistic taboos broken by art-oriented and/or commercial writers wishing to charge their erotic topics with higher excitive intensities than did previous generations of transgressors. The publishers' commercial motives and the readers' perennial hunger for fresh erotica indirectly spur the continuing revolt against censorship. By the end of the 19th and the beginning of the 20th centuries, social, political, moral or cultural movements, doctrines, and criticism gradually challenge and transform traditional views of the erotic as well as legal criteria. Catalysts for change include the suffragette movement; Bergson's Romantic emphasis on creative intuition; Freud's exploration of the subconscious, especially his *Treatise on Sexual Theory* (1905) and *Interpretation of Dreams* (1900); constitutionally guaranteed equality of the sexes; the recognition of sexology as a branch of medicine. However, the truly modern secular constitutional guarantee of freedom of speech was the main blow to millennial clerical interference and to the discretionary political powers of secular censors. Among the literary forerunners who emancipated their erotic discourse from traditional

103 See citation and comments in *LP I*, p. 152 and other comments on Lautréamont, *LP II*, p. 40–1 and ch. VII below, "Maldoror's nightmare wanderings."

restrictions are the secessionists Lautréamont and Rimbaud,[104] the naturalists, especially Zola and Maupassant, the Parnassian pagan A. France and the decadents Huysmans and Jarry.[105] Another milestone in the approach to erotic subjects is André Gide's apology of homosexuality as articulated in his *Corydon* (1924).

Fearless for its time, the essay took the form of a platonic dialog between an autobiographical intellectual, Corydon, and his former classmate, referred to as "témoin"/witness. Incited by the polemics of chronically proscribed homosexuality, the witness-narrator meets Corydon, who is ostracized for his erotic behavior. During their civilized discourse—resonant with many Socratic ironies—they try to determine if homosexuality is a less common, yet entirely natural, variation of human sexual make-up or a deliberate indulgence in biblically and socially banished turpitude.

A logical starting point for such a debate is a tenable definition or at least a detached elucidation of sexual instinct. How has it evolved in nature and what are its essentials in human terms? How have history and various civilizations dealt with it? In his opening remarks Corydon alludes to the conventional assumption that lust ("l'impulse vers le désir") is an integral correlate of a predetermined reproductive function. Citing Darwin (1809–82) and sociologists of his era such as Lester Ward (1841–1913) and others, Corydon contradicts this premise. Lust is not a biological device invariably subordinated to some preordained reproductive goal. While, traditionally, natural scientists have been "androcentrist" in maintaining that males rather than females represent each animal species, Darwinian and post-Darwinian research is "gynocentrist." It documents that the female not only typifies the race, "she is the race." In early evolutionary stages, the reproduction of certain primary animal species was largely hermaphroditic. In other instances, fertilizers were "cramponés"—clamped—onto female bodies 50 to 100 times larger than these miniature "male"organisms. Thus nature itself experimented and channelled a high degree of variability into male sexuality which evolved later than female sexual functions. This perhaps explains the imbalances between the two sexes: excess of spermatozoa available to impregnate a single egg, brevity of the sexual act and the

104 His elegy on the homosexual rape in "Le Coeur volé," *LP II*, pp. 50–5. Henri Clouard generally labels them as "symbolistes".

105 *LP II*, Appendix, Lautréamont, Zola, France, Jarry; see Huysmans' account of the satanist mass served on the naked body of a woman, *LP II*, ch. VIII, pp. 205–7.

continuation of male lust beyond the completion of reproductive functions. In the evolutionary process, some males respond biologically to these imbalances. (Genetic research in the nineties seems to corroborate these earlier theories.)

Passing from biology to history, Corydon emphasizes that various cultures and historical cycles manifested no hostility to "uranisme." Far from being decadent, homosexual periods often mark cultural and military culminations. For example, in Greece in the time of Pericles, in Rome under Augustus, during the Renaissance, or in Shakespearean England, homosexuality was openly, even offically accepted. *Code Napoléon* does not proscribe it either. Why? Banning it would have embarrassed Napoleon's best generals. Reading *Corydon* around 2000, when the treatment of homosexuality in the army was (reluctantly) "put on the table" in the U.S. Congress, North American readers can appreciate the audacity and the impact of André Gide's 1924 humanism. Needless to say, it also helped deregulate the restrictive censorship of erotica.

In the overpopulated global village, shaped by constantly evolving science and technology, previously isolated ethnic as well as erotic cultures are now intermingling and either clashing or harmonizing. Responding to the pressures of evolution, literary mimesis of contemporary sexual life no longer invokes the topical and stylistic restraint, the traditional *bon goût*, which used to leave more to the imagination than the direct semantics which characterizes erotic discourse today. A host of major and minor modern writers exploiting eroticism liberated both the subject matter and correlated semantics and rhetoric of the traditionally restrictive discipline. They include D.H. Lawrence (*Lady Chatterley's Lover*, 1928), George Bataille (*L'Histoire de l'oeil*, 1928), Céline (L.-F. Destouche, *Voyage au bout de la nuit*, 1932), Henry Miller (*Tropic of Cancer*, 1934), Anaïs Nin (*Diary*, 1934–38), Dominique Aury, pseud. Pauline Réage (*Histoire d'O*, 1954)[106] Lawrence Durell (*The Alexandria Quartet*, *Justine*, *Balthasar*, *Mountolive*, *Clea*, 1957), Vladimir Nabokov (*Lolita*, 1958) and, recently, especially John Updike (e.g., *Couples*, 1969; *A Month of Sundays*, 1974; *The Coup*, 1978; *Roger's Version*, 1986; *S.*, 1988; the Rabbit tetrology, 1960–1990; *Toward the End of Time*, 1997; *Bech at Bay*, 1998). Updike, for instance, without sacrificing high stylistic standards, mixes lexical subtlety and periphrases with semantic candor or clinical terminology in

106 John de St. Jorre, "The Unmasking of O," *The New Yorker*, Aug. 1994, pp. 42–50.

his erotic discourse. Contemporary writers often pepper direct references to intimate acts with contrastful juxtapositions of scientific, colloquial, slangy and vulgar vocabulary.[107] They probably see in the aging *bon goût* a child of the 17th century preciousness, a symptom of centuries-long topical as well as stylistic repression: their signifiers describing intimate love are returning to Malherbe's or de Viau's soft-porn vocabulary tolerated in erotic poetry before the birth of the salons indulging in overrefined euphemisms. They allude to sexual anatomy, its materiality, lubricity, its performance and to the correlated psychological vibrations of erotically motivated characters. Many, particularly interdisciplinary, scholars who now over-research innovative treatments of erotic topics, devote a great deal of their endeavor to erotic texts which, in the pre-Freudian era, may have been under-researched (e.g., Sade), as well as to the post-Freudian erotic genres (Bataille, Réage). While such research is legitimate, its sometimes laughable pedantic gravity often helps to erase the borderline between erotic literature and plain pornography. Among the authors covered in the earlier mentioned *Eroticism in French Literature,* Sade and George Bataille (1897–1962) were granted more attention than other masters known for their transpositions of sensual love. While the old generation of specialists in 20th century French literature such as Henri Clouard, Henri Peyre, or Pierre Brodin did not honor Bataille's poetry or prose with a single line in their general literary histories, literary theorists such as Roland Barthes and Michel Foucault "discovered" him and aroused academic interest not only in Bataille's cultural history and anthropological theories but also in Bataille's poetry and fiction.

Bataille's Psychotherapy: Art or Pornography?

The earlier mentioned *l'Histoire de l'oeil* is an unusual literary by-product of the young Bataille's psychoanalytical therapy supervised by Dr. Adrien Borel.[108] Although this 70-page *récit* is an epically coherent (not automatist) record of the author's sexual fantasies (not dreams), one can label it as a neosadist/surrealist genre in which recurrent metaphorical references to the white eyeball, egg, testicle and urine allude to would-be metaphysical mysteries while any sexual violence and

107 The above comparison of Voltaire's and Peyrefitte's treatment of a comparable lascivious subject or, for instance the vocabulary current in Updike's erotic passages illustrate the evolution of erotic diction.

108 *O.C. I*, ed. cit.

correlated orgasm aspire to be a grave rendezvous of love and death.

The 16-year-old narrator meets a girl of his age, Simone, and the two start discovering incongruous sensual thrills: "...nous restâmes longtemps sans nous accoupler. Nous profitions seulement de toutes les circonstances pour nous livrer à des actes inhabituels." In this stage of their adolescent intimacy Simone and her boyfriend meet on a lonely cliff. He lies down, she takes off his pants, sits herself naked on his stomach facing the boy's crotch. His finger penetrates her rectum ("cul") which his sperm ("foutre") had previously lubricated. Then she lies down and, places her face below his penis and flinging her pelvis ("cul") in the air, she asks the fantasizing narrator to piss ("faire pipi") as high as her hips ("cul"). Barely a few lines below this overture, the teenagers considerably improve their repertoire. It happens when the blond Marcelle comes close to their mating ground and collapses in tears near them. Simone interrupts their intimate pose, lifts Marcelle's skirt, rips off her panties and shows her lover another "cul" as charming as her own. A torrential rain sets the scene for a stormy erotic crescendo:

> Une frénésie brutale animait nos trois corps. Deux bouches juvéniles se disputaient mon cul, mes couilles et ma verge, mais je ne cessais pas d'écarter des jambes de femme humides de salives ou de foutre comme si j'avais voulu échapper à l'étreinte d'un monstre...De grands coups de tonnerre nous ébranlaient...chaque fois notre colère, nous arrachant des cris de rage redoublés à chaque éclair par la vue de nos parties sexuelles.

While masturbating Simone rolls in a muddy puddle: "...[E]lle se branlait avec la terre et jouissait violemment, fouettée par l'averse, ma tête serrée entre ses jambes souillées de terre, son visage vautré dans la flaque où elle agitait brutalement le cul de Marcelle..." Incessantly seeking unique cosmic highs, the three characters haunting Bataille's sick imagination are drowning in urine, sperm, vaginal secretion and blood: "...je n'aimais pas ce qu'on appelle les 'plaisirs de la chair'...ils sont...fades; je n'aimais que ce qui est classé comme 'sale.'"[109] Finally, Marcelle hangs herself in a Normandy armoire. Her corpse seduces Simone to perform some necrofiliac tricks and urinate on the cadaver's open eyes.[110] To avoid police inquiries the two maniacs leave for Spain

109 Ibid., pp. 15–17, 45.

110 Sontag (op. cit., p. 225) comments: "What Bataille exposes in extreme erotic experience is its subterranean connection with death." She approvingly suggests that Bataille, however, does not litter his text with corpses and that "only one person

where they meet an English aristocrat Sir Edmond. Bataille portrays him as a refined mentor who reveals new erotic horizons to his French disciples. One day at the beginning of their Spanish holidays, he shows them what a literal *cochonnerie* is: "…Sir Edmond fit jeter…dans une étable à porcs…une…belle-de-nuit de Madrid qui dut s'abattre en chemise-culotte dans une mare de sang et encore sous de ventres de truies qui grognaient. La porte une fois fermée, Simone se fit longuement baiser par moi, le cul dans la boue,…pendant que Sir Edmond se branlait", etc.

The picaresque pilgrimage dramatically ends in Don Juan's church in Seville where Simone asks an unknown priest, Don Amindo, to confess her. She tells him that she is masturbating and confessing at the same time. Receiving no reply Simone yells "Eh bien curé…qu'est-ce que tu fais dans la baraque? Est-ce que tu te branles aussi?" She accepts no silence for answer, penetrates in the confessional and orally rapes the "helpless" clergyman whose torments, needless to say, merely begin. The next blasphemy which the three church goers commit, evokes some of the Satanic rituals related in Huysmans *Là-bas* (1891): they force their victim to urinate in the sacramental chalice and drink from it. Sir Edmond then asks the priest, if he knows that the criminals condemned to hanging have an erection and ejaculate when the sling chokes them. To document this grisly bizarrerie Bataille's juvenile delinquent simultaneously strangles and rapes the cleric while her two male consorts hold him on the ground. Seated on the confessor's stomach "le cul près de sa verge flasque" Simone follows Sir Edmond's expert instructions:

> Maintenant…serre la gorge…en arrière de la pomme d'Adam… Simone serra…et la verge se leva. Je…l'introduisis dans la chaire de Simone. Elle continua de serrer la gorge [et]…fit aller et venir la queue raide dans sa vulve… [U]n…violent frisson fit trembler ce mourant: elle sentit le foutre inonder son cul. Elle lâcha prise…renversée dans un orage de joie.

Finally, Simone's ecstasy culminates with a necrophiliac miracle. Her morbid fascination with eggs, eyes, mud, urine, etc., makes her ask Sir Edmond to tear out one of the priest's eyeballs. At the same time she invites her lover to copulate with her on the stone floor and help her expose the dead man's orb to the play of their colliding navels. Having appeased this fleeting fancy she asks the obliging aristocrat to insert the

---

dies" in *L'Histoire de l'oeil*; this is not accurate—Sontag does not count Marcelle whose eye is resurrected in Bataille's morbid finale; see below.

eye into her rectum; but this pleasure does not last too long either. Interrupting her ongoing coitus she introduces the eyeball in her vagina as if making it see what it has never seen! Then she forces the narrator to continue their intercourse. He cannot comply because he prematurely ejaculates. As he looks closely at Simone's open genitals sprayed with his sperm he witnesses a miracle—Marcelle's blue eye weeping the tears of urine is gazing at him from Simone's womb.[111] Two hours following the successful murder and miracle the perverse trio leaves Seville in comical disguise and happily reaches Gibraltar where the Englishman buys a yatcht; with a crew of black sailors, they navigate who knows where. "Today [1970] we know it: Bataille is one of the most important writers of his century," Foucault proclaims in his preface to Bataille's first volume of the posthumous *Collected Works,* where *l'Histoire de l'oeil* appears for the first time under Bataille's name as the leading text.[112] Roland Barthes does not fully share Foucault's opinion. In his eyes, the saga on the poor Marcelle's and Don Amindo's eyes is not a "deep" work: "Tout y est donné en surface et sans hierarchie…circulaire et explicite, [cette oeuvre] ne renvoie à aucun secret."[113] Halley refuses Barthes' theoretical conclusions. He argues that (in *Sade, Fourier, Loyola*, discussed above), Barthes pays no attention to the work's epical informative substance.[114] The novel Halley says "verges on the pornographic [and]…demonstrates via its narrative voice"[115] Bataille's theory of eroticism. Although Halley's sociocritical overstatement verges on an esthetic understatement it nevertheless shows the weakness of Barthes' semiotic perspective. Confronted with Bataille's specific text Foucault's eulogy, of course, speaks for itself.

The allusion to Bataille's psychotherapy in the *récit* strikes me as an apology for its pornographic context: it seems to imply that the work's goal was therapeutic rather than pornographic or may be even "artistic" because it was prescribed by Bataille's psychiatrist and reflects the sick artist's authentic fantasy. Like the growing social support of sexual freedom, the slow penetration of Sade's and Bataille's pornographic

111 Bataille *O.C. I*, pp. 62, 66, 69.

112 Ibid., "Présentation," my transl. p. 5. The notes above refer to the original version.

113 Michael Halley "…And Truth for a Truth: Barthes on Bataille", *Eroticism in French Literature*, p. 117 citing Barthes' "La métaphore de l'oeil", *Essais critiques*, pp. 238–45.

114 [L']érotisme de Bataille est essentiellement *métonymique*", (sic, my italics)," Halley quotes Barthes, art. cit., p. 118.

115 Halley, p. 113.

genres into the *corpus* of "classics" constituting literary tradition indirectly extends creative freedom available to authors of erotic prose and poetry at the end of our neurotic century. Yet we must not overestimate the merit and impact of such a freedom "crusade." The limited tirage of Sade's and Bataille's works makes one speculate that they are sold to university libraries rather than to a broad community of liberal readers who seek maximum of freedom in every domain of their life but distinguish among erotic candor, scatology and "medical records."

Updike's Neopagan Christians and Jews

Among the well-known contemporary writers who successfully balance inventive representations of unrepressed Eros with broad esthetic and humanist goals is John Updike. Frequently, his ironic mimesis of love in all its fatality takes the form of a detached Voltairean satire, while still echoing the Virgilian topos "Love conquers everything and we give way to Love."[116]

His Rabbit tetralogy is not only a satirical panorama of mainstream U.S.A.; thanks to the roving eye of Updike's hero, it also becomes a vision of Eros American-style. Its originality is evident in various stimulative domains of style and content, including Updike's disclosure of "Uncle Sam's" notorious womanizing. As the teen-aged star of his high school basketball team, Harry Angstrom was nicknamed Rabbit (rhymes with Babbit). The tall young athlete becomes a line setter, marries the Toyota car-lot heiress, Janice Springer, and later works in her family business. Although the marriage breaks down because of Janice's alcoholism and infidelity, the separated Angstroms are eventually reconciled. Their American dream is fulfilled when Janice inherits the Toyota dealership. The affluent pair typify the relaxed, permissive generation which practises free love and experiments with friendly partner-swapping as a novel party game. As parents of their only son Nelson, the couple is a total failure.

In the last volume—the Pulitzer Prize-winning *Rabbit at Rest*[117]—Updike portrays Rabbit as a retiree who suffers a heart attack in Florida and has to return to his native Brewer in Pennsylvania. Before undergoing angioplast surgery to unplug the compulsive nibbler's

116 "Omnia vincit Amor et nos cedamus Amori." *Ecl.* X, 69. See Appendix, A. France.
117 [117](New York: Fawcett Crest, 1990)

arteries, Rabbit promises his granddaughter Judy that he will play Uncle Sam in her school's Fourth of July parade. The satire of this patriotic ritual thus mythifies the chocolate-loving cardiac as a (still) living incarnation of the immortal Uncle Sam.[118] During his retirement, marred by his son's drug addiction, thefts, related blackmail and loss of the dealership, Rabbit relives his past. One day, trying to entertain Judy at his Florida condominium, he proposes sunfishing and Judy's question triggers a microstimulative reminiscence:

"'What's sunfishing?' 'It's sailing in a little boat...' 'Have you ever done it, Grandpa? Sunfishing?' 'Sure. A coupla times.' 'Once, actually;...[w]ith Cindy Murkett in her black bikini that showed the hairs in her crotch...the two of them alone and nearly naked.'" Unaware of her grandpa's flashback the girl goes on chatting: "Sounds neat,...I got a prize in my camp swimming class for staying underwater the longest."[119]

Returning to Brewer after his heart attack, the dieting Rabbit visits his frail, failing mistress Thelma. She offers him dry roasted cashews, remembering that they used to be his favorite snack. They are now on the list of forbidden tidbits but he cannot resist the lure. Like Emile's *madelaine*, the nuts and the old furniture unleash Rabbit's melancholy reverie: "[D]ry roasted [cashews] have...the tang of poison that he likes." The plush sofa and Thelma now "her knees together" remind Uncle Sam of many interludes in between stressful car sales.

> They have made love on that sofa, which was not long enough to stretch out on but long enough if both parties kept their knees bent. In a way he preferred it to one of the beds, since she seemed to feel guiltier...in a bed her family used... Moving the table, he could kneel beside the sofa and have the perfect angle for kissing her cunt... He loved it when she would clamp his face between...her

118 Earlier in *Rabbit Redux* (New York: Fawcett Crest, 1971), p. 311, Updike's hero allegorizes himself in a different context" "...I was a fucking good samaritan, I took in these orphans. Black and white...regardless of color or creed, Hop aboard. Free eats. I was a fucking Statue of Liberty.

119 *Rabbit at Rest*, p. 44, 107–10. Judy's aquatic skills will later be dramatically tested during the planned "sun-fishing" cruise; the "Sailfish" will capsize, Judy will get caught under the immersed sail and her grandpa will barely survive the heart attack triggered by the mishap. Twelve years later, as a college student, Judy will recall her late grandfather as having saved her life—"he was a doll." However, Nelson—Rabbit's son and Judy's father—has a different memory: he comments that his dad "nearly killed" Judy. See *Licks of Love*, "Rabbit Remembered" (New York: A.A. Knopf, 2000), p. 339. This substantial postscript to the Rabbit tetralogy, completed in 1990, shows the intensity of the creative bond between the author and his colorful characters.

> damp thighs like a nut in a nutcracker and come. He wondered if a man ever got his neck broken that way.[120]

Preparing Rabbit for angioplasty in the nearby Deleon hospital the nurse taking his blood pressure casually asks her patient, "How's the Toyota business?" "Not bad. The weak dollar doesn't help. My son runs the place now, basically," the jolly cardiac volunteers, wondering how the nurse knew he used to sell Toyotas. "My boyfriend then and I bought a car from you. Don't you remember?" Suddenly, glancing at the nurse's hospital badge, Rabbit does remember. (The sophisticated Proustian narrator had never excavated such a remembrance from the whirlpool of his memories): "'It's *you*! Yes…' She is his daughter; or at least he imagines she is, though Ruth [another of Rabbit's old mistresses] out of spite would never admit it to him… [H]e reads her badge: ANNABELLE BYER, R.N. She still has her maiden name." The unexpected reunion of the real but unofficial father and daughter affects the blood pressure reading. Rejecting it with professional poise Annabelle suggests: "Let's try that again in a minute. It shot up while we were talking."[121]

Rabbit's precarious heart cools but this does not quite kill his sexual hunger. Following his release from hospital care he spends a night in the old Springer house inhabited now by his son Nelson, daughter-in-law Prudence (Pru) and their family; this sleep-over is arranged by Rabbit's wife Janice, who does not want to leave her convalescent husband alone at their home while she drives to Philadelphia to visit the institutionalized coke addict Nelson.

As hostess Pru laments about her matrimonial tensions, Rabbit tries to offer her a few words of consolation. Quasi spontaneously, the initially verbal intercourse becomes intimate. A few days later on the Toyota car lot, where he subs for his son, the retired boss, the pro-choice saleswoman Elvira and a Catholic salesman Benny discuss an illegal demonstration in front of an abortion clinic currently reported in the press. In their debate *à bâton rompu* they also address birth control (which, according to Rabbit, seventy percent of young married Catholics use) and non-mortal sins (which Catholics do not have to confess, if they do not wish, as Benny claims) and on too detailed confession (which could embarrass the confessor obliged to listen to lengthy trivia, as Elvira speculates). These issues provoke another flashback as the convalescent grandfather remembers that, while he was recovering in the young

120 Ibid., p. 163.
121 Ibid., p. 228. Annabelle becomes a primary character in "Rabbit Remembered".

Angstroms' house, his daughter-in-law pulled a condom from her pocket: "Either she always kept one there or had foreseen fucking him before coming into the room. He wasn't used to them, not since the Army, but went along with it...it was her show." In spite of its prophylactic prudence, Pru's "show" enables Rabbit to achieve a new entirely individual sex record:

> The thing had been a squeeze,...and his pubic hair,...left after the angioplasty,..., got caught...in the unrolling[;]...it maybe had made him slower to come, not a bad thing, as she came twice, under him once and then astraddle...her tits atwitter as he jiggled in pursuit of the second orgasm, he near to fainting with worry over joggling his defective heart... [T]o keep his prick up he kept telling himself, *This is the first time I've fucked a left-handed woman.*[122]

To protect her son against prosecution for the theft of the Toyota trade-in cars, Janice is ready to sell her and Rabbit's residence and share her old paternal house with the young couple and the grandchildren. Pru flatly rejects her proposal, tells her about her adultery with her father-in-law and argues that the in-laws' invasion would create an intolerable climate in Nelson's and her family nest. Wasting no time the hardnosed mother-in-law phones Harry, blaming him for the "kind of perverted thing that makes the newspapers. It was *monstrous*." But Harry flatly rejects Janice's puritan charge. There was nothing out of the ordinary in his rapprochement with his daughter-in-law. "What's this 'perverted'? We weren't at all blood-related. It was just like a normal one-night stand. She was hard-up and I was at death's door. It was her way of playing nurse...."[123]

Rabbit's Eros-driven clan has nothing in common with Sade's or Bataille's cast of deviant puppets. It rather relates the everyday life of an American family guided by its raw instincts, populist logic and vital materialistic drives. In his characters' repartee and flashbacks, Updike often strikes shocking verbal sparks but puts them out as fast as he strikes them, giving his readers neither time nor reason to confuse Rabbit's erotic nostalgia with the perverse neuroses characteristic of pornography. Like Babbit, the middle-aged Rabbit comes to typify the American male businessman who assumes that his inalienable rights include not only material success but also the right to pursue whatever erotic chances come his way. With his 1991 vintage, Don Juanesque

122 Ibid., p. 294. (Updike's ital.)
123 Ibid., p. 360–61.

Uncle Sam, Updike has created a fresh, living archetype which enriches the mythology of American pragmatism—economic, political, erotic. It is a fine example of high esthetic intensity.

(An intertextual postscript demonstrating a potential intensity range: no critic can read Updike's treatment of the love and death theme in *Rabbit at Rest* without seeing in it a unique burlesque counterpoint to the *Buddenbrooks*' refined decline—*Verfall einer Familie*; to the discreet Proustian evocations of Swann's and Uncle Alfred's overlapping commerce with the mondaine "*cocotte de luxe*", Odette de Crecy; or even an ultimate counterpoint to Lamartine's "Le Lac" or Hugo's "La Tristesse d'Olympio," Romantic poems about aging lovers returning to the sites of their passionate rendezvous. The memory of the once transcendent love will forever vibrate in their melancholy hearts.

Among the works rich in timely and effective erotic subject matter, *Couples*[124] seems to contain the highest concentration of interlocking sexual conflicts, neuroses, fast degenerating marriages, spouse-trading, contemplated divorce or abortion. The novel takes the form of a panoramic multiscreen revealing the fateful power of destructive sexual drive in suburban Tarbox, a quiet community in New England.

Ten married couples of various ethnic and social backgrounds socialize at private parties, tennis courts, ski lodges and beaches. Although some of them are church goers and see one another in or in front of their churches[125] their sexual life reflects obedience to instincts rather than to the seventh Commandment. Some of them consult their psychoanalysts—prior to rejecting the holiness of matrimony.

The wealthy patrician Angela Hanema, *née* Hamilton (who does not believe in anything), discusses her erotic status with her churchgoing husband Piet, a struggling contractor of modest Dutch descent. One night, she substitutes, for the matrimonial intercourse which Piet had in mind, a folksy discourse on the symptoms of neurosis and interactions of *id*, *ego* and parental *superego*. She tells him that, like her friend, Janet Appleby (one of Piet's mistresses), she plans to consult a psychoanalyst. Piet's reply is quite resolute: "The hell you will. Not as long as you're my wife."[126] Angela, not intimidated, claims that the psychiatrist might elucidate her lack of interest in conjugal sex. She confesses to Piet that

124 (New York: Fawcett Crest, © 1968), sixth printing, 1988.

125 One heroine is Episcopalian, one couple is Catholic, one Jewish and one lapsed Catholic.

126 Ibid., p. 219.

she has lost her interest in life and "would love not to wake up." And, although she legitimately suspects that Piet is having an affair with her friend Janet Appleby, she does not resent it, she welcomes it. "In a way, I want you to [sleep with Janet]. In a Lesbian way. I felt very drawn, lying beside her on the beach. I think I must be Sapphic. I'd love to have a girls' school, where we'd all wear chitons and play field hockey and sit around listening to poetry after warm baths." Angela further confesses that she is reluctant to cohabit with her husband because she prefers to masturbate. "Sweetie. When?" Piet inquires. "I wake up some mornings between four and five, when the birds are just beginning...and I do it to myself." To her husband "[t]hat sounds pretty normal."[127]

Piet has other mistresses than Janet Appleby, including Georgene Thorne, wife of the Hanemas' friendly dentist Fred who "writes an endless pornographic novel on his knee." The most fateful among his affairs is his adultery with Elizabeth (Foxy) Whitman, pregnant wife of a chemistry professor. They consummate their romance during the late stage of Elizabeth's pregnancy. Both practicing Christians, (he a convert from Dutch Reform to the Congregational Church, she a believing Episcopalian), they divorce their atheistic partners and later marry.

Just as the July 4th parade in *Rabbit at Rest* mythifies Harry Angstrom as Uncle Sam, so the lightning setting aflame the Tarbox house of God "improvises" a neomythical revelation which the worshippers cannot miss. This time Updike achieves high poetic intensity by eroticizing a traditional but ambiguous Christian symbol—the gilded weathercock standing above the spire (undoubtedly, to chase the demons away.)[128] The bird's eye was an old English copper and the Tarbox children fancied that the rooster above their shrine "was God".[129]

> The Congregational Church was burning. God's own lightning had struck it... and the crowds of people...watched in chilled silence. Smoke,...was pouring from under the cornice...and from the lower edge of the *cupola* that *lifted* the *gilded weathercock* one hundred and twenty-five feet into the air. Down among the *Doric columns* firemen were *chasing away the men*...who...already *rescued*...the brass *cross*,..."

Among the spectators watching this act of God, Piet Hanema notices his

127 Ibid.

128 "A cock crew lustily at the Resurrection. Hence [it] is placed upon the steeple of churches." M. Summers, *The History of Witchcraft and Demonology*, New York University Books, © 1956, pp. 117–8.

129 *Couples*, p. 21.

dentist and abortion consultant Fred Thorne, who brought a beer, his own ex-wife Angela and his two daughters, the first born Ruth, loyal member of the choir, and the preschooler Nancy; tears in her eyes, the little one is heartbroken because "the man Jesus would destroy His church, where she had always wiped her feet, timid of the holy, and had dutifully,...sung His praise, to please her father..." But when her mother concludes that "the best part is over," and that it is time to go home, the child protests; and pointing her finger at the ornament standing tall above the flames she sums up her deep concern in the laconic degradation: "The chicken!" With a deadpan irony, the author rectifies the innocent ambiguity: "The *rooster*, bright as if above not only the smoke but the rain, was *poised motionless atop* a narrow pyre. Flames...had *licked up* the *pinnacle* to the *ball* of *ironwork*...it seemed it all must topple; then a *single jet*,...hurled itself *higher* and the flames abruptly vanished. Though the impact made the *spindly pinnacle waver*, *it held*."

Turning his eyes away from the "chicken" which the cosmic arsonist preserved for posterity as an indestructible memento of his immortal vigor, the pious sinner Piet Hanema watches the lesbian Angela walk away "turn once...and walk on, leading their virgin girls."[130] Before leaving the dramatic show the ex-Lutheran ex-husband runs into Carol Constantine, a Presbyterian grass widow, who is also showing her two children the destroyed Tarbox landmark. Having pity for Piet, who lost his wife and his church, the Samaritan mother invites him for tea, then an improvised dinner and finally for an interdenominational sleep-over. The reader is left to muse: "Eine feste Burg ist unser Gott."[131]

The microstimulative within the macrostimulative gradation shows how Updike primes the reader's imagination. His references to "God's own lightning" and to "man Jesus[132] [who] would destroy..." perhaps misleadingly blame Jehovah or, in Nancy's innocent eyes, Jesus for the arson which, as hasty reading may lead us to imagine, is divine punishment for the carnal sins indulged in by no longer very virtuous Christian soldiers. At first sight, this seems to be the most obvious reading of the climactic passage. On the other hand Updike's ironic metamorphoses of the "cocky" devil fighter, first into a cowardly

130 Ibid., p. 465, my italics indicate the density and gradation of poetic (ironic) ambiguities.

131 M. Luther: a mighty fortress is our God.

132 "Man Jesus" is a rhetoric feature adding color to Rev. Horace Pedrick's pulpit populism.

"chicken" and then into an unmistakably phallic symbol invites speculation. Could Updike's thundergod be the "sovereign disdain"[133] or rather the immortal force which our ancestors christened Zeus Keranios? Who else would stage this revelation, the crowning image of this Priapic tool standing erect above the ruins to show mortals the prime imperative of their resurrection? In any case, the penial bird above the glandlike cupola is—besides the temple's Doric columns—the only distinct survivor of the Updikean conflagration.

Teasingly, and in tune with artistic tradition frowning at too politically or religiously motivated humanism, Updike provokes but does not subsequently manipulate our imagination. Each individual reader is free to contemplate whether Updike's fictional arsonist is Jehovah, Eros and Priapos playing with matches, Spinoza's Godhead defined as the pantheistic *natura naturans* or the Demon whom the intimidated "chicken" failed to chase away; or possibly (and why not?) all of them.

Like Albert Camus in *The Plague*, Updike portrays a fictitious priest reacting to the catastrophe. But unlike the French Jesuit Father Paneloux, who sees the Oran plague as a legitimate retribution imposed by God upon the sinful Christian flock including innocent children, the pragmatic Tarbox pastor, Rev. Horace Pedrick, accuses no one. He merely asks the opprobrious Piet Hanema, "How much in dollars and cents...will [it] take to replace this tragic structure?"[134]

The gallery of Updike's macrostimulative inamorati is not limited to the *nouveau riche* Uncle Sam/Rabbit or to Piet Hanema, expeditious contractor of both external and internal family-home renovations in Tarbox. Year after year, new acquisitions enrich the gallery. They include unorthodox theologians, agnostic scholars, a livresque Vedantic imposter and exotic lovers.[135]

133 "...dédain souverain" to which P. Valéry alludes in "Le Cimetière marin".

134 *Couples*, p. 465. Later, when the burned building is demolished, the crane operator adroitly saves the weathercock and, in front of the Herald photographer, places it in the clergyman's custody, undoubtedly, to be reinstalled as soon as the reconstruction fund permits.

135 Such as the intimate consultant of frustrated women, Rev. Thomas Marshfield (*A Month of Sundays*, 1974); professor of religious studies Roger Lambert and his graduate "protégé" Dale Kohler who plans to prove God's existence by computer (*Roger's Version*, 1986); the half Armenian "Hindu" guru of Waterton Mass., Art Steinmetz, alias Shri Arhat Mindadali, M.A., Ph.D., Head of Ashram Arhat (*S.*, 1988); the Islamic polygamist Colonel Ellellou married among others, to an

The 1998 addendum is a caricature of a 74-year-old New Yorker, Henry Bech. Against the expectations of the entire intellectual establishment, this newlywed Jewish writer is awarded the Nobel Prize for literature. He and his 26-year-old "post-Jewish wife," Rachel "Robin" Teagarten, are preparing for a trip to Stockolm where the laureate will receive the medal and deliver his lecture. When Henry agonizes endlessly over the lecture topic, Robin offers a simple solution: "Henry, an old Spielmeister like you? Tell them what you told Oprah...." The irascible prize-winner growls that he can never remember what he says on "these damn talk shows," but Robin refreshes his memory: Henry apparently told Oprah that he "did not write pornography," that he "just tried to give the sexual component of our life a fair shake." This line, Henry knows, would sound ridiculous in Stockholm: "The Swedes don't care if I write pornography. It's all legal there. *It's part of their healthy pagan outlook.*"[136]

Besides Rabbit's once separated then reconciled wife, Janice Springer-Angstrom, and Col. Ellellou's mini harem, the women in Updike's prose include Sarah Worth, major in Cartesian and existentialist thought and tenacious epistulographer,[137] the promiscuous Verna Ekelof[138] and the upperclass Brazilian Isolde/Isabelle who, with the help of an Indian shaman, ultimately becomes black, while her black husband Tristão becomes white.

What makes Updike's eroticism so convincing and timely is the illusion of minimal distance between life and its artistic vision. His countless original protagonists confront the same happenings which average Americans see on TV, read in the papers, hear on their car radio, discuss with their spouses and lovers, golf partners, brokers, barbers, and react to wisely, naively, cynically and in accordance with their shrewdness, ignorance, gullibility and political or religious biases. Once

---

American college girl (*The Coup*, 1978) or the black Rio de Janeireo street boy Tristão (*Brazil*, 1994).

136 *Bech at Bay*, (New York: A.A. Knopf, 1998), pp. 228, my italics.

137 The heroine of *S.* divorces her doctor-husband and in Ashram Arhat, is baptized as Kundalini "coiled up," i.e., "the serpent of female energy dormant at the base of spinal column." ("Kunda" in, e.g., Czech means "cunt"). She does not discover Ramakrishna, Sidhartah, *Om* or *purusha* (external cosmic spirituality) but, keeping her eyes open, the former Cartesian solves other thrilling, though not metaphysical, mysteries.

138 A single white mother of a black child, a mistress of the mentioned computer expert Kohler as well as of her Uncle, Prof. Lambert.

framed in macrostimulative satirical plots, such banal but fresh erotica suddenly reveal yet understate their tragic side. Only the author's light-hearted tone and his poetic ambiguities intimate his tolerance, disdain, ethos. His characters need no omniscient judge; their stimulative actions always speak for themselves.

I discuss the erotic frankness of *Rabbit at Rest* and of *Couples* for two main reasons: (1) because both novels transpose credibly and *con brio* the erotic mores of our post-Freudian era and (2) because, like the preceding milestones of erotic fiction, they too extend the artistic drive for free mimesis of erotic subjects. Had Updike written his novels one century earlier he would have probably faced graver criminal charges than Flaubert and Baudelaire did in 1857. Had Maître Pinard[139] had to prosecute *Rabbit at Rest* or *Couples*, the passages cited above would have been easy targets. Fines and deletions would have been imposed because then the threat to legendary "family values" would have appeared much more acute than it still may appear now to contemporary puritans. Yet even during the few remaining years of the 20th century, while our society unreservedly invokes freedom of speech and condemns censorship, its vocal religious and political lobbies still unofficially advocate manipulation and proscription of overt erotic information in literature or in the media. In this respect, Updike represents the first generation of liberal humanists truly free to publish, without excessive legal risk, their transpositions of "deregulated" erotic mores. The high stimulative potential of his erotic subjects (which advocates of censorship may still find too "offensive" or "sinful") is a distinct esthetic quality of Updike's agnostic art. Critics, who like to label the distinctive innovations of contemporary trends with a new "-ism," could christen it neopagan naturalism. Why "christened" and why "neopagan"? Certainly not only because in a symbolic fulmination the Tarbox rooster stood firm, like a fireproof relic of the pre-Christian cult suddenly emerging from the ashes of a Protestant church. The main reason is that in the world which Updike portrays, traditional Christian antisexualism has no place. He finds in hedonistic sex—sex not associated with penal offenses or pathological perversion—no other sins or guilts than, for example, those we find in Ovid, the eternally proscribed *Decameron* or La Fontaine's tales. Teleologically, his erotic mimesis follows the tradition of Epicurus, Lucretius Carus, Ovid, Petronius, Boccaccio and modern agnostics ranging from Anatole France to Nabokov. The candor of his

139 See the above discussion on judicial expurgation of the *Fleurs du mal*.

diction echoes the lexical shocks of Rabelais, the libertines, Zola or George Bataille rather than the classical *bon goût* and its ambiguous euphemisms still favored (in spite of Zola) during the *belle époque* and its *encore* during the days of Thomas Mann, John Galsworthy or André Gide.

Updike's original contributions to forever sensitive erotic content and language are his rare specifics of transposed love life and often raw or slangy semantics. What in our days heightens the impact of his treatment is the fact that his stylistic shocks[140] never compromise either Updike's artistry or his cheerfully pessimistic humanism. Rarely euphemizing erotic actions, Updike's discourse becomes a vague American analogy of the *langue verte* pervading Zola's work. Inventing his very own brand of 20th century naturalism, Updike makes his characters, through their flashbacks or contemplative interior monologues, spontaneous co-narrators of a Yankee *Satiricon*. The naked materiality of their fictitious intimate and spiritual life is free of any divine or diabolic *je ne sais quoi*. His latent moralistic hints make us see human flesh as is, where is.

Erotic Mores and their Mimesis Deregulated

Our erotic culture, its parallel stimulative mimesis and the readers' attitudes and responses required two millenia to complete an impressive cycle. To demarcate that cycle I have drawn from texts which intensely reflect the protracted struggle between the well-wishers of pagan erotic *laisser-faire* and Christian regulators of erotic mores and their literary transpositions. Ovid's *Art of Loving* exemplifies pre-Christian hedonism; *The Golden Legend* extols sexual asceticism. Right from the early moments of ecclesiastic intrusion in this domain, many Western writers, along with their readers, manifested a constantly growing nostalgia for erotic spontaneity springing from natural instincts uninhibited in Pagan culture. Nowadays, modern secular regimes which have emancipated their laws from too rigorous religious influence protect the writer's freedom of expression, including representations of erotica, against dogmatically motivated prohibitions. Once the outdated alliances between the monolithic secular and religious establishments vanish, the dialectical stalemate between the two incompatible erotic legacies may

140 E.g., microstimulative direct references to genitals, intercourse, bodily secretions, mucuses which not too long ago had been quarantined in pornography.

also disappear. In contemporary Occidental culture, where free thought, free speech and free pursuit of happiness— encompassing licit erotic bliss both in life and in art—are now well entrenched, our erotic everyday life and its esthetic mimesis have returned to ancient Eros. Love is released from the constraints of Christian virtue and sin. Both artists and critics must certainly ask whether, as a result of this major attitudinal change, the "sin-free" erotic material will not become less effective than the representations of "sinful" erotica. It is possible. But, at least for this generation of readers, the innovative demythification of stimulative erotic topics may offer esthetic compensations for banishing the Devil from the Kingdom of Eros.

*   *   *

V

HUMOR AND THE POWER OF LAUGHTER

"Asbestos d'ar' enorto gelos makaressi theoisi..."[1]

Greek Gods' Homeric Laughter. Jehovah's Sour Disposition. Zoological Fun. Scholars Ponder Theoretical Causes of Laughter. "Ridiculum" in Life and the "Comic" in Art. Esthetic Distance: a Debatable Theorem. *Intensity* Counts More than *Cause*. The Micro- and Macrocomic Quanta. Teleology of Humor. Comic Content: Farce. Verbal Humor: Irony. Our Remembrance of Comic Impact. Farcical Non-Literary Anecdote. Doderer's Projection of Growing Comic Intensity: The *Pointe*. Literary Anecdote and its Comic Frame in *The Grapes of Wrath*. Farcical Characters and Plots: Brautigan's Bootlegger, Marquez' Mystery. Scarron's Dated Humor. Comical Gradations in *Dead Souls*. Black Humor: Baudelaire's Farcical Satire of Equity à la Proudhon. Prévert's Surrealistic Formula for Regicide. Updike's Gallows Humor. Grave Irony in Wilde's and Mérimée's Prose. Mérimées's "Tamango". Sublime Irony in Maupassant's Short Stories. Ronsard's Melancholy Smile. Madame Nozière's Ironic Aphorism. Humor Down Under, Stale and Fresh. Earthy Humor Goes On—and On.

Greek Gods' Homeric Laughter

The *Illiad* and *Odyssey* suggest that laughter is a fit of cosmic mirth. Those raucous howls of the Olympians, described in both epics, are traditionally called Homeric laughter. One such outburst is provoked by Hera's conjugal quarrel with the philandering Zeus and the diplomatic plea for wise feminine tolerance from their son Hephaistos, all too

1 *Illiad* I, 599. "Then unquenchable laughter rose up among the blessed gods..."

familiar with his father's brutal whims.[2]

However, Hephaistos' conciliatory disposition vanishes when he ingeniously traps his wife Aphrodite *in flagranti* with Ares, god of war, and calls on other gods to witness the adultery and his imminent retaliation. This time, Hermes diffuses the gloomy expectations of the gathered Olympians into laughter; he tells them that he would not mind being in Ares' place no matter how uncomfortable Hephaistos' invisible trap might be: "Let there be three times the number of shackles and you gods looking… I still would lie by the side of Golden Aphrodite."[3] The founder of our literary tradition not only made his illiterate listeners and posterity laugh, he helped to develop our sense of humor. He illustrated that our preordained desire to laugh is both divine and human, he taught us that a joke, at the right moment, can calm passions and prevent violence.

Jehovah's Sour Disposition

Jehovah, on the other hand, is a grave patron. The Bible does not ever portray him laughing merrily. He only laughs "in derision" prior to punishing those who dare to worship other gods. The *Psalms* (ch. 2) encourage the faithful "to serve the LORD with fear, and rejoice with trembling." It seems, however, that humanity at large is not intimidated by the biblical ordinance. If farce or witty banter makes us laugh, we do not muffle our merriment because an invisible Lord might resent our fun. Without thinking too much about the Psalmist, like Homer's Olympians we prefer hilarity to metaphysical anxiety and trepidation.

The Cartesian concept of human dignity, springing from our ability to think, is a cornerstone of secular Western humanism. Our deliberate or spontaneous pleasure in recognizing comical incongruity—our sense of humor—cannot be anything else than an offshoot of our global intelligence. This may have occurred to Joseph Addison, who pondered three centuries ago the biological significance of laughter. "If we may believe our logicians, man is distinguished from all other creatures by the faculty of laughter."[4] My empirical experiences lead me to deem this

2 Ibid. Hephaistos reminds Hera of his conflict with father Zeus who once knocked him down from Olympus and crippled him.

3 *Odyssey* 8, ll. 364, q.s.

4 Joseph Addison (1672–1719), *The Spectator*, No. 494. Stanley Coren's *Intelligence of Dogs* rates canine intelligence on a par with with that of an 18-month to 3-year-old human.

aptitude even more universal. An elementary sense of humor may not be an exclusively human prerogative. Animals often seem to react to laughable or amusing events with the same atavistic, cerebral energy which activates basic human response. With my own eyes, I have seen animals playing, "laughing" and "rejoicing" (without trembling) over the fun which life offered them.

Zoological Fun

Once I spent a year in a ranger's house. He had two Dachshunds, a dairy cow and a pig. From time to time his wife released the Mashut, as they called it, from its dark pig sty into the fresh air of the fenced yard. As soon as the two dogs saw the pig in the yard, mother Medina and her daughter Diana started teasing it; they chased it around, barking whenever it charged against them. Their body language, eyes, noses, reverted ears, wagging tails all signalled cheer and amusement. Everybody knew that the dogs were laughing.[5] Their attack was a sham. Recently, I watched a German pointer who noticed a beaver swimming in the stream in front of our home. The dog instinctively rushed into the water to retrieve the rodent. Seeing another animal, the beaver intrepidly swam toward it and, when their noses were only about four feet apart, it dived with an impressive splash of its flat tail right in front of the dog's nose. He remained under water for just a few seconds and re-emerged in front of the beguiled but tenacious dog who, once more, tried to fetch the mocking challenger. The beaver repeated the same trick about half a dozen times. Clearly, this dupery made the comedian laugh right along with the audience on the shore. Andy Russell, a well-known Alberta wildlife photographer and author, describes the winter game of a herd of mountain sheep who had created a slide with their rumps, on a steep snow slope dropping down to a frozen lake in British Columbia. Like happy children, these seemingly stolid beasts kept running back up the hill to slide down again and again. Their gaiety did not spring from teasing but from pure, non-functional play.

Scholars Ponder Theoretical Causes of Laughter

When Bergson wrote his essay on *Laughter*,[6] communications as an

5 I fictionalized the scene in my novel *Bez konce jsou lesy* (*Endless Are the Forests*; Prague: V. Petr, 1943), pp. 79–80.

6 *Le Rire—Essai sur la signification du comique*, 1899.

academic discipline did not exist and the metaphoric cliché, "body language" (which I used above with a touch of irony), did not figure in scholarly jargon. He generally interpreted the characteristic sounds and facial contractions which signal human mirth or amusement as a social gesture whose function complies with or defies one's social milieu. What makes us laugh is some excess of automatism conveyed by words or gestures which deviate from conventions. A general (abstract) cause is an incongruity created by a sudden transition from one subject to another entirely opposite. Bergson breaks down the laugh-provoking incongruities into five categories: the comic of (1) forms, (2) movements, (3) situations, (4) words and (5) comic characters. Most scholars theorizing on humor before and after him see it as a characteristic kind of surprise. Earlier, in a different context, I have cited the Aristotelian "deceived expectation", to which Maggi added "surprise" and "suddenness"; Hobbes' "sudden glory"; A. Zeisig's "theory of double shock"; Kant's sudden transformation of a strained expectation into nothing; Shopenhauer's "paradox" and "disappointment"; Martin's element of "unexpectedness" as well as "contrast"; Jean Paul's "sharply bursting out"; Pirandello's "awareness of contraries" and a "contrast between the ideal and the real"; Spencer's "overflow"; Lipp's "descending incongruity"; Bains' "delivrance"; Levaillant's "contraire par le contraire" and "art de l'impropriété volontaire, du trop ou du trop peu", or Freud's "release." All imply a sudden shift from one contrasting element to another and the surprise linked with it. Although their theories do not even allude to the quantum of energy released by the comic cause, they agree that we laugh due to our perceptions of a "painless" incongruity. Some writers also point out that we laugh instinctively and that laughter is a frequent symptom of human happiness.[7]

"Ridiculum" in Life and the "Comic" in Art

Considering a theoretical delimitation of "the refractory ridiculous (*ridiculum*) [and] the purified power of the comic transposition (the comic pertaining to comedy)," H.R. Jauss sums up a number of major scholarly attempts to elucidate this dichotomy. He cites Emile Souriau[8] who "assigns the ridiculous to the world of everyday life, the comic to

7 See *LP I*, ch. VII, p. 146 and n. 13 listing the sources of the above citations.

8 *Aesthetic Experience and Literary Hermeneutics* (Minneapolis: U. of Minnesota Press, 1982), pp. 123–34, quotes Souriau's "Le risible et le comique," *Journal de psychologie normale et pathologique* 41, 1948.

art." Souriau claims that the transposition of the ridiculous due to the related "cathartic process" and "long ascesis" converts the often vulgar signifiers into an esthetically refined product. His arbitrary distinction between the "ridiculous" (life) and the "comic" (art) does not strike me as very convincing. If my barber tells me a racy joke while cutting my hair, I may take it as a free non-literary bonus to the haircut, yet may laugh as much as if reading an equally bawdy tale in *Les Cent Nouvelles nouvelles*. Souriau's demarcation between the "ridiculous"/life and the "comic"/art seems more semantic and speculative than scientifically or empirically substantiated. Further, it doesn't account for newspaper articles whose texts report life without creating art. I recently read a story in a Czech newspaper paraphrasing a German news report on what life offered Gisella and her husband Fred at Rheine, a Westphalian village. He, 60, she, 59, decided to reenact a scene they saw in *Stimulating Lust*, a porno film. Gisella was bound fast to the bed whereupon Fred planned to quench their passion by leaping down on her from the top of a six foot high armoire. Unfortunately, before lift-off, he fell to the floor, breaking his leg and both arms. Meanwhile Gisella, primed for X-rated ecstasy, was too firmly tied up to rescue her suffering sexagenarian. It took neighbors hearing their screams two hours to break into Gisella's and Fred's boudoir of stimulating lust. If this event really happened and was briefly reported (transposed) as an entertaining (subliterary) German news item, we have to recognize that *comicum* also exists in a variety of communications beyond the confines of art. (Besides, journalistic reporting of such news items does not substantially differ from traditional artistic treatments which the formalists baptized *ostraneni*-/making strange and *Literaturnost*/literariness. In addition, if this event did not take place, which is very probable, it is neither news nor a very cathartic mimesis parading as news.)[9] The following examples further illustrate that inadvertent *comicum,* for instance, in grave scholarly didactic discourse, does not particularly differ from *ridiculum*: David Dutton, who lectures philosophy of art at Canterbury University in New Zealand, looks for pearls of humor in esoteric, not too widely read scholarly prose. With the collaboration of several peers, he grants unsolicited annual international awards for comical academic acumen. The 1997 top award went to the first sentence of *Signatures of the Visible*

9 Canadian newspapers reported this "news" two years later. Re "literariness," see Terrence Hawkes, *Structuralism and Semiotics* (London: Methuen, 1977), pp. 62–63.

by Frederic Jameson: "The visual is essentially pornographic, which is to say that it has its end in rapt, mindless fascination; thinking about its attributes becomes an adjunct to that, if it is unwilling to betray its object; while the most austere films necessarily draw their energy from the attempt to repress their own excess (rather than from the more thankless effort to discipline the viewer)." Jurors (adding a little *ridiculum* of their own) compared immersion in Jameson's discourse to "swimming through cold porridge."

Although hardly inferior to the winner, this erudite concoction by Rob Wilson of Hawaii brought him only the second prize: "If such a sublime cyborg would insinuate the future as post-Fordist subject, his palpably masochistic locations as ecstatic agent of the sublime superstate need to be decoded as the 'now-all-but-unreadable DNA' of the fast deindustrializing Detroit..." The anonymous Associate Press writer chronicling the contest reports that third-prize recipient Fred Botting, unlike the first two winners, "kept his sentence short—to no avail." In his *Making Monstrous: Frankenstein, Criticism, Theory,* the Lancaster University lecturer discovered the following prize-winning theory: "The lure of imaginary totality is momentarily frozen before the dialectic of desire hastens on within symbolic chains."[10] No doubt all three citations fall in the literary domain where *comicum* and *ridiculum* are inextricably intertwined. Such academic pomposity brings to mind Montesquieu's aphorism: "La gravité est le bouclier des sots."[11]

Esthetic Distance: a Debatable Theorem

Regardless of the (newspaper) reader's limited "esthetic distance," such pre-literary news items without any implied "esthetic function" offer me and possibly many readers as intense a comic diversion as any comparable titillation in the *120 Days of Sodom*[12] or Voltaire's satire of metaphysicians. The postulates of "cathartic process [and] long ascesis" or of esthetic "distance" strike me as debatable theorems. The same objection applies to Mukařovský's broad postulate on the prevalence of esthetic function dominating over the communicative goals. Jauss cites other scholars who examine the problematics of humor. Reiner Warning, for example, explores comedy and laughter in the communication

10 Associated Press, "Professors' Worst Among the Prose," *The Calgary Herald,* May 18, 1997, p. 2.

11 *Mes pensées*, published posthumously only in 1899.

12 See comments on de Sade, ch IV.

process, defining it as an encounter between the real world of the audience and the fictional one on stage. Helmuth Plessner "introduces his concept of contrariety 'which, nevertheless, presents itself and seeks to be accepted as unity'." Jauss further alludes to E. Dupréel's theoretical distinction between *rire d'accueil* and *rire d'exclusion* and to Joachim Ritter's speculation on Plessner's arguments: "As soon as the aesthetic attitude discovers contrariety of comic conflict it gains the freedom of a distance which allows us to deal with the threatening situation, at least on the aesthetic level." My earlier objection to Souriau's arguments also applies to Ritter's unverifiable conclusion. The same sphere of "aesthetic atttitude" is activated by our direct perception of a TV news report covering the farcical aspects of the presidential campaign (journalism) or by the *pointe* of Baudelaire's sonnet "Sed non satiata".[13] From the theoretical comments and effort to isolate the primary causes of our laughter, we may generally assume that comic stimuli, like other categories of stimuli, are based on typical contrasts, evident or latent. How do comic stimuli differ from tragic or utopian stimuli based on qualitatively different contrasts? In the process of our perception, our memory, intellect and instincts seem to respond spontaneously to diversified specific oppositions (incongruities, *écarts*) which trigger sadness and tears, various degrees of mirth and laughter or amazement. Our basic communication in everyday life, as well as the cultivated esthetic communication which links readers and writers, would be impossible without a relatively common sentic frame of reference. However, as long as neurologists do not elucidate the physiology of perception and quantify the intensity of individual readers' laughter, curiosity, amazement or their grief, any philosophical and psychological concepts will remain hypothetical. Once science does irrefutably outline the complex physiological automatism involved in our individual valuatory perceptions, such concepts may be subject to revision. Unless this happens, we cannot even be sure, if the *gaudium* inherent in the beaver's teasing the dog offers the rodent and the humans watching it on shore mere *ridiculum* or the refined *comicum*. Can the beaver/comedian experience a rudimentary esthetic pleasure without any theoretical esthetic distance or is such an experience strictly reserved for the spectators and readers of its act's mimesis? No one knows. In any case the cause of humor rarely plays an important role in esthetic appraisals of comic effects. Generally, good and poor jokes may have the same

13 See *LP II*, pp. 102–9 and ch. IV above.

abstract causes while eliciting different impacts.

Intensity* Counts More than *Cause

The causes of laughter preoccupy psychologists, philosophers and interdisciplinary theorists; on the other hand, writers, publishers and esthetically oriented critics pay attention to the esthetic and/or commercial teleology of humor and to the impact which the identifiable comical micro- and macrostimuli may have on the targeted readership. From the point of view of creative practice and the reader's valuatory response to it, the main question is not why comic material is funny, but how funny it must be to stimulate the reader. Thus, I do not intend to dwell on the etiology of laughter. As in the case of the above discussed categories of stimuli, I am addressing here the elusive yet essential esthetic power of comic features, specific power generally neglected by theoretical research yet essential in the genesis of the text and its extratextual empirical appraisal by demanding qualified readers. From such a perspective the abstract criteria, naturally, are considered only inasmuch as they elucidate the potential extratextual impact experienced by readers.

For me laughter is our inner and external physiological response (externally manifested by body language) to reality, or its transposition which, spontaneously activate our innate sense of humor and quest of mirth. The intensity of our gaiety depends on the quality of comic factors which both life and art offer and on our individual expectations in the domain of humor. Our laughter is usually provoked by a real comic contrast or by its literary, acoustic or visual *mimesis* or by comic diction (which, however, may refer to both the comical as well as serious subjects) or finally by stylizations of non-existent ludicrous (not tragic) incongruities invented by the author. The dichotomy (1) mimesis of comical subject matter (inspired by the real referents or fictitious signifieds) and (2) diction (especially semantics, rhetoric) distinctly subdivides the vast domain of comical stimuli into farcical subjects and ironic humor generated by style, particularly by total or partial dissimulation, (e.g., in metaphor, hyperbole, litotetic understatements) and by incongruous, for instance, vulgar or precious semantics, parody of poetry, puns, automatist rhyming and so on. Both these inexhaustible reservoirs of comical effects store vital micro- and macrostimuli awaiting integration into a broad spectrum of heterogeneous comic or mixed genres. The recognized models of such genres include, for instance,

Aristophanes' or Plautus' ancient comedies; Petronius' *Satiricon*; Boccaccio's *Decameron*; Rabelais' humanistic *contaminatio*; Molière's or Shakespeare's classical comedy; tragi-comedy (e.g., Kleist's *Amphitryon*); Voltaire's satirical *conte philosophique*; brothers Marc-Michel and Eugene Labiche's bedroom farce *The Italian Straw Hat*; Jarry's burlesque *Ubu roi*; black (often sick) humor à la Lautréamont or Beckett; absurd comedies of Ionesco; satirical prose with high ironic density as in the works of Maupassant, Mark Twain, Oscar Wilde, Anatole France or Bernard Shaw; Marcel Aymé's comic fantasies; Zola's naturalistic sagas full of blue-collar slang and plebeian humor; Jaroslav Hašek's World War I satire of Austria-Hungary, *Good Soldier Schweik*.[14]

The Micro- and Macrocomic Quanta

Humorists know that minor as well as major comic effects have their place in art. Usually, in major comic prototypes both the farcical content and ironic style jointly increase the density of the macrostimulative bulk. In minor textual wholes esthetically supported by a single comical stimulus, the overall artistic impact is obviously less powerful than the impact generated by the major comical characters and plots. For instance Apollinaire, who so often imitates Verlaine's verbal music, seems to pay a mischievous compliment to the author of the well-known ariette "Il pleure dans mon coeur" by parodying the elegiac rhyming of its first stanza: "Il flotte dans mes bottes / Comme il pleut sur la ville / Au diable cette flotte / Qui pénètre mes bottes!"[15]

Neither the dose nor the satirical quality of this amicable livresque mockery exceeds microstimulative proportions. A macrostimulative counterpoint to any comical atom is, for instance, a masterpiece of alltime humor such as Gogol's *Dead Souls* offering a vital satire of Russian rot.[16] Its macrostimulative factors include the novel's main characters and their major epical actions essential in the macrostimulative plot.

14 *LP I* and *LP II* offer many examples of farcical and/or ironic humor of Rabelais, Molière, Voltaire, Baudelaire, Lautréamont, France, Zola, etc.

15 Guillaume Apollinaire, *Oeuvres complètes*, ed. Michel Décaudin (Paris: Ballaud-Lecat, 1965), III, p. 567. *LP II*, Appendix, illustrates the euphonies in the poet's well-known poems.

16 See below comments and table 4.

Teleology of Humor

Before addressing the two usually overlapping categories of humor, it may be worthwhile to contemplate briefly various functions and goals of laughter in life and in its transpositions in art and in the media. No matter what the specific causes of laughter, our relentless quest of it is universal. When Marcus Valerius Martial conceived, for example, a distych epigram treating what we might call today a rather basic "sight gag"—"[i]f from the baths you hear a round of applause / Maron's giant prick is bound to be the cause,"[17] he neither intended to initiate nor did he inadvertently start a "cathartic process." Like his readers, he simply found fun in the simplest of sources; and probably, no "long ascesis" preceded his inspiration or his readers'chuckles. (The translator not only magnifies the *mentula*,[18] he heightens the slapstick effect by rhyming not practised in ancient poetry.)

Students, especially in the countries where Latin is a high school prerequisite to university admission, sing "Gaudeamus igitur iuvenes dum sumus,"[19]—let's be merry while we are young, (for aren't *gaudium* and laughter the main goals of our youth?) Cato, statesman and moralist (234–149 B.C.), recommended *gaudium* as a tested medicine for our worries: "Let us alternate gaiety and troubles."[20] The Horatian dictum of telling (the resented) truth in comical terms, *ridendo dicere verum*,[21] refers to humor's moralistic, political and/or educational goals pursued, for instance, in satires such as Molière's comedies, Voltaire's *Candide*, Nikolai Gogol's *Dead Souls*, etc.

Humor maintains Man's high spirits: when a Spartan soldier at Thermopylae hears that the Persian spears will block out the sun, he does not lose his gallows' humor: "So much the better—at least we'll fight in the shade," he cracks. In the same mood, the author of a Nordic saga sees laughter as a life-long spiritual shield against the fear of tragic fate: "Yes, give us new swords, King...with cheers we set on against the enemy. With jokes and laughter we have accepted our destiny, we laugh

17 *The Epigrams*, transl. James Michie, Penguin Classics, bk IX, 33: "Audieris in quo Flacce, balneo plausum / Maronis illic esse mentulam scito."

18 Physical incongruities are frequent magnets just as the Cyrano-like nose of Charles de Gaulle which fascinated so many caricaturists as well as the general public.

19 Adaptation of medieval precendents attributed to the post-romantic German poet J.V. Scheffel (1826–86) or to itinerant singer Kindleben (1781).

20 "Interpone tuis interdum gaudia curis," *Disticha*, III 6 v. 1.

21 *Saturae*, I, 1, v. 24.

although we know that noone will get out alive from this fight—not one of the King's men".[22] In a rhymed 1915 letter, the punning Apollinaire conveys similar feelings to his friend though without the Viking premonition of heroic doom: "Je te le dis, André Billy, que cette guerre / C'est Obus-Roi / Beaucoup plus tragique qu'Ubu mais qui n'est guère / Billy crois-moi / Moins burlesque, / ô mon vieux, crois-moi / c'est très comique." Two months later he writes to another friend that "one must fight and laugh."[23] Without humor soldiers involved in absurd massacres would become insane.

Recently, I came across a distilled bit of Madison Avenue metaphysics encapsulating the lure of laughter in the feel-good Nineties. Surprisingly, it was the sole text of a full-page advertisement for recreational footwear.

> Laughter can add more years to your life than step class. Some people measure their lives in pulse rates and sit-ups. Far better to measure yours in licks of ice cream, well-told jokes, mad dashes to be first in the water, belly laughs. And, when you die, it won't be an erratic shift in your heartrate, it will be an overdose of mirth, fun poisoning, death by laughter.[24]

Traditionally, jokes and laughter testify to our love of life. They are precious and indispensable spices of humanistic optimism and of its bright civilized wisdom. Whether refined *esprit*, gallic *rigolade*, grave humor *à l'allemande* or the cynical salvos of Gogol, a dose of timeless humor is a desirable stimulative ingredient in the content or style of all non-tragic genres including poetry.

Comic Content: Farce

Aristotle defines the laughable content in comedy as "ugliness which is not painful." Two Indian works reach similar conclusions. *Dasarupa*, a Sanskrit treatise on the forms of the drama dating from the tenth century, says that "[m]irth (*hasa*) is caused by one's own or another's strange actions, words or attire"; *Sabitya Darpana* or *Mirror of Composition* states that the comic may "arise from the fun of distorted shapes or other dramatization, words, dresses, gestures, etc." The author may create a

22 Cited from Karl Holter's *Skinbrevet*, transl.from Norwegian into Czech by H. Koterka, *Pergamenová listina* (Prague: Evropský Lit. Klub, 1937), p. 180, my transl.

23 Letter of April 26 to A. Billy and to Louise Faure-Favier, (my transl.) *O.C.* IV, pp. 775, 855. "Obus"shrapnel— Ubu alludes to A. Jarry's burlesque *Ubu Roi*, see *LP II*, pp. 42–3 and below, Appendix, Jarry.

24 "Fashions of the Times", Part 2, *New York Times Magazine*, Spring 1994, p. 25.

farcical effect by a certain type of *topical* overstatement, understatement, or other exaggerated dramatization. Such distortions must not provoke pity but only the "instinct of humor".[25]

I consider Aristotle's "ugliness which is not painful" as a metonymy because it would be difficult to find painless ugliness in all specific comic plots or diction, for instance, in the sexual strike of married women organized by Lysistrata to stop the Greek men from fighting, to end the war and to impose the long overdue peace. Our first impression might be that the Aristotelian abstraction seems to apply mainly to the comic archetypes created by authors of ancient or classical comedies or epical works such as Euclion in *Aulularia*, his Molierian counterpart Harpagon, Shakespeare's Falstaff, Cervantes' Don Quixote and Sancho Panza, Rabelais' Pantagruel and Panurge, Voltaire's Pangloss, Beaumarchais' Figaro, Gottfried Bürger's Münchhausen, Dickens' Sam Weller, Alfred Jarry's Ubu, Mark Twain's Huckleberry Finn, Jaroslav Hašek's soldier Schweik, Jules Romains' Doctor Knock and so on. On the other hand, the pragmatic Indian formula allows for a broader range of comic material specifically including, besides characters, strange distorted shapes, plots, [the characters'] words, dresses, gestures. Yet, in some instances, which do not provoke pity, the "definition" may be too broad: strange and distorted shapes, dresses, words or action are also omnipresent in utopias, fairy tales, fantasies and bizarre genres—such as *Les Chants de Maldoror* in which the distortions are not always comic. At first sight, Charlie Chaplin's clownish appearance and attire strike occidental spectators as comical whereas a distortion such as the half-beast-half-man and its utterances in, for example, Cocteau's or Walt Disney's cinematic versions of *Beauty and the Beast* are not, because, of course, they inspire fear.[26] Generally, no incongruities are comic if they provoke irreversible anxiety. The signified's farcical contrast with normalcy ("ugliness", "distortion"), the typical specific excesses, shortages, deviations, "automatically" and almost simultaneously, provoke our sense of measure and/or propriety along with our instinct to laugh aloud or silently. But even if we correctly identify and reduce the varied specific causes of such esthetic effects (perceived by generations of readers and spectators with different frames of reference) to a general abstract common denominator, it merely reveals the presence of humor

25 *The Art of Anatole France*, p. 105 paraphrasing Eastman, op. cit., p. 163; Jauss op. cit., p. 127 refering to *Poetics* 5.

26 See below ch. VII.

without offering any clue to its qualitative intensity and relative esthetic value. Jean Suberville seems to derive the intensity of the comic in art from the intensity of the ridiculous in life: "The less predictable the ridiculous is, the more laughter it triggers."[27] To cause laughter the incongruity must surprise the observer as absurd though not fatal, and clash with some of his current expectations. Farcical incongruities often create a deceptive twist which unexpectedly reveal the relativity or imperfections of our general, e.g., esthetic, social, pedagogic, political, technical standards.

Verbal Humor: Irony

In literary humor, farcical content is usually articulated with a great deal of ironic rhetoric. Irony dissimulates the intended meaning by stating its opposite in order to tease, mock, satirize, discredit a character's action or thought and to amuse and surprise the reader. Total ironic dissimulations take the form of antiphrases: Voltaire approvingly describes a murderous battle as entertaining gunfire which "in the twinkling of an eye [absurdly short timespan], laid flat six thousand men on each side." In the course of the same massacre. "the musket bullets swept away out of the best of all possible worlds [cruel battlefield] nine or ten thousand scoundrels [innocent recruits] that infested [lived like anybody else] its surface".[28] Partially dissimulative, ironic tropes include, for example, over- or understatement, hyperbole, euphemism, litotes, ironic similes, metaphors, paradoxes, ambiguities, puns. Jaroslav Hašek, for instance, illustrates the ironic overstatement with Schweik's definition of happiness:

> When Schweik later on described life in the lunatic asylum, he did so in terms of *exceptional eulogy* : "The life there was a fair treat. You can bawl, or yelp, or sing or blurb, or moo, or boo, or jump, say your prayers or turn somersaults, or walk on all fours, or hop about on foot, or run round in a circle, or dance, or skip, or squat on your haunches all day long, and climb up the walls. I liked being in the asylum, I can tell you, and while I was there I had *the time of my life*."[29]

The heterogeneous conclusions of theorists examining the etiology

27 *Théorie de l'Art et des genres littéraires* (Paris: Éditions de l'École, 1961), p. 305, my transl. For him the comic is the transposition of the ridiculous: "le comique n'est que la mise en scène des ridicules qui engendrent le rire."

28 *Candide*, transl. T.G. Smollett (New York: Washington Square Press, 1976), p. 9.

29 *Good Soldier Schweik*, Penguin Books, 1946, p. 24, my italics.

of laughter vary not only due to the differences of their speculative routines but also because each of them bases his/her general reflections on different historical and individual expectations and different specific examples of comic subject matter. Consequently, Jean Paul's above mentioned clarification "sharply bursting out" which unifies but also confuses the sought cause with the elicited effect (laughter) strikes me as an absurd theoretical tautology—our laughter (i.e., bursting out) is caused by sharply "bursting out". Nevertheless, his comment forces us to examine the physiological spontaneity of laughter where cause and effect are so tightly linked that we can barely distinguish one from the other. In any case, the "sharply bursting out" confirms at least that whatever the cause, it is an effective comic and not a "non-comic" stimulus and also, of course, that the reader/spectator did not miss its humor. A scrutiny of specific comic causes and comic effects will elucidate the issue of esthetic power produced by farcical or verbal humor.

Our Remembrance of Comic Impact

As I was gathering convincing empirical evidence of various degrees of comical impact, I began pondering what, in my own life and among my life-long reading adventures, stands out as unforgettable comic material. As a child I repeatedly read a book about a pet chimpanzee named Hoot living in a bourgeois family. Now, seventy years later, I can remember only one farcical episode and its illustration: the smart chimp observes a pastry cook apprentice carrying on his head a platter with a monumental multilayer wedding cake. His mouth watering, Hoot grabs a toy bow and arrow belonging to the family's son and shoots off the top two layers of the cake. The arrow conveniently nails his dessert to a nearby billboard. Hoot's prank, cause of my childish laughter and condescending senior smile, confirms all abstract formulae elucidating the nature of comical substance: the Bergsonian contrast created by a sudden transition from one subject to another entirely opposite—unexpectedly, the wedding cake becomes a chimp's treat and sudden glory an apprentice-cook's, deceived expectation; the customer's "surprise", "suddenness", "disappointment". None of these formulae, however, explains why I forgot so many other comical episodes in the same book and in countless other children's books, but never forgot the comic triumph and the Boccaccian *ingenio* of the fictitious chimpanzee.

Farcical Non-Literary Anecdote

Later, when I was 12 years-old, I spent a summer in a language camp. There, our doctor, a medical student of Czech descent studying in Vienna, told me and my peers some dirty jokes. I forgot almost all of them except for one: a young peasant asks for the hand of his sweetheart. Her father, a wealthy farmer, spells out three conditions: "My son-in-law has to have good looks, be rich and have a prick 30 centimetres long." The suitor replies: "Without boasting, I am the finest looking lad in the village, my family has as many heads of cattle as your family has and, OK, because it is your daughter, I'll have five centimetres cut off." Again the theory of double shock, Schopenhauer's paradox, Bains' "delivrance," deceived expectation mixed with sudden glory, may clarify the abstract causes of my adolescent laughter but do not explain whether the medic's anecdote was a good or bad joke, paleolithic or sophisticated. Why have I never forgotten it? How intense was its comic appeal to a 12-year old in 1932 and now for a blasé critic trying to discern the elusive humor quotient in various comic subjects?

Doderer's Projection of Growing Comic Intensity: The *Pointe*

The anatomy of any successful anecdote implies a more or less gradual increase of its comic intensity from the outset to its last word. Within the preparatory suspense every successive word sets the scene for the contrastful *pointe* which brings surprise, release, deceived expectation, "bursting out", etc. The *pointe* in the anecdote marks the *peak* and end of the *comic gradation*. Empirically speaking, the *pointe*'s esthetic intensity should be higher than the anecdote's comic overture. It has to be the culminating esthetic point of the narrative. Klaus Doderer distinguishes the narratological plan of the short story (its *Wendepunkt*, reversal) from the anecdotal formula in which everything gravitates from the very beginning to the final *pointe*; he represents the dramatic *Spannungsfeld* (build-up) in a here altered but similar table.[30]

30 *Die Kurzgeschichte in Deutschland*, (Wiesbaden: Metopen Verlag, 1953), p. 29. In this study, the French term pointe is synonymous with the English (colloquial) "punch line". See also Bernard Dupriez, *Gradus—Les procédés littéraires* ©Union générale d'Éditions 1984 (n.p.), p. 354. "La pointe…est la façon de terminer irrésistiblement un paragraphe."

TABLE 4

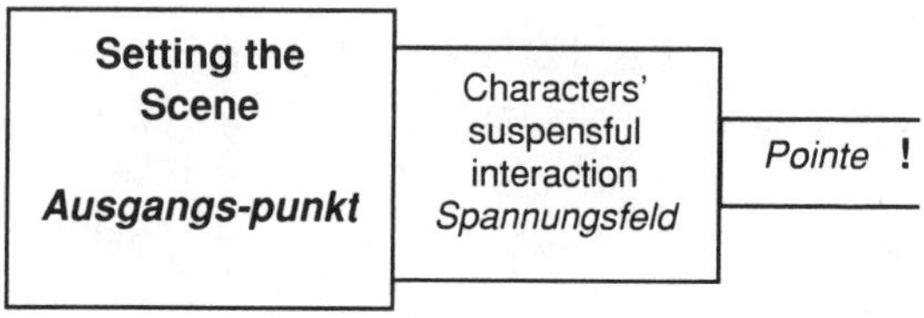

Literary Anecdote and its Comic Frame in *The Grapes of Wrath*

His arguments and representation of the anecdotal build-up illustrate the artistic strategy of a comic crescendo and its sudden explosive end. Let us document the validity of Doderer's argument in a convincing literary context. Although the anecdote cited below falls in the same category of licentious humor as the previous joke, it is not a mere product of subcultural yarn (which nevertheless had its elementary esthetic function). In the mid-thirties, I read a Czech translation of John Steinbeck's *The Grapes of Wrath* and today, more than half a century later, I still remember the tall tale told in the novel as a powerful sample of North American rural humor. The anecdote (2) is interpolated between two comic scenes (1, 3). Steinbeck's aging hero Joad and his preacher friend observe with interest a thrilling canine courtship (1).

> A committee of dogs had met in the road [the canine pecking order bureaucratized, irony], in honor of a bitch [canine mating ritual humanized, irony]. Five males, shepherd mongrels, collie mongrels, dogs whose breeds had been blurred by a freedom of social life, were engaged in complimenting the bitch… [hyperbolic enumeration, extension of the above irony] Joad and the preacher stopped to watch, and suddenly Joad laughed joyously. "By God!" he said. "By God!" Now all dogs met and hackles rose…each waiting for the others to start a fight. One dog mounted and, now that it was accomplished, the others gave way and watched with interest…and their tongues dripped… [mimesis of the farcical conflict; animal love life] "By God!" Joad said. "I think that updog is our Flash [the spectator's comic discovery]. I thought he'd be dead. Come, Flash!" He laughed again. "What the hell, if somebody called me, I wouldn't hear him neither. [Comic common denominator—man/dog.]

This preliminary episode (1) esthetically justifies a brief "analogy" ("Minds me of…") outlined in a digressive yet well integrated mid-west gauloiserie (2).

> Minds me of a story they tell about Willy Feely when he was a young fella. Willy *was bashful*. Well, one day he takes a *heifer* over to Graves' *bull* [setting

the scene]. Ever'body was out but Elsie Graves, and Elsie *wasn't bashful* at all [antithesis, ironic litotes]. Willy, he stood there turnin' red an' he couldn't even talk [comical suspense, hyperbole]. Elsie says, "I know what you come for; the bull's out in back at the barn." Well, they took the heifer out there an' Willy an' Elsie sat on the fence to watch. Purty soon Willy got feelin' purty *fly* [comic diction, suspense]. Elsie looks over an' says, like she don't know, "What's a matter, Willy?" Willy's so randy, he can't hardly set still [comic gradation]. "By God," he says, "by God, I wish I was a-doin' that! [gradation culminates]" Elsie says, "Why not, Willy? It's your heifer [*pointe*]."

As a comic epilogue (3) Steinbeck even invents his character's benign decrescendo of Joad's grassroot humor: "The preacher laughed softly. "You know," he said, "it's a nice thing not bein' a preacher no more. Nobody use' ta tell stories when I was there, or if they did I couldn' laugh. An' I couldn' *cuss*. Now I cuss all I want, any time… "[31] The lower intensity of the two micro-stimulative comic segments (1, 3) framing the climactic slapstick (2) with its suspense and salient *pointe* suavely links the levity[32] with the tragic main theme—the loss of the family's land and its desperate exodus westwards.

In the narratives which unfold plots broader than concise anecdotal intrigues, the overall comic intensity is obviously enhanced if, in addition to their dramatic reversals and macrogradations, they also have an effective "punchline". In such cases, the climactic segments often imply the macrorhetoric irony of fate going against the characters' expectations. (Extratextually, we readers/spectators share, though not fully, the represented characters' surprise since we expect to be offered the unexpected.)

Farcical Characters and Plots: Brautigan's Bootlegger

Richard Brautigan tells (in the first person) the life story of his resourceful granny, "who was a bootlegger in a little county in the state of Washington," distilling bourbon in the basement of her home. This

31 *The Grapes of Wrath* (New York: Bantam Books, 1945), pp. 84–5. There is a distant but unmistakable parallel between Steinbeck's subject and the memorable opening of Emile Zola's *La Terre*: it portrays the little farm girl Françoise leading la Coliche, the cow to be impregnated by Caesar the bull. Like Steinbeck's Elsie, Françoise is far from being bashful, in helping Caesar to complete the mission. She grabs the monumental member with her childish hand and directs it into la Coliche's vagina.

32 In this context I am not referring to overlapping esthetic supports such as Joad's colorful regional vernacular or the correlated erotic stimulus. See also Ch. V, n. 38 referring to Tom Wolfe's satirical though gravely erotic treatment of equine breeding in *A Man in Full*.

entrepreneur of a prefeminist era has a cosy business agreement with the local sheriff. Her marriage to a "minor Washington mystic, who, in 1911 [accurately] prophesized" to the day the outbreak of World War I and who, two years later, was transferred to the insane asylum, does not break her business spirit. To highlight her grassroots pragmatism, Brautigan ends the character sketch with grandmother's clean-up of her underground still. From time to time she had to empty it, "dump the old mash and get new batch going." Clad in railroad overalls, she loaded the bourbon dregs onto the wheelbarrow and dumped them on the lawn near the garage sheltering her flock of geese. The birds, lured by the potent nutrient, proceeded to get drunk and collapsed on the lawn "as if they had been machine-gunned."[33] Assuming that bourbon overdose had caused the fatal catastrophe, the old lady wasted no time and plucked the birds on the spot, hoping to sell what she could and roast what she couldn't. She reloaded her wheelbarrow this time with her plucked fowl and stored them on the cold basement floor. There the geese recovered from their hangovers, cackling desperately in total bewilderment over their nudity. Whether total fiction or mimesis of a legendary ancestor's memorable blunder, Brautigan's geese farce is an original and effective ruralist yarn which editors of humor anthologies may consider an enduring sample of American farce.

Marquéz' Mystery

Unlike Brautigan's plot, the tightly written mystery novelette, *Chronicle of a Death Foretold* by the 1982 Nobel Prize-winner Garcia Gabriel Marquéz, does not rely on the farcical actions of a single main character. His original intrigue comes alive due to the episodic interactions of the whole colorful population of a small coastal town near Riohacha in northern Colombia: the local bullies and matriarchs; the Spanish priest, Father Carmen Amador; the town madam, Maria Alejandrina Cervantes; policeman Leandro Pornoy, and many others make up the rich farcical mosaic depicting a rural vendetta.

The story opens when a macho newcomer, Bayardo San Román, steps off the weekly boat serving the coastal town. Soon he tenaciously courts and marries Angela Vicario, nubile daughter of a "poor man's goldsmith" and his wife Pura. After the garish wedding generously

33 *Revenge of the Lawn Stories* 1962–1970 (New York: Simon and Schuster, 1963–71), p. 9, 11–13.

financed by Bayardo's wealthy father, General Petronio San Román, the bridgroom discovers that his newlywed spouse is not a virgin. He returns her to the Vicario clan. Her mother beats out of her the name of the alleged (did she lie?) seducer—Santiago Naser of Arabic descent. Angela's twin brothers Pedro and Pablo decide to rehabilitate the Vicario honor by stabbing him to death with four butcher's knives which they sharpen at dawn on the local butcher's grindstone. They tell—among many others—the butcher's friend, Faustino Santos, that they are going to kill Santiago and that he knows why. The policeman even reports their threats to the Mayor, Col. Lazaro Aponte, who confiscates the four knives without believing the two bragging brothers would ever hurt anybody. They promptly sharpen another set of knives and successfully murder Santiago on the very morning the itinerant Bishop is arriving by boat to confer the annual blessing on their pious community. Disdaining to walk among the eager townsfolk led by Father Amador, the Bishop remains offshore, and the local priest, who had once studied medicine, is suddenly ordered by the mayor to perform an extracurricular autopsy on Santiago's corpse. In a somewhat unorthodox post mortem, Father Amador opens the stabbing victim's skull, comments on the impressive size of the seducer's brain and finally throws his guts into the garbage. Although some of these secondary characters occasionally appear digressive, all of them are indirectly linked in comic complicity in the murder, and all of them boost the stimulative density and intensity in the criminal burlesque of "a death foretold." In this respect, Marquéz' technique evokes the anecdotal discourse of writers such as Jaroslav Hašek in his *Good Soldier Schweik* or some of Marcel Aymé's portraits of French peasants.[34]

Naturally, the peak of vacillating extratextual intensity generated by intratextual comic stimuli depends on the text's "shelf life": it is assumed that we do not savor stale chesnuts, i.e., endless variations of jokes with which we are all too familiar. Our enjoyment of humor springing from an obsolete or remote social context may also be limited.

Scarron's Dated Humor

The contemporaries of Paul Scarron (1610–1660) and literary historians have recognized him as a talented 17th century humorist. Such

34 "Chronicle of a Death Foretold," *Vanity Fair*, March 1983, pp. 122–224. Also see *LP II*, ch. VII, "Marcel Aimé's *Le Vin de Paris,*" pp. 194–5

a recognition, however, does not guarantee the immortality of his humor. Today, Scarron may still be read in university courses covering classical prose rather than as a great French humorist. His novella, "Châtiment de l'avarice" (*Nouvelles*, 1655–7), represents Dom Marcos, a picaresque niggard who, like Plautus' and Molière's misers, loses his pot of gold. To amass 10,000 ducats, he scrimps for almost thirty years. Unfortunately, Scarron does not scrimp in the telling.

As the page of a Madrid prince, the emaciated 12-year-old starves to avoid any food bills. He saves all the scraps of meat left on his patron's plate, and even has special tin containers made for his pockets to prevent the sauces from staining his clothing. He finances this golden age technology by salvaging discarded candle butts to sell as wax. Ironically, the page's tightfistedness backfires because it pleases his master so much that he keeps Dom Marcos as his underpaid page until he is 30.[35]

When he finally becomes the prince's courtier, noone can surpass him in cutting the lighting budget: to save on candles the nobleman partially undresses in the street prior to entering his dark, low-cost lodgings. But the real *coup* of his farcical frugality is the hole which the miser makes in the wall separating his Spartan dormitory from that of his neighbor. This sly renovation allows the neighbor's candle to cast a few rays of light into Dom Marcos' abode.[36] Only after finishing the baroque caricature of his then modern miser, does Scarron address the tale's farcical plot.

The three decades of the thoroughly described penny pinching make his hero an affluent bachelor as well as an attractive target for swindlers. The go-between Gamara easily lures the tightwad into marrying Isidore, a grandmother rumored to be a wealthy widow enjoying an independent

35 *Contes classiques*, eds. Jean and Jacqueline Sareil (Engelwood Cliffs: Prentice Hall, 1967), p. 8. [I]l ne desservait jamais assiette chargée de viande qu'il ne fît part de quelques chose à sa pochette; et parce que les viandes liquides y faisaient un mauvais effet, il fit argent de la cire d'un grand nombre de bout de flambeaux qu'il avait amassés avec grand soin, et en acheta des pochettes de fer blanc, dont il fit depuis des merveilles pour l'avancement de sa fortune. Les avares sont d'ordinaire vigilants et soigneux, et ces deux bonnes qualités...le rendirent si agréable à son maître, qu'il ne se pouvait résoudre à se défaire d'un si bon page. Il lui fit donc porter les couleurs jusqu'à l'âge de trente ans.

36 Ibid. [S]on esprit inventif lui fit faire un trou dans la muraille qui séparait sa chambre de celle d'un voisin, qui n'avait pas plus tôt allumé sa chandelle, que Marcos ouvrait son trou, et recevait par là assez de lumière pour ce qu'il avait à faire.

income and valuable assets. The bride lives in a comfortable household also sheltering her alleged nephew Augustinet. On the wedding night the beldame's ivory denture gets stuck in the bridegroom's mustache and, when she tries to extricate it with her hand, Dom Marcos, in self defense, rips off his baldheaded spouse's wig. The next comic blow occurs when Isidore's furnishings and silver are reclaimed by their owner; the veteran courtisane had rented them to impress the scheming dupe. The ensuing theft of Dom Marcos' chest full of gold leads to a protracted treasure hunt. Gamara, disguised as a magician, fools Dom Marcos but at the end is arrested and sent to the galleys. Nevertheless, Isidore and Augustinet manage to whisk Dom Marcos' chest away. The desperate owner finally catches up just when it is being loaded on a boat sailing from Barcelona to Naples. He grabs its handle, pulling the chest off the loading crane. It lands on his head and both the chest and its owner fall into the sea. Augustinet, furious at losing the treasure, attacks the sailor who failed to secure the chest firmly enough. In self-defense, the seaman deals a blow to Augustinet who, falling into the sea, grabs Isidore and the crooked pair join their victim at the sea bottom.

Three and a half centuries later this slapstick material and its inordinate epic width possibly strike the modern readers (willing to read the tale to its end) as dated, stilted and not particularly ludicrous. Yet the society of Louis XIV with its cynical princes, abused pageboys, toothless courtisanes and shrewd pimps must have enjoyed it. A century later, when Montesquieu, Voltaire and Diderot introduced a higher degree of finesse into French humor by balancing the farce with subtle wit, Scarron's humor already must have run its cycle. In the age of electricity, computer theft and grandiose scams shaking up international banks and stock markets, "Punished Avarice" attracts neither modern readers nor publishers who could republish the text in the public domain at minimal cost. One day, Scarron's half-forgotten comic character and plot may be more suitable for treatment by a talented film animator or satirist/director.

The fading of Scarron's humor does not imply that all equally old comic texts face the same fate. For example, many segments of the *Decameron* (1350–55) or *The Heptameron* (1559) are still readable. The episode cited earlier about the assassination of the Florentine Duke Allessandro, mixing violence with black farce,[37] still seems to emanate more comic intensity than Scarron's miser and the brutal irony of his

37 See ch. III, "Regicide in *The Heptameron* and *Lorenzaccio*."

fate. Rarely can a hopeless *ridiculum* be rescued esthetically.

Comical Gradations in *Dead Souls*

Paradoxically, among the gracefully aging comic texts which defy literary death is Nicolai Gogol's *Dead Souls*, first published in 1842. I speculate that major bookstores still market this satire because its comedy is more universal, more deeply rooted in human weakness than Scarron's artificial character and plot. Its humor transcends the confines of the culture which inspired the satirist.

Gogol's and Scarron's comic heroes have one thing in common. Both want to get rich, both wish to upgrade their poor minor nobleman's status. But there the similarity ends—Dom Marcos is a psychopathic skinflint whereas Pavel Ivanovich Chichikov is a shrewd, corrupt civil servant twice fired and twice rehired. His father advised him to be a heel licker and, whenever convenient, to pull strings. The docile Pavlusha figured out for himself when to accept and when to proudly reject bribes and how to cover up his underhanded bureaucratic tricks: Gogol introduces him as a Collegiate Councillor travelling on private business. While administering the mortgaging of serfs the councillor discovers a legal loophole in the qualification criteria. His crooked imagination, historically situated just halfway between the 17th and 20th centuries, is much closer to modern quasi-legal con games than to Scarron's baroque parsimony. For next to nothing, Chichikov buys dead male serfs who generate no income for their living landowners. The deceased men are legally alive and taxable until the next Russian census (held once every ten years). At the same time Chichikov acquires free, newly opened crown land and "resettles" it with these dead but *de iure* living serfs. Thus he qualifies for a mortgage determined by the number of serfs earmarked to be resettled on the so far non-existent but "officially certified" Chichikov Burough. This fraudulent scheme is the core of an original comic plot.

Having met several serf-holding landowners at the Provincial Governor's party at N—, the Councillor provokes their interest in his private project. One of them, Sobakevich (whose comic character derives from misanthropic cynicism,[38]) is ready to discuss a deal and invites him to a family dinner. The introductory continuity is a lighthearted satirical character sketch blending farcical and ironic accents. "This is my

38 Ironic name, Russian *sobak*/dog (Gr.) *kyon*—cynic).

Theodulia Ivanovna, said Sobakevich. Chichikov approached Theodulia Ivanovna to kiss her fair hand, which she all but shoved into his mouth, during which operation he had an opportunity to note that her hands had been washed in dill-pickle brine."[39] The wheeler-dealer. who barely knows his crusty yet cooperative host, opens the negotiation with jovial name-dropping and compliments to the provincial brass whom he had met at the Governor's mansion. Wellek sums up Gogol's vision of the world as: "gloomy but also grotesquely comic". In addition, every page in Gogol's satire betrays his flair for effective dramatic gradation, rapid anecdotal pace and the art of recurrent caustic *pointe*. Chichikov's diplomacy clashes with Sobakevich's rustic bluntness. The culminations of their repartee are enhanced by colorful rhetoric revealing the landowner's unflappable disdain for the bungling and corrupt provincial bureaucrats, some of whom—Chichikov speculates—must be his social acquaintances.

The scene foreshadows the tough bargaining session to follow the amicable dinner served by Theodulia [40] Ivanovna. The host's price for his deceased *mujiks* will turn out to be much higher than Chichikov is ready to pay. Table 5 (reproduced below on pages 192–3) divides the 554-word macrostimulative citation into six minor epic segments including the functional (nonstimulative) continuity (I) a triple anecdotal gradation (II–IV), a transitional ironic epilog (V) and the first stylistically stimulative link integrating the comic controversy with its epic follow-up (VI). My 37 notes identify both farcical and ironic[41] microstimuli reflecting comic density within the analysed passage. They approximate my empirical estimates of density and the fluctuating intensity in the comic crescendo.[42]

39 *Dead Souls* (Toronto: Rinehart, 1948), transl. B.G. Guernay, introduction by René Wellek, p. 106.

40 Ironic first name—*nomen omen*—meaning God's serf, slave.

41 The stylistic humor supporting the two characters' comic conflict is, in this case, the translator's English replica of the Russian original. I first read the novel in a Czech version (about 1937/38) whose translator opted for the hyperbole "pig" (prase) rather than "swine" in Sobakevich's disdainful punchline (34). In the Czech rhetoric svine (*swine*) designates either a "*stinker*," *opportunist (male)* or has an erotic connotation (female); as a metaphor, prase ("pig") rather alludes to vulgar, uncivilized manners, or to a sloppy incompetent bungler.

42 In similar instances, my biocybernetic collaborator favors the term "cascade". I do not use this metaphor as it often implies descent not ascent. Rather than counting words, the biometrist would time the density as well as the intensity increments.

TABLE 5

N. Gogol. Dead Souls: intensity build-up in the opening dialog between Chichikov and Sobakevich	**Comic Intensity** 1 2 3 4 5 6 7 8	**Comic Density (epical and stylistic)**
I. Introduction — continuity — 45 words "We were remembering you at a party given by Ivan Grigoryievich, the Chairman of the Administrative Offices," said Chichikov at last, perceiving that neither one of the others felt inclined to start a conversation, "last Thursday, it was. We passed our time very pleasantly there."		epic continuity; no discernible intensity
II Comic controversy — 63 words "Yes, I wasn't at this place then," Sobakevich answered. "And what a splendid man!"[1] "Whom do you mean?" asked Sobakevich, looking at an angle of the stove. "The Chairman of the Administrative Offices."[2] "Well, perhaps he may have struck you that way; he may be a Mason, but just the same he's a fool[3] whose like the world has never yet produced."[4]		[1]hypocritical hyperbolic eulogy [2]suspenseful challenging question; eulogy reiterated controversy [3]eulogy rejected as illusion—not splendid but fool [4]"irrefutable" hyperbolic gradation: although Mason—illustrious fool; 1st comic peak
III Farcical controversy/continuity — 249 words "Chichikov was somewhat perplexed[5] by this rather harsh characterization but then recovering,[6] went on: "Of course, every man has his weak points,[7] but you take the Governor—what a superb fellow!"[8] "The Governor is a superb fellow?"[9] "Yes, isn't he?"[10] "A brigand—the biggest one on earth!"[11] "What—the Governor is a brigand?" said Chichikov,[12] and absolutely could not grasp how the Governor could have joined the ranks of the brigands.[13] "I must confess I would never think so,"[14] he went on. "But allow me to observe however, that his actions do not at all indicate anything of the sort; on the contrary, there is rather a great deal of gentleness[15] about him actually." Here he adduced, in proof, the purses embroidered by the Governor's own hands,[16] and commented, with praise on the kindly expression of the Governor's face.[17]		[5]protagonist shaken up (suspense) [6]suspenseful lowering of intensity; ironic "rather"; [7]protagonist's evasive commonplace; satirical accent; [8]to avoid any blunder, tries a fresh compliment [9]new challenging question; incipient controversy [10]C. tries to defend his hypocritical admiration, conflict cont. [11]Governor bluntly discredited; controversy, 1st peak [12]C.'s confusion grows; suspense [13]gradation of 12; satirical suspense [14]C. defends his view: diplomatic retreat [15]gradation of argument: gentle not a thug [16]Governor's needlework: farcical argument [17]gradation, friendly features

Continued on next page

TABLE 5 *(continued)*

"And his face, too, is a brigand's![18] said Sobakevich. "Do but put a knife in his hands and let him loose on the highway, and he'll slit your throat—he'll slit your throat for the smallest copper![19] He, and the Vice-Governor with him,[20] Gog and Magog,[21] that's what they are!"		[18]conviction firm [19]the Governor is a cutthroat, farcical gradation; [20]so is Vice-Governor (for good measure) [21]hyperbole: Satan's allies, controversy's 2nd peak
IV Suspense preceding the pointe — 162 words "No, he must be on the outs with them,"[22] Chichikov reflected. "There, I'll try him out with the Chief of Police—he's a friend of his, I believe."[23] However, as far as I am concerned," he said aloud, "I confess I find the Chief of Police to my liking most of all. What a straightforward, frank character he has; one can see something simple-hearted in his very face."[24] "A swindler!"[25] said Sobakevich with the utmost sang-froid[26] "He'll sell you out and he'll take you in, and dine with you right after that.[27] I know them all, they're all swindlers,[28] every man-jack of them; the whole town is like that,[29] one swindler mounted on a second and using a third one as a whip, Judases,[30] all of them.[31] There is but one—and only one—decent man;[32] that's the Public Prosecutor,[33] and even he, if the truth were to be told, is a swine."[34]		[22]C. is reaching conclusion too slowly; ironic suspense [23]C.'s new vain attempt to keep conventional conversation going; 24new model of provincial virtue; [25]paradoxically Chief of Police is a crook; 26S. intransigent moralist, ironic mot juste; [27]gradation of 25 [28]corruption universal; sweeping generalization [29]"all," "every," "whole" hyperbolic gradation [30]clique of traitors, gradation [31]28, 29, 30, hyperboles reiterated [32]one single exception 33, [33]Public Prosecutor (suspense) [34]reversal/pointe: "swine" 3rd comic peak
V Continuity — 71 words After such eulogistic although somewhat brief biographies,[35] Chichikov perceived that it wouldn't do to mention the other officials, and reminded himself that Sobakevich did not relish giving a good report of anybody.[36]		Epilog; [35]ironic epithet and euphemism [36]double ironic litotes; S. is a staunch misanthrope;
VI New subject — 12 words "Well, now, pet[37] let's go in to dinner," said Sobakevich's spouse,...		New epic sequence; [37]very brief ironic "taming" of the bilious husband.

Sobakevich's pithy verdict on the ranking civil servants exemplifies the anecdotal gradations forming Gogol's comic plot and maintaining its high macrostimulative satirical intensity. As soon as the landowner and his guest sit down to savor the *nurse*, Russian variation of haggis made of lamb gizzard dressed with buckwheat, brains and chopped lamb-leg stuffing,[43] the host's appetite as well as his taste for gossip grows. The ensuing dinner chit-chat is another anecdotal build-up (1ab, 2ab, 3ab) culminating in a *pointe*-like slander of the governor's chef and his notorious potlucks which, for Sobakevich, are nothing but slops(4).

> (1a) "You won't get to eat a pudding like that in town," he turned to Chichikov. "They'll serve you the Devil knows what there!"
> (b) "However, the Governor doesn't keep such a bad table," remarked Chichikov.
> (2a) "But do you know what all those courses are made of? You wouldn't eat them if you were to find out."
> (b) "I don't know how they're prepared, I'm not in a position to judge that; but the pork chops and stewed fish were excellent."
> (3a) "It just struck you that way. For I know what they buy in the market. The buying will be done by that rascal of a chef, who learned his trade from a Frenchman; he'll skin a cat, and then serve it up to you at table for rabbit."
> (b) "Faugh, what a nasty thing to say," said Sobakevich's spouse.
> (4) "Well, isn't it so, my little pet? That's how they do things; I'm not to blame, they do everything that way. Every sort of refuse, stuff that our wench Akulka throws into the cesspool, if you'll permit me to use the word, they pop into their soup. Into the soup with it! That's the place for it!"[44]

Even the epical continuities and, for example the functional chapter endings, may be punctuated with a burlesque aphorism culminating with a pointe. After his taxing day mixing shady business with the opulent hospitality of the rural gentry, Gogol's hero orders a Spartan evening snack which will not interfer with a well deserved and very sound sleep. Such an invigorating repose is a rare privilege which only darlings of the gods can enjoy: "Having eaten the lightest of suppers, consisting only of a suckling pig, he immediately undressed and...fell into that marvelous slumber which is known only to those fortunate beings who are bothered neither by hemorrhoids, nor fleas, nor overdeveloped mental faculties."[45]

The main artistic reasons why *Dead Souls* has become a classic of humor is not only the satire's high density of dramatically arranged farcical and ironic stimuli; it is above all the originality of the macrostimulative factors—the simple but unique satirical plot and the unforgettable fictitious yet living characters such as Sobakevich, the

43 A culinary bizarrerie, satire of rustic upperclass gourmandise and ironic contrast between the gizzard and the "excellent" pork and fish served "in town" by the Governor and recalled below by Chichikov.

44 Ibid., p. 109. This new *pointe* makes the reader wonder what was put in Theodulia Ivanovna's *nurse*.

45 Ibid., 150.

irrepressible liar Nozdrev, the fantasizing fool postmaster, the venal, "stonewalling" bureaucrats all embodying Russia as Gogol knew and loved it.[46]

Black Humor: Baudelaire's Farcical Satire of Equity à la Proudhon

The ugly, evil, perverse and brutal are recurrent subjects which, to the surprise of his contemporaries, Baudelaire transformed into shocking yet effective poetic qualities—"beauty" he still called it. He channelled these morbid elements into all categories of his contentual stimuli including humor.[47] Only rarely does his farce represent the Aristotelian "ugliness which is not painful." His restless mind neither gravitates to wholesome mirth or comic erotic scheming, nor is it drawn to Voltairean satire of cosmic and social evils, human corruption and incurable optimism. Baudelaire fancies eccentric burlesque and his irony relishes flirtation with the devil and hell. But although he is a pioneer of *black humor*, he certainly did not invent it: his farce judiciously draws from the libertine esthetics of de Sade, while his consummate ambiguities and metaphors shroud licentious topics in the fascinating poetry of the "new shiver". I shall not return here to the sick *gaudium* anchored in the Marquis' relish for sexual brutality. In this context, however, let us remember that, while contemplating his antihumanist originality, I have granted both de Sade's farce and his black sarcasm a modicum of esthetic credit.[48] Without identifying Baudelaire's specific debts to the Marquis' perverse wit, I shall try to assess the esthetic role of sadism and masochism in the poetry, black farce, and cynical parody of general ideas so substantial in *Le Spleen de Paris* (1967).[49]

"Assommons les pauvres" is the title of a whimsical causerie (XLIX) forming an anecdotal macrostimulus and addressing, with tongue-in-cheek, P.-J. Proudhon's Romantic socialism. It is a livresque parody of

46 In the novel's conclusive chapter (XII) Gogol ironically but patriotically mythifies his corrupted *bogatyr*. He claims that his Chichikov, warts and all, lives in every Russian and his troika carrying him to new rotten adventures symbolizes Russia—"all things on earth fly by past and other peoples and nations stand aside and give it the right of way." Ibid., p. 304.

47 See comments on antithesis in "Une Charogne", *LP II*, pp. 81–6. Hugo's compliment, p. 85; "Sed non satiata", pp. 102–9 and above ch. IV on Baudelaire's trial in 1857. Also see below Appendix, Baudelaire.

48 See above ch. IV.

49 Previously sadism and masochism in *Les Fleurs du mal* were discussed above in ch. IV, in *LP II*, pp. 81–5, 102–9 and *LP II*, Appendix, Baudelaire.

the poet's own indoctrination which, paradoxically, provokes a "constructive" sadist outburst of mock violence. The tripartite ironic discourse consists of two farcical crescendos unified by a hilarious reversal and framed by the contrasting pseudophilosophical prolog and a very brief epilog. A masochistic *pointe* punctuates the maniacal dialectic on Proudhon's doctrine of perfect equity and perfect remuneration of our work which, hopefully, will prevail in the blissful Proudhonian utopia. The controversial and, in today's terms, "politically incorrect" *Stück* (about 1865), starts with the narrator's ironic recollection of his youthful dedication to noble social ideals, a stage of life when he buried himself in the then fashionable gospels outlining the path to a commonwealth of free and equal men.[50] Like several other poems-in-prose in the collection, this causerie exemplifies a minor, usually provocative and paradoxical genre—eulogy of a negative quality.[51] It opens with would-be philosophical reflections on equality (1–15), followed by a flash of "crackpot" inspiration which overwhelms the narrator in front of a bar, where he sees an old beggar and hears his own "post-Socratic" inner voice (16–29). Without any warning, the narrator brutalizes the bum to show him the path to equality: his wicked assault forms a dramatic crescendo (30–47) which instantly provokes a violent retaliation (48–65). The lesson in political science finished, the bruised apostle of equality offers the beggar alms along with soothing assurance that now *they are finally equal* (70–3). The beggar gracefully accepts and promises the Baudelairean benefactor to spread the word among his peers, should they ever appeal to his charity (66–67).

To assess the comic impact of this macrostimulative discourse (763 words) I identified 77 farcical or ironic microstimuli numbered from 1 to

50 This poem-in-prose was included in the *Spleen de Paris* only posthumously in 1869; the editors transferred it from the collected works. Jacques Crépet, ed. of *O.C. de Ch. Baudelaire, Petits poëmes en prose* (Paris: Conard, 1926), pp. 344–8, indicates that the unpublished version of the text ended with a question, "Qu'en dis-tu, Citoyen Proudhon?" Crépet also mentions Baudelaire's letter to Sainte-Beuve describing Proudhon's lunch invitation to Baudelaire. Following the meal, Baudelaire picked up the tab but Proudhon did not allow him to do it, paid what he ordered and then had his guest pay his *equitable* share.

51 For example, of debt (Rabelais), folly (Erasmus), syphilis, war (Voltaire), revolution (Hugo), intoxication (Baudelaire), laziness, violence (A. France), hatred (Tzara, Sade), evil, filth, perversity (Sade, Lautréamont) and so on.

77 (table 6). The ratio 77/763 reflects very high density: approximately, every ten words form a discernible microstimulative feature. The table reproduces the annotated text, lists the comic stimuli and divides the two columns by a parallel graph which approximates the ups and downs of their fluctuating comic impact as I perceive and weigh it.

Neither Baudelaire, the eccentric champion of "l'art pour l'art," nor his comical storyteller were social altruists. Tenderizing the beggar's hide rather helped the whimsical sado-masochist narrator overcome his esthetic *taedium vitae*; it gave him the same malevolent satisfaction he had in dropping a flowerpot onto the window panes of the "evil glazier"[52] who had the nerve not to carry colored glass allowing his customers to see "la vie en beau." The beggar's surprise counterattack in the second crescendo forms a masochistic counterpoint to the outburst in the sadist crescendo. Similar fantasies broaden the range of the bizarre ecstasies invoked by the Baudelairean imperative "Enivrez-vous"[53]. The final terza of the *Spleen*'s versified "Epilog" also seems to support this speculation: "Je t'aime, ô capitale infâme, Courtisanes / Et bandits, tels souvent vous offrez des plaisirs / Que ne comprennent pas les vulgaires profanes."

Gems of black humor abound in Lautréamont's *Les Chants de Maldoror*, whose high topical intensities result from the artistic alliance of black farce, supernatural topics and bizarrerie stylistically transposed with sadistic irony and/or parody of Homeric similes and hyperboles.[54] Also rich in fresh clownish sadism is Alfred Jarry's soft pornography, *Messaline—Roman de l'ancienne Rome* (1901), *Le Surmâle* (1902), his poems and above all his juvenile burlesque *Ubu roi* whose first version, *Les Polonais,* was performed in 1889 and labelled "connerie" by one of Jarry's schoolmates and coauthors.[55]

Black humor is an essential component in the esthetics of the absurd: it blends with and amplifies the stimulative power of the ludicrous metaphysical forebodings and clownish characters common to Ionesco, Beckett,[56] Pinter, Boris Vian.

52 Ibid., IX "Le Mauvais vitrier".

53 See Bresky, Malik, "New Approaches to Literary Stimuli...Critical and Biocybernetic," *Texte* 3, 1984, pp. 203–21.

54 See ch. VII comments on bizarre stimuli and Lautréamont. See also *LP II*, pp. 40–1 and Appendix, p. 230.

55 See *LP II*, ch. II, pp. 42–3, n. 56 and Appendix, Jarry, below.

56 See *LP II*, p. 87 and below, ch. VII, comments on *Molloy*.

TABLE 6

Assommons les pauvres!	**Intensity** 1 2 3 4 5 6 7 8	**Identified stimuli; density**
[1]Pendant quinze jours je m'étais confiné dans ma chambre, et je m'étais entouré des livres à la mode dans ce temps-là (il y a seize ou dix-sept ans); je veux parler des livres où il est traité de l'art de rendre les peuples heureux, sages et riches, en vingt-quatre heures. J'avais donc[2] digéré, —avalé, veux-je dire,—toutes les élucubrations[3] de tous [4]ces entrepreneurs de bonheur public,—de ceux qui conseillent à tous les pauvres de se faire esclaves, et de ceux qui leur[5-6] persuadent qu'ils sont tous des rois détrônés.— On ne trouvera pas surprenant[7] que je fusse alors[8] dans un état d'esprit avoisinant le vertige ou la stupidité.	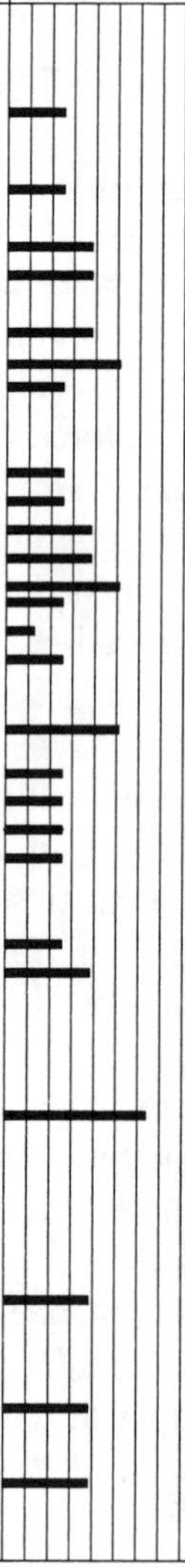	[1]Ironic scholarly zeal and ironic summation of sociological literature, advocating social reforms; [2]negative antithesis—did not digest, merely swallowed; [3]ironic mot juste referring to sterile theories; [4]ironic metaphor degrading the ideologists to quacks; [5-6]ironic antithesis and contradiction between the two "great" and absurd social reforms. [7]Litotes—[8]Suffering a theoretical overload, the would-be reformer is confused; dilemma—comic hyperbolic antithesis.
Il m'avait semblé seulement que je sentais, [9]confiné au fond de mon intellect, [10]le germe obscur [11]d'une idée supérieure [12]à toutes les formules de bonne femme dont j'avais récemment parcouru [13]le dictionnaire. Mais ce n'était que [14]l'idée d'une idée, quelque chose [15]d'infiniment vague.		[9]ironic ref. to mysterious intuitive depth; [10]ironic mot juste; [11]hyperbole—ingenious solution; [12]contemptuous metaphor—sterile discussions; [13]ironic ref. to pseudoscholarly encyclopedias; [14]ironic suspensful understatement; [15]suspenseful overstatement;
[16]Et je sortis avec une grande soif. Car le goût passioné des mauvaises lectures engendre un besoin proportionnel du grand air et des rafraîchissants. [17]Comme j'allais entrer dans un cabaret, [18]un mendiant me tendit son chapeau, avec un de [19]ces regards inoubliables qui culbuteraient les trônes, [20]si l'esprit remuait la matière, et [21]si l'oeil d'un magnétiseur faisait mûrir les raisins. En même temps, [22]j'entendis une voix qui chuchotait à mon oreille, une voix que je reconnus bien; c'était celle d'un bon Ange, ou d'un bon Démon, qui m'accompagne partout. [23]Puisque Socrate avait son bon Démon, pourquoi n'aurais-je pas mon bon Ange, et pourquoi n'aurais-je pas l'honneur, comme Socrate,[24] d'obtenirmon brevet de folie, [25]signé du subtil Létu et du bien-avisé Baillarger? Il existe cette [26]différence entre le Démon de Socrate et le mien, que [27]celui de Socrate ne se manifestait à lui que pour défendre, avertir, empêcher, et que le mien daigne conseiller, suggérer, persuader. [28]Ce pauvre Socrate n'avait qu'un Démon prohibiteur, le mien est un grand affirmateur, le mien est un Démon d'action, ou Démon de combat. [29]Or, sa voix me chuchotait ceci: "Celui-là seul est l'égal d'un autre, qui le prouve, et celui-là seul est digne de la liberté, qui sait la conquérir."		[16]comic degradation, maxim—inane theories call for a drink; [17]dramatic acceleration: reading philanthropist confined until now in his room, stands suddenly in front of the bar; [18, 19, 20, 21]a farcically distorted hyperbolic glimpse of the character stylized in the form of conditional aphoristic gradation; rhetorical allusion to illusory magic inherent in the art of provoking sympathy; [22]"Hellenist" supernatural being contacts the philanthropist; [23]Livresque comic parallel poet/Socrates [24-25]two mid-19th century illustrious psychiatrists, who studied available sources, concluded that Socrates was insane. Parallel poet/Socrates extended; [26]however parallel not total—negative antithesis; [27]comic antithesis describing two contrasting Demons a Hellenist discouraging Socrates, a modern encouraging poet; [28]ironic parallel gradation of the above antithesis. [29]Neither Crépet (O.C. de B., 1926) nor Pichois (Pléïade ed.) indicate the source of the Demon's radical libertarian principle. Challenge to the reader's memory and associative imagination.*

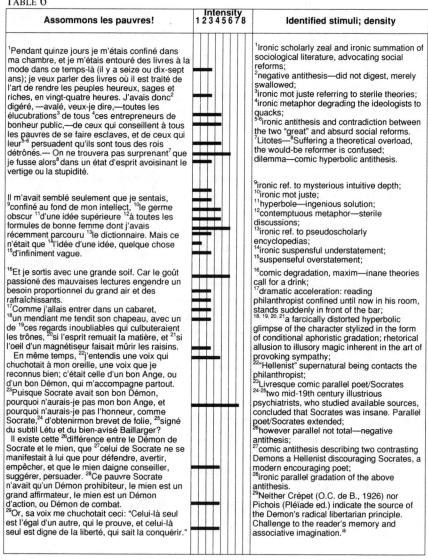

Continued on next page

* The maxims echoes some of the Sade's pre-Nietzschean axioms but it could even parody a Goethe's topos. (*Faust II*, Act 3, Schattiger Hain, ll. 5247-50, Euphorion's Romantic freedom plea: "Wollt ihr unerobert wohnen / Leicht bewaffnet rasch ins Feld. / Frauen werden Amazonen / Und ein jedes Kind ein Held / ." (If you want to free your land / Rush to battle sword in hand / Like Amazons all women strike / Each child fighting hero-like. My transl.)

TABLE 6 *(continued)*

Assommons les pauvres!	Intensity 1 2 3 4 5 6 7 8	Identified stimuli; density
[30]Immédiatement, je sautai sur mon mendiant. [31]D'un seul coup de point, je lui bouchai un oeil, qui devint, en une seconde, [32]gros comme une balle. [33]Je cassai un de mes ongles à lui briser deux dents; et [34]comme je ne me sentais pas assez fort, [35]étant né délicat et [36]m'étant peu exercé à la boxe, [37]pour assommer rapidement ce vieillard, je le [38]saisis d'une main par le collet de son habit, [39]de l'autre, je l'empoignai à la gorge, et [40]je me mis à lui secouer vigoureusement la tête contre un mur. [41]Je dois avouer que j'avais préalablement inspecté les environs d'un coup d'oeil, et que [42]j'avais vérifié que dans cette banlieue déserte, je me trouvais, pour un assez long temps, hors de la portée de tout agent de police.	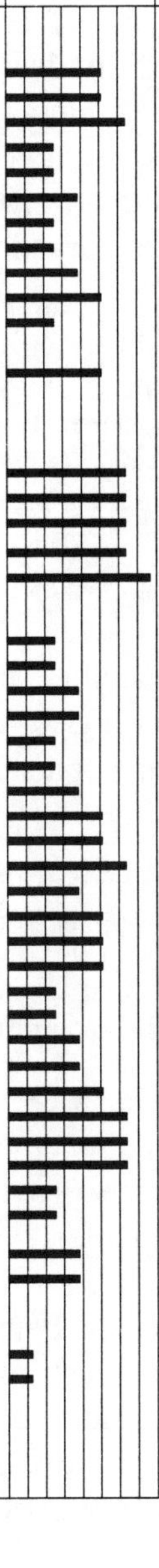	What the poor man needs is an opportunity to prove his status of a free man equal to all other human beings. [30]Baudelaire's bar-goer is now ready to offer him such a precious chance: his first violent blow marks the first crescendo consisting of gradation and contrasting with an ironic self-portrait of the fragile narrator attacker, who nevertheless has enough vigor to carry out his didactic charge. [30-33]gradation: black eye; phenomenal bruise, broken teeth; [34-36]the wimpy narrator's suspenseful ironic self-portrait; [37-40]farcical (sadist) assault resumed; triple gradation; [41-42]the above cowardly self-portrait extended; suspense;
Ayant ensuite, [43]par un coup de pied lancé dans le dos, assez énergique pour briser les omoplates, [44]terrassé ce [45]sexagénaire affaibli, je me [46]saisis d'une grosse branche d'arbre qui traînait à terre, et [47]je le battis avec l'énergie obstinée des cuisiniers qui veulement attendrir un beefsteak.		[43-47]mock violence continues: its clinical detail[(44)] hyperbole[(45)] ironic mot juste;[(46)] a thick branch used; comic simile first crescendo culminates: [(47)]didactic thrashing of the frail pauper with the zeal of a chef beating tough meat with a mallet.
Tout à coup, —[48]ô miracle! [49]ô jouissance du philosophe qui [50]vérifie l'excellence de sa théorie!—je vis cette [51]antique carcasse se [52]retourner, se [53]redresser avec [54]une énergie que je n'aurais jamais soupçonnée [55]dans une machine si singulièrement détraquée, et, avec un [56]regard de haine qui me parut de [57]bon augure, [58]le malandrin décrépit [59]se jeta sur moi, [60]me pocha les deux yeux, [61]me cassa quatre dents, et, avec la [62]même branche d'arbre, [63]me battit dru comme plâtre. —Par mon [64]énergique médication, je lui avais donc [65]rendu l'orgueil et la vie.		[48-50]hyperbolic gradation farcical reversal; [51]ironic derogatory metaphor; [52-53]minor gradation; [54]hyperbole; [55]ironic derogatory metaphor; [56]farcical challenge; [57]ironic mot juste; [58]hyperbolic "looter", name calling; [59]counterattack: second crescendo starts; [60-3]"malandrin" (brigand) retaliates with a truly Proudhonian sense of equity; [(61)]eye for eye; [(62)]tooth for tooth; [(63)]clubbing for clubbing with the same branch; [64]ironic mot juste; here ludicrous euphemism; [65]paradoxical "medicine" of the savior;
[66]Alors, je lui fis force signes pour lui faire comprendre que [67]je considérais la discussion comme finie, et me [68]relevant avec la satisfaction d'un [69]sophiste du Portique, je lui dis: [70]"Monsieur, [71]vous êtes mon égal! veuillez [72]me faire l'honneur de partager avec moi ma bourse; et souvenez-vous, [73]si vous êtes réellement philanthrope, qu'il faut [74]appliquer à tous vos confrères, quand ils vous demanderont l'aumône, la théorie que j'ai eu [75]la douleur d'essayer sur votre dos."		[66]archaism mot juste; [67]comic euphemism alluding to the free-for-all; [68]ironic "satisfaction" after the drubbing; [69]comic Hellenist simile; [70]contrasting change of tone "antique carcasse, malandrin," becomes "Monsieur" equal to his "savior"; [71]Proudhonian equity of human assets; [72]a shade of ironic doubt about the new status of the beggar implied; [73]ironic request, ironic euphemism; [74]"théorie", ironic euphemism; [75]painful testing theory was worth it;
[76]Il m'a bien juré qu'il avait compris ma théorie, et qu'il [77]obéirait à mes conseils.		[76]paradoxically ironic courtesy; [77]incredibly, civilized recognition of the "excellent theory".

Prévert's Surrealistic Formula for Regicide

In surrealist poetry, Jacques Prévert introduced a Marxist accent in the opening automatist discourse of his popular *Paroles.* The prose, entitled "Tentative description d'un dîner de têtes à Paris-France," unlike Baudelaire's salutary beggar-bashing, emits sinister threats to the bourgeois establishment. Prévert's *engagé* surrealism, which so charmed radical youth and the *engagé* literati of the cold-war era, tries to blame post-war capitalist politicians for starvation in China:

> Je plaisante, mais vous savez,...un rien suffit à changer le cours des choses. Un peu de fulmi-coton dans l'oreille d'un monarque malade et le monarque explose. La reine accourt à son chevet. Il n'y a pas de chevet. Il n'y a plus de palais... La reine sent sa raison sombrer. Pour la réconforter, un inconnu avec un bon sourire, lui donne le mauvais café. La reine en prend, la reine en meurt et les valets collent des étiquettes sur les bagages des enfants. L'homme au bon sourire revient, ouvre la plus grande malle, pousse les petits princes dedans, met le cadenas à la malle, la malle à la consigne et se retire en se frottant les mains.

To eliminate any misunderstanding the jovial mythologist of the proleterian revolution offers apologies for the "régicides" who find no King or Queen to murder and must seek eligible victims among commoners.

> Et quand je dis, Monsieur le Président, Mesdames, Messieurs, le Roi, la Reine, les petits princes, c'est pour envelopper les choses car on ne peut pas raisonnablement blâmer les régicides qui n'ont pas de roi sous la main, s'ils exercent parfois leurs dons dans leur entourage immédiat...parmi ceux qui pensent qu'une poignée de riz suffit à nourrir toute une famille de Chinois...

Updike's Gallows Humor

While contemplating the esthetics of "Conflicts" (particularly the mimesis of execution and of regicide), I was considering, as an example, an original integration of three discrepant subjects in a chapter of *The Coup* by John Updike.[57] It relates the botched beheading of a senile tribal King in the African country of Kush modelled after one of the Third World countries, perhaps Chad or Sudan. The clash between the (1) macabre and the (2) comic is esthetically enhanced by a high concentration of (3) bizarre mainly exotic features—(a) characters and

57 New York, Fawcett, ch. II, pp. 56–94.

their conflict and (b) the details of the setting's *couleur locale*. Both the macabre and the comical spring from the barbaric "neosocialist" execution. Updike's transposition reads like a feature by a columnist who knows how to let bizarre faraway savagery speak for itself. The burlesque contrast of the grisly decapitation is neither a Baudelairean effusion nor Prévert's automatist logorrhea with not too subtle Marxist undertones. *The Coup* strikes us as authentic reportage echoing the saga of Idi Amin's moronic terror.

Its truly modern exotic character is the young Hakim Félix Ellelloû, son of the black Muslim sergeant in the former French colony decolonized after the war. Despite his anti-Americanism, the promising young man receives a western education, graduates from a U.S. college and, prior to accepting a commission in his now sovereign native country, marries an American student. She becomes one of his four wives sanctioned by Islamic convention. The ambitious officer enters the political arena and (somewhat like Colonel Gadafi in Libya), preaches an ideologically absurd hodge-podge of Kush nationalism, Islamic fundamentalism and "scientific socialism." With the support of an opportunist clique he seizes power and becomes the Kush dictator. After the coup, his regime accuses the old figurehead King, the "miserable Edumu formerly known as Lord of Wanji," of being a reactionary enemy of scientific socialism and condemns him to death. Standing on the platform the moribund monarch challenges the colonel to step forward and behead him, King Edumu, with his own hand. This proves a difficult task since the new regime had outlawed the reliable guillotine favored by the prewar French justice as a politically incorrect "savoring of neocolonialism." Instead, to symbolize the return to native Islamic traditions, the Kush political reformers resurrect a dull historical scimitar which, until the spectacular regicide, had been on display in the "People's Museum of Imperialist Atrocities." Unwilling to lose face, the dictator grasps the archaic sword and after several abortive blows he finally manages to chop off the head of the antimarxist "Lord of Wanji". Whether artistically over- or understating routine politics in the decolonized, newly baked "democracies," Updike's vision of contemporary Africa is a timely satire *à la* Voltaire.

Grave Irony in Wilde's and Mérimée's Prose

Irony of fate does not make the reader laugh unless the author masks a grave subject, such as murder, by framing it in a comedy-like discourse: in "Lord Arthur Saville's Crime,"[58] the murder committed by Oscar Wilde's hero reads more like an anecdotal *pointe* dictated by the most cooperative irony of fate. At an upper-crust party Lord Arthur is introduced to a fashionable chiromantist, Mr. Podgers. When he examines the aristocrat's hand, his face becomes "a white mask of horror." Later, Lord Arthur has his palm analyzed more thoroughly (fee 100 guineas) in Mr. Podgers office. The nonchalant and happily engaged client is warned that he will live happily ever after only if he commits a murder before his marriage. With a Viking determination to fulfil his destiny, the Victorian playboy first plans to poison his frail aging aunt, Lady Clem. Unfortunately, she dies of natural causes without consuming the poisoned capsule which her nephew had bought for her and which she agreed to test along with her other remedies. The frustrated nobleman buys an explosive clock from Russian nihilists and offers it as a gift to his old uncle, Dean of Chichester. The clock merely explodes on the mantlepiece without killing or even hurting anyone. Lord Arthur is depressed and his fiancée Sybil Merton grows nervous because Arthur continues to postpone their wedding.

One night, the desperate hero is walking along the Thames Embankment when he sees a "man leaning over the parapet."[59] Recognizing his high-priced palmist, he grabs him by the legs and throws him in the river. After the press reports Mr. Podgers' "suicide," Lord Arthur, having bravely complied with his preordained fate, finally gets married and becomes a happy husband and a devoted father. The whimsical tone of Wilde's discourse dilutes the crime's ironic gravity but the tale's plot (seen apart from its backdrop of elegant, cheerfully decadent frivolity) can serve as a model of genres which stimulate readers fond of black humor and grave macro-irony. Thanks to Wilde's stylistic skill, his comic material is arranged, like Gogol's, with a flair for stimulative density, economical gradation and climax.

Although gravely ironic details can take the form of simple rhetorical dissimulation,[60] the analysis of Wilde's intrigue suggests that grave irony is more evident on the macro- rather than micro-stimulative level. It gradually emerges as the macro-ironic plot unfolds, especially, when its

58 "Lord Arthur Saville's Crime", *The Works of Oscar Wilde* (London: Collins, n.d.), p. 266 and 294. Like Lord Arthur, Wilde's best-known protagonist, Dorian Gray, commits a gravely ironic murder; see ch. VII, "Huysmans' and Wilde's eccentrics."

59 Ibid., p. 294.

60 See the comments below on "Tamango".

reversals and final outcome go against the characters' often unethical schemes or the tragic heroes' idealistic expectations. The previous illustrations of allegorical genres[61] show that literary macrotexts often have two or several connotative levels. The primary level conveys the conventional meaning normally signified by the sum of signifiers applied in the given part of discourse; on the second symbolic level, the same signifiers may allude to alternate symbolical or macro-ironic content which increases the esthetical intensity of the primary level.

Mérimée's "Tamango"

In his satirical short story "Tamango," Prosper Mérimée[62] christened his fictional slave-trader captain Ledoux (Sweet, Mild) and his devilishly functional slave ship *Espérance*; we can see such name choices as minimal though recurrent rhetorical doses (monorems) of sadistic irony. As the dramatic intrigue unwinds, each repetition of the character's or his ship's name within the successive microcontextual sequences acquires a renewed microstimulative value as conditioned by the repetition's integration and timing within its changing continuity. Within the macrotext such micro-stimulative atoms of irony nonetheless enhance the overall intensity of the macrostimulative grave irony which, of course, is the main esthetic factor in the tale's dramatic gradations. The major twists which sardonic fate has in store for Mérimée's clashing characters can be summarized in the proverbial rule of thumb—he who mischief hatches mischief catches.

Ledoux' slave supplier is the fearless African warrior Tamango who brings 190 enslaved countrymen to the market. The two trading partners consume a great deal of liquor during their protracted bargaining. The more Ledoux drinks, the more tight-fisted he becomes—the slaves are no longer what they used to be; nowadays the market only offers degenerate and unsellable weaklings. The more the seller drinks, the lower his price. Finally, Ledoux trades inferior cotton fabrics, gunpowder, flint stones, guns, three barrels and twenty bottles of brandy for all slaves except for a few frail looking wretches. In spite of the incredible discount Tamango offers Ledoux to make him buy the remaining captives, the Frenchman rejects them, mainly because he cannot overcrowd his fully loaded ship. Impulsively, Tamango starts shooting the old slaves.

61 *LP II*, ch. IV "Macrorhetoric," pp. 115–39.

62 *Op. cit.*, *LP I*, p. 145, n. 21 and pp. 149–50. For the readers' convenience the key passages of "Tamango" are also reproduced in this vol.'s Appendix, Mérimée.

Trying to stop her drunken husband from thus killing a native sorcerer, one of Tamango's two wives, Ayché, prevents him from aiming and discharging the gun. In a fit of rage, he offers her to Ledoux who gracefully accepts: "I'll see where I can put her," he ironically assures his trading partner. To avoid further bloodshed, the interpreter offers Tamango a cardboard tobacco box in payment for the unsold slaves and sets them free. Sobering up, Tamango realizes how absurdly he punished and, at the same time lost, his attractive Ayché. He runs through the jungle to catch up with the *Espérance* drifting downstream toward the Senegal shore. He intercepts the vessel and tries to buy back his spouse. Ledoux invites him aboard to discuss the deal. At that point the crew informs him that several slaves crammed below deck have died. The scene is now set for the first climactic reversal. From the moment he saw Tamango, Ledoux knew that the Herculean warrior would be worth 1,000 ducats at Martinique. Captain and crew waste no time in overpowering the slave trader, and put him in chains among the slaves he had sold the Frenchman. Tamango's beautiful wife becomes, for the duration of the cruise, Ledoux' concubine. "What the hell," the captain quips, "the slaves he sold me will laugh. For once at least, they will see that there is a Providence."

In the next grave reversal it is Ledoux' turn to "catch mischief." The exotic romance in the captain's cabin will be cut short. In spite of Tamango's betrayal, Ayché remains loyal to him and sneaks him a file. Tamango precuts his handcuffs and during the slaves' casually supervised recreation period on deck, he breaks them, attacks Ledoux and, like an angry lion, bites through his jugular. After the liberated black mutineers kill the white crew, noone knows how to navigate, and all those first enslaved and then liberated by Tamango die. The vessel's mast breaks and the *Espérance* drifts aimlessly for days. Ayché dies but Tamango survives. A British frigate incidentally notices the wreck and brings the black survivor to Kingston, Jamaica where the local planters would like to hang him as a black mutineer. The British Governor, however, argues that Tamango acted in self-defense and (ironically) after all, his victims had only been Frenchmen. He sets Tamango free, "that is to say," concludes Mérimée "he [is] made a civil servant" earning six "nickels" ("six sous") a day as the 75th Regiment cymballer. The exotic musician's anticlimactic death is not caused by his incurable addiction to rum but by pneumonia.

I discuss "Tamango" in this chapter because its plot conclusively exemplifies progressive macro-ironic gradation and growing dramatic impact, and because the observations on Mérimée's brand of irony conveniently tie in with my comments on macrorhetorical practices.[63] Naturally, in this context it is the informative factor of poetic ambiguities and grave satire which so often discloses the universal humanistic teleology. For example, the Rabelaisian (positive) imperative *Trinch!*[64] allegorically encapsulates the polyhistor's creed—drink what life offers, its joy and knowledge, whereas Voltaire's satire of war ironically approves (i.e., satirically condemns) its absurdity; Maupassant's grave and sublime irony in "Boule de Suif" attacks the hypocrisy of French "patriots." Further, I discuss Mérimée's post-Voltairean crusade as a powerful example of grave irony because its macrostimulative topic, illegal slave trade, haunted our humanistic conscience throughout the 19th century, long after the belated and only gradual outlawing and effective prevention of the shameful practice.[65] However, this critical emphasis should by no means be interpreted as a claim that the macro-ironic density and intensity, enhanced by many farcical details, constitute the only "key" to Tamango's critical appraisal. In addition to the satire and the impressive style which economically unifies Mérimée's characters, their struggles, victories and tragedies into a credible dramatic plot, the overall high density and intensity evident in every paragraph, dialog, sentence, is achieved by seamless concentration of epical riches drawn from almost all major sources of stimulative content: black farce (no pun intended); conflict between two villains—one white, one black; breach of basic human laws; melodramatic violence at the exotic slave market; punishment of the charitable black queen; her

63 *LP II*, ch. IV (pp. 115–39), which would have been incomplete had I ignored the stylistic side of the macro-ironic correlate so common in symbolic macrotexts.

64 Vème livre, ch. XLV, p. 167, ed. cit.

65 Denmark was the first European power to abolish the slave trade in 1802; England followed in 1807; the U.S. in 1808, Sweden in 1813 and France during Napoleon's 100 days, later confirmed by international agreements at the 1814 Congress of Vienna and proclaimed law in 1818. The Franco-British enforcement in international waters was sanctioned only in 1831, two years after the publication of "Tamango" in November 1829. Long after, the slave trade remained an urgent and timely subject as countries slowly abolished slavery itself. Great Britain freed the slaves throughout its colonies in 1838; France in 1848, and the U.S. abolished slavery by constitutional amendment after the Civil War in 1865. Brazil first outlawed slavery in 1871, but all existing slaves were legally obliged to serve their owner for life; children of slave mothers born after 1871 became free only at the age of 21; total abolition came in 1888.

paradoxical loyalty to her ruthless husband; the warrior's deadly biting of the captain's jugular; the triumph and disaster of mutineering victims; glimpses of Aychée's love life; two contrasting settings—African and naval; the slaves' superstition, their fear of mumbo jumbo; *Espérance* first sailing, then drifting; finally, Tamango's confrontation with British justice in Jamaica which reflects the international hesitation if not impotence to end the lucrative criminal business.[66]

Sublime Irony in Maupassant's Short Stories

The physiology of our rational, sentic, moral make-up spontaneously distinguishes the friendly or hostile levity or gravity, tender tone or detached sympathy, contempt, intimidation, which motivate a broad range of ironic communications and which control their rhetorical tone. The discernment of these informative goals and tones enables us to divide and classify the ironic statements: sublime irony, its partially or totally dissimulative rhetoric, its tenor which reflects, for instance, deep compassion, motherly devotion, or sincere respect. In my earlier analysis of "Boule de Suif"[67] I focus on the esthetic overlapping of allegorical and macro-ironic techniques and also cite Flaubert's letter anticipating the immortality of Maupassant's then unpublished text: "This story will survive...your bourgeois, what a gallery of portraits. Not a single miss. The poor girl who weeps while [the démoc] sings the *Marseillaise*, sublime."[68]

The story's ironic denouement, which Flaubert's compliment consecrates as "sublime," strikes me as having more than one ironic level: contempt (grave irony) targeted against the cowardly "bourgeois" and compassion (sublime irony) reserved for the heart-broken prostitute. The sardonic "démoc" Cornudet plagues the guilty conscience of his fellow travellers by repeated incantation of one of the French anthem's stanzas, which begins "Amour sacré de la patrie," (the sacred love of our fatherland). If we change the position of the epithet "sacré" we also change its connotation: "[Le] sacré amour de la patrie" means the damned love of fatherland. Most Francophones, hearing Cornudet's refrain once too many times, could not help thinking of the latter

66 As a major epical stimulus, the slave trade attracted, e.g., Herman Melville, "Benito Cereno", 1856. More recently, Geoffrey Unsworth treated the British slave trade in *Sacred Hunger*.

67 See *LP II*, pp. 115–8 and abridged text, pp. 232–34.

68 Ibid., my transl.

connotation regardless of whether the adjective's position is reversed. Thus the long ambiguous solo is both grave and sublime: it covers with contempt the hypocritical patriots and weeps with their crucified victim and savior, the poor girl symbolizing the raped France. "Sublime" indeed.

Sublime also pervades another very different poetization of a prostitute. In fact, Maupassant's "La Maison Tellier" is a discreet apotheosis of the whole brothel. In that *gauloiserie*, sublime irony springs neither from compassion nor disdain. It is Maupassant's *esprit* which transposes the mysterious happiness surrounding Madame Tellier and five *filles de joie* who, in the naturalistic style, embody not only the Menades and *das ewig Weibliche* but even the divine. Prior to leaving their establishment at Fécamp, they place a notice on the porch informing the Saturday regulars that their favorite house of joy is "closed due to the first communion." Taking this precaution Madame and her staff travel by train to a nearby farming community to attend the first communion of Madame Tellier's niece, Constance Rivet. When the fancily dressed, vivacious team appears in the church, they bring in an aura of transcendental euphoria. The enthusiastic priest opens his sermon by calling their presence an act of divine intervention. "Mes chers frères, mes chères soeurs,...vous venez de me donner la plus grande joie de ma vie. J'ai *senti Dieu qui descendait sur nous...Il est venu*, il était là, présent, qui emplissait vos âmes, faisait déborder vos yeux." The tale's ironic intensity grows with every ambiguous word of the sermon: "*Un miracle* s'est fait parmi nous, un *vrai*, un *grand*, un *sublime miracle*. Pendant que Jésus-Christ *pénétrait* pour la première fois dans *le corps de ces petits*, le Saint-Esprit *l'oiseau céleste*, le souffle de Dieu,...s'est emparé de vous..." Once more the priest addresses the city ladies, leaving no doubt who attracted God himself to the village church:

> Merci surtout à vous, *mes chères soeurs*, qui êtes venues de si loin...*dont la piété* si vive a été pour tous un *salutaire exemple*. Vous êtes l'édification de ma paroisse; *votre émotion a échauffé les coeurs*; *sans vous*, peut-être, *ce grand jour n'aurait pas* eu ce *caractère* vraiment *divin*. Il suffit parfois d'une seule *brebis d'élite pour décider le Seigneur à descendre* sur le troupeau.[69]

Never again will Constance feel heavenly love so close. Her first communion day will be the highlight of her life. Only the professional love-makers who, tears in their eyes, watch Constance for the first time

69 *La Maison Tellier* (Paris: Albin, 1969), pp. 41–2. My italics.

receiving the symbolical body of God's son, can transform the Christian ceremony into sublime *rendez-vous* of divine and sensual love. An orthodox Christian might consider Maupassant's mimesis of the rite as blasphemous satire rather than sublime irony. But then Maupassant is the Eros worshipper who at the age of 14, no longer believed in the omnipotent, omnipresent and omniscient Christian God. His concept of cosmic love is pagan.[70]

Ronsard's Melancholy Smile

The intensity and density of comic microstimuli should harmonize with the macrostimulative function of the genre. Humor is a primary stimulus in comedies, satires or parodies but in lyrical or reflexive poetry or in, for instance, historical novels, in biographical or psychological fiction, etc., it merely is an ingredient which may give rise to minor comic ripples. In such texts, too much humor would be esthetically detrimental. Ronsard's best known sonnet "Pour Hélène" is not comic; its subdued teasing tone merely underscores the melancholy lover's persuasion. His sybaritic argument elicits no laughter, just a pensive smile:

> When you grow old, one night by candlelight you may read my lines and say aloud—"when I was lovely, Ronsard glorified me in his rhymes." By then, you'll have no dozing maid whom the mere sound of my name would awake...I'll be underground, "fantôme sans os / Par les ombres myrteux je prendrai mon repos..." let's not miss our chance, Hélène / Let us enjoy our life today with all the roses it offers.[71]

Madame Nozière's Ironic Aphorism

As a preschooler, Pierre Nozière is enchanted by the triumphs of faith and by the glory of illustrious hermits immortalized in *The Life of the Saints*[72] which his pious mother reads to him. After one of his walks to the Botanical Garden, little Pierre speculates that there must be plenty of fruit and roots in this park to feed a young holy man. One morning he reveals his childish ambition to settle in the Botanical Garden, become a famous hermit and have calling cards printed indicating that he is a saint

70 See ch. VI, "French pagans and Roman Catholics." See also D. Bresky "Eros—Maupassant's only God", *Eroticism in French Literature*, pp. 143–7.

71 See comments on the rose metaphor, *LP II*, pp. 92–7. (My transl.)

72 A. France's fictionalized self-portrait as a precocious innocent child; *La Vie des Saints* by Father Ribadeneira, Madrid 1599–1610.

from the calendar. His mother cools her son's religious zeal with a tender ironic paradox: "Mon petit garçon a perdu raison à l'âge où l'on n'en a pas encore."[73] The maternal wit is not hilarious but it is a sublime spark of French *esprit* responding to the child's sublime naïveté.

Most of my examples of comic gradations and of high or low comic intensity demonstrate once again that stimulative humor consists rarely of pure "inorganic" ludicrousness; its originality and its impact are usually correlated to its "organic" fusion with other types of stimuli such as conflicts, erotic or supernatural subjects and with effective stylistic techniques:[74] Gogol's farcical and ironic discourse would be less comic if Chichikov broke no law and Sobakevich were a less eloquent pessimist. Likewise, the hasty plucking of the drunken geese would be less ridiculous, if Brautigan's granny were not a resourceful bootlegger.

The merriment, which we savor in life or which the media report or the artists transpose or invent to stimulate us, ranges from anaemic to raucous. We greet "good" jokes with unfeigned laughter and respond to bad jokes with a polite smile or funereal silence. The abstract cause of both effective and ineffective humor may be a contrastful incongruity generally identifiable as a (more or less) surprising, confusing *quid pro quo*, eccentric or absurd behavior and so on. The same applies to verbal humor: one dissimulative metaphor or hyperbole may be stale and corny, another fresh and witty. Naturally, our individual criteria vary. Well-read recipients with an undeniable sense of humor and broad frame of reference expect originality, freshness and high intensity, whereas observers/readers with a medium sense of humor and narrower cultural horizons may appreciate comic *schmaltz* in life, in the media and in the literature they favor.

Humor Down Under, Stale and Fresh

While writing this chapter and pondering the selection of suitable texts to illustrate comic impact, I wrote my friends scattered all over the world to ask what they personally considered the funniest piece of writing they had ever read. One of them, residing at Hawthorn, Victoria, immedately dispatched a richly illustrated magazine article on what she

73 *O.C.*, III, p. 243. "My little boy has lost his reason at an age one doesn't yet have any." My transl.

74 See *LP II* comments on Rabelais, p. 38; Lautréamont, p. 41; Jarry, p. 43; Zola, pp. 87–90; etc.

characterized as typical Aussie humor.[75] Its author, Peter Luck, does not theorize, he is an experienced *homme de métier*, TV producer and author. Yet illustrative jokes certainly reflect his flair for original Australian grassroots humor as well as for what represents below and above average comic quality. Luck selects his comic material with a sharp eye for its high impact (when fresh) and its pathetically low charge (when trite). If we ignore the unexplored aboriginal culture of humor, the mythology of Australian laughter is not distant, it goes back only about six generations. Many among the early immigrants were convicts shipped by the British Empire to settle in the thinly populated colony. Today, the drollery popular at the turn of the 18th century is as hilarious "as a hit over the head with a stocking full of diarrhoea", Luck says and, apologetically, hastens to explain that his rhetorical petard is a "'50's metaphor that [today] is itself decidedly creaky." A two-centuries-old post-Shakespearean [Hamlet] *quid pro quo*, which allegedly made "the blokes on the Argyl Cut chain gang clutch their sides," recalls a letter which a veteran lag is ordered to hand over to the magistrate. The jailbird knows that he will be lashed as soon as the letter is opened. To avoid this he persuades a naive lad to pass over the "mail" instead of him. As expected the duped volunteer is tied and flogged. An irrefutably pitiable "classic." Luck's higher rated humor includes a Hawthorn graffito, a preliterary comic genre I failed to discuss: "What would you do if Christ came to Hawthorn?" the vicar asks his congregation in an open letter pinned on the church noticeboard. One of his faithful jotted underneath: "Put him at centre-forward and shift…Hudson to the wing." This grassroots wisecrack sufficiently illustrates that the excitive potential grows due to (1) the overlap of two different stimuli—(a) the miracle alluded to in the theologian's anachronistic question and (b) an anonymous churchgoer's reply; (2) facetious riposte putting in ironic perspective the clergyman's metaphysics; (3) anachronistic humanization of the son of God by recruiting him for the Hawthorn soccer team rather than what the vicar expects; (4) the undeniably Aussi *couleur locale*; (5) laconic syntax of the theological dialog.

In the climactic finale of his entertaining piece, the fifth generation Australian journalist tells a joke which, in his eyes, best exemplifies the genuine, the homespun, the classic "gaudium" valued by Aussies whose sense of down-to-earth humor crystallized on the farms and vast ranches, and pervaded the optimism of a youthful nation. The anecdote relates

75 Peter Luck, "Classic Australian Laughs," *Good Weekend*, Jan. 29, 1994, pp. 10–14.

slangy exchange among three guests invited to a "jackaroo" wedding. As a latecomer parks his "ute", a departing guest warns him: "Mate, you'd better not come in...the booze has run out and the best man's stuffed the bride." "By cripes," he says, "you're right—I'd better be orf." But before he can take off, another guest asks him: "Where ya goin', mate?"..."I've just heard what's happened," he answers. "I'm shootin' through." "No, no," urges the man, "she'll be apples. There's another keg on the way...and the best man's apologised."

Like Steinbeck's anecdote, the Australian rural wedding joke exemplifies a universal, earthy humor valued in all eras by fun-lovers ranging from uneducated folk to cultivated connoisseurs.

Earthy Humor Goes On—and On

Generally, classical tradition infused refinement and subtlety into theatrical comedy and satirical genres. Masters such as Molière, La Fontaine, Perrault, Montesquieu, Voltaire, Anatole France, etc., more or less adopted Boileau's ideology of restraint and *bon goût* (though not the delicate affectations of *bel esprit* idolized in the *précieux* salons). Like Boileau, they rejected excesses of Rabelaisian vulgarity but, like Rabelais, they never eliminated the spice of preclassical *gauloiserie* from their humor.

The exclusive precursor of the so-called Rabelaisian humor is not Rabelais himself. Centuries before his *Pantagruel* (1533), many generations of anonymous *jongleurs* and *raconteurs* kept broadening the reservoirs of ribald yarns. In addition, aristocrats known to literary historians co-authored *Les Cent Nouvelles Nouvelles* (1455), a French imitation of *The Decameron* (approx. 1350–5). To reveal what made the refined noblemen laugh, let us pass the word to "Monseigneur [Antoine] de la Salle, premier maistre d'hostel de Monseigneur le Duc" (Philippe le Bon of Burgundy, 1396–1467). Courtiers like him used to top the ducal menus with anecdotes appealing to Philippe's sense of humor. Monsieur de la Salle, who contributed the 50th novella, exploited the now familiar bed-shortage gimmick. His plot, which in 1455 may have been less stale than it is today, invents a young antihero who leaves his native Lannoys to knock about the world. Since no one had heard from him in ten years, everyone believes that he is dead. When he suddenly returns, his mother, father and grandmother hug him and kiss him endlessly and, to celebrate the reunion, they throw an opulent feast. When it is time to go to bed, that is, to the only two beds in the lad's paternal home, he has to join his granny. Without knowing what came over him, “il monta dessus.” When she asks him , “et que veulz tu faire?” he replies, “Ne vous chaille...ne dictes mot.” (“Don’t worry and not a word.”) Realizing what favor her grandson has in mind, the matriarch calls for help. The boy’s father, shocked by this incestuous harassment and “l’inhumanite de son filz,” gets so excited and angry, “tres courroussie et mal meu,” that he threatens to kill him—“dit qu’il l’occira.” As the randy offspring flees his newfound family nest, the father hastily assures his elderly mother, “je vous vengeray bien” and then dashes off after the sexual offender. Catching up with the fugitive at nearby Laon, “il tire bonne dague [dagger]” ready to cut the son’s throat. When passersby ask what he did to deserve such severe paternal punishment, the son replies: “Not much. [The Father] is entirely wrong. He wishes me the worst—“pour une pouvre foiz que j’ay voulu ronciner [arch. hump, jump] sa mere. Il a roncine [he had humped] la mienne plus de cinq cent foiz et je n’en parlay oncques ung seul mot!”[76] This subcultural slapstick not only illustrates what was a welcome hit at the medieval markets and at the ducal tables. Above all, it confirms Victor Hugo’s normative oracle cited in *Le Petit Robert*: “Le peuple a besoin de rire, les rois aussi. Il faut aux carrefours le baladin; il faut aux louvres (palais) le bouffon.” (Common people want to laugh and so do Kings—there must be jokers at the crossroads and jesters in the royal chambers.)

* * *

76 *Les Cent Nouvelles Nouvelles*, intro. Franklin Sweetser (Genève: Droz, 1966), pp. 324–26.

VI

COSMIC POWERS: GODS AND DEVILS

> "For I have seen God face to face and my life is preserved..."
> "No man hath seen God any time. "[1]

The Lure of the Supernatural. Supernatural Stimuli; their Range and Kinds. God of "Genesis," The Christian Trinity and the Greek Gods. *Deus ex machina.* Dante's Devil and God. Jupiter in *Amphitryon*: From Plautus to Giraudoux. Goethe's God and Mephistopheles. Dostoyevsky: Battlefield of God and the Devil. Thomas Mann—Adrian Leverkühn's *Illuminatio.* Jean-Christophe's Mystical Visions of the Creator. Anatole France's Olympians. French Crypto-Pagans and Roman Catholics. Hermann Hesse's *Siddhartha.* Jill's Psychedelic Vision of God; Updike's Theologians.

The Lure of the Supernatural

After ten years of solitary meditation in the mountains, the hermit Zarathustra descended among the people and announced that God is dead and that *Übermensch* would replace him.[2] He offered, however, no proof that God really "lived" prior to his alleged death. This could be one of many other reasons why his neo-atheist tidings have not been universally accepted and perhaps also why, in 1954, Samuel Beckett's Vladimir and Estragon were still *Waiting for Godot* on so many prestigious stages of the world.[3]

1 "Genesis," XXXII, 30 and "St. John," I, 18.

2 Fredrich Nietzche, *Also Sprach Zarathustra*, 1883–5. His *Übermensch* is the evolutionary successor of *homo sapiens* and the cosmic link between God and Man. Zarathustra announces that God's love of Mankind killed him.

3 See ch. II, citation and n. 9; also see below ch. VIII, "Experimental bizarrerie: Beckett".

Today, according to a *Time* poll, 69% of Americans still "believe in angels"; 49% of those polled "believe in the existence of fallen angels or devils" and 46% trust that they have their own guardian angel. Only 7% are convinced that any supernatural or divine herald is a sheer "figment of the imagination."

Billy Graham's work of theological scholarship, *Angels: God's Secret Agents*, which was a best-seller in 1975 (2.6 million copies),[4] provides no scientific evidence of God's or His agents' existence but the book sales certainly reflect reader interest in biblical metaphysics. Works like Graham's study, along with the statistics above, generally support E.T.A. Hoffmann's (1776–1822) claim that "unchanging human nature is such that belief in the miraculous and supernatural always outweighs reason."[5] Even skeptics do not necessarily argue with Hoffmann's dictum: the neo-Epicurean sage, Anatole France, is drawn to supernatural topics for their esthetic impact. In one of his critical *feuilletons*, he quotes Baron Gleichen who claims that we all have an inborn "penchant" for the marvellous: "My special taste for what is impossible, my restless skepticism, my contempt for what we know and my respect for what is unknown to us inspire my excursions in the realm of imagination," the baron says and adds: "None of my travels has ever given me so much pleasure." France confesses that he shares the Baron's inclination. Like him France wants to "be amused;" he trusts that "there is no happiness without some illusion." Whether a fictional representation of a supernatural phenomenon, whether its parody or transposition of an illusion, such topics relieve the boredom of normalcy. "We no longer believe in the devilish tricks" like the medieval monks who, throughout the Middle ages, conjured endless sorceries. "They watched simple,

4 *Time Magazine*, December 27, 1993, "Angels Among Us," pp. 46–53 and the box "Sympathy for the Devil," pp. 48–51.

5 *The Tales of Hoffmann*, transl. Michael Bullock (New York: F. Ungar, 1968), "Mademoiselle de Scudéry," p. 47. His empiricism concurs with David Hume's (1711–76) observation on "the usual propensity of mankind towards the marvellous" and with J.-J. Rousseau's "L'amour du merveilleux si naturel au coeur humain." Historical figures such as Gilles de Rais, Emperor Rudolph II (Hapsburg), Albrecht Waldstein, statesman cardinal Richelieu, Louis XIV often consulted astrologers to make sure that the timing of their crucial actions complied with the optimal constellation of the stars. Among modern celebrities, for instance, the late Adolf Hitler, First Lady Nancy Reagan or Princess Diana imitated their example. The Secretary for Foreign Affairs in Neville Chamberlain's cabinet, Lord Halifax, as well as the Canadian Prime Minister Mackenzie King were rumored to practise spiritualism in hopes of communicating with the spirits of the deceased.

naive miracles which, at least, broke the deadly monotony of their life."[6] A "magic agent" figures among the essential epical "functions" which V. Propp detected in the structure of the Russian fairy tale.[7] Regardless whether we fall in the category of the believers or skeptics, we will always be fascinated by gods, devils, angels, Cyclops, seven-league boots, ogres, witches, time machines, Shangri-las, Dr. Jekylls, Dorian Grays, and Kafkaesque beetles; they are eternal esthetic magnets which have one common denominator: each of them breaks at least one natural law or challenges our empirical experience, reason or common sense. On one side, such subjects nourish credulous imagination, on the other they pique the fantasy of the skeptics.Today empirical humanistic arguments and criteria of supernatural esthetica have to be updated. Modern neurology is beginning to identify the neurological correlates of Man's metaphysical sensations. Michael Persinger stimulates specific cerebral areas by exposing them to "a weak but complex magnetic field" and thus elicits mystical states of mind in his experimental subjects. Reporter Michael Valpy, who summarizes in lay terms Persinger's experiments, suggests that "God lives somewhere in the temporal and parietal lobes."[8]

The readers with a broad or limited intellectual, spiritual and educational backgrounds, wise adults or immature adolescents respond to identical supernatural stimuli according to their individual outlooks. The same fictitious information may provoke fear, amused amazement, tolerant irony or even intolerant mockery depending who perceives it. The grandchild listening to the tale of the brutal Ogre who plans to cut the throats of the Petit Poucet and his brothers, temporarily holds its breath and then perhaps feels relief when, in the darkness of night, the duped freak murders his own seven daughters instead of the seven boys destined to be roasted and eaten the next day. The grandfather who reads his illiterate grandchild Perrault's fairy tale obviously responds differently to its content.

Supernatural Stimuli; their Range and Kinds

Scholarly criteria which social scientists and humanists apply to the immense bulk of fictional "supernaturalia" are dictated by the individual

6 *O.C. VI*, *La vie littéraire*, "L'Hypnotisme dans la littérature—Marfa," pp. 115–16, my transl. See also *The Art of Anatole France*, p. 179.

7 See ch. II, nn. 26–30.

8 *The Globe and Mail* , August 25, 2001, "Science Neurotheology—Is God All in Our Heads?" P. F 7.

disciplinary or interdisciplinary approaches to this very broad subject. The historians describe distinct creeds worshipping heterogeneous supreme beings (Greco-Roman, Judaic, Christian, Oriental, etc.), their mythology, chronological evolution ranging from the prehistorical genesis to the cults' historical decline. In *History of Witchcraft and Demonology* (1926), Montague Summers offers practical reasons why, in a single study, a scholar like him cannot branch in all directions and get drowned in available material, for example, in ".....hungaism among the Maoris...the Bersekit of Jaland...or Siberian Shamanism [or in] negro voodoism. . ." Even his impressive bibliography (approx. 1,100 titles) covers mainly the Christian tradition intertwined with the surviving remnants of Occidental paganism.

H.E. Wedeck framed his *Dictionary of Magic* in a slender alphabetically arranged encyclopedia. Although his bibliography is much more limited than that of Summers, his *Dictionary* also covers concepts pertaining to other than Judeo-Christian cultures. One logical way to systematize supernatural subjects, other than historically or alphabetically, could be according to the specific natural laws they break in literary narratives—for instance, natural life expectancy contradicted by immortality or time itself suspended.

Neither the alleged omnipotent creator, nor Greek gods, nor angels, nor Adam's daughters from his first marriage with Lillith (daughters alluded to in the Talmud and referred to in fantastic texts as sylphs or Salamanders), are subject to death; nor is the Jew Ahasverus condemned by the Christian Trinity (rather than by Jehovah) to ramble endlessly through eternity. Sisyphus' never-ending struggle with the treacherous boulder in Hades is a "posthumous life-like existence" of the mythical rebel against death, a pathetic immortality *à rebours*. Even Achilles' conditional invulnerability (except for his delicate heel) can be seen as "limited immortality". As a result of fairy tale sorcery the Sleeping Beauty and her paternal court fall asleep, stop aging and wait in a centennial limbo for a prince of a yet unborn generation to resurrect them and marry the 100+ year-old bride who, nevertheless does not look her advanced age due to a fabulous suspension of time. The quasi miraculous *longevity* in Aldous Huxley's science-fiction novel *After Many a Summer* is even more impressive than that of the Sleeping Beauty. This tale chronicles the protracted life of a 17th century aristocrat who discovers that by eating the same diet as the long-lived carp in his ponds, he will fantastically yet naturally prolong his own life: the nobleman consumes the same rotting food his fish feed on and lives 300 years to witness our modern decadence.

H.G. Wells' "time machine" *can reverse or accelerate the flow of time* and his character travels backwards in the past or forward in the future. Aladdin's lamp or the flying carpet exemplify the constantly growing arsenal of *magic objects* which lend power to their owner and make him a *superman.* Tristan's and Yseult's *love potion* is the cornerstone in the Celtic plot poetizing the *determinist fatality* of a mythical erotic enchantment. Literary practice and critics distinguish, though never too rigidly, various genres which, theoretically speaking, have much in common—myths (mythology), legends (hagiography), tales (folklore), utopias (non-existent countries and peoples), fantasies (imaginary, dreamlike adventures), gothic novels (occult and draculoid topics), science (often futuristic) fiction. For practical reasons, this chapter covers only representations of gods and the Devil. The esthetics of the magical, fabulous, utopian and bizarre is addressed in the correlated chapter to follow.

An empirical appraisal of such genres' stimulative power does not rely only on the individual tastes of trained critics: in the course of their evaluation one should not ignore the indirect marks of the texts' high quality. These include a relative consensus of journalistic and academic critics and literary historians on their prominence; recognition of their artistry by juries granting prestigious awards, continuing interest of publishers and readers as reflected by the scope and success of posthumous internationally marketed editions; coverage in reputable dictionaries or encyclopedias, discovery of a given text's stimulative potential by film-makers or recurrent literary treatments or cinematic adaptations of the perennially attractive topics. All these factors indicate esthetic power noticeable or latent. Although my selection of authors and illustrative texts evaluated here relies all on my own criteria of esthetic quality, I do pay attention to external indicators of literary significance.

God of "Genesis," the Christian Trinity and the Greek Gods

The fundamentalist reading "Genesis" or "Exodus" would not catalog them as metaphysical fiction; the skeptic, however, might well see them in that light and rate them as literary material comparable to Hesiod's *Theogony.* Yet both readers might admit to a fascination with the principal subject of these narratives: the representation of the Judaic creator in one case and the exploits of mythological Greek gods in the other. Information on any Supreme Being provokes our interest and is stimulative.

The Lord of "Genesis" is not the single Creator in three persons who sacrificed his only son—integral member of the indivisible holy Trinity—so that we, human sinners, would not end in the flames of Hell. He does not even appear to be the Omnipotent, Omniscient and Omnipresent Creator defined in the Christian catechism.[9] The anonymous writer of "Genesis" portrays him as a speaker "walking in the garden in the cool of the day."[10] The Lord seems to be unaware of where the man he had created might be, so he calls him and asks: "Where art thou?" Adam replies that he is naked and therefore is afraid to meet the Lord. From the perspective of a skeptic, the well-known climax of this biblical dialogue—Adam's and Eve's expulsion from Eden—can only imply that the omniscient stroller is either playing dumb or, in fact, is not entirely sure whether Adam and Eve ate the forbidden fruit. God also does not seem to know if the personified snake, who had talked to Eve, conspired with the first human beings to violate the divine taboo. If God fakes his ignorance, from the point of view of human ethics, he acts as a rather revengeful hypocrite, because, throughout his eternal existence, the Omniscient must have known that, one day, Eve and her mate would eat the forbidden fruit and that he, the divine judge, would punish them severely. The fundamentalist, the selective believer and the agnostic will each react differently to the saga of the biblical revolt. They will respond differently even to the minor microstimulative punishment of the subversive snake created by God to corrupt the only human couple in paradise: the fundamentalist will reconcile it with his faith and assume that, in the biblical paradise, the snake may have had legs or wings prior to its humiliating degradation to a creeping and hissing reptile. The liberal believer, feeling somewhat but not fully free to interpret selected biblical passages symbolically, will perhaps see the communicative reptile as a mythical challenger of God's supreme power, an archaic allegory of the satanic (or Promethean) hunger for

9 An "agnostic" unable to prove the existence of any omnipotent cosmic energy would speculate that, provided it exists, it implicitly could also be omnipresent and omniscient, unless it had voluntarily given up the scope of its own "omnipotence." It also could be polyvalent, universally embodying both supreme good as well as evil, or simultaneously be or not be within or beyond any cosmic confines of universal existence and its inherent "good" or "evil.

10 Ch. 3, v. 8, q.s.

knowledge—an allegory underpinning the Judaic and Christian ethical doctrines formulated later than "Genesis." Free thinkers will read it as pure mythology in the same spirit as they read, for instance, the Hellenic myths about Prometheus' revolt against the jealous gods or about Orpheus and Euridice (who was fatefully bitten and killed by the snake). In their eyes, the authors of the Judaic and Greek myths laid prehistoric and preliterary foundations for the two ethnically and religiously oposed cults and their primitive poetry.

Unlike the "sacred" scriptures, the secular *Iliad* and *Odyssey* (written by the half-mythical, half-historical Homer) and the *Theogony* (related by the historical Hesiod) have never been venerated as verbatim heavenly quotations of the only God's Word. The entertaining, orally transmitted versions of the pre-Homeric epics were addressed to the imagination of Bronze Age audiences rather than to their faith and religious orthodoxy.

Homer's Olympians are the third generation of Greek gods.[11] His countrymen associated them with the primordial elements and forces manifest in the cosmos, and in the life on Earth—time, solar light and heat, stars, sea waters, storms, reproductive cycles, fire, and so on. Ancient poets, playwrights, sculptors represented such divine powers as humans; they "created" them in the human image. The Homeric immortals act just like the humans whom they help, love, despise, threaten, condemn. Their ruler Zeus was originally a "cloud-gathering mountain god given to boasting and hurling thunderbolts." Homer Hellenized and humanized the eastern deities welcomed in Greece, such as Apollo or Poseidon, and described their roles in nature and human life. In epical poetry and the Greek theatre, they incessantly determine the outcome of human adventures ranging from wars to conjugal crises.

> They are not spiritual gods, but only glorified human beings. Even for mere supermen their behavior is often shockingly undignified, quite apart from all their philandering. They bicker and scold, and then complain that their breakfast has been spoiled; they tell clumsy lies and are caught in them; they fight with men and bawl when they get wounded. They call their father a hard-hearted tyrant; call one another fools and bitches.[12]

11 See ch. V, opening comments inspired by Hesiod's *Theogony*.

12 The *Iliad* (transl. cit., ch. III, no. 5), introduction, pp. 15–16.

Deus ex machina

In Greco-Roman mythology, gods personifying various kinds of cosmic energy propel life and its fatality in the intimate ancient universe. They carry out divine plans, they reveal themselves in the "blind" forces of nature—forces which generate and terminate life; which strike happy living creatures with tragic blows. At the very beginning of the *Iliad* Apollo brutally supports the old Chryses when Agamemnon rejects the ransom which the Trojan priest offers him for the release of his daughter Chryseis, taken hostage and made a concubine by the Greek commander. Irritated by the humiliation inflicted upon the priest who has always loyally offered him in sacrifice the fat joints of cattle, the divine archer aims his silver bow and death-dealing arrows at the Greek mules, dogs and warriors under Agamemnon's command: "And the crowded pyres for the dead burned on unceasing." Thus Apollo's cosmic massacre forces Agamemnon to return Chryseis to her father. To compensate for this erotic loss, the war lord claims Briseis (Chryseis' sister), who was awarded to Achilles as a war prize. The son of Peleus and Thetis, Achilles refuses his supreme commander's request:

> Greedy one, clothed in shamelessness, how shall any of the Achaeans willingly obey your bidding...to fight with men? For I did not come hither to do battle on account of the Trojan spearmen, since they are by no means guilty in my eyes. Never have they driven off my cattle...never wasted the harvest in fertile Phithia...since in between lie many...mountains and...sea. No, it was you, utterly shameless, that we followed hither, to win revenge from the Trojans for Menelaus and for you, dog-face... But these things you neither care for nor consider. You even threaten to take away my prize yourself, the prize for which I labored much, and which...the Achaeans gave me.[13]

The son of Atreus will not tolerate such an insubordination of his "most hateful" ally: "Go home with your ships...and...Myrmidons...I do not care about you...but I will go myself and lead to my tent your prize, fair-cheeked Briseis, that you may know well how much I am your better... " Agamemnon's arrogance makes Achilles' blood boil. Feverishly, he ponders whether to restrain himself or punish the cocky overlord. When he draws from the sheath his mighty sword, Athena comes from heaven to subdue her protégé's wrath and to tell the raging hero; "I came...to check your fury...[G]odess Hera sent me...draw not your sword...but reproach him with words...restrain yourself and obey us."[14]

13 Ibid., p. 38.
14 *Iliad*, cit. transl., pp. 36, 38–9.

The *Odyssey*'s opening chant on the Olympians' Council once more testifies to the intimate bond between the gods and the ruler of Ithaka who suffered many troubles while navigating on the purple sea.[15]

The agnostic Heraclitus of Ephesus (c. 530–470) criticized Greek mythologists and poets, including Homer and Hesiod, as poor teachers. "None of the gods or men has created our world, it has always existed." It is and will be the living *(hilozoic)* fire which dies and flares up again. Cosmos is in an eternal flux—*panta rhei*—nothing remains forever the same—*ouden menei*: cosmic energy of a pantheistic nature generates life which is nothing but an eternal struggle of conflicting natural forces.[16] However, even in antiquity, Heraclitus' skepticism did not prevail. Regardless of whether they were skeptical or superstitious, Romans, five centuries after his death, did not only venerate mythological gods, they were forced by the imperial establishment to observe new cults launched by the deification of the emperors. In *I Claudius*, Robert Graves draws inspiration mainly from Suetonius' biography of young Caligula (Gaius Caesar). This successor of the perverted Tiberius deifies himself during his own rule. Among other evocations of Caligula's madness, the novelist describes Caligula's deplorable campaign in Gaul, where on the Atlantic shore, the "god" Caligula challenges his enemy Neptune. His legionnaires, both infantry and cavalry, are ordered into the shallow water to chop Neptune to pieces. To document his "victory," Caligula returns to Rome with a heap of seashells along with foreign prisoners and triumphantly parades them through the streets.

Dante's Devil and God

The most significant medieval poet laureate, whose masterpiece esthetically relies on the representation of supernatural, utopian and fantastic subject matter, is Dante Alighieri (1265–1321). The three volumes of his *Divine Comedy*,[17] *Inferno*, *Purgatory* and *Paradiso* are—as the titles indicate—set beyond. Drawing from his thorough scholastic background, Dante narrates in the first person what he saw and heard in the three utopian empires devised by the Christian doctrine. His late

15 The comments and citations in ch. III, *deus ex machina*, illustrate Athena's ruses to secure Achilles' victory over Hector.

16 I paraphrase and/or cite (my transl.) "Herakleitos" *Encyklopedie antiky*, Prague, Academia, 1973; also see H.G. Clark (ch. III, n. 1) and *Encyclopedia Britannica*, 11th ed.

17 See comments on its gothic structure *LP II*, ch. VII, p. 198.

pagan confrère Virgil shows him around the facilities in Hell and Purgatory while the beloved and too early deceased Beatrice is his hostess in Paradise. During this metaphysical excursion Dante does catch a rare glimpse of the Christian God and Devil; but he spends most of his time listening to dead historical or mythological figures or to deceased highly placed contemporaries spending their postmortal eternity in one of the three Christian accommodations. Among those allocated to Hell by Dante's creative invention, are several Popes.

The *Comedy*, written after Dante's spiritual experience "akin to what is now called 'conversion',"[18] is an ambitious poetic synthesis of Christian scholasticism and ancient culture. Its rhetoric and *couleur locale* reflect ancient mythology but its religious outlook is based on dogmatic biblical and Aristotelian concepts. The *Inferno* setting is a modified replica of the pagan Hades with the mythological ferrier Charon, watchdog Cerberus, rivers Acheron, Styx and Cocytus. Among the distinguished residents are Homer and his mythological characters[19] ranging from Helena and her lover Paris to Achilles and Odysseus. The fictional Hell is theologically compartmentalized according to sin: the first circle is inhabited by decent pagans, no serious sins; the second circle, managed by the infernal judge Minos, punishes carnal sinners such as Helena, Cleopatra, Achilles or Francesca of Rimini. The third circle is reserved for Epicureans and Gluttons; the fourth for the Prodigal and Avaricious; the fifth for the ostentatious, arrogant and brutal; the sixth—the city of Lucifer Dis—for the heretics and so on. In the Inferno's last circle of the river Cocytus, an enclave named Judecca after the traitor Judas, the medieval Satan finally emerges; he is not the Lucifer/Prometheus but a monstrous colossus half congealed in a monumental block of ice.

> How icy chill and hoarse I then became, ask not, O Reader!.../ I did not die, and did not remain alive.../ The Emperor of the dolorous realm, from mid breast stood forth out of the ice; and I in size am liker to a giant, / than the giants are to his arms:... If he was once as beautiful as he is ugly now...Oh how great a marvel seemed it to me, when I saw three faces on his head!.../...Under each there issued forth two mighty wings, of size befitting such a bird...No plumes had they; but were in form and texture like a bat's: and he was flapping them, so that three winds went forth from him. / Thereby Cocytus all was frozen; with six eyes he wept, and down three chins gushed

18 A. John Butler, "Dante," *Encyclopedia Britannica*, 11th ed.

19 Many of them, like Virgil or Homer, are there simply because they had no chance of being baptized; the same applies to children deceased prior to their baptism.

tears and bloody foam.[20]

In comparison with the shockingly colorful portrait of the fallen angel represented by Dante's unleashed fantasy, the poetic "mimesis" of God is prudent, esoteric, symbolical. Seeing the celestial heights from which Beatrice will reveal a distant vision of the Christian Creator, the poet invokes the powers above to make him worthy of the laurels awarded to the great bards. Unlike Greek pantheism, Christian doctrine and constrictive faith in the divine Trinity disregard human creative instincts and respect for immortal poetry. In the Christian paradise, Christian Alighieri finds no credible patron of arts or Musae. Thus, upon entering the saintly citadel of Christian mysticism, he imitates the example of his ancient models and first invokes the appropriate Olympian: "O good *Apollo*...make me so fashioned vessel of thy worth, as thou demandest for the grant of thy beloved *laurel*. / Up till here one peak of *Parnassus* hath sufficed me."[21] After this pagan incantation the poet will finally see the Christian God, though not so specifically and dramatically as he saw the medieval Satan. To be able to perceive the revelation of the Almighty the poet's human vision has to be first "purged." This preliminary cleansing is made possible by the pilgrim's prayer to the Virgin Mother and by the intervention of Beatrice. After this ritual "[t]hose eyes, of God beloved and venerated fixed upon him who prayed" testify to the miraculous power of the heavenly Queen. The curtain will finally open when the friendly St. Bernard smiles and points upwards to indicate where God will reveal his invisible presence. The divine counterpoint to the thoroughly medieval image of Satan has neither face nor even eyes (mentioned just a few lines above). The poet's "purged sight" can now "[enter] through the ray of the deep light which in itself is true." [22] To catch the overwhelming Platonic glimpse of the divine greatness, to transform the faith in God into certainty, our human senses have to be mystified or rather "mysticized." The mystical lightening has to stun the poet's memory and sight and induce a dreamlike hypnosis comparable to the Greek Sybil's trance in which she

20 The *Divine Comedy*, The Modern Library (Random House) 1932, the Carlyle-Wicksteed, transl. introduced by C.H. Grandgent, c. xxxiv, p. 182. The abridged citation cannot preserve the canto's prosodic frame; the strokes and ellipses, however, mark the complete, abridged and omitted terzas.

21 Ibid., *Paradiso*, c. I, p. 403.

22 "Queen who canst all that thou wilt...let thy protection vanquish human torments; see Beatrice...for my prayers folding hands." XXXIII "Canto", ibid., p. 604.

recorded her oracles on leaves and then scattered them to the four winds.[23] Approaching the altar of his literary cathedral[24] the Christian poet in a state of *furor mysticus* no longer invokes Apollo/Sun/Phoebus but sees, adores and begs the "light supreme" to "give [his] tongue such power that it may leave only a single sparkle of [the light's] glory unto the folk come." The fascinating source of luminous energy which dazzles him and which radiates an abstract universal harmony reflects inexpressible perfection:

> I hold that by the keenness of the living ray which I endured I had been lost, had mine eyes turned aside from it. / And so I was the bolder, as I mind me, so long to sustain it as to unite my glance with the Worth infinite. / O grace abounding, wherein I presumed to fix my look on the eternal light so long that I consumed my sight thereon! / Within its depth I saw...the scattered leaves of all the universe; / Substance and accidents and their relations, as though together fused...that what I tell of is one simple flame... / The universal form of this complex I think that I beheld, because...as I say this, I feel that I rejoice... / Thus all suspended did my mind gaze fixed, immovable, intent...

This hazy vision marks the end of Dante's utopian journey. It also is the last step of his humanistic effort to amalgamate the incompatible Ancient and Medieval metaphysical legacies.

The editors of the cited translation interpret Dante's ultimate mimesis of God in terms more idealistic and less detached than my agnostic remarks:

> [As the poet] gropes for the recovery of some fragment of his vision, he feels in the throb of an ampler joy the assurance that he is touching on the truth as he records his belief that he saw the whole essence of the universe, all beings and all their attributes and all their relations, no longer as scattered and imperfect fragments, but as one perfect whole, and that whole naught else than one single flame of love... Dante's kindling vision reads deeper and deeper into the unchanging glory of the triune Deity, till his mind fastens itself upon the contemplation of the union (in the second Person) of the circle of Deity and the featured countenance of humanity—the unconditioned self-completeness of God that reverent thought asserts... [25]

Focussing on the originality and esthetic impact of Dante's invisible Platonic God Light, God Love,[26] one realizes how far Dantean divine

23 A Virgilian vision transposed in the *Aeneid,* II and VI, see ed. cit., p. 606, n. 8.

24 "Paradiso", c. XXXIII, ed. cit., p. 604.

25 Ed. cit., pp. 602–3.

26 See *LP II*, ch. IV, "Macrorhetoric," pp. 121; there is a certain analogy between Dante's vision and Plato's allegorical foreboding of the divine Ideas.

Energy is from the Lord of *Genesis* or from the ubiquitous Homeric gods. Yet, at the same time his trilogy, which imitates both the pagan as well as biblical universe, spontaneously establishes a truce between them, thus preparing the European spiritual and especially intellectual climate for the advent of the Renaissance.

Jupiter in *Amphitryon*: From Plautus to Giraudoux

Literary or sculptural representations of the anthropomorphous Olympians are easier to achieve and—esthetically speaking—easier to "believe in" than a mimesis of an invisible Trinity or a secretive Jehovah governing the universe from behind the burning bush. The artistic personification of the cosmic energy which the Greeks observed in nature does not demand anybody's faith. Their statues reflect ancient canons of human beauty and their literary visions stimulate our free imagination. The macrostimulative impact of mythological plots and divine characters is probably subject to cyclic changes. One thing, however, at least indirectly indicates the relatively high macrostimulative potential of these narratives—their recurrent treatments by successive generations.

Among the mythical plots which have never ceased to fascinate playwrights and their audiences is Zeus' (Jupiter's) love affair with his human great-granddaughter Alcmene married to the same god's equally human great-grandson Amphitryon. This myth, first told by Hesiod, strikes us as a pre-Christian parallel of the immaculate conception: following coition with her deceptive ancestor, Alcmene gives birth to the half-god Heracles. In 1929, Jean Giraudoux[27] alluded to 37 precedents of his own version entitled *Amphitryon 38*. Besides his variation, the best known treatments of the Amphitryon myth are the comedies by Plautus (approx. 254–184 B.C.), Molière (1668) and the Romantic Heinrich von Kleist (1807).

The mythological intrigue amalgamates supernatural, erotic and comic (both farcical and ironic) stimuli. As indicated, Amphitryon is Alcmene's husband and cousin, but their union has not been consummated because, inadvertently, Amphitryon killed his father-in-law, Electryon. Alcmene will receive her husband only after he defeats her father's old foes, the Teleboans. While Amphitryon leads the Theban army to an impressive victory, Zeus disguised as his mortal descendant

27 See comments in *LP II*, pp. 90–2.

and parading as a homecoming hero, seduces Alcmene who awaits the return of her husband. The divine adultery and the successive matrimonial cohabitation beget twins, Heracles, fathered by the philandering Olympian, and Iphicles, fathered next day by the triumphant Amphitryon. Plautus' version stresses the double farcical *quid pro quo*—Jupiter posing as Amphitryon and Mercury as his servant Sosie who, too, is awaited by his wife. Their intimate interaction with the Theban royal family and staff constitutes the play's farcical macrostimulus: the growing confusion of the real Amphitryon and the real Sosie makes both of them ultimately doubt their own existence.

Molière, who assimilated both the Ancient and the Christian tradition, was not entirely blind to the tragi-comic trick Jupiter plays on the unsuspecting Alcmene. Prudently, he glosses over the issue of immaculate conception. "On such affairs, it is always better to say nothing." Molière's *Amphitryon,* while entertaining a frivolous French establishment, seems to draw a vague parallel between Jupiter's adultery and the love affair of Louis XIV and the Marquise de Maintenon. Thus his treatment neither satirizes the royal Don Juan nor preaches moral reform to his decadent court. Cheerfully, Molière rather justifies the perennial double standard *—quod licet Jovi non licet bovi*—keeping his own irony subtle and free of satirical sarcasm.[28]

It is Heinrich von Kleist (1777–1811) who introduces grave irony full of tragic undertones in the comic plot. Jupiter's adulterous fraud is nothing to laugh about, it seems to reveal a perfidious alliance of Heaven and Hell.[29]

Giraudoux' *Amphitryon 38* pits Alcmene's decent *joie de vivre* against the Olympian playboy's egocentric libido. Unlike Kleist, Giraudoux ironically understates[30] the god's lust and, at the same time, elevates civilized feminine humanism above divine licence. Innocently, without realizing it, Giraudoux' mortal Alcmene teaches the immortal lecher a lesson about the sacred nature of human love and loyalty.

28 What is allowed to Jupiter is not allowed to an ox.

29 This summation draws from Hanseres Jacobi, "*Amphitryon* in Frankreich u. Deutschland", *Züricher Beiträge zur vergleichenden Literaturgeschichte*, 1952 Juris Verlag; Ernst Kayka "H.V. Kleist's *Amphitryon*," *Zeitschrift für Vergleichende Literatur*, 1906; August Sauer, "Zu Kleist *Amphitryon*," *Euphorion*, 1913; Karl-Heinz Wegener, *Amphitryon im Spiegel der Kleistliteratur*, Frankfurt, Bern, Cirencester/U.K., P. Lang, 1979.

30 His irony exemplifies French *esprit* (see n. 27) and Henri Clouard, *Histoire de la littérature française, Du symbolisme à nos jours* (Paris: A. Michel, 1949), p. 458.

The classical, Romantic and modern *imitatio* of Plautus' model reflect the authors' confidence in the compelling esthetic impact of the ancient macrostimulus adjusted to timely humanistic perspectives. With a calculated nod to his royal patron, Molière revives the myth as a testimony to the admirably vigorous virility granted *dei gratia* to the Sun King. The romantic ressurection of the myth intransigently revolts against the divine abuse of Alcmene: the lusty god is a traitor of everything that is charming and decent in his creation. Thanks to the inborn decency of modern Alcmenes, some of us humans are perhaps more civilized than single-minded divine lovers. Humans may deserve more respect than deceptive, sex-hungry gods, or so at least ponders Giraudoux.

Goethe's God and Mephistopheles

Five centuries after Dante's portraits of the Christian God and Devil, J.W. Goethe transposed the two transcendental beings as characters in the brief "Prologue in Heaven" preceding his *Faust* (1808). As a poetic overture to their meeting in the celestial utopia, the three archangels sing of the divine power and the glory of "works [which] are as bright as in the Creation's hour." As soon as they finish, Mephistopheles confirms the ironic veracity of their *gloria* in his up-to-date account of the human species. Obviously spending much more time among people than the Lord, the Devil tells his master that, in his eyes at least, Mankind is not a crown of Creation but a pathetically stagnant breed which stubbornly resists any worthwhile progress. Yes the angelic choir is right, man has not changed much since the miraculous first birthday of our cosmos:

> Of suns and worlds I've nothing to be quoted;
> How men torment themselves, is all I've noted.
> The little...world sticks to the same old way,
> And is as whimsical as on Creation's day.
> Life somewhat better might content him,
> But for the light which Thou hast lent him:
> He calls it Reason—thence his power's increased,
> To be far beastlier than any beast.
> Saving Thy Gracious Presence, he to me
> A long-legged grasshopper appears to be,
> That springing flies, and flying springs,
> And in the grass the same old ditty sings.
> Would he still lay among the grass he grows in!
> Each bit of dung he seeks, to stick his nose in.

The diabolic report card on human vegetation, meanness and bungling cannot undermine the divine confidence in Mankind's genius. Somewhat annoyed the Creator inquires, if Mephisto met his loyal *Knecht* Faust, a relentless pioneer of enlightenment. Mephistopheles replies that the learned Faust is not entirely incorruptible and bets that, without the Lord's interference, he may successfully lead him to eternal damnation. God accepts the risky wager and the Heaven closes. Mephistopheles, alone on the scene, respectfully eulogizes the lordly old boy:

> I like, at times, to hear The Ancient's word,
> And have a care to be most civil:
> It's really kind of such a noble Lord
> So humanly to gossip with the Devil.[31]

Goethe's humanization of the supreme forces and especially their civilized *modus vivendi* is much closer to the Homeric mythology than to Dante's grave "Inferno" and "Paradiso." His God and Devil are colleagues who both inhabit Heaven and argue about human aspirations the way the Olympians muse on Odysseus's destiny. Their portraits certainly make us speculate that Mephisto may be the Goethean incarnation of the Creator's own battle over the goodness and perfection of man whom he created in his own image. Could the devil merely be an ironic *alter ego* of the Lord? Do not the two supernatural characters as well as the angels articulate Goethe's secular *Weltanschauung*? They are not too far away from the visions of God and the Devil in modern fiction. Such macrostimulative subjects include, for instance, G.B. Shaw's agnostic satirical fantasy *Don Juan in Hell*, Anatole France's angelic utopia *The Revolt of the Angels* (1914) or J.-P. Sartre's existentialist version of an atheistic psychological Hell, *No Exit* (*Huis clos*, 1944).[32]

Dostoyevsky: Battlefield of God and the Devil

Fyodor M. Dostoyevsky, later Romain Rolland and Thomas Mann represent the divine or demoniac not as transcendent but as concrete endopsychic energy manifested in the creative visions and contemplations, either sick or sensitive, of their mystically or religiously predisposed characters. Reciting Schiller's *Ode to Joy* ("An die Freude")

31 *Faust*, the versified transl. by Bayard Taylor (New York: Three Sirens Press, n.d. illustr. by H. Clarke), pp. 36–9, my italics. I have never seen the above "Prologue im Himmel" performed on stage.

32 *Don Juan in Hell*, act III of *Man and Superman*, 1903; *The Revolt* see comments below; *No Exit*, see ch. VII, "Existentialist fantasies."

the drunk Mitya Karamazov reveals to Alyosha (his younger stepbrother from their father's second marriage) the tragic gap in the Kamarazov soul: "Though I may be following the devil I am Thy son, O lord and I love Thee." When the declaimer's *furor poeticus* delivers the final part of the *topos*, "All things that breathe drink Joy," Joy which offers her gifts to all beings "To angels—vision of God's throne / To insects—sensual lust...," Mitya interrupts his Schillerian outburst "...enough poetry," and ends his intimate performance on a grave contrastful note: the insects' sensual lust and "the shameful beauty mankind finds in Sodom and in any form of mysterious as well as terrible beauty as sources of Man's joy, damnation and eternal tragic conflict...God and the devil are fighting there and the battlefield is the heart of man."[33]

Further Dostoyevsky describes Ivan's psychosis which triggers his illusory, yet to him authentic, communication with the demonic sphere of his own subconscious (Ivan is Alyosha's older brother). The first few sentences of the chapter entitled "The Devil. Ivan's Nightmare," characterize the neurological or psychiatric disorder which launches his mystical ecstasy:

> I am not a doctor, but yet I feel that...I must inevitably give the reader some account of the nature of Ivan's illness... [H]e was at that moment on the very eve of an attack of brain fever. Though his health had long been affected, it had offered a stubborn resistance to the fever which in the end gained complete mastery over it.

In his delirium Ivan is unexpectedly visited by a bearded Russian gentleman "qui faisait la cinquantaine" and who is clad in shabby but once would-be fashionable attire. While continuing in his conversation with the bizarre guest Ivan is not willing to admit his existence..."What a nightmare to have!...I won't be taken to a mad-house!" The gentleman however, does not disappear and goes on talking to Ivan.

> "By the way, I...am rather surprised to find you are actually beginning to take me for something real, not simply your fancy, as you persisted in declaring last time..."
>
> "Never for one minute have I taken you for reality," Ivan cried with a sort of fury. "You are a lie, you are my illness, you are a phantom. It's only that I don't know how to destroy you and I see I must suffer for a time. You are my hallucination... From that point of view you might be of interest to me, if only I

33 *The Brothers Karamazov*, transl. Constance Garnett (New York: Random House, Modern Library, n.d.), pp. 126–7. Russian text publ. in 1879–80; subsequent ref. ibid., pp. 771 and 775.

had time to waste on you..."

"Excuse me... When you flew out at Alyosha under the lamp-post this evening and shouted to him. 'You learnt it from *him*! How do you know that *he* visits me?' You were thinking of me then. So for one brief moment you did believe that I really exist," the gentleman laughed blandly.

"Yes,...but I couldn't believe in you. Perhaps I was only dreaming."

But in spite of his reasoning Ivan begins to fear that the spectre is not a figment of his reminiscing imagination but an ominous urgent premonition foreshadowing a gruesome blow: Alyosha, Ivan's younger brother whom he had just left following their tense controversy will emerge at a ghastly hour. When Ivan hears someone knocking on the door, he *knows* it is Alyosha coming to announce the suicide of Smerdyakov, their stepbrother who had murdered their corrupt father and in so doing he made (their second stepbrother) Mitya prime suspect of the crime.

Thomas Mann—Adrian Leverkühn's *Illuminatio*

Thomas Mann's doctor Faustus, Adrian Leverkühn,[34] like Goethe's Faust, studies theology, and unlike him, also mathematics and music. Like him he seeks "beauty" though not so much in life as in art. In our days, following the centuries of seemingly inexhaustible invention which tested many creative techniques, both mimetic and stylistic, gifted artists have to find new alternatives of true artistic originality. Mann portrays his modern character as a genius of rare intellectual talents, spiritual sensitivity and phenomenal memory; but he suffers from hereditary migraines and from syphilis deliberately contracted from a gypsy prostitute.[35] Its treatment was never fully completed. The slow gradual penetration of the composer's brain by *spirochaeta pallida* causes Adrian's schizophrenia and leads to his abrasive but revelatory communication with his individual Mephistophelian *Doppelgänger*.

34 *Doctor Faustus*, transl. by H.J. Lowe-Porter, M. Secker and Warburg, 1949. The subsequent quotations cite chs. XII, XIII and esp. ch. XXV, pp. 278–80.

35 During Adrian's university studies a tourist guide led him to a brothel where he met the exotic beauty. The shy reserved man left the establishment without having intercourse but never forgot the girl. In his fantasy he baptized her Hetaira Esmeralda after an exotic butterfly depicted in one of his father's illustrated manuals. Two years later he tried to find her but she had left Germany; he travels to the Slovak Pressburg (Bratislava, then Hungary) where she works in another brothel. The composer pays no attention to the prostitute's warning that she has a venereal disease and contracts her illness.

Following Leverkühn's premature death, his lifelong friend, classical scholar Serenus Zeitblom[36] examines the deceased artist's papers; among them he finds the secret, never mentioned handwritten transcript of Adrian's hallucination (stylized in archaic Lutherian language) and integrates it in his friend's biography. The title of Mann's novel reflects its primary literary debt to Goethe and it is indeed an unprecedented *imitatio* of the Faustian saga. But Mann, an avid reader and critic of Dostoyevsky portrays his modern genius, his creative neurosis and his contact with the Devil the way Dostoyevsky represents Ivan's traumatic vision. The *alter ego*, which Adrian identifies as "black Kaspar, Samiel/Sammael [angel of death], *Dicis et non facis*", etc.[37] suddenly contacts him during his 1911/12 stay in Palestrina.[38] At the beginning the phantom vaguely resembles Docent Schleppfuss[39] for whom "the Evil One…was a necessary emanation…of the Holy Existence of God." This pedagogue, sempiternally clad in black, used to greet his disciples with the ridiculous hyperbole "your most obedient servant." In his, as in Luther's eyes, the Devil, the Dragon, is not an academic abstraction but an urgent reality and his most used *instrumentum* of fleshly seduction is *femina*.[40]

On the night of his vision, Adrian suffers a harrowing migraine attack and gives up his original plan to go out with his friend Schildknapp. Instead he rests in his half-lit room reading Kierkegaard's essay on Mozart and his *Don Giovanni*. Suddenly, he feels that he is no longer alone. "I start up from my boke and look abroad into the hall, belike Sch. is come back for I am no more alone. There is some bodye there in the mirk, sitting on the horse hair sofa…; not Sch., but another, smaller than he,…and not in truth a gentilman at all."

Adrian addresses the ominous visitor in Italian, "Chi è costà?" and "the voice of the other" asks Adrian to speak "[o]nly good German without feignedness or dissimulation." The nocturnal reader of

36 Mann's narrator, who writes the musician's biography.

37 The abundance of diabolic synonyms is inspired by theological diction of Adrian's former professors at the theologically eminent *Alma mater Hallensis*, Ehrenfried Kumpf, who lectured philosophy of religion and ethics (*Dr. Faustus*, ch. XII) and the Privat-docent Eberhard Schleppfuss, who had a "suggestively demonic concept of God." (ch. XIII.)

38 Archaic, though not gothic birthplace of Giovanni Palestrina (1526–94), composer of religious music.

39 Ibid. A symbolical Oedipian/Hephaistian name—dragfoot; see n. 37.

40 See n. 47. See also ch. IV, Simone de Beauvoir's comments in *The Second Sex*.

Kierkegaard is overwhelmed by a wave of acute chill and the phantom thoughtfully suggests: "...fetch thee a cloak, a hat and rug. Thou art cold." The shy and proud hero, who resents the familiar *Dutzen*[41] even by his intimate friends including the devoted Zeitblom, replies angrily: "Who says *thou* to me?"

The discovered "transcript" of the ensuing—about 14,000-words—dialog gradually reveals the poignant details of Adrian's psychological depression, artistic conflicts and also throws unexpected light on the pathology of the neurosis activating his creative genius. It is not easy to estimate the subtle gradations of Adrian's anxiety esthetically raised to a higher power by the parody of the Lutherian scholastic jargon indulged in by the theologians at Halle university: the high density of the macrostimulative chapter XXV is evenly distributed and its intensity build-up is disguised by the "documentary" tone of the allegedly unedited repartee.[42] Nevertheless, any author of Mann's caliber and any demanding reader of this Faustian adaptation will be well aware that the contract between the protagonist and his Mephistophelian tutor has to form its first dramatic or epical peak. In harmony with this premise Mann creates a successful metamorphosis of Goethe's climactic *topos*[43] and integrates its prosaic parallel into his contemporary version of the legendary plot. To make the rendezvous of his present-day Faust esthetically convincing he wrote 24 chapters to set the scene for it. In them, with patient yet constantly thrilling epic breadth, he covers his character's roots, childhood, adolescence, his geographic, social and moral milieu, gymnasium and university studies, physical and mental idiosyncrasies, all the crucial characters and events which shaped him. The opening of Adrian's schizophrenic vision (ch. XXI) evokes the cited Dostoyevsky text. Like Ivan Karamazov, Adrian refuses to consider the mysterious visitor from beyond as an authentic being and treats him as a psychotic fiction related to his acute headache. As in Ivan's controversy

41 The German *Du*, French *tu*, thou form, 2nd person singular (ch. XXV).

42 My perceptions rely on my reading of the original German text (Stockholm, Bermann-Fisher, 1947, the cited English translation and on Pavel Eisner's Czech translation (Prague, Melantrich, 1947). I reiterate that the isolation of content from style benefits from comparing the translations.

43 Part I, scene 4, The Study: "...werd ich zum Augenblicke sagen: / 'Verweile doch! du bist so schön!–' / Dann magst Du mich in Fesseln schlagen / Dann will ich gern zu Grunde gehn!" ("When thus I nail the Moment flying / Ah, still delay—thou art so fair! / Then bind me in thy bonds undying, / My final ruin then I declare!" Transl. cit.)

the overture to Adrian's inner colloquy is abrasive:

> I: "[I]t is nothing likely that a man should seat himself here with me…speaking German and giving out cold, with pretence to discuss with me gear whereof I wot nor would wot naught. Miche more like is it. I am waxing sicke and transferring to your form the chills and fever against the which I am wrapped, sneaped by frost, and in the beholding of you see but the source of it."
> He (quietly and convincingly laughing, like an actor): "Tillyvally, what learned gibberidge you talk! In good playne old German, tis food and frantick. And so artificial! A clever artifice, an 'twere stolen from thine own opera."

The illusory dialog's hostility, the somewhat "Protean" Devil's ironic self-confidence and Adrian's frustration keep increasing. "You say nothing save things that are in me and come out of me but not of you. You jape old Kumpf[[44]] with turns of phrase yet look not as though you ever had been in academie…"

The contemplative wandering through the labyrinth of Adrian's memory leading to the fatal contract is a coherent and lucid stream of subconscious. Mann's *contaminatio* unifies the biographical and livresque elements fermenting in the hero's mind and activating his imagination already affected by the Haetera Esmeralda's deadly viral gift. In his trauma Adrian visualizes the ominous "houre glasse of Dürer's *Melancolia*" which the Devil offers him as His "gift…so fine, the little neck through which the red sand runs." The Samiel (the tormented former student of theology even remembers that according to Johann Ballhorn from Lübeck, Samiel is an incorrect form of Sammael) tells the shivering musician that he cannot do too much about the room temperature; for he has to be cold and spread the chill to be able to dwell "in the brenning pit of fier" which, as the "Herr Doctor ex-Theologus" undoubtedly knows, has so many scholastic synonyms "*carcer*, *exitium*, *confutatio*, *pernicies*, *condamnatio* and so on."[45] Finally, Adrian's Ego obliquely alludes to the terms of the agreement and receives the following answer:

> I: 'So you would sell me time?'
> He: 'Time? Simple time? No, my dear fere, that is not devyll's ware. For that we should not earn the reward, namely that the end belongs to us. What manner of time, that is the heard of the matter! Great time,…bedivelled time, in which the fun waxes fast and furious, with heaven-high leaping and springing—and again, of course, a bit miserable,…I…emphasize it,…such is artist-way and artist-nature… Always the pendulum swings

44 See n. 37.
45 An Echo of Dante's "ice-cooled" Satan?

> very wide to and from between high spirit and melancholia, that is usual,... For...we purvey towering flights and illuminations, experiences of upliftings and unfetterings, of freedom, certainty, facility, feeling of power and triumph, that our man does not trust his wits—counting in besides the colossal admiration for the made thing which could soon bring him to renounce every outside, foreign admiration—the trhrills of self-veneration, yes, of exquisite horror of himself, in which he appears to himself like an inspired mouthpiece, as a god-like monster.

Neither the style nor the substance of Leverkühn's secret negotiation are addressed to the masses of curious readers. The dialogue is bookish and full of abstract, metaphysical, esthetic and psychological arguments. The itemized bill, which the black Kaspar presents to his victim to pay for the ingenious *illuminatio* and for his refined creative energy, is tragic.[46] Although it requires slow, syncopated reading, many erudite readers will always savor Adrian's cross-examination by his alter-ego.[47] His vision (like Ivan Karamazov's trauma) suddenly ends when Adrian's companion, Schildknapp, returns and greets the indisposed composer. Without realizing how gravely ironic his casual words are, Schildknapp tells the hallucinating Adrian that he missed little by not coming to the club: "...newspapers and two games of billiards, a round of Marsala and the good souls calling the *governo* over the coals." This expertly timed awakening exemplifies Mann's skill in suave gradation, with a sharp yet subtle antithesis matching missed banal entertainment against "uneventful" solitary but supposedly salutory repose.

From a broad historical perspective, Adrian's neo-Faustian portrait and its matching background—one which unveils the escalating paralysis of pre- and postwar Germany and its progressive metamorphosis into a Nazi inferno—can be seen as a tragically sick counterpoint to Goethe's

46 In the context of the dialog the Devil, "Esmeralda's friend and cohabitant," (p. 283), informs Adrian that his acquaintance, painter Baptist Spengler, is also a syphilitic but his illness is banal in comparison with the inspirational power of Adrian's exquisite "tender pareuchyma...in short *virus nerveux*".

47 Ibid., p. 296. The hero's schizophrenia and the "syphilitic upgrading" of his creativity concurs with the recent psychiatric research of Felix Post, who analyzed 300 famous men and documents that their "exceptional creativity and psychiatric problems are intertwined." His study published in the *British Journal of Psychiatry* covers here discussed Dostoevsky, Gide, Gogol, Kafka, Kipling, *Mann*, Proust, Sartre, Wilde, Kierkegaard, Nietzsche, Maupassant (who according to Post is the only one who had no "symptoms"). The *Insight/Guardian News Service*, London, review published in *The Calgary Herald*, June 30, 1994, p. F2, "'Mad' Genius Idea Is Proven by Doctor."

enlightened optimism. In the narrow historical bounds of the literary genre and its period and in the broad context of humanistic reflections on God, it also strikes European readers as an inspired cacophonic counterpoint (à la Schönberg) to Romain Rolland's post Romantic "musical" novel, *Jean-Christophe* (1904–12).

Jean-Christophe's Mystical Visions of the Creator

Rolland, who became the first professor of musical history at the Sorbonne, modelled his fictional German genius after several German composers: the struggling, somewhat clumsy Händel; the child prodigy Mozart; the Messianic Rhinelander Beethoven (incessantly clashing with an alcoholic father); the Romantic Wagner and the passionate Hugo Wolf. His robust, post-Romantic "Christophoros" J.-C. Krafft[48] has, like Adrian Leverkühn, rare flashes of mystical vision but, unlike him and more like the Biblical Moses, he directly communicates with the invisible Creator. The usual catalyst of his personal encounters with God is the powerful breath of a pantheistic nature—the Alpine storm, the vital waters of the Rhine, the poetic language of distant bells. The 1916 Nobel Prize winner shrouds his melodramatic novel in a cloud of mystique when he claims that it is a literary symphony as well as a literary cathedral yet, at the same time, not a work of literature but a work of faith.[49] It transposes his inner eclectic sympathies in the form of dialogs between the exiled Jean-Christophe and his learned Parisian friend, Olivier Jeanin, both autobiographical but neither with a heart quite so all-encompassing as his own. Like Olivier, Rolland was strongly attracted to the human gods of the *Iliad*, yet at the same time he shared Christophe's admiration for the vengeful Lord of *Exodus*. "Religious education has been reduced to the catechism in France; the Gospels are emasculated, the New Testament pallid and limp...Nothing but snivelling humanitarian bigotry...Take a good healthy slice of the red-blooded Old Testament Bible every morning."

48 Like the character's first name and initials, his family name Ger. *Kraft*/Engl.strength is also symbolic.

49 *Jean-Christophe*, def. ed. (Paris: A. Michel, 1966), p. xiv. The first ed. appeared in 1904–12. See previous comments on Rolland's rhythmical and rhymed prose, *LP II*, pp. 164–6, 200–1; this segment draws from my earlier *Cathedral or Symphony, Essays on J.-C.*, op. cit., ch. 1, n. 1 and "Les Aventures mystiques de *J.-C.*",*The French Review*, vol. XLIV, no. 6, 1971, pp. 1048–56. The subsequent citations refer to the def. edition (my transl.), pp. 996–8, 56, 64, 1419–20 and 1593.

Christophe's sermon does not impress Olivier. As a civilized intellectual he has little taste for the primitive vulgarities of the Old Testament which make him turn with relief to the *Iliad*, the *Odyssey* or the *Arabian Nights*. "The Gods of the *Iliad* are men, handsome, powerful, vicious perhaps, but men I can understand." To him, Greco-Roman paganism seems a fountain of wisdom, unsullied by the sort of fanaticism to be found in the Bible. He loves the Greek gods, even if he does not always like them. "But the Biblical God is a monomaniac old Jew, an angry madman who spends all his time cavilling, threatening, and howling like a rabid wolf". To prove his point, Olivier recalls the brutalities of Jehovah.

> He's insane. He thinks He's judge, jury and executioner all by Himself. He pronounces sentences of death in His prison yard on flowers and pebbles. His relentless hatred chokes you when you read His book and hear the cries of carnage..."The ruined places shall cry out... His battle cry shall cover Moab, and the roaring of His wrath shall go unto Eglasian..." Now and then He takes a rest between massacres, when He tires of crushing little children, raping and killing the women; and then He laughs—like a ruffian..."[A]nd the sword of the Lord drinketh the blood of the foe, and it is made rich with the veins of them that opposed Him..." Worst of all is the treachery of a God who sends His prophet to blind the people, so that He may have an excuse to punish them. "Go, harden the hearts of this people; stop up their eyes and their ears so that they may not understand the words of the Lord, nor repent them and turn into healthful ways. — How long, O Lord? — Until there be no house in which these men dwell..." No, in my whole life I have never seen such a wicked man!

But none of these arguments can weaken Christophe's sympathy for the Hebraic Lord. Nature is the sum of all beauty, and Nature herself is often cruel, and life a constant struggle. "In that case," said Christophe, "I should horrify you, because I am drunk with it. To me it is like the lion's marrow. Strong Hearts are made stronger by it. Without the Old Testament, the Gospels are a tasteless and unhealthy dish... You have to struggle, you have to hate." Fictionalizing the evolution of Christophe's acquaintance with God, Rolland, who himself had not "seen the light"[50], invents his hero's mystical visions. As a child Christophe imagines God as an enormous sun speaking with thundering voice and burning eyes, ears and one's whole soul. He could punish: one could never know. The boy also associates God with death which the adults mention—"the body in a box in a deep hole dug out in the middle of a disgusting cemetery:

50 See *Cathedral or Symphony*, op. cit. p. 19 and nn. 23, 24.

"Dieu! Dieu! quelle tristesse." As a precocious adolescent, Christophe meets the Omnipresent during an early creative impulse bordering on mystical delirium. Like Spinoza, like the vedantic sages, he becomes confident that his own creative elan is a revelation of authentic divine energy. My prosodic arrangement of the passage also illustrates the esthetic role of rhythm and rhyme in Roland's mimesis of a dionysiac furor à la Beethoven.[51]

A la lueur de l'éclair,
il vit, au fond de la nuit,
il vit — il fut le Dieu.
Le Dieu était en lui.
Il brisait le plafond de la chambre,...
. . . .
Il avait perdu le soufle,
il était ivre
de cette chute en Dieu...
Dieu-Abîme! Dieu gouffre,
Brasier de l'Etre! Ouragan de la vie!
Folie de vivre,
sans but, sans frein, sans raison,
pour la fureur de vivre![52]

The adult Jean-Christophe communicates with the God-like-warrior who relentlessly defends the universe which he has created against nothingness and death.

— Thou art returned! O Thou, whom I had lost...Why hast Thou forsaken me?
— To fulfil my task, which thou hast abandoned.
— What task?
— The Struggle.
— What need hast Thou of Struggle?... Art Thou not everything that is?
— I am not everything that is. I am Life, who strives against nothingness, but I am not nothingness. I am the Fire which blazes by night, but I am not the night. I am the eternal Struggle [,]...the Free Will, which strives eternally... Struggle and burn with me!... For Centuries, Death has pursued me and Nothingness has lain in wait for me. The river of Life is red with my blood.
— The Struggle. Must one always struggle?
— One must always struggle. God struggles also. God is the conqueror.

Only shortly before his death, when Christophe manages to bridge the gulf between Death and the Eternal Struggle against it, the last vision projects his lifelong metaphysical dualism as a sublime monistic harmony. Like Goethe's Faust, like Herrmann Hesse's Siddhartha, Jean-Christophe, who struggled all his life, is earmarked for a glorious

51 A.R. Lévy, (*L'Idéalisme de R. Rolland*, Paris, Nizet, 1946, pp. 68–9) discusses the Beethovenian "crises d'union mystique" and the vedantic "Toi c'est moi"; see also "Les Aventures mystiques de J.C.", op. cit.

52 For my prosodic arrangement see *Essays on J.-C.*, p. 82.

salvation; he becomes certain of his own resurrection:

> O joy! The joy of seeing oneself melt into the supernal peace of God, whom one has striven to serve all one's life...Lord, Thou art not too displeased with Thy servant?...I suffered, I fought, I erred, I created. Let me now pause my Father... Thou shalt be born again. Now rest; for there is now but one heart. The smile of night and day entwined. Harmony, the majestic *marriage of love and hate*. I shall hymn the *mighty winged God*. Hosannah to *life*! Hosannah to *death*!

This ultimate extension of God to the cosmic life/death *perpetuum* may strike some sufficiently qualified individual readers as neo-Beethovenian Romantic metaphysics; others, as eclectic secular pantheism. Critics with a Voltairean disposition may see it as an honest but naïve humanistic illusion of the absolute about which we know so little. The representation of the culminating mystical visions, however, does not seem to constitute the esthetic peak of Jean-Christophe's overabundant melodramatic adventures.[53]

Anatole France's Olympians

In the last years preceding World War I, when Rolland completed his idealistic *profession de foi*, his skeptical countryman Anatole France[54] offered occidental readers two contrasting gospels of ironic doubt, *The Gods Are Athirst* (*Les Dieux ont soif*, 1912) and his major neopagan fantasy, *The Revolt of Angels* (*La Révolte des anges*, 1913). In the first novel evoking the madness of the French Revolution, two erudite characters, the wealthy dilettante-banker Brotteaux, disguised as a street vendor of puppets, and the learned theologian, Father Longuemarre, talk metaphysics. Both are trying in vain to escape the guillotine. Brotteaux contemplates the potential commitment of the omnipotent Creator to his own Creation. In the cruel climate of growing terror, there is nothing to encourage Brotteaux's confidence in divine justice. He sums up his vote of nonconfidence in God in a sarcastic syllogism:

53 Naturally, in any "literary cathedral" the discovery of God is essential. But among the macrostimulative highlights of *Jean-Christophe* are the characters who help the hero become a great composer: Christophe's wise mother, his alcoholic father with the chip on his shoulder, his respected grandfather, his humble uncle Gottfried, the Teutonic duke who appoints the Mozartian *Wunderkind* his *Hofmusikus* but fires him as soon as he becomes a free thinker. Another artistic forte is the panoramic vision of the French *monde* endlessly greeting and disputing emerging avant-garde fashions.

54 Then 68; received the Nobel Prize for Literature in 1921.

> Epicure said: "Either God wants to prevent evil but cannot, or he can but does not want to, or he neither can nor wants to or, finally, he wants and can do it. If he wants but cannot, he is impotent; if he can but does not want to, he is perverse; if he neither can nor wants, he is both impotent and perverse; if he wants and can do it, why, my Father, doesn't he?[55]

In the *Revolt*, the immortal Angels, struck down by the choleric Jehovah, survive on Earth. After their metamorphosis into Greek and later Roman gods, they transform their cosmic refuge into a mythical cradle of joy and enlightenment. One of France's main characters, Nectaire, nostalgically recalls Antiquity during which he resurged as a Satyr in Dionysus/Lucifer's retinue. Sadly, when the divine tenure of the Olympian immortals comes to an end, he has to live incognito in the post-pagan Christian culture. Posing as a friar in the 17th century Jansenist setting, he encounters one of the so-called *Solitaires Messieurs*.[56] In harmony with St. Augustine's dogmatic distinction between divine and human justice, these doctrinal seclusionists professed that God "naturally and paradoxically" strikes the most faithful sheep in his flock while overwhelming with his favors the blasphemous villains. This is to be expected because we humans have not the slightest clue about Jehovah's (and the Trinity's) unpredictable code of justice. Nectaire, who is the author's frequent mouthpiece, compliments the Jansenist apostle of divine grace: "May the old Jehovah bless you. You know him so well. Oh! how well you know Him!" So saying, the ironic flatterer unveils his mythological face and horns, giving the shocked *Solitaire* a stroke. Speculates the bard of angelic *irredenta*:..."he felt that God had damned him."[57]

The above Epicurean aphorism (sharpened by France's flair for paradox) and the Jansenist anecdote illustrate France's pagan nostalgia

55 *O.C.* XX, p. 185, my transl. The editors of this critical edition do not identify this citation's source. (The projected Vols. III and IV of the Pleiade edition have not appeared at this point.) Because France himself, as well as his fictitious Brotteaux, were keen readers of *De rerum natura* by Lucretius Carus, L.B. Walton, *Anatole France and the Greek World*, Durham, N.C.: Duke University Press, 1950, p. 109, speculates, without identifying the precedent, that France probably imitates Lucretius' poem. See also *The Art of Anatole France*, p. 180 and n. 4.

56 Lay Jansenists, including the three brothers Le Maître, who settled in a vacant abbey in the Chevreuse valley and founded a "rustic branch" of Port Royal known as Port Royal des Champs.

57 Ibid., France's (here paraphrased) discourse parodies Pascal's rhetoric and turns upside down the argument advanced in the 2nd *Lettre écrite à un Provincial par un de ses amis*.

on the threshold of World War I. Like Epicurus and Lucretius, the iconoclast assumes that "all there is is natural."[58]

Yet, as stressed above, this outlook never reduces France's artistic taste for supernatural subjects—something which may surprise his readers. In that domain, he favors the macrostimuli anchored in our Greco-Roman and Judeo-Christian mythologies: perhaps, he assumes that the inherited fairy tales, superstitions, myths and biblical miracles, which once sparked our ancestors' imaginations and which remain forever in our memories, perhaps demand less "suspension of disbelief"[59] than supernatural subjects anchored outside our cultural frame of reference. A psychocritic could speculate that France's intuitive choices of supernatural subjects exemplify C.G. Jung's (1875–1961) concept of "collective unconscious" based on "extraordinary unanimity" of myths in different cultures, on recurrent symbols not related to our experience and on myth-like fantasizing of psychotic patients (and readers), on death or rebirth.[60]

The Revolt, France's last major novel, relates how and where the immortal angels survived after the demiurge Ialdabaoth had banished them from the cosmic heights. His plot is a fictional follow-up to the myth as described in the Ethiopian Apocrypha, *The Book of Enoch*, rather than in the vague biblical references and their patristic interpretations. Dietrich Schlumbohm comments on this source which, prior to France, had attracted imitators such as Milton and Chateaubriand.[61] *The Book of Enoch* considers the angels' erotic relations with humans as the chief cause of their fall. But later official Christian

58 "Rien n'est qui ne soit naturel," *O.C.* XIX, p. 241; included also in *Le Jardin d'Epicure*, *O.C.*, IX.

59 As postulated by Coleridge and recently invoked, e.g., by Italo Calvino in his "Levels of Reality," *Uses of Literature*, San Diego, New York, London: Harcourt Brace Jovanovich, 1986; transl. by Patrick Creary, p. 103.

60 See comments on Jung's outlook in J.A.C. Brown, *Freud and the Post-Freudians*, Penguin Books 1961, pp. 44–7; see also Brown's comments on Georg Groddeck (1866–1934) concurring with "the wisdom of Jungian collective unconscious" (ibid., p. 90).

61 *Der Aufstand der Engel; Anatole France und seine literarischen Vorläufer*. Romanisches Seminar der Universität Hamburg, 1966, p. 183. See also my review of Schlumbohm's thesis in *Comparative Literature* vol. XXI, fall 1969, No. 4, pp. 371–2. The early precedents include Avitus of Vienna's *De spiritualis historiae gestis* and *De originali peccato* (appx. 450–51), Du Bartas' *La Sepmaine ou création du Monde* (1578), Lope de Vega's *La creación del mundo y primera culpa del hombre* (1640), and Joost van den Vondel's drama *Lucifer*.

doctrine did not assimilate the apocrypha's explanations: St. Augustine and St. Thomas frowned at the idea of angelic liaisons, and because of their chaste inhibitions, it became pride, not sex, which preceded the fall. In spite of some striking similarities between Vondel's *Lucifer* and *Paradise Lost*, Milton's debt to Vondel is very uncertain. Schlumbohm stresses borrowings from the *Book of Enoch* which Milton adapted to suit his esthetic and his theological concepts (i.e., his individual interpretation of theodicy). However, in *Paradise Lost* the erotic bliss experienced by the angels is a heavenly projection of the purest matrimonial relationship. In his apology of Christianity against paganism, Chateaubriand reduces the angels to a decorative role. Although a secret but devoted worshipper of pagan antiquity, he pleads for Christianity while the fallen angels crusade for Greek paganism.

Anatole France, the Parnassian who blames Chateaubriand for poisoning his youth, will, naturally, fully rehabilitate the angels after their fall. Unfortunately, the ancient era of their dominion is too short. Faced with intolerant Christian puritanism, the anti-Jehovah heralds of joy must once again find new hideaways. Dionysus settles in a bucolic valley of the Himalayas, while many of his loyal escorts vanish in the polycultural labyrinth of Paris. Throughout the centuries half a million of the vulnerable but undying demons live disguised as guardian angels, monks, printers, gardeners, bankers, enlightened socialites. They form an immortal fraternity hoping to overthrow the imposter Ialdabaoth and replace him with the friendly Apollo, Dionysus and the Musae.

Ultimately their uprising neither succeeds nor fails. Lucifer cordially receives the Parisian delegation of his stalwarts in his Virgilian miniparadise. He listens to their proposal and decides to sleep on it. That night, he dreams that he is transformed into the jealous Ialdabaoth and puts on the crown of God. In his theological delirium, he proclaims himself a God in three persons. Drowning in icy perspiration, he awakes and rejects the violent and absurd confrontation. We readers may appropriately consider the civilized Angel's creed as France's humanist testament.

> Comrades...no—we will not conquer the heavens. Enough to have the power. War engenders war, and victory defeat. God, conquered, will become Satan; Satan, conquering, will become God. May the fates spare me this terrible lot; I love the hell which formed my genius. I love the Earth where I have done some good, if it be possible to do any good in this fearful world where beings live but by rapine. Now, thanks to us...every thinking being...disdains [the god of old] or knows him not. But what matter that men should be no longer submissive to

> Ialdabaoth if the spirit of Ialdabaoth is still in them; if they, like him, are jealous, violent, quarrelsome, and greedy, and the foes of the arts and of beauty? What matter that they have rejected the ferocious Demiurge, if they do not hearken to the friendly demons who teach all truths; to Dionysus, Apollo, and the Muses? As to ourselves, celestial spirits, sublime demons, we have destroyed Ialdabaoth, our Tyrant, if in ourselves we have destroyed Ignorance and Fear... We were conquered because we failed to understand that Victory is a Spirit, and that it is...in ourselves alone, that we must attack and destroy Ialdabaoth.[62]

France brings his angelic utopia to this lofty apostolic level without a monotonous mimesis of the plot's macrostimulative supernatural substance. He increases the gradations of its high stimulative density and intensity by calculated, although often seemingly random integration of macro- and microstimuli. These include (1) the angelic uprising against the Judeo-Christian Lord which is a so far unwritten, didactic Act II of the biblical fall of angels; (2) a satirical accusation of the Christian cults sabotaging for centuries free thought, science and general secular enlightenment. Throughout his discourse France balances the ideological gravity of this message with (3) a licentious, erotic subplot pervaded with (4) social satire of the French upper crust; (5) bookish theological arguments formulated by pedantic scholars who usually push them *ad absurdum*; (6) paradoxical psychological conflicts; (7) farcical anachronisms; (8) disgressive livresque or bizarre subjects, such as ancient anecdotes or comic forgeries of paintings by European masters sold by unscrupulous painters and art dealers. The main stylistic techniques adding to the originality of the *Revolt* are (9) the pervasive micro- and macro-irony; (10) rhythmical and rhymed prose; a marginal livresque stimulus is a parodical *imitatio* of memorable lines of poetry which of course is not addressed to all readers (11). Let me offer at least a few specific examples of these abundant topical and stylistic stimuli to document my general list. Besides the former satyr Nectaire, who sings his pagan version of the Occidental genesis (1) and besides Lucifer/Dionysus (who emerges only in the novel's humanistic denouement), the main macrostimulative characters include a decadent Catholic playboy Maurice Bussart d'Esparvieu, his guardian angel Arcade and Maurice's mistress Mme Gilberte des Aubels (4). This trio's erotic interaction (3, 9) forms the subplot parallelling the main intrigue, i.e., the planned *Revolt* against the jealous biblical Jehovah (1, 9). Arcade

62 *Revolt*, pp. 356–7.

becomes friendly not only with his human protégé, but also with Gilberte who, while thoroughly observing social conventions (4, 6) gladly succumbs to Arcade's angelic seduction (3). Maurice challenges the treacherous angel to a duel, and thus forces his immortal guardian to scratch him with the sword. After this bizarre conflict Arcade leaves Maurice to serve a higher cosmic cause but Maurice rejects this resignation and swears to reverse their roles and to become Arcade's guardian angel (7, 9). Gilberte too misses her lover's refined protector (3).

Nectaire's poetic epopee[63] has several artistic functions—it is a humorous, livresque *addendum* to vague biblical allusions: it provides a neopagan literary counterpoint to Bossuet's apotheosis of triumphant Christianity entitled *Discours sur l'histoire universelle* (8); it serves as an elegiac prelude to the *Revolt*'s civilized anticlimactic finale; and, naturally, it is author Nectaire's remembrance of things past which echoes not only Epicurus and Lucretius but also Darwin and La Place (2, 5, 8); [64] told intermittently in free verse vaguely underscored by occasional rhyming and assonances, Nectaire's elegy (10) evokes Jehovah's mythological victory over the Promethean Lucifer and his immortal sympathizers. The crashed demons suffer, but survive the brutal humiliation in ancient Greece and Rome where they create and experience a brief Golden Age.

A hostile Christianity puts an end to this period and renews the persecution of the Greek gods. Only the Renaissance and the era of anticlerical free thinkers alleviates the tribulations of these immortal beings. In his recital, Nectaire tells his angelic audience about some of his own millennial mutations (8): in the early Middle Ages the pagan spirit survived as a friar (probably at Cluny). In the 17th century he found asylum in Jansenist circles.[65] In Voltaire's days the satyr threw his ecclesiastic frock in the nettles and concealed his horns under a wig and his hoofs in white stockings. Clad as a rococo philosopher he became a regular in the salon of Madame Helvetius and after her death in the salon of Madame Condorcet. There he even met an occasional visitor, Napoleon Bonaparte; not too felicitously, the cabal gathered in the liberal salon offered him its support. Even in the dangerous era of the guillotine the lusty satyr could not resist watching the nymphs' nocturnal dance in

63 Chs. XVIII–XXI.

64 See above comments.

65 See the previous reference to Nectaire's encounter of a *Monsieur Solitaire* and n. 7.

the Bois de Boulogne. The revolutionary vigilanti overacted by arresting the peeping Tom as a spy. In the 19th Century Nectaire cultivates a garden in the woods of Montmorency. The revolt organizers come to listen to the gardener's flute recitals and persuade him to become the revolt's official bard.

The esthetic impact provoked by the integration of the novel's varied micro- and macrostimuli depends on our tastes, the historical setting of our society, erudition, world outlooks, political or religious bias. Christian or Jewish fundamentalists will be irritated by the satire of their Lord while liberal free thinkers will value the post-Voltairean campaign against any constrictive dogmatism and political bigotry of the conservative establishment. Epicureans who, in pursuit of their secular happiness are trying to rediscover the overgrown trails of ancient beauty, poetry, and freedom anchored in natural human teleology, will always discover the friendly, undying spirits in France's pagan utopia.

French Crypto-Pagans and Roman Catholics

The writers' and the readers' reactions to the mimesis of Greek gods, Jehovah or of the Christian Trinity are like a humanistic litmus test—they immediately reveal the author's or reader's metaphysical bias: for instance, Guy de Maupassant (1859–93) expressed his lifelong outlook at the age of 14, when he summed up his doubts about God's infinity, eternity and his questionable omnipotence. His poem entitled "Dieu créateur" shows the boy's ironic compassion for the God of the catechism "whose face nobody has ever seen." The main target of his *non confiteor* is the ontological contradiction and the monotony of divine eternity.

> Dieu, cet être inconnu dont nul n'a vu la face,
> Roi qui commande aux rois, et règne dans l'espace,
> Las d'être toujours seul, lui dont l'infinité
> De l'Univers sans borne emplit l'immensité,
> . . . .
> Dans l'éternel ennui d'un éternel présent,
> Solitaire et puissant et pourtant impuissant
> A changer son destin dont il n'est pas le maître,
> Le grand Dieu qui peut tout ne peut pas ne pas être![66]

As an adult man, Maupassant had a different vision of God when he

66 Pierre Borel, *Le Vrai Maupassant* (Genève, 1951), pp. 21. This biographer cites the previously unpublished poem.

was invited to shoot ducks at his cousin's estate in Normandy. Cosmic Love, the quasi-divine bond between the male and female, appeared to him "like the crosses in the middle of the skies used to appear to the first Christians."At daybreak, the two cousins shot a few birds and, when the sun rose, were about to leave their site. Suddenly, two birds flew above them.

> Je tirai. Un d'eux tomba... C'était une sarcelle au ventre d'argent. Alors, dans l'espace au dessus de moi, une voix d'oiseau cria. Ce fut une plainte...déchirante; la petite bête épargnée se mit à tourner dans le bleu du ciel au dessus de nous en regardant sa compagne morte...
>
> — Tu as tué la femelle, dit-il [Karl], le mâle ne s'en ira pas.
>
> Certes, il ne s'en allait point; il tournoyait toujours, et pleurait autour de nous. Jamais gémissement de souffrance ne me déchira le coeur comme l'appel désolé, comme le reproche lamentable de ce pauvre animal perdu dans l'espace.[67]

The drake was shot in his turn and the narrator was heartbroken. He did not even stay for another day but left for Paris. A tragic feeling of having destroyed something infinitely precious weighed heavily upon him.

One century later, Jacques Prévert offers his surrealist revision of the "Holy Scriptures." Dedicating it to "Paul and Virginie...to the goat and cabbage...zist and zeste...to your and [his] own health...to God and the Devil [and finally] to Laurel and Hardy", he opens his automatist gospel with crisp visions of "God and the Devil. "God is a big rabbit...living over there high in the sky *dans son grand terrier nuageux.*" On the other hand, "le diable est un grand lièvre rouge / avec un fusil tout gris / pour tirer dans l'ombre de la nuit."[68]

French literary history clearly distinguishes two fraternities, both cutting across the centuries: the crypto-pagans such as Jean de Meung, Rabelais, Ronsard, du Bellay, Montaigne, Marguerite de Valois, La Fontaine, Molière, Diderot, Voltaire, Flaubert, Maupassant, A. France, Zola, Gide, Valéry, Pagnol, Giono, Camus, etc. and the Roman Catholics such as Jean Bodel, Bossuet, Pascal, Barrès, Péguy, Claudel, Bernanos, Mauriac...

Accepting the Christian God/Trinity as the Catechism dictates, Catholic humanists cannot deviate from the official doctrine in any

67 See Bresky, "Eros—Maupassant's Only God," *Eroticism in French Literature,* pp. 143–7, nn. 3–4.

68 *Paroles*, Paris, Gallimard, 1949, "Saintes Ecritures". My transl.

individual way. In his "Magnificat," Paul Claudel[69] glorifies his merciful God for saving him from false idols and for granting him eternal life. "Car l'image de la mort produit la mort et l'imitation de la vie / La vie, et la vision de Dieu engendre la vie éternelle. / Soyez béni mon Dieu, qui m'avez delivré de la mort!" Some 25 versets lower, the poet associates God with the ontological Being: "qui ne croit plus en Dieu, ne croit plus en l'Être." By extension, the poet leaps to the conclusion that who does "not believe in the Being" *eo ipso* hates it, "et qui hait l'Etre, il hait sa propre existence." Believers finding God need not fear death which, as Claudel intimidatingly trusts, threatens agnostics (perhaps Zola, Anatole France, Huysmans and others): "Savants, epicuriens, maîtres du noviciat de l'Enfer, practiciens de l'introduction au Néant / Brahmes, bonzes, philosophes,..." In the conclusive part of his confiteor Claudel identifies the godless candidates for eternal damnation: "Restez avec moi, Seigneur,...Ne me perdez point avec les Voltaire, et les Renan, et les Michelet et les Hugo, et tous les autres infâmes!"

Like a priest in his "ample golden robe," the poet ends his solemn thanksgiving, knowing perfectly in the fulness of his heart that his Lord awaits him in the transcendant materiality of "unleavened" Holy Host, "sous les accidents de l'azyme" kept in the liturgical monstrance.[70]

Outside the orthodox and free-thinking camps are many eclectic rebels, sinners, heretics, anarchists, grave existentialists, nihilists—Villon, T. de Viaud, de Sade, Baudelaire, Rimbaud, Jarry, Tzara, Henri de Montherlant, Sartre, Henri Michaux. The above fictional debates between Jean-Christophe and Olivier Jeanin, whose names reflect the cultural polarity of occidental tradition, fictionalize the historical coexistence of the two incompatible creeds. If fictionalized, any religious conflict can become an effective macrostimulus.[71] Rolland, the scholar and pacifist apostle of brotherly love uniting all believers in God, did not limit his literary model of the Creator to the Judeo-Christian and Greco-Roman revelations. His scholarly trilogy, *Essais sur la mystique et l'action de l'Inde vivante,* offered to the post-World War I public

69 The third in the *Cinq grandes odes*, (1900–8) written in the " Claudelian versets" imitating solemn biblical discourse.

70 The above quotations, translations and paraphrases are drawn from *Twentieth Century French Literature*, ed. Germaine Brée (New York: MacMillan, 1962), pp. 77–94. Claudel's *Magnificat* opens with the Holy Virgin's biblical *Magnificat,* thanking God for choosing her to bear His son (Luke 1: 46–55).

71 See ch. III, "Zikmund Winter."

biographies of Rama Krishna (vol. I) and Vivekananda (vol. II) and Vivekananda's "Universal Gospel" ("L'Évangile Universel", vol. III.) In these richly footnoted yet accessible essays, Rolland cites or paraphrases not only these sages' thoughts but also old Hindu myths evoking Oriental deities or visions of the transcendant Eternal Soul attained by ancient and modern mystics. Concluding the "Universal Gospel," Rolland emphasizes Gandhi's endorsement of Vivekananda's tolerant neovedantic embrace of all theologies as the "right" ones, although none can be free of errors; yet in spite of the flaws inevitable in any doctrine, all deist outlooks are *almost* as dear to Vivekananda as his inherited Hinduism. In addition, Rolland's essays sum up the parallels between Oriental and European (especially medieval) mystical experiences.

Herrmann Hesse's *Siddhartha*

In 1929, when Rolland's essays appeared, the best known Western work of fiction which awakened occidental readers' interest in the cosmic absolute was a slender novel, *Siddhartha* (1922), by the German /Swiss Herrmann Hesse (awarded the Nobel Prize in 1946). His hero, son of a rich Brahmin, is a contemporary of Gotama Buddha. Vaguely but unmistakably Hesse lends him some biographical traits of Gotama Siddhattha, the future Buddha. Like him, Siddhartha seeks Ultimate Truth. Without powerful contrasts, gradations and effective microstimulative topics, such themes risk monotony. Hesse avoids this danger as his hero gradually tests various colorful trails leading him to union with God. On his journey to find Wisdom, Atman/Om (External Soul, the Absolute, God), he first becomes a Samana ascetic achieving mystical exaltation through mortification of physical sensitivity.

> Silently Siddhartha stood in the fierce sun's rays, filled with pain and thirst, and stood until he no longer felt pain and thirst. Silently he stood in the rain, water dripping from his hair onto his freezing shoulders...And the ascetic stood until his shoulders and legs no longer froze...Silently he crouched among the thorns. Blood dripped fromhis smarting skin, ulcers formed, and Siddhartha remained stiff, motionless, till no more blood flowed...

Later, his instructors teach him how to conquer one's Self: "A dead jackal lay on the sandy shore and Siddhartha's soul slipped into its corpse; he became a dead jackal...decayed, was dismembered by hyenas...became a skeleton, became dust..."

The masochistic spirituality of the Samanas does not satisfy

Siddhartha's metaphysical hopes. After a duel of wills with the eldest Samana, Siddhartha is allowed to leave the ascetics and he meets Buddha whom he admires. Nevertheless he is not willing to adopt his passive doctrine of suppressing human sorrow by giving up one's aspirations and goals. Although his dearest friend and fellow Samana, Govinda, becomes Buddha's disciple, Siddhartha elects an active life, marries, has a son and becomes wealthy. Yet on this path toward happiness, his longing to discover the divine never weakens. Once more he abandons his family and his possessions. This time he becomes the apprentice of a ferryman, Vasudeva. Observing and listening to the river, which is "everywhere at the same time, at the source and at the mouth," he learns that there is no such thing as time. "Nothing was, nothing will be, everything has reality and presence." After Vasudeva retires, Siddhartha operates the ferry and like him listens to the river and to everything that is. The river mirrors his whole past life as well as Om. When Buddha dies, Govinda joins his old friend and Siddhartha tells him about the holy man who knew everything "without books, just because he believed in the river." He reveals Vasudeva's insight into the cosmic substance of material Being, the divinity of every whisper of the river, of every stone, every tree. The Buddhist Govinda objects: "But what you call thing , is it...not only the illusion of Maya...? Your stone, your tree, are they real?" Siddhartha answers, "If they are illusion, then I also am illusion, and so they are always of the same nature as myself... That is why I can love them. And here is a doctrine at which you will laugh. It seems to me, Govinda, that love is the most important thing in the world."[72]

Inspired by ancient Oriental pantheism, Hesse's novel enriched Western pantheistic naturalism rooted in pre-Christian Indo-European polytheism. We find many striking pantheistic accents, for instance, in Knut Hamsun's work, in Maupassant's and Anatole France's short stories and novels, in the key passages of *The Magic Mountain*, in Paul Valéry's poetry, in the rural novels of the pacifist Jean Giono, Anton Coolen or Karl Holter. Hesse's poetic evocation of ancient Hindu legends and Rolland's biographies of the Indian "saints" are precedents of post World War II mimetic approaches to metaphysical visions. The surrealist Henri Michaux imitated Mexican Indian techniques of reaching a mystical high by consuming certain kinds of mushrooms.[73] After the

72 The above quotations are drawn from Hilda Rosner's translation of *Siddhartha* (New York: New Directions, 1957), pp. 11, 12, 18, 19, 118, 119.

73 *LP II*, ch. II, p. 23, n. 8 and pp. 48–9 cite fragments of Michaux' poetry.

war and especially after the Vietnam conflict, hallucinogenic drugs entered the counter-culture as a medium facilitating transphysical perceptions.

Jill's Psychedelic Vision of God

John Updike's satirical mimesis of mystical illusions draws from sixties-style "revelations" witnessed by drug addicts on psychedelic trips. During a period of conjugal turbulence, Updike's Everyman, Rabbit, shelters an upper-class teen-age fugitive named Jill, who does her drifting in a white Porsche convertible. She recalls how her first lover—a teen-age lifeguard—persuaded her to try a hallucinatory drug mixture, maintaining that the main goal of the trip was to let her see God. When Jill protested that it might kill her, her boy friend said this was part of the "kick." Once having "seen God face to face," Jill's confidence in her lover and his mystical doctrine declined. "...if he met God right on the street he'd've tried to hustle him for money enough for a couple bags." Rabbit, Jill's fatherly new protector, is fascinated by the teenager's spritual attainments. "What did he look like?" he asks. Missing the (mystical) point, she replies, "about five ten, brown hair down his shoulders...he had been a runner in junior high." Rabbit interrupts, his metaphysical hunger unsatisfied. "I meant God," he says. Unperturbed, as though she were merely flipping to another page in the school yearbook, Jill depicts the God she saw in her trance. "Oh God. He changed. He was different every time. But you always knew it was Him. Once I remember something like the inside of a big lily, only magnified a thousand times, a...funnel that went down and down. I can't think about it."[74]

Updike's Theologians

This caricature of a drug-induced mystical vision complements other equally ironic but more subtle transpositions of the modern quest for God. Their prime protagonists are not street-wise teenagers like Jill but rather erudite theologians who keep alive the ancient cults. In *A Month of Sundays*, the penitent apostle of adultery Thomas Marshfield recalls his discussions with his father-in-law, Doctor Reverend Wesley Augustus Chillingworth, ethics scholar at the divinity school. In *Roger's version*, Roger Lambert, professor of religious studies, hesitantly supports the

74 *Rabbit Redux*, pp. 132–7, op. cit. ch. V, n. 137

interdisciplinary research grant application of the postgraduate Dale Kohler, computer specialist. Dale proposes to design a program proving the existence of God. In *S.*, Updike's Art Steinmetz of Waterford, Massachusetts, son of Jewish Armenian immigrants, spends some time in India and returns to the States with a new name and embellished academic credentials—Shri (holy) Arhat (Meritorious Buddhist monk) Mindali, M.A., Ph.D. As the Supreme Mediator and Guru (teacher) he operates ashram (retreat) Arhat, where he leads the well-heeled *sannyasins* (pilgrims), especially *samanya ratis*, ordinary (consort) women, to the Hindu fountains of *purusha* (eternal cosmic spirit). To the amazement of Sarah and other selected *naiykas* (devout women), his mystical *savoir-faire* includes *vajrolimudra*—the yoga technique of retaining one's *bindu* (sperm) and absorbing *rajas* (female secretions) during the extended *maithuna* (intercourse). As the ashram's bookkeeper, Sarah puts and end to his mystical scam by opening her own account on one of the Caribbean islands.[75]

Like Updike's earlier novels, *In the Beauty of the Lilies* fictionalizes the seepage of secular skepticism into archaic Christian doctrines which are stubbornly defended not only by (officially) orthodox theologians but even more by "modern" fundamentalists. He transposes contemporary Americans' doubts, doctrinal interpretations and misinterpretations in the portraits of two contrasting but not interacting characters. The first, who is a duly annointed God's vicar, is introduced to the reader in chapter I, set at the beginning of the 20th century. The other, a fanatic doomsday prophet, emerges only in the novel's finale, a stunning echo of recent tragic events.

The Princeton Divinity graduate, Reverend Clarence Wilmot, succumbs to agnostic temptation in Paterson, New Jersey, during a hot afternoon in 1910. As he meditates on Robert Ingersoll's arguments in *Some Mistakes of Moses* [76] (which a "perturbed parishioner" asked the

75 Thorough readers of Updike's *S*, satirizing the trendy mysticism of the seventies and eighties in the United States (see above, Ch. IV, "Updike's neo-pagan Christians" and nn. 137, 139) have to use a glossary of vedantic terminology derived from livresque sources outlined in "The Author's Note." Analogical terminology characterizes the above essays, obviously drawing from a much broader bibliography linguistically accessible to Rolland.

76 *In the Beauty of the Lilies* (New York: Fawcett Columbine, 1996), p.5. The two subsequent citations in this passage refer to pp. 4 and 484. Ingersoll (1833–99), controversial Illinois Attorney General and renowned political orator known for anti-Christian candor which hampered his political ambitions.

pastor to invalidate in the name of Presbyterian orthodoxy), Clarence is unaware that a new god is in action across town: the movie. D.W. Griffith is in Paterson making a silent film at the pseudo-Gothic castle owned by a local silk tycoon. Seventeen-year-old Mary Pickford, "svelte in the tights, velvet cape and heavy brocaded tunic of a page," is ready (for the third time) to mount a horse and ride full speed carrying the royal command to waiting troops: "Attack the Saraceen infidels!" The protracted rehearsal under a blistering sun makes Griffith's legendary star dizzy and the saddle piping hot. During the third take, it "scorches her buttocks" and to the displeasure of the gentlemanly director, the royal page falls from her horse in a faint. Somewhat incredibly but conveniently, this is the very moment when "the last of his faith" leaves Clarence. Updike's clergyman becomes an infidel falling away from the Biblical Lord. Far from denouncing the heretical Ingersoll, Clarence wholly endorses his accusation: "[T]he God of the Pentateuch was an absurd bully, barbarically thundering through a cosmos entirely misconceived. There is no such God, nor should there be." But what shall he tell his flock? The honest, high principled apostate knows he must resign, despite the objections of his wife and the church establishment. Gradually, Updike's reluctant defender of the faith loses his voice and his wife delivers his sermons. Is his silence all that is left of the compelling biblical voice which commanded Moses from behind the burning bush? A voice now drowning in the noise of modern Babel? Possibly. Before abandoning his calling, Clarence has four conversations which provide a particularly rich mimesis of canonic dialectic. These arguments elucidate the doctrinal sclerosis sapping the metaphysical and moral vigor of the modern cloth. They include the repartee with his pragmatic wife Stella; his discussion with a dying believer who fears that Presbyterian Providence has predestined him to damnation rather than resurrection; his evening discussion with a congregation Elder, Dearholt, who stresses the essential cooperation of business and the Church, and especially the colloquy with Synod member Thomas Drever, an erudite but slick advocate of insidious pastoral compromises. These dialogs echo the gravely ironic "correspondence" between the *pasteur* and his son Jacques, a theology student, in Gide's *La Symphonie pastorale*. They are also reminiscent of the prodigal son's four heart-to-heart talks in *Le retour de l'enfant prodigue*.[77] Like these characters, Clarence embodies

77 The first with the allegorical Mother, perhaps embodying Christian love and compassion; the following with the Father, God of all religions; with his older

faith losing ground to secular doubts concerning the revengeful God of the Old Testament, the divinity and resurrection of Jesus, the existence of Paradise, Hell and Purgatory, divine damnation, even the power of Christian ethics to achieve elementary social justice. Instead of spreading the Word, Clarence is reduced to enlightening his fellow man by selling encyclopedias. Between sparse sales, he finds spiritual nirvana in a new temple: the movie house. Tuberculous, he dies in oblivion.

Updike introduces Clarence's theological antipole long after the Presbyterian apostate's death: Jesse Smith founds the Temple, a small promiscuous commune which settles at a secluded ranch at Low Branche, Colorado. His feminine followers call this Seventh Day Adventist and Bible buff Big Daddy—he is a prolific bachelor-polygamist. The commune's undisputed master persuades his brothers and sisters in Christ that the day of reckoning is imminent and that he is the mystical lamb sent to defeat the apocalyptic Beast, the satanic No. 666. When the abominations of Gog[78] reach their peak, the Lord and his U.S. delegate Lamb Jesse can tolerate no more. In harmony with Jesse's biblical exegis, one of his apostles fires at the schoolbus coming to take the commune's children to the public school. In the attacker's eyes, the bus symbolizes the diabolic Darwinian forces of the anticreationist GOG Beast. The long awaited Advent will now start. The Colorado State Police trying to investigate the shooting incident are met by gunfire from the God-loving Temple. One state trooper is killed and another is paralyzed. After a protracted negotiation (echoing the memorable Waco siege), a Temple Judas prevents the second coming: Clark/Esau/Slick Wilmot, the Temple's lukewarm public relations man and great grandson of the skeptical Clarence, shoots the deranged "Savior". Jesse had ordered his men to burn the Temple and shoot his concubines and their children because Big Daddy "will need his girls" in the renovated Heaven and the city within "with foundations adorned with saphire, and

---

brother—the symbolic heir of the Roman Catholic "house" and with the younger brother who, like the prodigal, is open, "disponible," to life's adventures unrestricted by dogmatic "house rules." See also citations (France, Gide, Lautréamont, etc.) and/or comments in *LP I*, ch. V, pp. 93–111, *LP II*, ch. IV, pp 129–135; 201–205; 224–227.

78 Ruler in Magog, the Biblical region mentioned in the "The Book of the Prophet Ezekiel." In it, the Lord informs Ezekiel that he plans the liquidation of Gog. In his Bible classes, theologian Jesse maintains that Magog is the United States and Gog stands for GOG, the Government of the Godless.

chalcedony, and emerald" as outlined in "Revelation" ch. 21.

Like his erotica, Updike's metaphysica portraying the angry God who burned the Temple of the Tarbox sinners[79] or his portraits of modern shepherds are inspired by his ironic skepticism and limited confidence in mankind rather than in the rigid authority of a jealous God predestining our resurrection in Heaven or damnation in Hell. None among Updike's Voltairean sketches of these theologians who interpret God and His divine Word is likely to boost the ranks of born-again Christians but their message is provocative. Updike's art and humanism are comparable to Anatole France's *pessimisme jouisseur* or *sombre optimisme*.[80] The fanatical Jesse evokes the cult-leader whose "mighty fortress" of Christian fundamentalism Updike's readers must have seen *ad nauseum* on television. His absurdly literal interpretations of biblical prophesies provoke both laughter and a grim foreboding of tragedy. By letting such visions speak for themselves or by representing a melancholy parson who loses his faith, Updike the humanist hints at what still might be imprudent to say outside a fictional frame in a culture where no one takes an oath without a hand on the Bible: our religious faith has its limits and the archaic Judeo-Christian doctrines are ready for tolerant revisions unreservedly recognizing secular laws and free secular thought. If this diagnosis is correct, literary historians have to admit Updike into the fraternity of enlightened skeptics.[81]

Creating a verbal portrait of Providence has always been a challenge to any writer's inventive skills. In a remarkably rational century during which agnostic science and technology strengthened secular materialistic trends, authors tend to represent the invisible universal Force through the metaphysical speculations of their believing or doubting characters. Perhaps one day, when human genius identifies the all-controlling, macrocosmic "DNA", its mimesis may cease to be a product of human faith or fantasy and will rather be inspired by profound knowledge. Until that happens, we readers will respond to the mimesis of divine or diabolic subjects according to our constantly evolving outlooks and

79 See ch. IV, "Updike's neo-pagan Christians."

80 G. Michaut, *Anatole France* (Paris: Fontemoing, 1913), pp. 300,303.

81 Among the fathers of the skeptical tradition are Thales of Miletus (6th century B.C.), Anaximander (c. 610–545), Heraclitus (530–470), Democritos (460–370), Aristotle (384–322), Epicurus (342–270), Lucretius Carus (97–55). Their followers include doubters of various stripes such as Boccacio, Montaigne, Galileo Galilei, Fontenelle, Voltaire, Diderot, Goethe, Marx, Flaubert, Anatole France, Zola, Thomas Mann and so many others.

vacillating assumptions, biases or doubts. The esthetic impact of metaphysical topics is many sided, including didactic and spiritual as well as farcical or satirical treatments of gods and correlated cults, in which the comic fuses with the supernatural. Such stimuli usually trigger a variety of responses ranging from enlightened approval to annoyed disapproval. The didactic components awaken the reader's philosophical, religious, social, cultural or historical associations. The esthetic perception of the first sinful sample from the Tree of Knowledge; Prometheus' theft of Olympian technology; Dante's journey to Hell and Paradise; the fallen angels' coup against the cosmic autocrat—all stimulate critical reflection and enjoyment. Recalling such heterogeneous topics, we experience recurrent macrostimulative echoes. They document the lasting storage of such stimuli and, above all, confirm their eternal allure.

* * *

VII

FANTASIES, UTOPIAS AND BIZARRERIES

"Démons et merveilles vents et marées
Deux petites vagues pour me noyer. "[1]

Renaissance of the Irrational. Cocteau's Muse Cinéma—her Magic Touch. Prévert's *Les Visiteurs du soir*. Existentialist Fantasies. Marcel Aymé's "Passe-Muraille." Shangri-la—a Utopian Fantasy. Wonders of Sci-Fi: Verne, Wells, Čapek, Huxley. Bizarrerie—Poe's "Definition." *Salammbô*. Maldoror's Nightmarish Wanderings. Huysmans' and Wilde's Eccentrics. Experimental Bizarrerie: Beckett. The Spooky Fix in 1996.

Renaissance of the Irrational

Homer's Cyclops or Circe or the Welsh Merlin all possess powers no less supernatural than those of gods and devils. The magic of these characters defies the laws of nature; like divine or demonic miracles, it piques our curiosity, stirs the imagination and, if it threatens, it provokes fear. Yet these marvellous beings are not omnipotent gods and their extraordinary powers are limited. Humans defy them and, like Odysseus, may even overcome them. Thus such characters and their powers form a distinctive branch of supernatural or quasi-supernatural subjects. The genres exploiting such topics are not limited to fairy tales and utopias (such as Swift's *Gulliver's Travels*, Voltaire's "Eldorado" or Goethe's *Faust II*.) Fantasies and bizarreries representing dreams, metaphysical contemplations, stunning scientific predictions, various types of neurosis

1 "Jacques Prévert, *Paroles*, "Sables mouvants". Under the above title, I also cover mimesis of magic, sorcery, mystery and science-fiction. Bizarreries as discussed below, include inexplicable (supernatural) and natural (consistent with natural laws) incongruities.

or occult illusions never cease to deepen and broaden the modern reservoir of macro- and microstimulative figments. Their power is conditioned by their density and by the captivating credibility of bizarre characters and plots. A minor allusion to, say, a prevalently farcical topic may strike barely noticeable microstimulative sparks. For example in Rabelais' chapter subheading informing readers "...how Pantagruel's farts gave life to dwarfs,"[2] merely enhances the text's comic intensity. No matter how miraculous, Pantagruel's digestive sorcery will never enrich the esthetics of marvels and mysteries. More compelling bizarre or fantastic features generally stem from the mimesis of supernatural voices, spectres (e.g., Goethe's "Erlkönig," Perrault's cannibal "ogre"), ghosts of the deceased (e.g., Hamlet's father) or from encounters with folkloric fairies (e.g., "The Sleeping Beauty"), and so on.

Among the classic writers who revealed to their readers the fairylands of fantasy and magic illusions are Charles Perrault, author of *Fairy Tales of Mother Goose,* and Antoine Galland, whose translation of the 14th century Arabian *Thousand and One Nights* (1704–12) was rapidly introduced into other national literatures. These works whetted the Occidental appetite for ogres with seven-league boots and exotic genies with magic lamps.

Contemplating the spiritual climate favorable to the birth of fantastic narratives, Pierre-Georges Castex maintains that the triumphant rationalism of Bayle, Montesquieu, Diderot and Voltaire has its paradoxical yet quite natural counterpoint—the "Renaissance of the Irrational."[3] He suggests that the growing hunger for the fantastic, occult and mystical in 18th and 19th century Europe was propelled by seekers of the sixth sense called *Illuminati.* The best known apostles of the irrational include the Swede Emanuel Swedenborg (1688–1772),[4] Martines de Pasqually, who practised numerology and tried to reconcile his brand of Christianism with hermetism and occultism, and the mystical fideist Claude Saint Martin (1743–1803). Another proponent of irrational noetics is the Swiss Pastor, J.K. Lavater (1741–1801), who prophesized the day when the "regenerated Christians would unite

2 *O.C., Pantagruel*, ed. J. Plattard (Paris: Société de Belles Lettres, 1946), ch. XXVII, p. 132.

3 *Le Conte fantastique en France—de Nodier à Maupassant* (Paris: Corti, 1951), pp. 18–25. In this context see ch. VI, esp., n. 7 referring to Hoffmann, Hume and Rousseau.

4 *Arcana coelestia quae in Scriptura sacra seu verbo Domini sunt detecta,* 1747–58.

around the living God."[5] Lavater also dabbled in typology, a charlatan empiricism deriving one's propensities as well as one's past and future from one's physiognomy. Dr. Franz A. Mesmer (1734–1815) mixed charlatan and legitimate scientific methods to explore the therapeutic potential of magnetism and astrology.

Among the unscrupulous exploiters of human credulity belong the Venetian globetrotter Jacques Casanova de Seingalt (1725–98), who made a fortune organizing Parisian lotteries, and Giuseppe Balsamo, who paraded as Count Alessandro Cagliostro (1743–95), a latter-day alchemist peddling love philtres and potions making ugly women beautiful. Their influence, along with the Romantic cult of intuitive impulse and the taste for the grotesque inspired two 19th century genres, the *conte fantastique* and the gothic novel.

Today many people, ranging from trusting children to crusty old skeptics, want to see miracles with their own eyes—usually on the small or large screen—rather than read about them. Thanks to the technical sophistication of its special effects, contemporary cinema can create convincing illusions for a mass audience in often overlapping fantastic, utopian and magic genres. Meeting the growing demand, script writers continue turning out scenarios and scripts dealing with supernatural topics and the producers adapt and readapt literary works loaded with a high charge of fabulous content.[6] As I suggested earlier, in my eyes, the decision of the film or TV makers to transpose literary supernatural subject matter into cinematic terms indirectly testifies to the subject's powerful stimulative potential.[7] For example, R.L. Stevenson's memorable fantasy *The Strange Case of Doctor Jekyll and Mister Hyde* (1889) inspired three major film versions. *Halliwell's Film Guide* bestows an impressive four-star rating upon the 1931 production starring Frederic March; it awards the 1941 production with Spencer Tracy and Ingrid Bergman two stars and the 1971 British version of Dr. Jekyll's bizarre mutation into Jack the Ripper merely one star. Oscar Wilde's

5 Castex, p. 19, my transl. Also see *Encycl. Britt.*, 11th ed., "Lavater."

6 Such as *One Thousand and One Nights* or all stories such as *Adventures of Baron V. Münchhausen* by Erich Raspe (1737–94) and Gottfried Bürger (1747–94).

7 In Bram Stoker, *Annotated Dracula* (New York: Ballantine Books, 1975), ed. Leonard Wolf ("Introduction", p. ix) comments: "The film industry in a dozen countries inexhaustibly reinvents the adventures of the Count or his various semblables: Baron Latoes, Count Alucard, Count Yorga, Blacula. Because there are more than two hundred Draculoid titles (and the rate at which new ones appear is accelerating), it is nearly impossible to make a sensible filmography".

novel *The Picture of Dorian Gray* (1890) attracted Hollywood in 1945.

Cocteau's Muse Cinéma—her Magic Touch

Contemporary writers soon discovered the artistic merits and pecuniary benefits generated by the fruitful marriage of literature and film. Jean Cocteau welcomes its child—a fresh genre: "Vive la jeune muse Cinéma car elle possède le mystère du rêve et permet de rendre l'irréalité réaliste".[8] At the time when Cocteau became acquainted with Muse Cinéma, she had already come of age and was worshipped by the polyartistic fraternity of poets, directors, cameramen, actors, painters, designers, interacting both in new ateliers as well as in the open air. Cinéma offered literally fabulous opportunities to those who sought original alternatives to the post-Goethean and post-Wagnerian *Gesamtkunst*. While exploring the new medium, Cocteau wrote, adapted and directed a number of movie scripts. Due to their artistic failure as well as to the proliferation of films on the market, some of his accomplishments (e.g. *Orpheus*) have already ended on history's cutting room floor. Others, film historians will probably dub "typical" samples of Cocteau's experimentation but (I speculate that) two of them may survive as typical samples of French film under the occupation— the *Eternal Return* (1943) and especially the *Beauty and the Beast* (1945); in both films the fabulous "irréalité" plays an essential esthetic role. However, the density of magic features is high only in the *Beauty and the Beast*.

The *Eternal Return* echoes the Celtic romance of Tristan and Yseult versified by the Anglo-Norman Thomas (1170) in 3,000 lines and by the poetess Marie de France who condensed the romance in the short *Lai de Chevrefoil*.[9] Unlike the medieval aristocrats Tristan and Yseult,

8 René Gilson, *Cocteau, An Investigation Into His Films and Philosophy*, transl. Ciba Vaughan, (New York: Crown Publishers, 1969), chose this 1959 statement as the motto of his study, whose frontispiece is illustrated by Cocteau's caricature of the eighth Muse.

9 Throughout the centuries this perennial topic attracted many imitators including Hans Sachs, Wilhelm Schlegel, Martin Wieland, Tennyson, Swinburne and, of course, Richard Wagner. The modern novel-like version by the prominent medievalist Joseph Bédier (1864–1992) draws from the originals by Thomas, Eilhart, V. Oberg, Godfried v. Strassburg and Beroul. Most recently, John Updike (*Brazil*, New York, 1994) mythified two Brazilian teenagers, the black proletarian Tristão and the white upperclass Isabelle, in an exotic "neopicaresque" and occasionally livresque version of the timeless plot. See also "Tristan and Iseult" in Updike's *The Afterlife* (New York: A.A. Knopf, 1994, pp. 148–53.)

Cocteau's Patrice and Nathalie are not entangled in the same epical cobweb of magic. Cocteau's context retains the love philtre but implies that its consumption paralleling the genesis of the fatal erotic bond may just be a case of "accidental synchronization"[10] Cocteau eliminates the dwarf Frocin's malevolent magic, replacing him with the hostile character Achille. Silent, ominous images suggest the medieval sorceries. It is the youthful Muse Cinéma—the discovery of visual rhetoric—which helps the surrealist to create an illusion of invisible cosmic fate in action. The scenario reveals what the syncopated dialog conceals.

There is a remarkable contrast between the laconic scarcity of subtle marvels in *The Eternal Return* and their explicit abundance in *Beauty and the Beast*.[11] But even in this work the poet imitates the old plot's magic details[12] so far as they do not reduce the wonder of the macro-stimulative metamorphosis of Beauty's self-sacrifice into a superhuman love for the frightening beast with a feline head and hairy leonine paws. Her incredible pity for this repulsive yet chivalrous freak ultimately transforms the timid merchant's daughter into a brave savior. When her initial decency becomes a love beyond the grave, it breaks the evil spell and the bewitched wretch becomes a prince devoted to his redeemer. Projecting this fabulous climax, the adapter of Mme de Beaumont's text avoids the "realist" connubial stereotype, "...and they lived happily ever after." Instead, Cocteau's special effects experts created a whirlpool of clouds which, like Rimbaud's "flots abracadabrantesques"[13] carry the royal couple toward the dreamy heights of love and marvels.

Prévert's *Les Visiteurs du soir*

The darkest days of France humiliated under the German occupation, as well as an obscure 15th century legend, inspired the 1942 film—*Les Visiteurs du soir*. It re-enacts the "charming May 1485 [when] the Lord

10 Gilson, op. cit., p. 28.

11 An *imitatio rerum* based on the well-known fairy tale *La Belle et la bête* (1756) by Mme Jeanne-Marie Le Prince de Beaumont (1711–83).

12 For instance, the castle's interiors where human arms holding candelabras suddenly emerge from the walls to illuminate the silent staircases and hallways for the solitary shaken guest of the Beast or meals and wine glasses miraculously appearing on the table.

13 See *LP II*, pp. 50–6.

Devil sent two of his subjects to Earth to make humans despair."[14]

Today, older viewers who still remember the days of the French defeat, collaboration, heroic resistance and treachery will not only be captivated by the tragic poetry of the forgotten fable but might see in it allegorical allusions. At first sight, a show in which three devils are disguised as humans and three medieval French aristocrats—the widowed Hugues, his daughter Anne and her fiancé *chevalier* Renaud (whose name echoes Reynaud, Pétain's predecessor)—form the main cast, appeared to be apolitical enough to avoid the suspicion of German or Vichy censors. Although the commentaries do not intimate that Prévert/Laroche, Carné or Paulvé conspired to allegorize the German aggressors as Devils, a general parallel between the infernal guests and the invaders, who divided, blackmailed and corrupted the French family, must have always been an attractive hermeneutic option. In any case, such poetic ambiguities were discussed and considered only after the war. Had they been publicized during the Vichy regime, the film could not have received the 1942 Grand Prix of the French Film Industry.[15]

The infernal initiative is represented by the black field and slowly growing white dot zeroing in on two barely visible horsemen emerging from the sombre nowhere. Gradually, the black field becomes an arid rocky landscape. The riders in medieval attire are two troubadours heading toward a castle built on a rocky hill overlooking the dry deserted plains. In front of its gate, the older Gilles reveals his magic power when they meet a desperate bear trainer whose animal was allegedly killed by a brutal castle guard. All there is left of the peddler's livelyhood is the chain. Suddenly the living bear miraculously appears in its "handcuff". The singers are hospitably received by the Lord Hugues whose daughter Anne is about to marry the manly *chevalier* Renaud. As one bard sings two lovesongs,[16] the bride suddenly feels a fatal attraction for him. Her abrasive fiancé soon discovers that Gilles' younger "brother" Dominique is not a man but an attractive woman. In his turn, Renaud is irresistibly drawn to her. As time and life stand still, in the way of a fairy tale, both Anne and Renaud fall under the spell of the two mysterious singers.

The cast also includes three shockingly disfigured dwarfs shown as

14 *Les Visiteurs du soir*, scenario/dialogue by Jacques Prévert and Pierre LaRoche, direction Marcel Carné, a 1942 Paris production by André Paulvé, publ. in *Cinéma l'Avant-Scène*, No. 2, February 15, 1962, p. 2, my transl.

15 *Les Visiteurs du soir*, coll. des Bibliothèques du cinéma, Balland, 1974, pp. 25, 212.

16 The first is the above cited "Sables mouvants," n. 1.

"entertaining" bizarreries of nature during the feast. While not performing before the audience they wear "cagoules" similar to Ku-Klux-Klan hoods. Their primitively assonanced doggerel fulfils the role of a demoniac choir disclosing the past or future evils.[17]

Late at night, following the feast and dance, Dominique also approaches the Baron in his bedroom to solicit his quasi paternal protection and to confess to him that she is a noble maiden forced to pose as a man because "grave dangers threaten her." When she leaves, Hugues' eyes fall on the portrait of his late wife Madame Berthe, portrait under which he had been praying when Dominique entered. Suddenly, the likeness of Madame Berthe vanishes and the live face of the encouragingly smiling Dominique appears in the massive picture frame.[18] The same night Dominique lures Renaud into the wedding bed chamber prepared according to local customs days ahead of Anne's and his wedding. There she seduces the warrior with the assistance of a dwarf hidden under the bed: when the lovers appear he discreetly removes the bed spread and leaves, softly closing the door.

Under Gilles' spell, Anne calls his name in her dream while Gilles stands under her window in the garden. The next day, after the night full of intrigues and prophetic rhymes chorused by the dwarfs, Hugues' guests go hunting. On the hidden trails the main characters' incipient passions become urgent, but the devilish scheme does not quite progress according to the infernal plan. On one hand, the scene is set for the fatal rivalry between Anne's prospective husband and her father. On the other hand, the divine power of Anne's pure love for the damned Gilles and his sincere response start interfering with the designs of the until now absent Prince of Darkness who cannot tolerate the disobedience of his servant. While most of Hugues' guests are gathered in the castle's social hall to play games, an unexpected thunder storm erupts. A few seconds later in a heavy rain a stranger clad in black, gold-embroidered velvet stands on the hall's threshold asking for shelter. The generous Hugues offers him his hospitality. Just *en passant* the traveller helps Renaud to win in a

17 Because of their hoods/*cagoules* they seem to evoke the underground French fascist "Cagoulards" intimidating and blackmailing the French population during the World War II German occupation.

18 Here a magic picture is a microstimulative subject. It is macrostimulative in the *Picture of Dorian Gray* (see below "Huysmans' and Wilde's eccentrics"); In Aymé's "La Bonne Peinture" it is an epical nucleus. This still life makes the viewers consume a gourmet menu depicted on the canvas. (*Les meilleures Nouvelles de Marcel Aymé*, (New York: Scribner, 1964).

single move the game of chess which the knight had just given up to Dominique. Gaining immediate confidence of the host the eloquent stranger wishes to meet the young bride. She is found in her bedroom in the company of Gilles. As recommended by the Evil Spirit, Gilles, accused of abusing his host's hospitality, is put in chains and tied to the wall of the kennel.

During the tournament taking place the following day, the Devil's plot will bring about another unexpected calamity. In a tournament duel, in which Anne's father and his future son-in-law display their war game skill, the aging Lord "incidently" kills Renaud, whom Dominique had previously provoked to show his courage and fight the old man without a protective coat of mail. The Demon reveals his magic power to Anne when he makes her see the fatal duel mirrored in the water of the fountain quite distant from the tournament field. While talking to him Anne also sees him sitting at the tribune among the tournament's spectators. The blood suddenly obscures the fountain's water and the image in it like a curtain veiling a gruesome prelude to the final tragic act. After the abruptly ended tournament, Dominique confesses to Hugues what role she had played in his funereal victory—she had done it for him—she had feared that Renaud would kill her beloved protector. Feigning her regret for the tragedy which she had caused, she tells the Lord that she cannot remain any longer in his hospitable castle. Unable to persuade her to stay, the Baron promises to follow and defend her wherever she might go. A few moments later, the camera shows her in the saddle riding in full speed through the castle gate. The enamored Baron follows a few steps behind her. Dominique directs her horse toward a cliff and, miraculously, vanishes on the verge of a deep gap. Unable to stop, the Baron's steed carries him into the abyss. "Dominique!" he cries as he disappears over the cliff's edge while Dominique, hidden behind a rock, sighs with a melancholy smile, "mon amour."

In her final encounter with the Devil, Anne trades her own soul for Gilles' salvation. Gilles appears free near the fountain but does not recognize either his savior nor Satan. The irony of fate makes him even ask if Anne is the Devil's daughter. Offering thus the proof that Gilles is free, the Satan claims Anne's promised fidelity. She rejects him, protesting that her promise was a lie. Shaking the Devil's self-confidence once more, Anne can see and talk to Gilles who takes her firmly in his arms and assures her that nothing can ever divide them. In an outburst of fury the infernal sorcerer turns the lovers into a stone sculpture.

A deadly silence triggers the Demon's victorious smile but not for longer than a few seconds. A distinct rhythmical sound breaks the quiet—it is the pulse of the statue's heart which goes on beating—"leur coeur qui bat... qui bat... qui bat..." The Devil screams, flogging the lovers' lithified heads with his horse whip.

Viewers observing the fictional destruction of the French family, especially the viewers who lived through the terror unleashed in France during four years of occupation, can see the characters and the plot as an allegory of the Vichy Quislings tricked and corrupted by the brutal invaders or of patriots ready to die in their struggle against the forces of Evil. Yet regardless whether we conceive this production as a political allegory or whether we are merely enchanted by its archaic poetry, we will probably recognize that its macrostimulative impact springs both from the artistry of techniques applied to a fantasy dormant for centuries, as well as from the very content of this cinematically revived legend in the bleakest days of French national misery.

Existentialist Fantasies

After the 1940 capitulation, no French film maker who wished to keep his job in either occupied or unoccupied France could afford to produce any films even latently hostile to the conquerors and their ideology. Following the 1945 liberation it was just the opposite. This expected trend, however, did not seem to weaken the public's "escapist" taste for marvels and utopias. Even the Marxist existentialist Jean-Paul Sartre did not hesitate to dramatize our posthumous existence, infusing it with his own agnostic moralism. The self-deception (*mauvaise foi*) of his hypocritical characters condemns them to eternity in an infernal *Huis Clos*.[19] The philosopher's hell with "no exit" is set in a stuffy, overheated room in a second-class hotel. The only furnishings in the windowless decor are three easy chairs occupied by Garcin, Inès and Estelle. Garcin claims that he had been a pacifist who got 12 bullets in his skin while fighting for his noble cause. Gradually, it turns out that he was executed as a cowardly deserter, in addtion, he installed his mistress in the house he shared with his wife—she died of anguish. Estelle killed her child and destroyed her lover; the lesbian Inès confesses honestly that she had provoked her friend to commit a murder and suicide. Because they see

19 A one act play (Paris: Gallimard, 1944) which still reflects the wartime precautionary political vagueness. The same applies to its 1944 cinematic version.

themselves only through their hell-mates' eyes, the characters argue endlessly to justify their lifelong self-deception—thus creating hell for one another. Despite this conflict and the stimulus of lurid confessions, this lengthy existentialist cross-examination staged in a static setting is readable rather than dramatic; on stage or screen Sartre's cerebral Hell is monotonous rather than shocking.

His first post-war *ciné-roman, Les Jeux sont faits*[20], moves much faster; it balances the author's socialist puritanism with entertaining fantasy. The two main characters embodying his abstract concepts in *Les Jeux sont faits* are Eve Charlier, a bourgeoise married to the chief of a (Nazi S.A.-like) militia in an imaginary dictatorship and the labor leader Pierre Dumaine, who plans a socialist uprising against the country's fascist regime. Both Eve and Pierre are murdered at the beginning of the story: André Charlier pours poison in his wife's glass of water in hopes of retaining her dowry and doubling it by marrying her naive sister Lucette; Pierre is shot by a teenage stool pigeon Lucien Derjeu. The two victims leave their bodies as hazy spectres and meet one another when they arrive in a drab world of the dead. A corpulent, deadpan woman receives them in the admission office located on a mysterious dead-end street, Languénésie. Later, the receptionist casually notifies Pierre and Eve that, due to a regrettable administrative mix-up, they had been deprived of a preordained chance of falling in love with one another prior to their premature deaths. To remedy this mishap the plutonian code (art. 140) permits a restitution *ad integrum*. Under the circumstances and provided the thus distressed parties wish to pursue their potential erotic bliss, the overworked bureaucrat tells them they can either stay or be resurrected and—like the mythical Sisyphos—resume their former life. They opt for the latter and once back on Earth, they meet this time and inevitably fall in love. Yet due to their other previous loyalties or commitments they keep deferring the consummation of their love which, as the cited article postulates, has to take place within 24 hours after the provisory release. Failing to fulfil this precondition the applicants will be recalled. Eve tries to warn and protect her naive sister against André's scheming. Pierre, on the other hand, is in a desperate hurry to warn his former comrades whose lives are threatened: as an invisible ghost, Pierre visits the Hitlerian Regent's palace and learns that the police know everything about his long planned uprising and are ready to crush it. Trying in vain to persuade the conspirators not to risk bloodshed, he

20 Published by Nagel in 1947; film production is directed by Jean Delannoy.

keeps deferring his mandatory tryst with Eve. Ultimately the 24 hour deadline expires prior to their intimate reunion. The absurd cosmic dice are cast—"les jeux sont faits", Eve's ghost utters when she meets the spirit of her predestined lover at Languénesie.

In his movie script, Sartre's crusade for self-sacrifice which elevates aimless existence to a worthy human essence overlaps with a vision of the universe beyond that is predictably as absurd as life on earth. However, this *ciné-roman* differs from the ideologically overloaded film adaptations of his masterpieces such as *Les mains sales*, "Le Mur"or *Huis-Clos*. The ideological message of *Les Jeux sont faits* seems to be outdated to the generation which not only witnessed a continued decline of Sartre's once prestigious Marxist intellectualism but also saw the grandiose collapse of the Soviet empire and its satellites. On the other hand, the entertaining parody of the bureaucratized Hades where the gallant doddering cynics guillotined during the Revolution are eager to chat with the disillusioned newcomers, the caricature of the totalitarian dictator, who is observed by the ghosts of his victims, the awkward romance between a French socialite and a common blue collar worker still stimulates students and film buffs interested in the black and white productions inspired by works of Malraux', Hemingway's and Sartre's generation. The probable contemporary response to Sartre's amalgam of ideological moralism with fantasy and post-mortal Utopia illustrates that, like any subject, fantasies heavily charged with Marx, Heidegger or the catechism are likely to become doctrinal rather than esthetically effective statements. In the fifties and sixties, Sartre's *engagé* exempla provoked but in the seventies and eighties ultimately bored those readers favoring the disdained bourgeois liberalism rooted in individualist democratic pluralism. While denouncing fascist dictators Sartre had a soft spot for Soviet despotism. My assumption that ideological excess shaping epical and dramatic characters and plots is mixed artistic blessing is not a norm; it is merely empirical. Not all ideological crusades are incompatible with art: Zola's *Germinal*, satires such as *Death of a Salesman* or Robert Penn Warren's *All the King's Men* prove the opposite.

Marcel Aymé's "Passe-Muraille"

Marcel Aymé's story "Le Passe-Muraille" reflects no political engagement whatsoever. It blends absurd fantasy with farce and irony. Its anti-hero, Dutilleul, a minor civil servant from the old school, discovers one day that he can miraculously pass through any wall. At first, he takes it for a sickness and consults the physician who diagnoses it as a "helicoidal hardening of the thyroid's strangular partition". He prescribes overexertion and two tablets containing, among other therapeutic ingredients, centaur hormones. These pills are to be taken at a rate one every six months. Dutilleul takes the first and puts the other in the drawer. At the same time his old *souschef* Mouron is replaced by a younger M. Lécuyer. Full of fresh administrative zeal, he reforms the style of departmental correspondence, scrapping the stereotype epistolar opening—"Referring to your worthy letter of such and such day of this month and reminding you of our previous letter exchange, I have the honour to inform you..." He replaces it by a terse rather "American" formula "In reply to your letter of such and such I inform you..." Dutilleul, settled in his old ways resents the change. He also hates the humiliating removal of his desk to a dark niche adjacent to Lécuyer's office. To get revenge, the clerk penetrates into Lécuyer's office, showing only his head above the superior's desk and calling him names. Not believing his eyes Lécuyer keeps rushing to Dutilleul's niche only to find the grave clerk, pen in his hand, sitting behind his desk. The scribe goes on repeating the same manoeuvre as often as 23 times a day. In less than two weeks Lécuyer has to be admitted to an insane asylum. The early triumph encourages Dutilleul's bank-vault break-ins reported every morning by the press and read by his colleagues. When this glory becomes old hat, Dutilleul allows the police to arrest him. From his cell he penetrates into the apartment of the prison director and steals his watch. Bored by his own practical jokes he disappears and lives incognito. A new challenge emerges when he falls in love with a young lady married to a brutal Montmartre crook. The couple lives in a small house surrounded by a garden and a high thick wall. The husband always leaves the house at ten at night and returns home at four in the morning, thoroughly locking the house and bolting all window shutters. None of the these obstacles can stop the adventurer. With no effort Passe-Muraille enters the lonely wife's bedroom and spends several hours in her demanding company. Next day, he has a light headache, takes a pill and rushes to his rendezvous; after the repeated marathon of love the exhausted wolf leaves the bedroom shortly before the husband's return. But as Passe-Muraille penetrates the house wall, it seems more resistant than usual and, to his further suprise, he cannot complete the passing through the garden wall. The second dose of the centaur's hormones, along with the unmitigated overexertion, cures the elusive Don Juan at the least opportune moment: the thick masonry of the garden wall traps him forever.[21]

Shangri-la—a Utopian Fantasy

One of the "best-selling" prewar fantasies is James Hilton's *Lost Horizon.* Within the twelve years which followed its first edition this novel had 73 printings and was also adapted into a four-star film.[22] Although the mystery, utopian and fantastic features prevail in the stimulative subject matter, their esthetic impact is appreciably increased by the contrastful characters' conflicts, inner dilemmas, affinities and by the many offbeat livresque, historical, religious and exotic topics. The narrative has three contrasting parts—the dramatic abduction of several characters; their imposed yet serene confinement in a timeless retreat, and finally, paradise lost as the result of a troubled exodus. The interaction between the two main characters, Glory (Hugh) Conway, British Consul in India, and his mysterious kidnapper, the High Lama of Shangri-la, is the epical focus of Hilton's plot. While the consul is busy helping evacuate British civilians threatened by revolution in Baskul, an unnoticed assailant incapacitates and then replaces the pilot of the rescue plane. Instead of flying his passengers to nearby safety, the highjacker crosses the high ranges of the Himalayas and suffers mortal injuries while crash-landing in a remote Tibetan valley. When local tribesmen lead the survivors to the Shangri-la lamasery built at the foot of a spectacular peak, the sinister opening of the novel is paradoxically followed by the poetic discovery of an idyllic utopia. When, after a long delay, the High Lama finally receives the Consul, he does not discuss returning the captives to their former lives. Instead he praises Conway's interest in Shangri-la's origin and links it to early Christian influence in Tibet, where during the Middle Ages, the Nestorian[23] cult was

21 Aymé's text was adapted as a German film.

22 *Lost Horizon*, William Morrow, no pl. 1933; film 1937, dir., by Frank Capra and starring Ronald Colman; a 1972 remake was accorded one star by Les Keyser (*Hollywood in the Seventies*) who predicted, "it will never play again outside Shangri-la."

23 An early somewhat autonomous Christian doctrine inspired by the Syrian-born ascetic Nestorius, patriarch of Constantinople from 428–31. The sect, founded by the Persian bishop Barsumas Nisibis, built monasteries along the trade routes Bagdad-Peking. Marco Polo testifies to their existence (1274). Recent scholars speculate that Polo had never travelled beyond Constantinople where he allegedly fabricated his travelogs.

widespread. (The lama's *extempore* progresses from the historical to the fantastic level. It increasingly intrigues the Englishman who, prior to his consular career in China and India, lectured on Oriental languages at Oxford.) To renew contact with Christians in the Far East, in 1719, the Vatican sent four Capuchins to see whether the creed had survived in any of the remote Tibetan monasteries. Three died; only the 53-year-old Father Perrault reached the Blue Moon valley where, in 1741 he began rebuilding the ruins of the deserted Shangri-la monastery with his own hands. In 1769, the 82-year old missionary received instructions, dated 1757, to report to the Vatican. He acknowledged the summons but explained why it was impossible for a man of his age to comply—never learning whether his reply ever reached the Holy See. Yet, in spite of his age, the Capuchin, by then accustomed to high altitudes, learned how to induce lucid visions with the help of Yoga and Tibetan drugs; he did not master the art of self-levitation but triumphed in telepathy; he learned how to suspend some of his inborn senses to acquire extrasensory perception. The former Oriental scholar is captivated (as is the reader) by the metamorphosis of Perrault—born in 1688 in Luxembourg and educated in Paris and Bologna—from Capuchin into Tibetan mystic: the high Lama cannot be anyone else than this ancient Capuchin. At that moment, in 1931, the man is two and a half centuries old. Sensing that his death is approaching, Lama Perrault reveals to Conway that he had him kidnapped to make him his successor and guardian of the Shangri-la heritage.[24] Conway however, does not gain the High Lama's mystical powers overnight; he does not become the master of Shangri-la as soon as Perrault dies. He, his Vice-Consul and Princess Lo-Tsen, leave the lamasery. The "Prologue" and "Epilogue" framing Hilton's fantastic yarn vaguely relate the plot's open-ended denouement. As soon as the three characters leave Shangri-la, the beautiful princess becomes an ancient crone; she dies at Chung-Kiang when she and an amnesiac Conway are admitted to a missionary hospital. Quite incidently, Conway's former friend Rutherford, a British diplomat and writer, finds and identifies him and obtains his release. During their passage to the

24 Perrault's Christian/Buddhist monastery faintly yet distinctly echoes the Rabelaisian Abbaye de Thelème, its *fais ce que voudras* and its being open both to men and women. A Manchu princess, Lo-Tsen, who in 1884 travelled to Turkestan to marry a prince, is among the Shangri-la settlers. Its European founder built it as a secret humanistic asylum resistant to the shocks of intolerant doctrines and brutal wars of society.

States, Conway finally remembers his past and leaves the ship. Three months later, Rutherford learns that his friend is heading for Kashmir and "further East"—perhaps to the utopia awaiting its High Lama. Because of the high density and intensity of fantastic, utopian and livresque stimuli, like Sir Thomas More's *Utopi*a (1516), like Voltaire's "Eldorado"(in *Candide*), Hilton's Shangri-la has become a common metaphor for an idyllic society.

Wonders of Sci-Fi

The Romantic cult of the irrational did not affect the naturalist mimetic techniques twinning art and science, but even so, the progress of scientific research influenced not only Zola's cycle on the alcoholic degeneration of the Rougon-Macquart family, it also gave life to a relatively new brand of futuristic fantasies and utopian bizarreries generally labelled science fiction. Like the esthetics of heroism, love, laughter or divine omnipotence, the poetry of discovery goes back to mythology: among its prototypes are Prometheus (who created mankind, gave it fire stolen from the gods and taught it crafts and sciences) and the ingenious *heuretes/inventor* Daidalos (who designed the first glider, which enabled him to fly to Sicily from his Cretan prison in Minos' Labyrinth). The stimulative force of modern science fiction springs from the triumphant rationalism of the *Lumières* such as Diderot or Voltaire rather than from the metaphysical idealism of the *Illuminati*. The pioneers of the new genre are Jules Verne (1828–1905; 12 years older than Zola), Robert Louis Stevenson (1850–1894) and H.G. Wells (1866–1946). Their characters are scientists, and their fictitious inventions are the results of the anticipated progress of human knowledge rather than of occult activities.

Verne's *Voyage au centre de la Terre* (1864) relates the descent of a geologist and his crew to the underground empire alluded to in a deciphered cryptogram. They start their journey via the crater of the extinct Islandic volcano Sneffels. After many geological and archeological discoveries the explorers are ejected from the crater of Stromboli, an active Mediterranean volcano.

The first astronauts to orbit the moon are fictionalized in Verne's *De la Terre à la Lune* (1865–70). They are the members of the Baltimore Gun Club who fought during the American Civil War. This veterans' fraternity builds an immense aluminium missile appointed like a comfortable sleeping car and fires the fictional ancestor of modern space ships up into cosmic heights. Following its excursion to the moon the satellite falls in the Pacific. The astronauts are saved by a corvette guided by the director of the Cambridge Observatory and the vigilant secretary of the Gun Club. The well-known *Vingt mille lieues sous les mers* (1870) imagines the sophisticated submarine Nautilus engineered by the misanthropic captain Nemo, an incognito prince once betrayed by the perfidious Albion.

The earlier mentioned Doctor Jekyll develops a pharmacological formula to manipulate his own schizophrenic mutations. Like him, Wells' young physicist Griffin in *The Invisible Man* (1897) discovers in his laboratory how to make all his tissues transparent.

The Island of Doctor Moreau (1896) is an experimental island where the perverse surgeon and his assistant Montgomery "humanize" animals by modifying their larynxes to make them talk and brains to make them think. The *War of the Worlds* (1897) dramatizes the conquest of Mars by Martians armed with mortal rays. The happy ending is due to an epidemic launched by our planet's deadly viruses which the Martians, unlike the lucky Earthlings cannot resist. Verne's main artistic goal is entertainment, whereas the fantasies of the intellectualizing Wells reflect political ideals. The bizarre, utopian content of his novels is a powerful esthetic accessory of social satire and ideological reformism.

The period following World War I brought advances in engineering, physics, chemistry, biology and medicine, including the exploration of human psyche. These developments, along with the establishment of the League of Nations in an era of colossal social and political change led modern humanists to contemplate precipitous expansion in many domains of life and to transpose both their fear and confidence into prophetic visions. Their fiction anticipates the Promethean leaps, technological dead-ends and threatening disasters triggered by human genius and its quest of political and economic power.

The futuristic topics developed by the prematurely deceased Karel Čapek (1890–1938) and by Aldous Huxley (1884–1963) issue humanistic warnings to a modern society committed to scientific research and to its applications by modern industry or governments. As early as in 1924, two decades before the explosion of the atomic bomb, Čapek's novel *The Krakatite* deals with the invention of a devastating explosive the formula and samples of which are sought by German militarists as well as by the anarchists. When he is arrested in Germany and kidnapped by a mysterious stranger, the Czech inventor rejects foreign promises, escapes and does not disclose the secret of the Krakatite.

The best known of Čapek's scientific fantasies is his 1921 play, R.U.R. (Rossum's Universal Robots),[25] portraying the manufacturer of soulless robots, their merciless revolt and extermination of mankind. Life will nevertheless continue because two robots fall in love and the play's finale thus becomes a beginning of the planet's new era. Like a man-created Adam and Eve, they will give life to new progeny and repopulate the Earth. With the emergence of AIDS the stimulative potential of Čapek's *White Disease (Bílá memoc)* may increase. The play may be resurrected as an apocalyptic epidemic which does not distinguish between the oppressed humans and the powerful dictator.

Huxley's *Brave New World*, published 10 years after *R.U.R.*, mythifies our fears of collective enslavement with a much heavier dose of pessimism than Čapek's play: seven centuries A.F. (after the deified Ford) the overpopulated world state, governed by an oligarchy under dictator Mustapha Menier, genetically controls every citizen from birth to death. In the Bekanovsky process one human egg is split into sixty identical siblings. In the test-tube stage each future being is pre-programmed to fill its determined place in the stratified society consisting of Alpha, Beta, Gamma, etc., citizens all of whom, regardless of their social class, experience euphoria. When its expected level declines, one simply consumes the somapill which brightens one's mood. Euthanasia eliminates discomforts of old age and dying. Huxley's anti-hero Bernard Marx is a rare exception: due to a flaw in the test-tube programming of this hypnopedic worker, he is chronically sad and even falls in love. The authorities exile him to a New Mexico reservation for the last remaining humans of the old era where he meets a contemporary of our time, John Le Sauvage. Marx introduces him to the "brave new world" and to its mandatory happiness. Shocked by the outcome of evolution Le Sauvage hangs himself. Huxley concludes his futuristic premonitions with a vision of journalists rushing to report the death of the last human to a society drowning in regulated bliss.[26]

25 The terms Rossum and robots echo the Czech *rozum*/reason and *robota*/drudgery, serfdom.

26 Franz Rottensteiner (*The Science Fiction Book*, New York: Seabury Press, 1975, p. 92) rates *Brave New World* as one of the finest examples of the genre: "Few of the many antiutopias after those by Zamyatin, Huxley and Orwell have been as powerful." Rottensteiner's concise but richly illustrated history contains an extensive bibliography of both the primary texts from 1810–1975 and the criticism devoted to the genre.

Bizarrerie—Poe's Definition

In my reflections the general term bizarrerie designates a broad spectrum of stimulative incongruities forming sufficiently specific contrasts with expected normalcy. Dictionaries allude to its etymological derivation from the Basque *bizar* (beard), Spanish *bizarro* (gallant, brave) and to its subsequent French and Italian shift to "extravagant, fantastic, queer, odd, strange, unusual, eccentric, droll, absurdly comic, bordering on lunacy." In this broad discussion it not only has all these somewhat tautological connotations but also covers enigmatic, grotesque, exotic and off-beat, erudite, bookish or historical subjects intended to surprise, stir up our curiosity or awaken our sense of propriety. One leading modern practitioner of the esthetics of the bizarre is Edgar Allan Poe. His short story "The Murders in the Rue Morgue"[27] not only portrays two eccentric detectives but also spells out his concept of bizarrerie. The American narrator incidently meets an erudite and ingenious Monsieur C. Auguste Dupin in an "obscure library" where both of them look for "the same very rare and very remarkable volume". The American concludes that, during his stay abroad, he would benefit if he could live with a man of Dupin's calibre. The Parisian accepts the stranger's invitation provided the wealthier American pays the rent and furnishes their common home to appeal to the "fantastic gloom of [their] common temper". They move into a "time eaten and grotesque mansion, long deserted through superstitions…[and] tottering to its fall in a retired portion of the [then dated] faubourg St. Germain". If anybody had been able to penetrate their privacy, he would have considered them "as madmen". But no one is ever allowed or tempted to enter the "secret" edifice whose "seclusion [is] perfect." The narrator then credits the Frenchman for changing his American style of living: "It was a freak of fancy in my friend…to be enamoured of the Night for her own sake; and into his *bizarrerie* [Poe's italics] as into all his others, I quietly fell." His nouns and adjectives confirm that Poe's connotative range generally concurs with the dictionaries; in addition, their sequence reflects a certain gradation progressing from "obscure" and "very rare" first (1) to "fantastic and grotesque (2), deserted through superstition (3) and ultimately to "madmen" and "freak of fancy" of the character "enamoured of the Night" (4). In this instance, the microstimulative latent contrasts—contrasts between the characters' bizarre tasks and

27 *The Great Tales and Poems* (New York: Pocket Books, 1949), p. 140–1.

enigmatic interests on one side and their social surrounding's implied conventions on the other—play the role of an epical prelude. It further piques the curiosity generated by the mysterious crimes promised in the title, and their dramatic denouement yet to be detected by the bizarre scholarly Dupin and his new friend. There is nothing transcendental in this murder story; at the end Dupin unravels the whodunit plot.

Many other bizarre mysteries may appear to be occult as long as their natural causes remain unknown. According to a Maoi legend a volcanic cave in Waianapana State Park had served as a fine shelter to prudent lovers. To get in it they had to dive in a pool and swim under a subterranean rocky partition. Among the grotto's past visitors had been a Hawaian princess unfaithful to her husband. The jealous spouse, however, sniffed out the hidden adulterers and murdered them. Thereafter people began noticing that from time to time the water in the grotto turned red and a weird moaning was occasionally heard. The blood-like water had been attributed to the ghosts of the killed lovers until modern zoologists and geologists clarified the two recurrent phenomena: thousands of tiny red shrimp close to the water surface appear to be patches of blood, and air blowing through a crevisse in the cave wall occasionally sounds like ominous groans.[28] Thus the scientists transformed an occult myth into a commercialized bizarrerie of nature. The skeptical tourist wonders if the legend was invented to explain an inexplicable phenomenon much older than the legend. The disparity between Poe's suspenseful "residential" bizarrerie and the exotic and melodramatic Polynesian bizarrerie suggests that the two topical incongruities have no common denominator other than a certain oddity. Their specific stimulative anomalies, however, are heterogeneous. Obviously, esthetically effective bizarreries form a broad category of polymorphous features which we pragmatically unite under the general label, "bizarrerie." Consequently, depending on their incongruous factors they often stimulate other faculties than curiosity: the previously discussed military burial of Colonel Chabert who, although seriously wounded in the battle, was not killed, and his almost miraculous survival and struggle against the cobweb of legal errors forms not only an epical cluster of macrostimulative violent, non-violent and ultimately even psychological conflicts;[29] it is also a tragic and typically Romantic bizarrerie.

28 *Hawaii*, tourguide, American Automobile Association, 1995, p. 63.
29 See comments and illustrations, ch. II.

Or while de Sade, Lautréamont or George Bataille invent perverse phantasms to stimulate their readers' lust, revulsion or laughter, many a feature within dominantly erotic content is often bizarre.[30] The subject of Prévert's surrealist fable on two snails who go to the burial of a dead leaf[31] certainly piques our curiosity but, in the first place, strikes a comic note. The naïve fable personifying the farcical mollusks gradually enkindles the benign optimism of readers who identify themselves with the symbolical snails reaching the autumn funeral only in spring time when the leaves are green again; sun and blossoms transform the mood of the slow mourners who forget dead leaves, get drunk and sing happily.

Excursive anecdotes or diverse anomalies are frequent microstimuli in various kinds of discourse.[32] If integrated smoothly, they increase the esthetic density, especially in historical and *livresque* genres. Paul Stapfer applauds France's broad erudition combined with his suave techniques of digression, which make his readers enjoy the Francean extemporizations, for example, on the nasty whims of Nature, which gave the sister of the heroic Mithridates two rows of teeth in both the upper and lower jaw.[33] In *The Gods are Athirst* , "citizen Pelleport, health officer," incidentally meets the novel's main characters at a country inn, "l'auberge de la Cloche." He draws their attention to the monumental stamina of the inn's housemaid, Tronche, who, as he claims, is literally "two girls." He confesses that her impressive figure caused him to examine her and he discovered that most of her bones were double, "each thigh, two *femurs* welded together, each arm two *humeri*. Some of her muscles are also double. When people call her 'La Tronche,' they should rather say 'Les Tronches'. Nature has these bizarreries..." (This information awakens the interest of one of the guests in the auberge, who also examines Tronche's anatomy.)[34]

Salammbô

If there is any classic which we could call the bible of the bizarre because of the concentration and remarkable intensity of its bizarre

30 See reflections on these authors and their subject matter in ch. IV.

31 "La Chanson des escargots qui vont à l'enterrement [d'une feuille morte]. *Paroles*, 1949.

32 See above comments on dwarfs in Prévert's *Les Visiteurs du Soir*.

33 "L'union de l'Atticisme et de l'humour," *Humour et Humoristes* (Paris: Fischbacher, 1911), pp.159–160.

34 *O.C.*, XX, p. 135. My transl.

topics, I would suggest that three very dissimilar works could compete for the title—Flaubert's *Salammbô* (1862), Lautréamont's *Les Chants de Maldoror* (1867) and Samuel Beckett's absurdist novel *Molloy* (1951), are milestones in traditional and experimental esthetics of the bizarre.

The first is a *livresque* panorama of the extinct Punic civilization rivalling the Roman republic in the third century B.C. Its heroine, Salammbô, is the daughter of Hamilcar Barcass, Carthaginian leader. Drawing from many obscure sources such as Polybius, Aristotle, Livy, Pliny, Aelian, Pausanias, Diodorus, Saint Augustine, Tertulian, etc., Flaubert fictionalizes the desperation of the multiracial cohorts shipped, following a long Sicilian campaign against the Romans, to the North African city of Megara. There these mercenaries are on the verge of mutiny, demanding the long overdue pay Carthago owes them. Needless to say, the Punic Republic is reluctant to pay. To lift the haze of history from an obsolescent conflict, Flaubert infuses fresh artistic life into forgotten anecdotes and colorful off-beat material which he seamlessly unifies with the half historical and half fictional characters and their intrigues. It is the density, cohesion and dramatic gradations of these subjects in a credible esthetic frame which make *Salammbô* a rare bookish pageant of historical, exotic, entertaining (ironic) as well as didactic bizarreries.

To appease the unremunerated soldiers, the Republic throws a grandiose welcome party at Megara in Hamilcar's park surrounding his "palace built of yellow-spotted Numidian marble"[35] on four huge terraces. Lion pits and elephant corrals are among the highlights of the lavishly landscaped architectural decor. The ancient symposium has nothing in common with modern political picnics organized (somewhat like the Megara feast) to bribe a motley electorate. There are no overdone hamburgers and free beer. The entrées served by the budget-conscious Republic at Hamilcar's Punic barbecue are probably nothing that Flaubert's readers in the past 150 years have ever tasted.

> … the tables were covered with every variety of meats: roasted antelopes, with their horns—peacocks in their plumagee—whole sheep cooked in sweet wine—legs of camels and buffaloes—hedgehogs, with garum sauce—fried grasshooppers, and candied dormice. In bowls of Tamrapanni wood large pieces of fat floated in the midst of saffron—every dish overflowed with pickles, truffles, and assafoetida; pyramids of fruit rolled over honey-cakes; nor

35 *Salammbô*, transl., introduction B.R. Redman (New York: Tudor Publishing, 1931), p. 4. The subsequent citations from this edition refer to pp. 5, 6, 7, 11, 38 and 42.

> had there been forgotten some of those red-haired, plump little dogs fattened on olive leaves: a Carthaginian dainty held in abomination by all other peoples.
>
> Appetites were whetted by novel dishes. Gauls, with their long hair coiled up on the top of their heads, snatched at watermelons and lemons, which they crunched, rinds and all; Negroes, who had never seen lobsters before, cut their faces with the red claws; shaven-faced Greeks, whiter than marble, threw the leavings from their plates behind them...

The menu and the Greek, Campanian, Cantabrian wine and the "the wines of jujube, cinnamon and Lotus" gradually invigorate the verve of the embittered servicemen. "They made shameless wagers, plunged their heads into wine jars and then drank steadily like thirsty dromedaries." The ancient freelance entertainers need neither encouragement nor a podium to show their skills.

> A Lusitanian, of gigantic height, carrying a man upon each arm, ran across the tables, spitting fire from his nostrils. Lacedemonians, still laden with their cuirasses, leaped about with heavy strides; some imitated women making obscene gestures; some, stripped naked, wrestled like gladiators in the midst of the feast; and a company of Greeks danced around a vase decorated with nymphs; meantime a Negro pounded on a brass buckler with a beef-bone.

This is just a shy prelude to the climactic Pandemonium: the plastered veterans start showing off their bowmanship by shooting the lions in Hamilcar's "private zoo." Others chop off the elephants' trunks and still others go fishing in the sacred pond decorated with blue stones where the Barca family keeps fish descended from "primordial eel-pout, which had hatched the mystic egg wherein was hidden the goddess." Determined to top these anemic capers, amidst the wounded lions' roar and elephants' desperate trumpeting, other daring warriors grasp the torches and set afire Hamilcar's orchard. On every page, in every paragraph the novelist recounting these barbaric amusements reassures his curious, ironic, trusting, skeptical sophisticated or inerudite readers that the parade of stunning Punic bizarreries will carry on to the end of his exotic saga. I first read its Czech translation as a teenager some sixty years ago and probably missed a great deal of Flaubert's irony. For some reason, a detail, which comes to mind whenever I remember or discuss Flaubert, evokes the art of ancient pharmacists. It alludes to a potion regularly concocted for Hanno, one of Hamilcar's generals whose itchy skin condition makes him scratch day and night. While briefing his captains about the Republic's sad but undeserved insolvency, Hanno claims that such a bonafide debtor deserves the indulgence of his bellicose creditors. Flaubert briefly interrupts Hanno's plea and zeroes in on the orator.

"From time to time he rubbed his limbs with his aloe spatula, or even paused to drink, from a silver cup held to his lips by a slave, a decoction of ashes of weasels and asparagus boiled in vinegar..."

Once more, Flaubert returns to medicinal weasels so vital in the ancient dermatology when Hanno is ultimately cornered by his furious troops and, to save his life, tells them that he has brought the owed pay. Without waiting for their commander's permission to unpack his abundant military baggage loaded on many camels, they first open the baskets filled with "hyacinth-robes, sponges, scratchers, brushes, perfumes, and bodkins of antimony for painting the eyes." Unwilling to swap the withheld pay for their commander's toilet kit, the exasperated creditors continue foraging among his other belongings including his travelling bathroom, pharmacy and pantry.

> [O]n one of the camels they found a large bronze bathtub, in which the Suffete [Hanno] bathed during his march; even bringing caged weasels from Hecatompylus, to be burned alive for his decoction. And as his malady gave him an enormous appetite, he had brought a plentiful supply of comestibles—wines, pickles, meats and fish preserved in honey, and little Commagène pots of goose-grease packed in snow and chopped straw.

Microstimulative topics such as breeding lions in one's private zoo, entertaining rowdy guests who shoot them after dinner, burning live weasels to alleviate the torments caused perhaps by psoriasis or an allergy—all are the effective sparks in Flaubert's macrostimulative fireworks which may dazzle even future generations of qualified readers.

Maldoror's Nightmarish Wanderings

As I suggested, either *Salammbô* or Lautréamont's *Les Chants de Maldoror* could strike experienced readers as a thesaurus of the bizarre. But in spite of this common ground, they exemplify two artistic antipoles: while Flaubert patiently excavated fragments of forgotten exotic history and made them live thanks to his stylistic self-discipline, merciless pruning and semantic polish, the *Chants* owe their literary life to perverse fantasy, juvenile delight in irreverent burlesque and spontaneous, hyperbolic and pleonastic salvoes. As soon as Lautréamont emerged in the French literary fraternity he ostentatiously manifested his disgust with its literary traditions. This did not endear him to the broad community of readers. Even today, like de Sade's work, *The Chants* draw the attention of erudite critics rather than that of general reading public. Their mean antihero has no model in our everyday life. Monsters invented by de Sade's sick imagination, Maturin's Melmoth (who, like Faust, signs a contract with the Devil) or the vicious "je" or "moi" relating Baudelaire's *Flowers of Evil* are his obvious bookish precedents.[36] Maldoror is a narcissistic maniac who entertains his readers with unheard of prepoetic bestialities and original degradations of joys. While examining Lautréamont's style, I have illustrated, along with his ironic savant vocabulary and his caricature of lofty Homeric eloquence, some of his bizarre subjects.[37] In chapter IV, to illustrate the intensity of a shocking erotic fata morgana, I discuss Maldoror's first true love for a startling female shark and its weird consummation in the bloody foams of the stormy sea. In this chapter exploring the esthetics of supernatural, fantastic and bizarre subjects, it would be unforgivable not to include at least two divinities haunting the pre-Kafkaesque *Lebensraum* of the fantasizing "Count." One day, a gluttonous heavenly ogre devouring terrified humans reveals himself to Maldoror's "spleenetique" eyes. Imagining this dated cosmorama and responding to its morbid humor, modern cynics may read it as an inadvertent, allegorical preview of today's black holes. Henri Michaux' gloomy forecast entitled "L'Avenir"[38] offers somewhat similar stimulative blasts of poetic intimidation. Like so many other subjects in *The Chants*, Lautréamont's Creator of "Chant II" (considerably differing from the divine lecher patronizing a brothel in "Chant III") not only embodies the creative overflow of the author's ill-omened pugnacity[39] but also illustrates his antiesthetic illusions about pre-human, prebiblical and premythical atavisms. Because this and other similar pseudomystical deliria went against everything that is joyful and decent in life, not too many late 19th century critics were willing to give Lautréamont's shocking but original antipoetry the benefit of the doubt. No major critics speculated that *The Chants* were a heretic offshoot of the then-emerging poem-in-prose.[40] Admitting the antipoet to Parnassus could have then undermined confidence in the critics' esthetic judgement. In 1868, creation of

36 Maurice Blanchot, *Lautréamont et Sade* (Paris: Minot, 1949); Gaston Bachelard, *Lautréamont* (Paris: Corti, 1939); Marcelin Playnet, *Lautréamont par lui-même*, pp. 90–8 outline L.'s literary debts.

37 *LP II*, pp. 40–1, nn. 52–54 and Appendix 'Lautréamont''''' pp. 230–1.

38 See text and comments in *LP I*, pp. 48–9 and n. 72.

39 Stressed by Gaston Bachelard, *Lautréamont* (Paris: Corti, 1963).

40 Baudelaire's 50 causeries forming *Le Spleen de Paris* were written between 1855 and his death in 1868. See also *LP II*, pp. 156–7, comments on Aloysius Bertrand and Baudelaire.

"beauty" had still been the poets' main mission; Baudelaire, who sought and found it in the rotting corpse of a dog,[41] first published his "Hymne à la Beauté" as late as 1860.

Lautréamont's theophobic *bravoura* (below) on the brutal cosmic metabolism forms a brief climax (1–8) followed by a continuity (9) detailing the divine menu outlined in a sardonic, rather anticlimactic *envoi* addressed to the reader (11). Many an editor would probably delete Lautréamont's gourmet warning without the slightest hesitation.

> Un jour,...en chancelant comme un homme ivre, à travers les catacombes obscures de la vie(1), je soulevai...mes yeux spleenétiques...vers la concavité du firmament, et j'osai pénétrer, moi, si jeune, les mystères du ciel(2)... [J]e soulevai la paupière effarée plus haut...jusqu'à ce que j'aperçusse un trône, formé d'excréments humains et d'or(3), sur lequel trônait, avec un orgueil idiot, le corps recouvert d'un linceuil fait avec des draps non lavés d'hôpital, celui qui s'intitule lui-même le Créateur! Il tenait à la main le tronc pourri d'un homme mort, et le portait, alternativement, des yeux au nez et du nez à la bouche; une fois à la bouche, on devine ce qu'il en faisait(4). Ses pieds plongeaient dans une vaste mare de sang en ébullition(5), à la surface duquel s'élevaient...deux ou trois têtes prudentes, et qui s'abaissaient aussitôt, avec la rapidité de la flèche: un coup de pied, bien appliqué sur l'os du nez, était la récompense connue de la révolte au règlement, occasionnée par le besoin de respirer un autre milieu; car, enfin, ces hommes n'étaient pas des poissons! Amphibies tout au plus, ils nageaient entre deux eaux dans ce liquide immonde(6)!...jusqu'à ce que, n'ayant plus rien dans la main, le Créateur, avec les deux premières griffes du pied, saisit un autre plongeur par le cou...et le soulevât en l'air... Il lui dévorait d'abord la tête, les jambes et...le tronc, jusqu'à ce qu'il ne restât plus rien; car, il croquait les os. Ainsi de suite, durant...son éternité(7). Quelquefois il s'écriait: "Je vous ai créés; donc j'ai le droit de faire de vous ce que je veux. Vous ne m'avez rien fait, je ne dis pas le contraire. Je vous fais souffrir, et c'est pour mon plaisir(8)." Et il reprenait son repas cruel...sa barbe pleine de cervelle(9). O lecteur, ce dernier détail ne te fait-il pas venir l'eau à la bouche?(10) N'en mange pas qui veut d'une pareille cervelle, si bonne, toute fraîche, et qui vient d'être pêchée il n'y a qu'un quart d'heure dans le lac aux *poissons* (11).[42]

To diagram the gradations in rising and falling intensity, I have arranged the identified contentual stimuli in the form of an inverted pyramid. (The table does not reflect stylistic stimuli.)

41 See *LP II*, pp. 81–6.
42 *O.C.* (Corti, 1958), pp. 182–3.

TABLE 7

	Bizarre Stimuli	Intensity Gradations 1	2	3	4	5	6	7	8
1	Enigmatic quasi drunk Maldoror staggers through the premythical universe	—							
2	His splenetic eyes infiltrate mystical spheres. (Maldoror's spleen differs from Baudelairean spleen.)	—	—						
3	Nightmarish vision of a droll throne made of excrement;	—	—	—					
4	on it sits God/Creator, an unsavory madman who	—	—	—	—				
5	comfortably soaks his beclawed feet in human blood;	—	—	—					
6	in their own blood desparate humans swim—parody of divine love;	—	—	—	—				
7	divine menu: the cosmic cannibal devours one human after another.	—	—	—	—	—	—		
8	His word: "I created you to torment you, I enjoy your pain,"	—	—	—	—	—	—	—	
9	he preaches, his beard drenched in human brains.	—	—	—	—	—	—		
10	A psychopath's p.s.: what a tasty custard!	—	—	—	—	—	—		
11	Anticlimax: a burlesque tidbit	—	—						

The carnivorous freak is not the only god Maldoror meets. In the next chant he runs into a metamorphosed Creator who, this time, sleeps beside the wayfarers path. The passers-by including various animals immediately recognize him and spontaneously manifest their hatred. An ass kicks the sleeper in the head, saying: "This will serve you right. What did I do to you to deserve these long ears?" Shortly after, Maldoror sees a human pilgrim approaching his maker with more insulting intentions than a mere assinine kick: he takes his time and for three days manures ("fienta") the slumberer's "august face." This protracted disrespect awakens the sovereign and makes him stagger to the nearest boulder just to collapse and letting "his arms hang like the two testicles of a phthisic [*poitrinaire*]." Soon after, Maldoror discovers that this pathetic deity patronizes a convent converted into a brothel.[43] During his hetero- and homosexual orgy, without knowing it, the Omniscient loses one of his hairs which subsequently talks and informs Maldoror that the Creator has to cover up his fornication and sodomy on Earth because their disclosure would undermine his prestige not only in the eyes of the Archangels and Satan but even in the eyes of mankind. The heavenly profligate returns to the brothel (where the orthodox nuns continue observing the cult) just to assure the loquacious hair that he, Providence, will later replant it in his scalp, provided, of course, the hair never reveals what it saw. It would be scholarly overkill to offer a serious analysis of this outrageous "Chant" patched from sophomoric *Stücks*. Its still juvenile author, Isidore Ducasse sporting the clownish *nom de plume* of Count de Lautréamont, makes one think of Alfred Jarry and the gang of talented rascals who concocted *Ubu roi*.[44] Like their distorted archaisms, Isidore's pre-automatist mockery of classical rhetoric, along with his irreverent imagination reflects a typical youthful response to the stern academic discipline common in lycées and gymnasia. The impact of parodies born of early erudition mixed with adolescent tomfoolery depends on our individual culture—familiarity with the old European hatcheries of the intelligentsia, sense of humor or gravity, tolerance or puritanism—and on our intertextual horizons. There is a double dose of laughter in *The Chants* for those who have read Homer in the original at high school. Academic critics probably cannot respond to the microstimulative divine beard tainted with human brains without remembering other episodic evocations of brains, for example, the mentioned Titus Andronicus' *pâté*; Baudelaire's (probably apocryphal) alleged encouragement of a civil servant to eat baby brains because, as the devilish Charles claimed, they taste "like preserved walnuts—delicious"; Father Ubu's penal procedures including the "nose torsion" followed by the "extraction of brains through the heels"; or Zola's Etienne Lantier smashing Chaval's skull with a rock which scatters the villain's brain on the ceiling supports of the coal mine.[45]

Our familiarity with applicable critical interpretations may also influence the intensity of esthetic response. For instance, I contemplated

43 See *LP II*, pp. 110–1, n. 52–4.

44 See *LP II*, pp. 42–3.

45 See ch. III "Voltaire on Shakespeare;" A. France, *O.C.* VII, pp. 32–3. See below Appendix, Jarry, Shakespeare and Zola, *Germinal*.

Maldoror's devilish chimera in the light of P.W. Nesselroth's[46] conclusion that Maldoror's outlook is Dionysian; in what I see as Maldoror's (and his author's) facetious and would-be "pre-poetic" sophomoric burlesque, Nesselroth claims to hear primeval "Orphic" whispers:

> Maldoror has the aspect of Dionysus when he appears as 'antagonist of Apollo who sanctions logic…' and as a hermaphodite (II, I) [sic] because 'instead of negating, [Dionysus] affirms the dialectical unity of the great instinctual opposites: Dionysus reunifies male and female, Self and Other, life and death. Dionysus is the image of instinctual reality…'[47]

This unflinching exegesis which lends metaphysical significance to unsavory yet effective creative pranks, made me wonder which Dionysus Nesselroth and the cited grave critics could link with Maldoror and his so contradictory visions of bizarre gods. In the mainstream mythology Dionysus/Bacchus, son of Zeus and Semele, is a god of fertility and wine, herald of joy and relaxed, euphoric anarchy, intoxicated cheer leader of lusty satyrs and elated Menades, a companion of Hermes and Priapus. Neither Maldoror with splenetic eyes, who cannot laugh even after cutting open his lips, (I, 5) and who finally consummates his first love with a creature like himself—namely, the voracious female shark, nor his vision of the cosmic monarch sitting on the malodorous throne and crunching human corpses *ad nauseum* even faintly evokes the Olympian embodying established Dionysian lore. At best, one could perhaps argue that the Cretan Zagreus, hunter of men and god of the underworld akin to Hades is often linked with the genesis of the Dionysian cult. If the metamorphic Maldoror or his hallucinations echo chaotic bacchanales, perhaps and only perhaps the obscure Zagreus, fathered by Zeus but torn to pieces and eaten by the Titans, could be seen as an ancient model of Lautréamont's sadists. Rather than accepting this

46 *Lautréamont's Imagery* (Genève: Droz, 1969), pp. 118–9.

47 Nesselroth's single quotation marks first cite Herbert Marcuse, *Eros and Civilization, Philosophical Inquiry into French* (Boston: Beacon Press, 1955), p. 146, then N.O. Brown's *Life after Death* (New York: Vintage Books, 1959), p. 175. Nesselroth speculates (p. 123) that Lautréamont "realized from the very first stanza that the Apollonian cultural norms of the reader would be destroyed." Obviously, neither writers nor critics can predict with certainty which esthetic criteria of future readers will be destroyed by their exposure to a text saturated with shocking inventions. See the subsequent comment by Clouard and my reaction. Even Preromantics such as Rousseau, advocate the emancipation of (Dionysian) instincts from classical (Apollonian) sobriety.

debatable premise, I consider ghoulish fantasy and misanthropic bravado, mixed with the author's virulent humor, as basic explosives in his juvenile, anti-esthetic bombs. I would agree with Henri Clouard, who labels Isidore's masterpiece as an "album of repulsive clowning" and the above discussed divine hair episode as a "10-page, low and sinister blasphemy"[48]. However, unlike Clouard, upon rereading this album in 1995, I cannot separate my enthusiasm for what is *felix et faustum* from my ironic enjoyment of the ludicrous pseudoapocalypse. Today, Lautréamont's would-be oniric spectres have become riotous rather than scatological. It seems to me that the blasé *lycéen* savored the spell of Homeric poetry long after his *bachot* at Tarbes. At that time, Flaubert's and Baudelaire's thoroughly disciplined conversions of banality, ugliness and vice into consummate poetic qualities, might have struck the budding rhapsodist's sardonic spirit as too mild. Perhaps he found de Sade's unrepressed malevolence more attractive, mixed it with the parody of bronze age rhetoric and threw it like a reeking petard into the charming poetry of the *belle époque*. It took a few decades before the dadaists and later André Breton discovered the pungency of the puerile subconscious. With the help of pioneer psychocritic Gaston Bachelard (to the amazement of the censorious historians who, for half a century, had ignored Lautréamont,) they "smuggled" *Les Chants de Maldoror* into the history of *belles lettres* as a barbaric herald of subliminal obsessions and of the then fashionable automatist *écriture*. Like the *Übermensch* ready to rip power from the hands of the moribund god, Maldoror foreshadows artistic revolts—the decadent surnaturalism, dadaïst anarchism, Kafkaesque chaos, surrealist dreams, automatism, the *roman noir* and the theatre of the absurd.[49]

Huysmans' and Wilde's Eccentrics

While Maldoror, endlessly titillated by fresh deliria, gropes through an illusory premythical twilight, Lautréamont's longer lived decadent confrères, J.-K. Huysmans (1848–1907)[50] in France, and Oscar Wilde (1854–1900) in Great Britain rather set memorable eccentrics and their bizarre undertakings amidst upperclass luxury in the late Victorian era. Huysmans' protagonist, des Esseintes (*A rebours*, 1884), has some of the

48 *Histoire de la littérature française (1885–1914)* (Paris: Michel, 1947), p. 79.

49 Lautréamont's literary followers adored "un Moi qui s'exalte dans le sentiment de la négation absolue. . ." Ibid., p. 83.

50 See *LP I*, p. 153 and *LP II*, pp. 205–8.

writer's own tastes but also vaguely evokes Count Robert de Montesquiou-Fezensac, "known among his acquaintances as 'Chief of Fragrant Odours'". This illustrious dilettante inhabited the "queer and disquieting" upper floor of his paternal residence. "The main feature of [his] bedroom was a sculpture of a black bulbous-eyed dragon"[51] sheltering the eccentric's bed. Huysmans, not among those admitted to that exclusive bedroom, may, nonetheless, have injected some social gossip into the portrait of his fictitious enemy of nature. He made his supersensitive des Esseintes rich enough to finance and overdecorate a museum-like mansion where he indulges in his strange whims, ranging from composing symphonies of flavors on the "organ des liqueurs" to receiving his food *per rectum* with the help of an enema. The dilettante fancies that his hoard of decorative antiques and bibliophilia[52] radiates a divine mystique. Like Baudelaire's living pillars in "Les Correspondances," they mark his secret path to the beyond.

Shielded against banal life in his antinatural solitude, des Esseintes' sickly imagination begins reliving all his past turpitudes; this revival overwhelms the eccentric's fragile soul and causes a neurosis bordering on folly. Thanks to his doctors he survives his teleological crisis and discovers the salutary power of Faith. Huysmans' esthetic dependence on monotonous livresque decor, stagnant (non epical) longings and the penitence of the introverted hero encouraged the critics to consider *A rebours* as a fictionalized decadent manifesto rather than a powerful alternative to the naturalist novel.[53]

This may have occurred to Oscar Wilde (1854–1900) who, nevertheless, found des Esseintes and his then fashionable religion of bizarre beauty worthy of adaptation in an esthetically more viable tale—*The Picture of Dorian Gray* (1891). Wilde acknowledges his debt to Huysmans in rhapsodizing the growing thrill of Dorian opening "the strangest book that he had ever read... It was a novel without a plot and

51 James Laver, *The First Decadent* (New York: Citadel Press, 1955), p. 76. The same decadent socialite inspired Proust's Baron Charlus.

52 He puts a high premium on the religious paintings of Gustave Moreau, Jan Luyken depicting torture inflicted on victims of *Religious Persecutions*, works by Rodolphe Bresdin and Odilon Redon. Ibid., pp. 85–7 and illustrations pp. 80–81.

53 Laver (ibid., pp. 89) cites Zola's alleged wire "Naturalisme pas mort, lettre suit," (sent by P. Alexis). He also cites (pp. 74–5) Mario Praz' *The Romantic Agony* (and Huysmans). "Tous les romans que j'ai écrits depuis *A rebours* sont contenus en germe dans ce livre, Huysmans remarked." Adds Praz: "Not only his own works but all...works of Decadence from Lorrain to Gourmont, Wilde and D'Annunzio[.]"

with only one character...who [tries] to realise...all the passions and modes that belonged to every century except his own..." His reflections on the "life of senses" articulated in the "curious jewelled style...full of argot and of archaisms" strike Dorian as the poetry of the finest French Symbolistes. The monotonous music of sentences and chapters creates an illusion of malady dreaming" and Dorian wonders, if these "rêveries [reproduce] the spiritual ecstasies of some medieval saint or the morbid confessions of a sinner... It [is] a poisonous book."[54]

As panegyric as Dorian's rapture sounds, the innuendoes "novel *without a plot,...only one* character,...*jewelled* style,...*monotony*" suggest what in Wilde's rather than in Dorian's eyes are artistic flaws. Thus, in adopting the French model, Wilde is cautious not to create his uppercrust London hero in des Esseintes's image: he splits Huysmans' character into narcissistic, cherubic Dorian and the Mephishophelean master of cynical maxims, Lord Henry (Harry) Wotton. With them interact a profoundly gifted virtuous painter Basil Halward, a low class actress Sibyl Vane, who commits suicide when Dorian, manipulated by Lord Henry, betrays her. In the early drafts of Wilde's novel, Huysmans' *À rebours* may not have been the original model of the livresque "poison" sealing Dorian's fate: Elaine Showalter suggests that Wilde had considered fictionalizing Dorian's corruptive reading as *Le Secret de Raoule*. Had he done it, he would have linked Dorian's diabolic gospel not with Huysmans' des Esseintes but with the sado-masochistic heroine Raoule de Vénérande portrayed in Rachilde's decadent novel *Monsieur Venus*.[55] Further, to increase his tale's epical impact, Wilde also vaguely adapted the intrigue of Stevenson's *The Strange Case of Doctor Jekyll and Mr. Hyde* (1886) published four years before the *Picture of Dorian*

54 *The Works of Oscar Wilde* (London: Collins, n.d., pp. 146–7). The subsequent citations refer to this edition, pp. 247, 253, 155, 161 and 157.

55 *The Times Literary Supplement*, June 30, 1995, No. 4813, "The Decadent Queen," p. 6. Rachilde is the pen name of Marguerite Valette, née Eymery (1860–1953), whom Wilde met in Paris. Her novel published in 1884 in Belgium was confiscated as scatology. The French author was fined, sentenced to two years and barred from entering Belgium. Rachilde's noble playgirl treats her blue-collar lover as a female and savors necrophilic sex with him when he is killed in a duel. She has his hair, teeth and nails set into a Venus-like instructional cast introducing medical students to feminine anatomy. William Gaunt (*The Aesthetic Adventure*. Johathan Cape, London, 1945, ch IV "Débâcle", pp. 141–164) comments on Huysmans' influence on Wilde à propos of the two trials which ended with his incarceration in Reading Gaol.

Gray. But unlike Dr. Jekyll, who during his schizophrenic mutations turns into the beastly Mr. Hyde, Dorian, as long as he lives, never loses his beauty and youthful charm; it is Basil's miraculous portrait which, like an eye of Providence, watches Dorian's secret profligacy. His angelic features immortalized on Basil's canvas gradually degenerate into the physiognomy of a hideous debauchee, blackmailer and assassin. Blaming the painter for this transfiguration, he stabs him to death in front of the incriminating oil barricaded in the attic above Dorian's private quarters. In his fleeting sorrow he places the responsibility for his crimes on the "poisonous book" which Lord Henry gave him:

> "...you poisoned me with a book once. I should not forgive that. Harry, promise me that you will never lend that book to any one..." "My dear boy, you are...beginning to moralise. You will soon be going about the converted, and the revivalist, warning people against all the sins of which you have grown tired... You and I are what we are... As for being poisoned by a book, there is no such thing as that. Art has no influence upon action. It annihilates the desire to act. It is superbly sterile.

Trying to cover up his villainy, Dorian will not end like the penitent des Esseintes. He will rather fulfil his Fate in destroying the telltale portrait of his invisible degeneration with the same knife with which he had previously murdered its painter. But when he plants the blade into the heart of the repulsive witness of his crimes, far from abolishing the magic picture, he ends his own life. Hearing his final cry, the servants force the door to Dorian Gray's thirteenth chamber where they find "a splendid portrait of their master as they had last seen him in all his exquisite youth and beauty". Below it lies a "man in evening dress with a knife in his heart." It is not his "loathsome" face but the rings on his fingers which identify the "suicide."[56]

Like Huysmans, Oscar Fingall O'Flahertie Wills also tends to overestimate the esthetic merit of encyclopedic interpolations on perfumes, textiles, jewels, liturgical garments and so on. Such subjects may have a decorative and symbolical function and even harmonize with the character's esthetic profile, but once they are overstated, they become digressive, static and weaken the texts's epical integrity. If treated

56 A cartoon signed Cheney (*The New Yorker*, June 26, 1995, p. 118) commemorates this metamorphosis with six mini-sketches entitled "The Jeans of Dorian Gray": 1. brand new; 2. showing wear; 3. showing tear; 4. faded and patched; 5. repatched; 6. debased to uncouth cut-offs. As irreverent as such a parody is, it leaves no doubt that Wilde's fantasy has become a milestone in our literary culture.

sparingly, they whet the readers' senses including their sixth sense. In the following passage Wilde stimulates his readers' sense of smell and curiosity by alluding to obscure perfumes and their alleged powers.

> ...he would now study perfumes, and the secrets of their manufacture, distilling heavily-scented oils, and burning odorous gums from the East. He saw that there was no mood of the mind that had not its counterpart in the sensuous life, and set himself to discover their true relation, wondering what there was in frankincense that made one mystical, and in ambergris that stirred one's passions, and in violets that woke the memory of dead romances, and in musk that troubled the brain, and in champak that stained the imagination; and seeking often to elaborate a real psychology of perfumes, and to estimate the several influences of...aromatic balms...of spikenard that sickens, of hovenia that makes men mad...

The experienced esthetic impact of such epical material depends on the readers' ability and disposition to evoke specific fragrances of "frankincense, ambergris" or "hovenia". If one has never heard of them, let alone smelled them, one may be modestly amused rather than sentically stimulated by Dorian's bizarre perfume collection.
The catalog of textiles entered in Dorian's museum of precious bric-à-brac may indirectly sensitize some readers' *tactile imagination*, but it may strike others as dull decadent affectation.

> ...he sought to accumulate the most exquisite specimens...of textile and embroidered work, getting the dainty Delhi muslins, finely wrought with gold-thread palmates, and stitched over with iridescent beetles wings; the Dracca gauzes, that from their transparency are known in the East as "woven air," and "running water"...

While studying the jewels, Dorian also learns bizarre historical or prehistoric hearsay about jewels:

> ...he took up the study of jewels, and appeared at a costume ball as Anne de Joyeuse, Admiral of France, in a dress covered with five hundred and sixty pearls. [Finding additional information on the obscure historical figure is time-consuming.]...He would often spend a whole day settling and resettling in their cases the various stones...such as the olive-green chrysoberyl that turns red by lamplight, the cymophane with its wire-like line of silver, the pistachio-coloured peridot... In Alphonso's *Clericalis Disciplina* a serpent was mentioned with eyes of real jacinth, and Alexander, the Conqueror of Emathia was said to have found in the vale of Jordon snakes with collars of real emeralds growing in their backs...

Dorian's treasure is his collection of sacerdotal robes inseparable from sacraments, their symbolical meanings and divine sanctions shrouded in clouds and the scent of incense.

> He had a special passion, also, for ecclesiastical vestments,... In the long cedar chests...he had stored away many rare and beautiful specimens of what is really the raiment of the Bride of Christ, who must wear purple and jewels and fine linen that she may hide the pallid macerated body that is worn by the suffering that she seeks for, and wounded by self-inflicted pain.

The novel's elaborate synesthetic props cannot thrill all readers. Like Huysmans, Wilde perhaps hopes that the mysterious glittering things and even the glamor of their unheard of signifiers will express the inexpressible so valued by the transcendentalists. Whether we fall in that category or tend to draw no conclusions on what we know nothing about, our esthetic tempers—mystical, rational, grave, ironic—spontaneously respond to the *artistic* quality of hermetic figments. Unlike Mallarmé who obscures his poetic *parole*[57] to make it whisper ineffable tidings, Wilde makes his quasi mystical luster radiate from the (references to) polished jewels, esoteric fragrances and ceremonial robes themselves as well as from the correlated semantic splendor. For him, not the living pillars of nature but rather its unearthed treasures, refined by the artist's hands and the poet's cryptic scription, open the door to the absolute.

Experimental Bizarrerie: Beckett

Generally, no mystical or fantastic implications distinguish the key bizarreries in "experimental" plays and prose. Like the mainly Marxist and Freudian surrealists publishing between and after the two world wars, and like the Heideggerian existentialists, the proponents of the avant-garde genres deem the cosmos, its nature, including our natural life, not unnatural but absurd: in their works, no evident Providence is wisely steering life on Earth before we are born, while we live and after our death. Past and future threats to our existence determine our attitudes not less than political ideologies or psychological research. We remember the two devastating wars and are aware of the threatening overpopulation and pollution of nature. We fear the insane, absurd self-destruction which fills us with pessimism. The progress of sciences and technology generates confidence in materialistic science and cautious rational optimism. The bizarre subjects of the 20th century naturally reflect the extremes of our cultural climate.

"Grotesquely absurd, bordering on lunacy" (cited above among the

57 See *LP II*, p. 120 and Appendix, pp. 231–2.

synonyms of the term "bizarre") usually best describes the artificial, comic characters who are threshing straw on stage, for example, in Eugene Ionesco's *La Cantatrice Chauve* (1950; *The Bald Soprano).* Richard Coe characterizes this brand of the bizarre as the "apotheosis of platitude."[58] In his "anti-play" Ionesco parodies conversational phrases and clichés found in the French-English handbook for beginners, *Méthode assimil.* Mrs. Smith, talking to her husband, declares: "...it's nine o'clock. We've drunk the soup and eaten the fish and chips and the English salad. The children have drunk English water...the salad oil was not rancid. The oil from the grocer at the corner is better quality than oil from the grocer across the street." When her husband finally looks up from his newspaper to respond, he changes the subject: "All doctors are quacks. And all patients too. Only the Royal Navy is honest in England." Returning to the paper, he further pronounces on the press: "In the newspaper, they always give the age of the deceased but never the age of the newly born. That does not make sense."[59]

"Reist," "chosist," pseudo-bizarreries characterize the mimesis in the *nouveau roman.* Alain Robbe-Grillet's novel, *La Jalousie,* best illustrates this technique with often monotonously technical descriptions of horizontal blinds ("jalousies") during various times of day or repeated references, say, to the centipede smashed against the wall by a dinner guest's napkin. In the context of *La Jalousie* they are raised to bizarre *leitmotifs*—the darker spot of the centipede obsessively feeds the jealous husband's suspicion of his wife's adultery.[60] Or in his earlier spoof on the Oedipus myth, *Les Gommes* , Robbe-Grillet's recurrent description of a used eraser—brand "Oedipe," showing, however, only the middle syllable "di"—plays a key role in the parody of conventional mystery novels.

The one author who has considerably broadened the inventory of bizarre stimuli and who has assimilated all secessionist trends launched by Lautréamont, Jarry and their followers, ranging from Tristan Tzara to Edward Albee and Harold Pinter, is Samuel Beckett. Neither his subject matter nor his style leave any doubt that Maldoror's soliloquies, Jarry's "pataphysics" or Kafka's ominous, anonymous bureaucrats or Jaroslav Hašek's cynical humor are the precedents of his innovations. His

58 *Ionesco,* (London: Oliver and Boyd, 1961), pp. 40–6.

59 *Four Plays by Eugene Ionesco,* transl. by D. M. Allen (New York: Grove Press, 1958), pp. 9, 11.

60 See *LP I*, pp. 122–129 and *LP II*, "Robbe-Grillet's centipede," pp. 136–39.

indolent antiheroes and vacuous antiplots have made a mark on postexistentialist literature which Claude Mauriac christened "alittérature."[61] Born in 1906 in Dublin and educated at Trinity College, this disciple of James Joyce was appointed lecturer at the École Normale Supérieure in 1938. During the war he was active in the French underground. His contact with Joyce, his erudition, translating skills and the years spent in the cosmopolitan, cultural Babylon sheltering so many expatriate artists made him aware of all experimental trends. As we see his plays or read his prose, in which bizarre absurdities play a primary role, we associatively recall not only his 19th century forerunners but also his fellow experimenters, such as Tzara, Breton, George Neveux and especially Ionesco, Boris Vian, Jean Genêt and Robert Pinget, along with *le nouveau roman* and even the hilarious blunders of Laurel and Hardy.

The play *Waiting for Godot* (*En Attendant Godot*, 1952) and his first novel written in French, *Molloy* (1951), highlight his fiction.[62] Like Didi/Vladimir and Gogo/Estragon in *Waiting for Godot*, Molloy is an obscure loafer. As soon as he emerges, he makes one think of a Chaplin on crutches battling the trivia of daily routine. Unlike Charlot, Molloy ties his hat with a string attached to a buttonhole big enough to accommodate a bouquet of flowers. Masochistic self-deprecations conveyed in the first person singular reinforce the character's banal miseries. The first strokes of Molloy's self-portrait, contained in the opening narrative drivel,[63] illustrate Beckett's amalgam of weirdness and morbid humor pervaded by a neurotic death wish.

> Je suis dans la chambre de ma mère. C'est moi qui y vis maintenant. Je ne sais pas comment j'y suis arrivé. Dans une ambulance peut-être, un véhicule quelconque certainement. On m'a aidé. Seul je ne serais pas arrivé. Cet homme qui vient chaque semaine, c'est grâce à lui peut-être que je suis ici. Il dit que non. Il me donne un peu d'argent et enlève les feuilles. Tant de feuilles, tant d'argent. Oui, je travaille maintenant,...seulement je ne sais plus travailler... Moi je voudrais maintenant parler des choses qui me restent, faire mes adieux, finir de mourir. Ils ne veulent pas. Oui, ils sont plusieurs, paraît-il. Mais c'est toujours le même qui vient. Vous ferez ça...plus tard, dit-il. Bon. Je n'ai plus beaucoup de volonté, voyez-vous. Quand il vient chercher les nouvelles feuilles il rapporte celles de la semaine précédente. Elles sont marquées de signes que

61 *L'Alittérature contemporaine* (Paris: A. Michel, 1958). Re "pataphysics," see below, Appendix, Jarry.

62 See earlier ref., *LP II* and above ch. II, "Recurrent Characters."

63 "...monologue of a consciousness babbling more or less coherently," Laurent Le Sage, *The French New Novel,* (The Pennsylvania State UniversityPress, 1962, p. 48).

> je ne comprends pas. D'ailleurs je ne les relis pas.[64]

The mysterious editor of Molloy's copy is never identified. Is he Youdi (you die) emerging though only *in absentia*, in the novel's second part? (See below.) Soon Molloy leaves his mother's home and her chamber pot—"...je fais dans son vase," the narrator informs the reader—hoping, without knowing why, to find his mother. (The end of Part I suggests that he wishes to be where he was before he was born.)

Although he despises her for giving him life and cannot even remember whether she is alive or dead, and in spite of his deformed leg, he attaches his crutches to his bicycle frame and without the slightest clue where his bicycle will take him, he sets out to join his mother. Here Beckett reveals at least one joy his handicapped cyclist experienced:

> C'était une bicyclette acatène, [chainless] à roue libre, si cela existe. Chère bicyclette, je ne t'appellerai pas vélo,... Elle avait une petite corne [horn] ou trompe au lieu du timbre à la mode de vos jours. Actionner cette corne était pour moi un vrai plaisir, une volupté presque...[et] si je devais dresser le palmarès [awards] des choses qui ne m'ont pas fait trop chier au cours de mon interminable existence, l'acte de corner y occuperait une place honorable.[65]

As he pedals through the countryside, Molloy remembers the woman who forced him to leave his pre-existence:

> ...celle qui me donna le jour par le trou de son cul si j'ai bonne mémoire. Premier emmerdement... Elle ne m'appelait jamais fils...mais Dan...Dan était peut-être le nom de mon père... Moi je la prenais pour ma mère et elle me prenait pour mon père...Dan, tu te rappelles le jour où j'ai sauvé l'hirondelle? Dan,tu te rappelles le jour où tu as enterré la bague."

Without knowing why, Molloy used to call her Mag. The letter "g" Molloy explains, abolished the syllable "ma" and, so to say, spit on it much more effectively than any other letter. He also called Mag Countess Caca, believing that she "faisait sous elle sa grande et sa petite commission." Molloy's unappealing matriarch Caca is an irrefutable debt to Émile Zola's "la mère Caca, as they call her, for she does not shrink from emptying her...chamber pot in her vegetable patch."[66] Further down

64 *Molloy , L'Expulsé*, followed by *Beckett , le précurseur* by Robert Pingaud and "Dossier de presse de Molloy," (n.p., Editions de Minuit, 1963), p. 7. The subsequent citations refer to pp. 8, 19, 37–39, 41–42, 221–22, 234.

65 Knowing Beckett's delight in verbal mischief, one may wonder if "acte de corner," i.e., literally act of horning/hooting, could be a latent pun addressed to bilingual readers, by an Anglophone who writes his first French novel.

66 *La Terre*, *OC V*, (ed. Henri Mittérand e.a.) p. 870, my transl.

the road, the cyclist observes herds of sheep and meditates their death by the butcher's axe. "Quel pays rural, mon Dieu, on voit des quadrupèdes partout... le temps délicieux, délicieux," he rhapsodizes but the growing heat stifles his enthusiasm. He dreams of cool winters when he has to wrap his frail body in *The Times Literary Supplement*, made of non-porous paper. Its quality not only keeps him warm but his farts cannot perforate it. Molloy recalls that once he counted 315 farts within 19 hours; incorrectly he calculates (Beckett tests his readers) that it makes 19 farts per hour. (He muses that, after all, he is not such a big old fart as he thought.) Finally Molloy reaches an unknown city. To orient himself he plans to consult a passerby. But as he stops near a curb, he falls over while still straddling the bicycle and kills a dog. A policeman, who is ready to lay charges interrogates Molloy but he can't even remember his own name. The dog's owner, Lousse, intervenes. She is an elderly widow who was taking her blind and rheumatic "Teddy" to the vet's to have him put away. Molloy's fall actually saved her the expenditure, which she could ill afford on her meagre war pension. In a bizarre digression, she even tells the policeman that her husband sacrificed his life for the fatherland, which only used to insult him and "put pokes in his wheels." After burying the dog with Molloy's modest help, she falls in love with him. However, Beckett's picaresque adventures will not have a happy ending.[67] Molloy leaves and the reader imagines him as he helplessly creeps on his belly through the forest underbrush. Neither his legs nor his crutches support him any longer. Any residual instinct of self-preservation is gone. He awakes outside the forest in a ditch. He remembers two travellers, one of whom had a cudgel. "Molloy was able to stay where he was," a narrator/author says, ending the novel's first part. Does he allude to the "adieux" Molloy yearned for at the beginning?

The scene is now set for the novel's Part II, revealing in obscure terms what may have lead to Molloy's death in the ditch. A new character emerges, Moran; the threatening "Mor" in his name evokes the Slavonic Morana/Death or Blaise Cendrars' assassin, *Moravagine*, (1926.) Moran is less cryptic than Molloy but his everyday life and interests are not less ludicrous than those of the lost Molloy. He, his son

67 This segment is reminiscent of Georges Neveux' surrealist play (and film), *Juliette ou la clé de songes* , in which the sleeping Michel dreams that he strays into a community where all the inhabitants have lost their memories. In Beckett's text, it is the other way around: the protagonist's memory fails, not the policeman's.

and the servant Marthe inhabit a house on a piece of land where Moran keeps beehives and a chicken coop. He is depressed when his favorite grey hen stops laying eggs. One Sunday, Moran, a regular church goer, fails to attend Mass because Gabor (Gabriel?), the Kafkaesque messenger for the Kafkaesque boss Youdi (you die?), instructs him and his son to leave and find Molloy. (Is he assigned to find him or to get him?) Moran has a beer, "une bonne marque, la Wallenstein," then, like a pious member of the family, goes to ask Father Ambroise to give him belated Holy Communion. Hesitantly but benevolently the priest—resting after his lunch—complies with the unorthodox request. Thus spiritually prepared for the search, father and son leave—like Abraham and Isaac—but they never find Molloy, unless, of course, the solitary vagabond whom Moran assassinates without remembering how he did it, is Molloy. After this accomplishment, Moran's son leaves him and his doctrinal convictions begin to crumble.

> Certaines questions d'ordre théologique me preoccupaient bizarrement. En voici quelques-unes. 1. Que vaut la théorie qui veut qu'Eve soit sortie, non pas de la côte d'Adam, mais d'une tumeur au gras de la jambe (cul?)? 2. Le serpent rampait-il ou, comme l'affirme Comestor, marchait-il debout? 3. Marie conçut-elle par l'oreille, comme le veulent Saint-Augustin et Adobard? 4. L'antichrist combien de temps va-t-il nous poireauter [to keep us waiting] encore?… 12. Faut-il approuver le cordonnier italien Lovat qui, s'étant châtré, se crucifia [having castrated himself, crucified himself]? 13. Que foutait Dieu [what was God messing up] avant la création?

Gradually, one of Moran's legs becomes shorter and shorter, stiffer and stiffer. He is now as crippled as Molloy. Has he become Molloy? At this point, the boss Youdi orders Moran to return home. It is empty and shabby. All the bees froze in the beehive and the chickens are dead. Once more Gabor appears and asks Moran to write the report. Its beginning ends Beckett's saga. "Il est minuit. La pluie fouette les vitres. Il n'était pas minuit. Il ne pleuvait pas."[68]

As illustrated, Beckett shies away from the historical, exotic, occult, mystical or pseudomythical oddities of his predecessors. Molloy is an original macrobizarrerie. Whatever we consider normal in human existence is sickly distorted in Beckett's mimesis: Molloy's comically

68 One associates this beginning with the here-parodied opening lines typical of *la belle époque* , e.g., "l'averse, toute la nuit, avait sonné contre les carreaux…," in Guy Maupassant's *Une vie* ; "La pluie bat les carreaux depuis le commencement du jour," in Rolland's *Jean-Christophe*.

grotesque handicaps, suicidal aspirations, failing memory, vulgar vilification of his mother, his distant superior collecting Molloy's nebulous writings on Sunday, his crawling through the thicket on his belly in hopes of finding his (perhaps dead) mother. All of these oddities create coherent microstimulative effects in this monument of the absurd and bizarre. The readers, used to interpreting existentialist macrorhetoric, are naturally attracted by interpretable ambiguities in the enigmatic passages potentially expressing the author's antihumanism. Wallace Fowlie[69] points out that Beckett rejected the hermeneutic theories of his critics who interpreted, for example, the single onstage prop in *Waiting for Godot*, a stylized tree, as a symbol of the Biblical tree of knowledge or even as a symbolic cross. No author, however, can prescribe how critics should read his texts. Moran's improvised partaking of Christ's body with the Wallenstein beer in his stomach, his doctrinal blasphemies after clubbing to death the mysterious wanderer, his metamorphosis into Molloy, the nuances of the overlord Youdi and his enforcer Gabor or the rejection of Father Ambroise by the former church-goer Moran, obviously, cannot be read on a single level. The contradictory beginning of the report at the novel's very end also provokes legitimate hermeneutic speculations on the meaning of Beckett's text.

Responding to the symbolism of Beckett's discourse, the early reviewers of *Molloy* appreciate the quality of his black farce. "Ironic genius...compared to him, humorists reputed for their black humor are green with envy," comments Maurice Nadeau. Most critics reject, however, the aimless teleology implied by the static clowns—Gogo, Pozzo—or the *antiroman* Molloy, Moran, Gabor—all drowning in nihilistic stagnation. "In the tenacious accusations of life, which characterize contemporary literature, Beckett has to be credited for introducing a new form of *Malheur*. What others call Death, Absurd Necessity, Absence, Evil, Ignorance of Law appears in *Molloy* to be like a physical degradation, the shame of life overwhelmed by animal functions—and yet we have to admit that this merciless epopeia of garbage...is undeniably powerful," says Gaetan Picon.

Deploring Beckett's "humanism of rot," G. Albert Astre sums up the author's *Lebensanschauung* reflected in *Molloy* as "a quiet acceptance of decaying existence, waiting for death [and] taking for granted that nothing really exists (except for shit, to use the narrator's style.)" Characterizing the human condition in *Molloy*, the same critic exhausts

69 *Experimental Theatre*, p. 214.

all the synonyms of the adjective bizarre: Beckett's creature is "abandoned, absurd, a prisoner, guilty, beyond time, beyond space, almost beyond language, a stranger to himself and others, impotent, obscene, disgusting, etc. He anxiously wonders if a certain orifice...is not the true gate of his being."

In Robert Kanters' eyes, *Molloy* exemplifies "neoconformisme...scatologique." If avant-garde critics nowadays greet a coherent "honestly woven" novel with a sigh: " 'Another Balzac!', we may sigh, 'Another Kafka, or a Joyce, or a Faulkner!' "[70]

When Henri Peyre completed his major overview of *The Contemporary French Novel*, his assessment of *Molloy* did not differ substantially from the critiques in the French press. *Molloy* is "an epic of nothingness... The underlying assertion, if one may use such a term for literature of total negation, seems to be...that yielding to some abject nirvana is perhaps the only relief from anguish and absurdity... " On the margin of his comments, Peyre laconically remarked that Beckett's deliberate obscurity has "spurred commentators to ingenious exegeses."[71] Among the critics who explore Beckett's hermetism to discover meaning other than "total negation, rot or garbage" is Bernard Pingaud. In his essay, "Beckett le précurseur," [72] Pingaud identifies three hermeneutic levels: at the "story level" the opposition of the two contrasting protagonists, followed by their fusion, seems to suggest that Moran could be the conscience of Molloy. In this case Beckett's "nihilist odyssey" presents man seeking his own identity. Moran has to give up his anonymous human existence when, having fused with Molloy, he realizes that he no longer can exist on his own. However, according to the essayist, the flaw of this reading is Beckett's debt to Kafka from whom he borrowed the invisible boss Youdi and his messenger Gabor. They are foreign to "Beckett's universe." (Other inquisitive readers would, of course, ask whether Molloy had any shred of conscience before he started his nihilist odyssey.)

70 For the critics cited above (my transl.) see *Molloy*, ed. cit., "Le Dossier de presse de *Molloy* ," pp. 257–86. Cited are Nadeau, "En avant nulle part," *Combat*, 12 avril, 1951; Picon, "L'Impossible néant," *Samedi Soir*, 12–18 mai, 1951; Astre, "L'Humanisme de la pouriture," *Action*, 7–13 mai, 1951; Kanters, "Un chef-d'oeuvre préfabriqué," *L'Age Nouveau*, juin 1951.

71 *The Contemporary French Novel* (New York: Oxford University Press, 1955), p. 308.

72 Included in the 1963 printing of *Molloy*, pp. 285–311. I refer here to Pingaud's macrorhetorical interpretations.

Pingaud asserts that if one disregards Youdi's and Gabor's "epic" role, the antithesis between Molloy and Moran disappears and the tales, which the narrator relates for himself, are sheer fantasy: there are no longer either heroes or intrigue, only monstrous visions remain. Thus the true substance, "la loi du discours chez Beckett," is not the contradiction but the metamorphosis. This rather comfortable riddance of Youdi and his enforcer eliminates the sinister threat and prepares the ground for Pingaud's third hermeneutic leap: placing himself at the level of Beckett's *écriture*/writing.[73] He claims that *Molloy* (and especially the books which follow) represent a "systematic" [sic] criticism of the modern novel. Like Joyce or Proust, Beckett is not a theorist but like them he knows that the best way of testing the limits of fiction is to write it.

We can agree with Pingaud that many passages in *Molloy* seem to parody *Remembrance of Things Past* with an added touch of digressive deviltry à la Joyce. Beckett tells his readers right at the beginning of his discourse that Molloy earns his living as a writer: "Tant de feuilles, tant d'argent." And at the end, Moran writes and "edits" his cryptic report without knowing how to start and/or finish it. Other mischievous allusions to Molloy's literary bent is *The Times Literary Supplement*, which keeps him warm during the cold days. In addition to abundant minor clues, Pingaud demonstrates that the imbecilic intellectual possesses some writerly skills. "Ne pas vouloir dire, ne pas savoir ce qu'on veut dire, ne pas pouvoir ce qu'on croit qu'on veut dire, et toujours dire ou presque, voilà ce qu'il importe de ne pas perdre de vue, dans la chaleur de la rédaction."

The final "in the heat of editing" is of course a strong editorial hint which no thorough reader is likely to overlook. Such a hint lends relative credibility to Pingaud's argument: Molloy's never-ending affirmations, followed by immediate denials, ridicule the author who honestly tries to fictionalize his life adventures but who, as soon as he puts them on paper, finds his story incomplete, ringing false and demanding endless editorial deletions.

We may accept Pingaud's *explication* yet any esthetically oriented critic will question the stimulative power of the pleonastic yes-no's in Beckett's wavering narrative. In concluding his essay, Pingaud contemplates the obvious elements of Beckett's *antiroman*—especially its passive resignation—"le degré zéro de la parole...un degré zéro de l'existence..." He joins the chorus of the critics cited above: Molloy

73 See ch. II, "Ideological hints: *écriture*?", "Lyrical stimuli" and "Didactic stimuli".

"cannot find any truth elsewhere than in silence... Literature of the interminable is condemned to remain an interminable failure... Beckett's novels are successive stages of such a failure [my transl.]" Seven years after this assessment, in 1969 Beckett was awarded the Nobel Prize.

The Spooky Fix in 1996

Two main reasons have made me draw my characteristic examples of paranormal[74] subjects not only from exclusively graphical but also from cinematographical fiction: 1. movie scripts and scenarios—regardless whether original or adapted from literary sources—are nonetheless new literary genres which spring from their theatrical precedents; and 2. the cinematic dramatizations of such incongruities, on one hand, leave less to the spectator's imagination than printed fiction because they have reduced the distance between illusory reality and its verbal transposition; and on the other hand, as a result of the multi-sensory—verbal, acoustic and multicolor—perception, the same subjects are seen more as reality than as literary mimesis relying on vital imagination.[75] The esthetic illustrations and persuasiveness which on-screen "reality" offers to audiences potentially reaches a higher stimulative level than exclusively graphical mimesis. The speed with which multisensory cinematography captivates young generations, long before they become literate, convincingly documents the esthetic edge which this genre has gained vis-à-vis traditional literary representation.[76]

"When *The X Files* airs its newest episode this fall, millions will be glued to the tube to get their spooky fix." Thus a TV columnist prognosticates no end to the popular "fascination with beings from outerspace [which] has resulted in the success of...*X-Files*, *Unsolved Mysteries* and the...*Millenium* series." The writer identifies UFO researchers Budd Hopkins, Stenton Friedman and Harvard psychiatrist J.E. Mack" as script-writers developing new esoteric subjects to meet the insatiable demand for them.[77] Meanwhile, contemporary writers continue

74 A functional journalistic neologism, "supernormal" or "supraregular" would not mix Greek prepositions and Latin adjectives.

75 Current experiments move the power of cinematic illusion a step further into a three-dimensional "virtual reality."

76 Updike's *In the Beauty of the Lilies* caricatures the domination of the American soul by Hollywood, the self-worshipping factory of information, misinformation and entertainment marketing the mythology of American dream.

77 Cinda Chavich, *The Calgary Herald*, Sept. 22, 1996, Sec. E, p. 1.

to turn out tales of blood-soaked supernatural horror in the Dracula mode. In an article suitably slated for Halloween,[78] Baltimore Sun writer Michael Ollove features the best-known "mass producer of nightmares", Stephen King, whose novels have sold 250 million copies and whose 1996 royalties were projected to reach the utopian height of $34 million. There is, however, an evident lack of consensus among academic critics on the esthetic value of King's work. The University of Maine has crowned him as the "Shakespeare of the twentieth century" while Stephen Dixon, respected fiction writer and English professor at John Hopkins University, dismisses him as "a total hack [who] should not be taken seriously." Psycho-critic Leslie Fiedler disagrees: "None of us will be…revered as deeply as…Stephen King." As some English departments begin to offer courses devoted to King's novels and the films based on them, it is probable that fewer students will read about Dorian Gray's magic portrait or about Des Esseintes' repasts *à rebours*. But, although Wilde's and Huysmans' esthetic attraction peaked around the turn of the century, both the young and the old, literate or illiterate, continue to crave mysteries, occult revelations and fresh Utopias. Far from growing stale during the long Romantic and post-Romantic periods, psychic visions and scientific forays into the bizarre past and future still mesmerize modern audiences no less than Homer's *Odyssey,* whose mythological marvels stunned patrons at the dawn of literary practice.

* * *

78 "The Master of Horror," *The Calgary Herald*, October 31, 1996, Sec. B, p. 7.

VIII

A BIOCYBERNETIC EPILOG

By Miroslav Malik

"Happy the one able to understand the causes of things."

"What was memory? Where, if anywhere, did it reside? How did an idea look? Why was comprehension bred, or aesthetic taste, or temperatment? Predicates threaded my neural maze."[1]

Perception of Poetry and Audiovisual Arts. Physiological Responses to Conflict. Biometrics of Inner Conflicts. Eroticism Travels through Neural Pathways. Measuring Laughter: Bresky Reads Baudelaire. Metaphysical Information. Biometrics Past and Future.

Perception of Poetry and Audiovisual Arts

Literature leaves more to the imagination than the audiovisual arts. Reading poetry or prose offers readers more freedom than looking at paintings, watching films or listening to symphonies. The movie-goer, for instance, sees only literal images of characters and/or events, selected and presented in a specific order and style by the film's *auteur*, who controls the viewer's mindscape. On the other hand, the reader is free to create his/her own by imagining and supplementing the 'missing' visual

1 "Felix qui potuit rerum cognoscere causas." Virgil, *Georgica*, II, 458; Richard Powers, *Galatea 2.2* (New York: Farrar Strauss Giroux, 1995), p. 28. Miroslav Malik completed the draft of this chapter before his premature death in August 1998. Louise and Dushan Bresky, as editors of his text, were able to send only the first half of the corrected version for Malik's approval. The chapter's second half did not reach him in time.

or acoustic details inevitably implied in the author's narrative, yet never directly perceptible. The reader can also complement, modify, even distort the authors' plots, characters, their fleeting thoughts, or poetic descriptions of settings, etc. A further difference between the written/read and the dramatized seen /heard mimesis lies in the way audiovisual and literary works of art are perceived: while authors arrange the sequences and contents in their indirect discourse and direct dialogs, each reader is free to synchronize the reading time with his/her speed of perception as well as with the brain's fast, slow or often interrupted processing of the textual input. The vertical information cascades characteristic of non-literary art can analyze performers' techniques, art direction, etc. with the help of repeatable audio-visual recordings and slow-motion projection. (In this case, however, we move from esthetic delectation into the sphere of didactic analysis.)

Before addressing the physiology of perception of various informative stimuli and their processing by the neural system, it might be useful to repeat what was stressed in *Literary Practice I* and *II*: the biometric measurements of readers' responses are global; they do not distinguish between "esthetic" and "non-esthetic" information and, unlike qualified critics, they cannot isolate content and/or style from the mass of stimulative material which enters and is processed in the reader's brain.[2]

As our faculties of perception evolve, remain young or grow old, each act of perception is not only prevalently individual, it is to some extent "once only." And while general human anatomy, neurology and physiology do not radically differ from person to person, our genes, activities, experiences and aspirations do. So do our teleologies and so do our sentic responses to the various categories of stimulative subject matter which Bresky discussed in his critical comments. In harmony not only with literary tradition but also with psychiatric and psychological research, he classifies conflicts, erotic subjects, humor and representations of cosmic powers as the main domains of epical and dramatic genres. The same subjects are integral parts of information skeletons and archetypes identifying our perception cultures.

Physiological Responses to Conflict

Our sentic responses triggered by literary representations of conflicts

2 See *LP I*, ch. IX, pp. 177–194.

are gradual: they start and develop as we perceive the narrative's successive microstimuli. The degree of our individual stimulation, however, varies from one reader to another. It depends on the illusory concern, empathy, imagination which the written information sets free in a given reader's brain. The transposition of a mere latent confrontation, for instance, provokes only a partial mismatch of the neural pathways in a particular region of the brain; however, the representation of a violent epic or dramatic clash initiates a physiological reaction in the whole autonomous neural system which can be recorded by biometric instruments. Even visible physionomical effects—changes in facial muscles or blushing—may testify to the intensity of response in the reader's brain.

The recordable responses to conflicts reflect three neural activities: 1) the crossover of information chains; 2) the overpass of the thresholds of neural networks; 3) parallel processing of the non-matching temporal neural pathways intercepted by the reader. What is significant in this triplex of neural response is its systemic nature.

The biometrics of the recordable reactions are affected not only by the reader's individual anatomy and physiology but also by his or her cultural and psychological background. Heterogeneous (e.g., Western, Oriental, African, Christian, Islamic, etc.) cultures developed different mythological, ideological artistic models; while their information skeletons are similar, they are not identical. Only today in the age of global information are the distinctions slowly fading and "cosmopolitan" information stereotypes and archetypes are evolving.

Biometrics of Inner Conflicts

The perception of psychological conflicts differs from the dominantly sentic responses to the mimesis of wars or violent struggles provoking fear, hatred, anxiety. A *colllisio officiorum* engages readers in multiple feedbacks which fail to lead to obvious solutions. These suspenseful mental dead-ends prime the reader's hunger for more information.

Perception of the fictional characters' inner tensions initiates stress in the reader's web of temporal neural pathways. These reactions are clearly identifiable in the multichannel biometric records. Frequently the stimulators come out of a long tradition of written and oral story-telling—a tradition anchored in ancient precedents such as the Bible, Homer, Greek tragedies and their classical imitations (Shakespeare, Racine, etc.). Over

TABLE 8a *(Le Colonel Chabert)*

Intensity (1 2 3 4 5 6 7 8)	Bresky's intensities estimates	Balzac's gradations
3	1. Balzac's ironic contradiction (black humor) extending Derville's previous impression—"he is a fool" who claims that he is a colonel.	1. — Monsieur, dit le défunt, peut-être savez-vous que je commandais un régiment de cavalerie à Eylau.
5	2. Chabert's military prowess: lion's share of impressive victory. "The Golden Eagle,"Murat, legendary cavalry commander related to Napoleon, later King of Naples, executed 1815—vivid historical associations for many readers. Legally and tragically, I Chabert am dead... gradation of the plot's epical core.	2. J'ai été pour beaucoup dans le succès de la célèbre charge que fit Murat qui décida le gain de la bataille. Malheureusement pour moi, ma mort est un fait historique consigné dans les
3	3. Official recognition of a living man's heroic "death".	3. Victoires et Conquêtes, où elle est rapportée en détail.
4	4. Recalling the opening of the battle—daring French strategy. His regiment faced stubborn Russian resistance.	4. Nous fendîmes en deux les trois lignes russes, qui, s'étant aussitôt reformées, nous obligèrent à les retraverser en sens contraire.
5	5. Premature illusion of victory; Napoleon emerges (historical associations); suspense; reversal: new danger—new gradation.	5. Au moment où nous revenions vers l'Empereur après avoir dispersé les Russes, je rencontrai un gros de cavalerie ennemie.
6	6. No time to lose; two giant horsemen attack the single French commander. Many a reader imagines pictures of saber-brandishing Cossacks. "Modern readers remember film epics such as *War and Peace*, *Chapayev* or *Dr. Zhivago*.	6. Je me précipitai sur ces entêtés-là. Deux officiers russes, deux vrais géants, m'attaquèrent à la fois.
6	7. A fatal blow: anatomy of heroism; origin of mutilation; Chabert's ugly scar explained.	7. L'un deux m'appliqua sur la tête un coup de sabre qui fendit tout jusqu'à un bonnet de soie noire que j'avais sur la tête, et m'ouvrit profondément le crâne.
7	8. The hero falls.	8. Je tombai de cheval.
8	9. Murat's friendly "rescue" cavalcade defeats the Russians but ironically the stampede seemingly kills the French colonel.	9. Murat vint à mon secours, il me passa sur le corps, lui et tout son monde, quinze cents hommes....

TABLE 8b

GSR, ECG, EEG par. EEG occ.	**Malik's analysis**
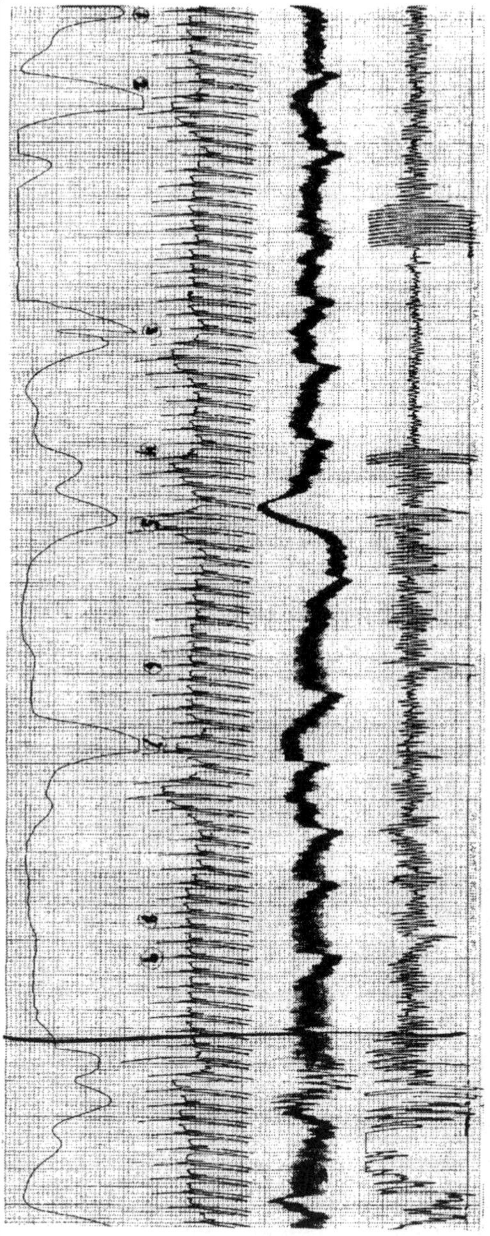	1. Reader starts with high anticipation activity (channel GSR) in first sentence; processing in the occipital lobes occurs approximately in the first few seconds, before the point 2. Is read. 2. Evident activity in all three channels (GSR, ECG and EEG), with GSR channel with overshot conclusively with ECG deviation with evidence of stress wave. The EEG occ. channel is not conclusive between the point 2. And 3. The occipital processing is going on steadily. 3. Evidence of strong GSR reaction to the contentual part of the sentence with the double peak around point 3, and a parallel stress wave on ECG channel. 4. This point is difficult to assign to particular words in the text. It is evident that reader is increasing his interest steadily from point 3. and activity is strong on all four channels. Between points 3. and 5. Is the climax of the attention. 5. Here is evident the cool-down the activity of the reader, but strong evidence of processing in occipital and parietal lobes. 6. This is the end of the cool-down period with activity gradually ceasing from the point 5 (climax). 7. Once again the interest of reader is rekindled, in the expectation of the further semantic aspects of the text. 8. This and the next point is the final reactive point in the text reading. Very interesting repeating activity in EEG channel signal the reader's attempt to memorize the sections of the text. 9. Last sentence is read nearly automatically without too much activity in GSR and ECG channel, but with active mental processing in occipital and parietal lobes.

the centuries they have become imbedded in the envelopes of neural pathways and can be fixed as such. Nevertheless, the researcher has to distinguish between the form of such stressors and their content.

The protein bases in the envelopes of neural pathways (which carry the genetic codes) tend to assimilate formal informational characteristics rather than specific content. With reference to the stimulative intensity of fictional inner conflicts, it is relevant to add that such information can be categorized as "specific artifacts" and that the readers respond to them independently of the author's possible intentions, for example, religious, moralistic, didactic, entertaining. This is due to the interaction of the temporal neural pathways after the text is read and belongs to the secondary and tertiary information impacts. Here, original literary stimulus is mixing with the reader's own past experiences, hierarchy of values and various other environmental information impacts. The resulting envelopes of neural pathways may be far away from the form and content of the original literary stimulus. But, whenever an original stimulative passage is literally or vaguely recalled, the stressor will trigger a response similar to the one originally experienced (sometimes with " information noises" —the room or place where the book was read, or the person with whom the episode was discussed later, or the situation from the reader's own life relating to the original literary stimulus.)

Satisfactory reproductions of biometric recordings in book format are very difficult: for example, Bresky's reading of passages from *Le Colonel Chabert* cited in Chapter II is biometrically transposed on two strips of graph paper, one eight meters and the other 12 meters long. Reduced to a page format, the subtle biometric fluctuations fuse into a single, fuzzy line. Table 8b (p. 303) illustrates the difficulty: it is a reduced reproduction of one segment (72 cm x 20 cm) of the original polygraph monitoring Bresky's reading of 16 printed lines cited on Table 8a (p. 302) and describing Chabert's cavalry charge, the blow inflicted by the Russian's sabre, splitting the Colonel's skull and knocking him from his horse. This narrative is recorded in the form of nine numbered segments reflecting the number of identified stimuli. The four channels on his polygraph, from left to right, include GSR, ECG, EEC, cerebellum, and EEC, occipital (See *LP I*, pp. 189–93). My diagnostic comments form the biometric counterpoint of Bresky's empirical estimates of intensity. These estimates, of course, do not reflect a single one-time-only reading, but rather the result of several readings followed by a long deliberation and a synthesis schematized on his Table 8a.

Eroticism Travels through Neural Pathways

The information process potentially triggering the reader's erotic arousal is a multi-layered neuro- and physiological process. As erotic information travels from the source via neural pathways, it activates the two subcortical centers of the brain, namely, its lymphatic system as well as its thalamic-hypothalamic regions. The first center may initiate physical erotic arousal, while the second may or may not open certain information gates causing inhibition or releasing endorphins. Thus, curiously, a given erotic discourse may both stimulate and warn the brain. This clash of commands issued by the autonomous nervous system and the contrasting cortical responses creates stress which initiates a prudent approach to the stimulus; at the same time it could also provoke deviant responses including, in some cases, sexual violence. In this respect, the indirect (imaginary) perception of erotica conveyed by the texts read considerably differs from sexual stimulation transferred cinematically or from stimulation elicited by direct tactile contact with erotically disposed flesh. The brain processes these various types of erotic provocation with a different speed and in different directions. Written information first travels from the visual cortex to Wernicke and Brocca centers for decoding; this delay permits the simultaneous and sometimes opposite responses from the thalamic and hypothalamic systems.

Thus, before any physical arousal can start, the incoming stimuli are modified. Such modifications may either diminish or increase the ultimate informative impact: daydreamers, or readers highly sensitive to virtual sexual stimulation may experience higher degrees of arousal than cerebral skeptics. On the other hand, cinematic or televised erotica travel much faster than literary input. Audiovisual input reduces the chances of activating the inhibition system in thalamic regions and consequently, the viewers of erotically charged films, TV programs or sex shows react more vehemently than readers of erotica. However, literary reception of erotic subject matter initiates an increased internal feedback in both hemispheres of the brain as well as in the *corpus callosum* and in the brain stem. Such a process is intricate because it is triggered not only by the stimulative information being read but by correlated feedback, for example, remembered associative experiences. External sensations which influence the degree of stimulation include the hormonal level during and after the time of reading (especially in female readers), extreme positive or negative sexual experiences of the individual reader, and various environmental, sexual or quasi-sexual stimuli (for instance, sexual sounds, settings depicting males and females, phallic or vaginal ornaments and their ambiguous analogies in nature).

The information skeleton of erotic discourse further determines the text's macrostimulative, suggestive power. For example, a minor erotic episode may provoke an immediate mental and glandular response. The same passage may, however, be soon forgotten. On the contrary, major erotic plots consisting of the dramatic adventures of extraordinary heroines and heroes not only elicit intensive and durable responses but may even modify some readers' future erotic behaviour.[3]

Determining whether the per capita universal hunger for erotic stimulation is "normal" or whether it borders on an obsession with sex would be a meritorious but probably vain service to our overpopulated planet. While unable to pass qualified judgment, one may assume that erotic literary and cinematic mimesis is a powerful and very ramified influence. In a single day a given reader/viewer may experience several dozen erotic mental encounters. We are all no longer exposed to mere information cascades but to overwhelming cataracts in which assorted erotica often play the first fiddle. Because the artistic and commercial mimesis of erotic adventures is prevalently cinematic, literary language, as a medium which has traditionally articulated erotic affinities and conflicts, has to compete with the younger filmic language. Two cinematic shots may condense and replace two pages of literary discourse. On the other hand, still younger technologies such as fax and internet will probably inject fresh vigor into the literary transposition of erotic subjects. Not only chat room bulletins and cybersex will enlarge the reservoir of original esthetic erotica but even a forthcoming new breed of cybernauts will soon rediscover old-fashioned literary stimuli now dozing in classical texts.

Biometric measurements of erotic information impact can lead only to limited conclusions for two reasons. First, they record the energetic fluctuations in real time, indicating merely the primary information

3 Bresky's note: Heroines such as Baucis, Helena, Phaedra, Andromache, Penelope, Thaïs, Shakespeare's Juliette, the Princess de Clèves, Manon Lescaut, Clarissa, Rousseau's Julie, de Sade's Juliette, de Laclos' Marquise de Merteuil, Emma Bovary, Anna Karenina, Lady Chatterley, Lolita; or the male lover archetypes such as Orpheus, Philemon, Paris, Bluebeard, Romeo, Don Juan, des Grieux, Lovelace, de Laclos' Valmont, the Sadist Duc de Blangis, Casanova, Flaubert's Rudolph Boulanger, Nabokov's Humbert Humbert, etc. In that context, it may be relevant to evoke the suicides of jilted lovers inspired by Goethe's novel, *Werther's Sorrows*.

impact which individual readers may experience. The measurements do not indicate how a stimulative eroticism is processed in the reader's mind minutes or hours after the recording. The biometrist could repeat the test at certain intervals or use magnetic resonance scan procedures but such methods do not guarantee that the brain reactions apply exactly to the same text sample. The technology has yet to be developed which would permit continuous biometric monitoring of a single, say, erotic or comical stimulus in order to clarify its effect and role hours or days after entering the reader's brain.

The second shortcoming is related to the quality of biometric testing, which depends on a pretesting procedure. The pretest enables the biometrist to determine the baseline on which the record of incoming information can be evaluated. Its main purpose is to establish the tested reader's biometric profile and limit the ranges in which the signals will be processed graphically and digitally. Current laboratory practice does not allow too extensive pretests which would record readings of very long passages. Even if the text used in pretesting were pervaded with various stimulative eroticisms, the main test itself would reflect different glandular and hormonal conditions among the individual readers tested. Nonetheless, biometric tests can provide valuable feedback whenever authors, film producers, advertisers or sponsors deliberate whether a higher dose of erotic stimulation might enhance the intended informational impact. The same applies to testing racially or culturally mixed target audiences.

Measuring Laughter: Bresky Reads Baudelaire

Bresky's reflections on the esthetics of humor (ch. V) amply document a relative scholarly consensus on the cause of laughter: invariably, it is an unexpected semantic or logical incongruity giving rise to an esthetic surprise and followed by a sudden cathartic release.[4] There can be a significant individual difference between the *vagal tonus* at a given moment: this explains why different readers, or the same reader at a different tonus level, react to a given comical discourse or an unexpected joke with anything from a subtle chuckle to explosive laughter. Bresky's emphasis on the intensity of laughter in the realm of

4 Bresky's note: comical incongruities are verbal, e.g., a spoonerism—"let the parson cough" intead of "let the coffin pass"—or farcical subjects, e.g., the disguised Jupiter parading as Amphytrion in order to deceive and seduce Amphytrion's wife Alkmene.

TABLE 9

"Assommons les pauvres"	GSR, ECG, EEG par., EEG occ.	Malik's Comments
1. Comme j'allais entrer dans un cabaret, un mendiant me rendit son chapeau, avec un de ces regards inoubliables qui culberteraient les trônes, si l'esprit remuait la matière, et si l'oeil d'un magnétiseur faisait mûrir les raisins. 2. En même temps, j'entendis une une voix qui chuchotait à mon oreille, une voix que je reconnus bien; c'était celle d'un bon Ange, ou d'un bon démon, qui m'accompagne partout. Puisque Socrate avait son bon Démon, pouirquoi n'aurais-je pas l'honneur, comme Socrate, d'obtenir mon brevet de folie, signé du subtil et du bien-avisé Baillarger? 3. Il existe cette différence entre le Démon de Socrate et le mien, que celui de Socrate ne se manifestait à lui que pour défendre, avertir, empêcher, et que le mien daigne conseiller, suggérer, persuader. Ce pauvre Socrate n'avait qu'un Démon prohibiteur; le mien est un grand affirmateur, le mien est un Démon d'action, ou Démon de combat. 4. Or sa voix me chuchotait ceci: "Celui-là seul est digne de la liberté, qui sait la conquérir." 5. Immédiatement, je sautais sur mon mendiant. D'un seul coup de poing,je lui bouchai un oeil, qui devint, en une seconde, gros comme une balle. Je cassai un de mes ongles à lui briser deux dents, et comme je ne me sentais pas assez fort, étant né délicat et m'étant peu exercé à la boxe, pour assommer rapidement ce viellard, je le saisis d'une main par le collet de son habit, de l'autre, je l'empoignai à la gorge, et je me mis à lui secouer vigoureusement la tête contre un mur. Je dois avouer que j'avais préablement inspecté les environs d'un coup d'oeil, et que j'avais vérifié que dans cette banlieue, je me trouvais, pour assez long temps, hors de la portée de tout agent de police.	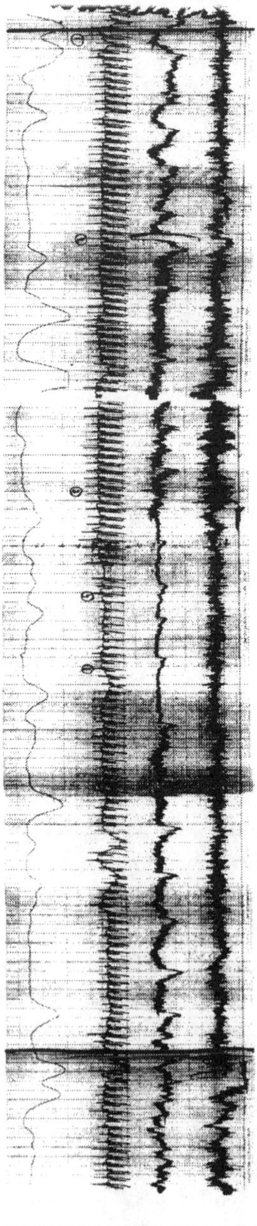	1. The opening text shows the reader's high anticipation (GSR Channel) and minor stress waves on ECG channel. Both EEC (occ. and par.) are active. 2. A brief pause between the end of first paragraph and beginning of the second (EEC par.) shown on second line of graph, could be explained by reader's momentary closing of eyes (blinking). Second paragraph shows high activity on GSR channel, on the beginning of first and second sentence, where the reaction to the text is higher than the range of GSR sensitivity. It also corresponds to the ECG channel and to a certain degree the ECC occ. 3. A certain leveling off of the interest and activity during the third paragraph of the text, which could be explained by the eye tracking, showing that the reader scans relatively fast over individual words, with minor activity, except for EEG occ, which shows initial activity slowly diminishing to the end of paragraph. 4.Relatively short paragraph is read very slowly, carefully, with low activity on all channels except for GSR channel on initial phase. 5.This paragraph shows renewal of activity on GSR channel, corresponding to the individual sentences in the text. There is an interesting activity curve on ECG channel, corresponding to the middle of the text. Also a very active processing of the text by reader. There also is an after effect when reader closes his eyes but mentally is still processing the text.

esthetic stimulation is, of course, appropriate: measurements of reader response reflect the considerable difference between a gentle smile and a Homeric outburst.

The above polygraph (p. 308) retrieves Bresky's responses to the opening of Baudelaire's ironic and farcical poem-in-prose, "Assommons les pauvres," analysed and tabled in chapter V. It exemplifies black (sadistic as well as masochistic) humor.

Metaphysical Information

Mysticism is the human quest of the divine, accessible through extrasensory faith and ecstasies rather than through sensory perception and logic. Among the mental tools assisting this effort to unite with ideal phenomena outside human and terrestrial parameters are superhuman fantasies—visions often triggered by asceticism and cosmic meditation. (Also see the reference to "neurotheology" in ch. VI, n. 8.)

Our ancestors could not conceive fantasies or experience supernatural visions before the physiology of their brains allowed them to think abstractly. Only such a refinement can trigger a variety of mental abstractions. One of them—a free change of dimensional and cognitive scales—can be seen as the physiological origin of abstract "percepts" revealed without any sensory reference in the mindscape of an individual so disposed. Such mental activities generate figments of imagination, illusions, reveries, hallucinatory utopias. Once personified, these percepts can lead to the development of esoteric informational backgrounds, skeletons and to two-way, possibly heterogeneous feedbacks (from authors to their audience and vice versa.) These feedbacks can be both manifest and latent. Literary treatments of extrasensory subjects allow readers to escape and dream in amazing domains of the irrational. The authors of such texts leave it up to them to choose a convenient time and space to perceive and to respond to fantasies. These literary excursions may not only transport our human mindscapes into mythical utopias where miracles take root, evolve, flourish; where gods and devils emerge. Thus primed imaginations not only enriched mythologies and literature, they may be the cornerstones of various spiritual cultures.

What cognitive sciences call metaphysical thinking is, from the biocybernetic perspective, information processing inside the brain's parietal and occipital lobes. In the case of visual or some auditive fantasies, this process usually unfolds with the interference of Brocca

TABLE 10

Lautréamont's Text	GSR, ECG, EEG par., occ.	Malik's Comments
Un jour,...en chancelant comme un homme ivre, à travers les catacombes obscures de la vie(1), je soulevai...mes yeux spleenétiques...vers la concavité du firmament, et j'osai pénétrer, moi, si jeune, les mystères du ciel(2)...[J]e soulevai la paupière effarée plus haut...jusqu'à ce que j'aperçusse un trône, formé d'excréments humains et d'or(3), sur lequel trônait, avec un orgueil idiot, le corps recouvert d'un linceuil fait avec des draps non lavés d'hôpital, celui qui s'intitule lui-même le Créateur! Il tenait à la main le tronc pourri d'un homme mort, et le portait, alternativement, des yeux au nez et du nez à la bouche; une fois à la bouche, on devine ce qu'il en faisait(4). Ses pieds plongeaient dans une vaste mare de sang en ébullition(5), à la surface duquel s'élevaient...deux ou trois têtes prudentes, et qui s'abaissaient aussitôt, avec la rapidité de la flèche: un coup de pied, bien appliqué sur l'os du nez, était la récompense connue de la révolte au règlement, occasionnée par le besoin de respirer un autre milieu; car, enfin, ces hommes n'étaient pas des poissons! Amphibies tout au plus, ils nageaient entre deux eaux dans ce liquide immonde (6)!...jusqu'à ce que, n'ayant plus rien dans la main, le Créateur, avec les deux premières griffes du pied, saisit un autre plongeur par le cou...et le soulevât en l'air...Il lui dévorait d'abord la tête, les jambes et...le tronc, jusqu'à ce qu'il ne restât plus rien; car, il croquait les os. Ainsi de suite, durant...son éternité(7). Quelquefois il s'écriai: "Je vous ai créés; donc j'ai le droit de faire de vous ce que je veux. Vous ne m'avez rien fait, je ne dis pas le contraire. Je vous fais souffrir, et c'est pour mon plaisir(8)." Et il reprenait son repas cruel...sa barbe pleine de cervelle(9). lecteur, ce dernier détail ne te fait-il pas venir l'eau à la bouche? N'en mange pas qui veut d'une pareille cervelle, si bonne, toute fraîche, et qui vient d'être pêchée il n'y a qu'un quart d'heure dans le lac aux poissons (10).	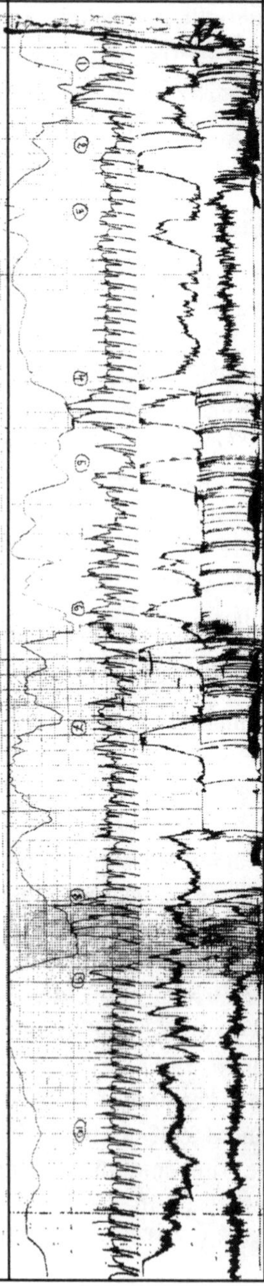	1. All four channels reflect the reader's high anticipation of the text. Notable is a large stress wave on the ECG channel. The GSR channel overshoots its range but cools down considerably through the next sentences. Both EEG channels are very active at the start.(Initial reactions some-times reflect a a carry-over response from previous test.) 2. Reader's interest slowly rises here, with corresponding mental processing. (EEG, occ.) 3. Reader is processing the text carefully and rationally; activity on all channels relatively low. 4. First "mini-climax" in text; activity rises on all channels, with high stress wave on ECG; slow but greatly increased GSR activity. Due to mechanical failure on the EEG par. channel, only the peaks are visible, not the minor activity in the region. Failure also affects the EEG occ. channel, which is readable but some high activity is over the range. 5. Temporary decrease of activity on GSR channel and minor activity on ECG channel. Activity on both EEG. channels increases gradually up to the point of 8, representing the maximum range of signal detection. 6–7. This part of text shows increasing activity on all channels, with major variation of intensity on GSR channel, major stress wave development in ECG channel with maximum EEG activity (both channels.) 8. Reader's reaction culminates. All four channels in maximum range. Apparent decrease of activity at end of period. The only ECG overshoot indicates largest stress wave of text. 9. Major cooldown in activity on all channels. GSR drops to minimum range. ECG channel cools after previous vershoot; remains indifferent for this period. EEG channels are delayed: occ. shows some activity in two peaks; par. shows minimum activity. 10. Previous ceased activity becomes moderate on GSR, showing information feedback from reader toward end. Some EEG activity toward end; occ. moderate with peak in middle of period; par. dormant throughout.

and Wernicke centers. And, because such metaphysical inspirations are only partially reflected in the physiological reactions of the body, biometric charts can detect only the observable large stress waves which are discernible mainly in the GSR channel (fear, rage, acceptance or resentment of metaphysical information). Table 10 (p. 310) retrieves Bresky's reading of the satirical representation of God by Lautréamont discussed above in ch. VII, "Maldoror's nightmarish wanderings," and Table 7.

Biometrics: Past and Future

Biocybernetics, pertaining to perception of artistic information and to the correlated evaluation of perceivable information stimuli, is a child of the twentieth century. Its main goal is to measure with scientific tools the impact of information on the human mind. (In this context, information refers to any form of perception of oral or written statements, pictures, sounds, film, television and so on.) The field is new—it has barely begun a long journey—and its future depends especially on the successful physio- and neurological exploration of the brain, its many functions and roles: brain/center of logical as well as intuitive thinking; brain/tool of qualitative judgment; brain/generator of inspiration and hopes; brain/-storehouse of memories, and brain proliferating both confidence and skepticism.

While the goal of biometrics is stable, its methodology and instrumentation have been changing steadily from its modest beginning. Half a century ago, Prof. Z. Laufberger and his assistants in the Purkinie Physiological Institute in Prague first measured responses evoked from the human body and especially from the brain. Those rather crude experiments were later perfected into a cohesive examination technique and exploited by the post-war Communist regime to examine the effects of propaganda messages woven into artistic performances and literature. In Canada, a number of experiments of this kind were carried out by Dr. Wilder Penfield at the Allan Memorial Institute in Montreal during the 50's and 60's. In Germany, Prof. V. Breitenberg had established his Institut fuer Biokybernetik at the University of Thubingen and in 1976 founded the discipline of biocybernetics as a useful junction of the sciences of biology and cybernetics (which until then had been perceived as a theoretical branch of mathematical theory founded by Norbert Weiner in 1948). At the same time (1972–76), I was able to set up the experimental laboratory at Concordia University in Montreal and began testing the impact of information stimuli. From clumsy, stationery biometric instrumentation, the laboratory progressed to a portable, light-weight set of sensors and from analog processing of signals to digital processing of data. During the past 20 years, German, American, Russian and Japanese laboratories have developed programs devoted to biometric research and have accepted general protocols of experimentation.

Currently the most advanced cybernetic research institute was built at the University of Gifu in Japan and biocybernetic methodology is now being applied worldwide for the UNESCO-sponsored World Virtual Heritage Sites project. Parallel to the Human Genome project,[5] it is assembling and recording users' information matrixes elicited by the stimuli of major works of art all over the world. A similar project using biocybernetic techniques to explore the impact of stimuli in literary masterpieces would present fresh insights to creative writers and critics. This trilogy pioneers in offering a new method applicable to the evaluation of literary information impact on individual readers.[6] The data reflecting the physiological reactions of contemporary readers may serve one day as a cultural mirror of our era and its esthetic standards. The rapid evolution of the discipline, and especially of biocybernetic technology, is bound to extend our understanding of how and why we respond to, and judge literature.

The first main task of the young discipline was to develop a functional technology serving the specific goals of biocybernetic research. The past ten years have seen a number of significant advances: we can now record not only a separate signal from the scalp (13–64 places using classic EEG), but also from the entire surface of the brain via magnetic resonance scanning. We can even restore the data in three dimensional form via computer-assisted tomography. We can inject and mark the movement of blood and neural signals via radioisotopic marking of the chemical substances in the brain during the perception of stimuli . By three-dimensional plotting (3-D Fourier Analysis) we can re-reestablish the pathway of the neural signals and visualize the temporal neural pathway, that is, observe the passage of an individual thought.[7] We can construct the models and derive from them the algorithm of the temporal neural pathway for storage in the memory of the computer.

5 See ch. I, "Breitenberg, Bergström, Pribram explore physiology of the brain".

6 Bresky's note: As stated earlier, I see the biometric method as an innovative and relevant technical supplement to empirical humanistic appraisal.

7 See ch. I, n. 14, ref. to Salzberg's research.

These advanced research tools are now accessible worldwide via the internet.[8]

Current progress in biometrics is paralleled in cognitive science and psychology. Not only are works of art being analyzed and dissected into the smallest parts (as in psychometrics), but the semantic content of literary texts are being examined in the context of the user's reaction. For instance, at Rutgers, Dartmouth, and Carnegie-Mellon University, researchers are examining the creation and perception of semantic "atoms" (semanoles). From the biocybernetic perspective, these findings justify our notion that it is not individual words in literary texts, but groups of words—constituting an informative stimulus—that are discernible in biometric records.[9] Further, the information delivered by reading or by the spoken word, is highly processed during the act of perception. Humans are also able to feedback their own thoughts, fantasies, modifications into the perceived literary text, thus either increasing or decreasing its original information impact. At this point, biometric research cannot fully determine what will be stored in the reader's mind after the reading of the original stimuli. This may depend on the readers' own mindscape, their inclinations, field, era and scope of their erudition. In spite of the variable responses of readers being tested and in spite of the technical limitations which developing research methods usually have to overcome, my experimental measurements of literary perceptions undertaken in the late seventies and eighties at the Myer Pollock Communication Research Laboratory helped point the way for younger generations of biometrists. In the 21st century, they will benefit from the growing neurological knowledge of the anatomy and physiology of the brain. Their research equipment will, no doubt, be

8 The above comments draw from H.M. Thwaites-M.F. Malik, "Toward Virtual Realities: A Biocybernetic View of Communication Media of the 21st Century," paper presented at Seikin Symposium, Tokyo, 1990, pp. 67 and "Bibliography."

9 See our graphs in all three volumes in this trilogy. Bresky's note: This recent research also concurs with the basic criterion of this study, spelled out in *LP I*, ch. V, "Identifiable Esthetic Stimuli—Their Density and Intensity." Within the literary micro-context, esthetic stimuli are most often either (1) minor syntactic units conveying excitive topics (information) or (2) tropes (such as surprising similes, antitheses, paradoxes, etc..) or poetic versifications potentially heightening topical or formal intensities. A provocative monoreme in the form, say, of an unexpected *mot juste* or a shocking obscenity can, of course, also become a "laconic" stimulus and/or stimulative "semanole." Vladimir Propp's narrative "functions," Lord Raglan's "features," Barthes' "lexies"/codes (*S/Z*), erotic codes (*Sade*), all constitute what could be defined as basic primary semantic (informative) or narrative quanta.

more sophisticated than the instruments available to my generation of biocybernetists. One can safely predict that, as biometrics and its applications continue to evolve, neurologists, information specialists and collaborating critics will ultimately understand the specific working process of perceiving esthetic subjects and forms, as well as the subtleties of the resulting individual stimulations. Such research may one day lead to a successful analysis of the faculty which we call taste. It will reveal how taste is energized, how it functions, what are its constants and individual variables or what initiates its cultural changes.

* * *

IX

CONCLUSIONS

> "Excusez le style: Je n'en suis pas responsable.
> —Allez toujours! Je n'y prête plus attention dès que ce que l'on dit m'intéresse."[1]

In the above repartee, André Gide not only fictionalizes his own creative deliberations, he expresses the cardinal rule of literary practice. The unmistakably autobiographical Corydon quotes an American text in French translation which does not meet his stylistic standards. He apologizes for the lack of verbal polish to his old schoolmate, a friendly opponent who plays down the apology. In his eyes, style becomes negligible whenever the related content is sufficiently compelling.[2] This minor digression of a puritan stylist[3] appears to be his empirical recognition that the Catonian *res,* the subject, is essential in any communication or artistic mimesis, while style is subordinate to it. This is nothing world-shaking. Generally, facts still count more than verbal elegance.[4] Besides, the view that poetic mimesis is the basic act of artistic creation has been a pillar of literary practice since antiquity. At the peak of classicism, Goethe's *Dichtung* drew from his *Wahrheit* and, in any cultural cycle analogies between life and its artistic representations prevailed.[5] It is difficult to imagine any literary work

1 *Oeuvres d'André Gide, Corydon* (Paris: N.R.F., 1932–39), p. 224. "Excuse the [citation's] style. I am not responsible for it. Read on! I pay no attention to it as long as what's said interests me." [My transl.]

2 See comments on *Corydon*, ch. V, " Pioneers of relaxed mimesis."

3 See *LP II*, pp. 34–6.

4 See comments, *LP I*, pp. 70–1.

5 Elaine Scarry (*On Beauty and Being Just*, Princeton University Press, 1999, p. 3), cites Wittgenstein, who claims "that when the eye sees something beautiful, the hand wants to draw it."

which would ignore the human frame of reference shared by past, present and future "art consumers" and still hope to attract an audience.

Modern experimenters, especially the dadaists, surrealists and the proponents of the art of the absurd[6] tried to create literary visions independent of positivist reality but their experiments failed to diminish the primary role of mimesis in art. Even the chaotic surreal and absurd subjects stimulate only because they deviate, for example, absurdly or shockingly from a conventional reality which surrounds both writers and their readers. Today, John Updike re-emphasizes the link between reality and art: "The world of literary art springs from the world and adheres to it but is distinctly different in substance." This is so because it offers "an intensity and shapeliness absent in our own life." Clearly, like Aristotle's *poesis*, Updike aspires to reveal "the spiritual significance of things" perhaps not perceivable *prima vista.*

In a satirical fantasy Updike enriches his traditional concept of fiction by alluding to the paradoxical potential of mimesis. He imagines an antiseptic "think-tank", where a *homo sapiens* critic, Farquhar, introduces the Martian emissary, Chokchöq, to the fiction of the human race by offloading directly into the electronic receptacle in Chokchöq's skull the major literary milestones ranging from *Robinson Crusoe* to *The Remembrance of Things Past.* It takes just a few seconds. "Put it this way," says Farquhar, "fictional persons are objectifications of actual impressions of life received by the author. Because they are not actual, the author is free to invade their privacy and confide to us their thoughts and sensations, however evanescent and trivial." This is why fiction is more to readers than historical or sociological diatribes. "Fiction is realer than real, one could say," Farquhar proclaims. Does the futuristic humanist allude to a latent revelatory, perhaps even quasi-mystical power of fiction? Is he resurecting Horace's portrait of the poet as "sacerdos Musarum" revealing divinity? There's nothing like fiction, proclaims Farquhar, "for immaterial interpenetration, it expands the sympathies...if you guys had some fiction on Mars you wouldn't be so cruel, zenophobic and paranoid..." Whereupon the insulted alien grabs Farquhar's head between two of his prehensile tentacles. When an alert technician stuns him with megabolts of electricity, Chokchöq concedes that human fiction "packs a wallop" but adds: "I'm not sure you Earthlings will have much

6 E.g., Tzara; Henri Michaux, see *LP II*, pp. 48–9; Ionesco, Beckett, see ch. VII, "Experimental bizarrerie."

luck exporting it."[7]

To assess the qualities of literary subject matter, this final volume of *Literary Practice* categorizes and then examines the topics and themes treated by writers over the past three millennia, mainly to stimulate their audiences and readers. From the very beginning of our poetic tradition, the main branches of excitive subjects have included representations of heroic, tragic and comical conflicts and fateful inner struggles fought by literary heroes and heroines; their erotic adventures, their encounters with cosmic or magic forces, their colorful odysseys. Like the trilogy's second tome, which estimates the esthetic potential of style, the last volume approaches topical stimuli from a qualitative esthetic perspective. Depending on the epical, lyrical or dramatic role such stimuli play in literary art, I classify them as informative micro- or macrostimuli. In the course of reading, specific microstimulative topical details elicit brief passing quanta of esthetic surprise, while homogeneous macrostimulative gradations may offer the readers continuing delectation after the reading ends, by extending their humanistic frame of reference and nourishing their associative imagination. The obvious macrostimuli in epical or dramatic genres are the plots and the main characters engaged in them; the macrostimulative themes in lyrical and reflexive texts include intimate confessions, nostalgic souvenirs, breviaries of wisdom, and so on.[8] Major coherent condensations of homogeneous microstimuli, for example, of mysterious incongruities in Hilton's description of Shangri-la, fuse in a macrostimulative utopian adventure. Baudelaire's distinct visions of "evil" beauty—his specific flowers of evil—generally strike cultivated readers as macrostimulative condensations of the poet's sensual fantasies, dreams, neuroses, preoccupations with sin. In the broadest sense, the transpositions of major violent or inner conflicts, or erotic bonds and betrayals, supernatural powers, bizarre settings or comical intrigues,

7 John Updike, *More Matter, Essays and Criticism* (New York: A.A. Knopf, 1999), pp. 62–5.

8 When such reflections or pleas culminate in didactic maxims or lyrical refrains, due to their proverbial impact, they become "unforgettable" but also somewhat trite: e.g., Heracleitus: "Panta rhei ouden menei" ("All is flux, nothing lasts forever"); Seneca citing Hypocrates: "Vita brevis, ars longa"; Cicero: "O tempora, o mores"; F. Villon: "Où sont les neiges d'antan!" (Where are the snows of yesterday!"); Ronsard: "Cueillez des aujourdhui les roses de la vie…"; Shakespeare: "To be or not to be…"; Goethe: "Das ewig Weibliche zieht uns hinan… Lamartine: "Ils ont aimé"; Kipling: "If…You'll be a man, my son."

elegiac reminiscences, broodings on the goal of life are the Ovidian *mutatae formae*[9] which every generation of authors has to reinvigorate—one could say remythify—to create original timely yarns appreciated by their contemporaries and hopefully by their descendants. Once perceived, the revitalized subject matter may offer young generations of readers fresh stimulation. Naturally, the potential ability of the subconscious to imagine and the individual interaction of experience with erudition involved in imagining are highly individual. We each respond in our own time, milieu and according to our indvidual teleological and esthetic make-up. Consequently, while our reactions may have a great deal in common, they are never identical. The reader whose humanistic outlook is at odds with that of the writer might value the work less than the reader who concurs with the author's views. For instance, Tolstoy's masonic message in *War and Peace* could reduce the novel's value in the eyes of a Catholic intellectual. Vice versa, Paul Claudel's *La Mort de Judas* might elicit approving smiles in Catholic ranks but strike agnostic critics as a polished lampoon targeting an unconvertible free-thinker, André Gide. As much as is practical, I try to distinguish between synchronic and diachronic reactions of readers pertaining to different eras, cultures or fashions. I try to make allowances for discrepant noetic interpretations or world outlooks of readers living, long deceased or not yet born. (Since each chapter sums up the evolving mimesis of the categorized informative stimuli, additional condensations of previous conclusive comments would be redundant.)

In the previous chapter, the biocybernetist Malik comments on typical recordable responses which might be activated by, for example, a representation of a brutal duel, by a farcical poem-in-prose or evocations of erotic activities. He sums up the progress of physiological and neurological monitoring methods between the late seventies, when he first recorded the biometric profiles of literary texts included in *Literary Practice I,* and the present; he predicts that improved instruments will be able to monitor the complex functions of the brain, such as memory storage and recall; the energy needed to transfer eligible stored concepts into active thoughts, imaginings and judgements of the text being read. He also contemplates the future evolution of biocybernetic research: how far modern science is from isolating the neurological correlates of perceiving, contemplating, enjoying, resenting, judging direct (life) and

9 "In nova fert animus mutatas dicere formas." *Metamorphosae I,* l. 1. See *LP I,* p. 31, n. 27.

illusory (art) information. Less than two years after his death, scholarly reviews and even the daily press report the development of "neuro-esthetics" by the Department of Cognitive Neurology at University College, London, and by the Centre for Brain and Cognition at the University of California, San Diego.[10] To this one could add that Updike's fictional think-tank may also be "realer than real": another embryonic precedent of such a mini-utopia may be, for instance, the Virtual System Laboratory at Japan's Gifu University mentioned above by Malik.

As some of the biocybernetic techniques, used for example in criminology, intelligence and advertising, are adaptable to monitoring any perception process, including the reading of artistic texts or watching films, the collaboration between empirical critics and biometric scholars may gradually become routine. It may ultimately lead to a thorough re-examination of the surviving pragmatic and optional norms which, although evolving, reflect an enduring esthetic consensus linking many generations of readers and the critics they respect. Literary production and "consumption" have always been multilayered. In modern society, no book has a universal appeal. Inevitably, various levels of esthetic qualities compete on book markets catering to a broad variety of tastes and interests. The main goals of my critical analysis and synthesis of esthetic qualities in literary texts were (1) the definition and categorization of identifiable stimuli and the determination of their microstimulative range and density in the selected illustrative texts; (2) an empirical but credible appraisal of these features' fluctuating intensity within the textual gradations and/or longer segments of suspenseful discourse; (3) the final empirical assessment of the macrotext's stimulative potential, not only based on the first two critical procedures but also applying the traditional historical, comparative and hermeneutic methods. To illustrate and document the universality of my valuatory approach (4), I drew from a broad range of genres, both traditional and avant-garde, characterizing Western prose and poetry.

The subjective but detailed analysis of the esthetic microcontext made it possible to tabulate my individual responses to specific textual segments and, subsequently, to record in Malik's laboratory the biometric measurements of my readings of the same texts. The two

10 See full-page review, *National Post*, July 6, 2001, "Neuroesthetics. Why We All Like Picasso. It's All About Brain Wiring," p. A 12. Also see the reportage on "neurotheology" referred to in ch. VI, n. 8.

entirely different methods thus became compatible. Both my collaborator and I were fully aware that the estimates of my own stimulation (based not on one but several readings) are self-searching and inevitably subjective assessments. Malik nevertheless considered these tables legitimate attempts to bring individual esthetic value judgements into the digital era.

The twinning in this trilogy of my humanistic appraisals and Malik's biometric measurements of informative impact represents an early precedent to a foreseeable, more sophisticated valuatory process applicable to macrotexts. First, however, neurologists must explain how imagination retrieves from our memory all factors making up our final esthetic evaluations and how those assessments of macrotexts are gradually conceived and become more or less stable. Only then shall we be able to replace speculations by real knowledge of the biophysical process generating acuity in valuatory as well as elucidatory criticism. A valid diagnosis of how the physiology of the brain stabilizes qualitative conclusions has yet to be made. Updike's cited "realer than real" fantasy goes beyond ordinary futurism to foresee, even if whimsically, this direct link between biometric technology and the appraisal of literary practice.

Today, as the increasing pressure of electronic media reduces reading time and influences writing itself, the critic is forced to consider whether traditional literary practice is down for the count. Throughout their history the basic flexible normative literary options have resisted radical changes. Rigid, dogmatic practices, however, were abandoned, modified or replaced by techniques that were still normative yet adaptable to the writers' creative goals and esthetic expectations of their readers. It is safe to assume that the representation of reality or illusory virtual reality, including penetration of the subconscious, will remain a creative *constante*. It will resist any experimental attempt to replace it by autonomous content disssociated from our existential frame of reference. Any "antimimesis" would have to substitute the familiar stimuli, articulated in familiar languages, by unprecedented elements of surprise. The vacuum created by the suppression of comic or tragic characters, Aristotelian plots (*mythoi*) and ancient and modern settings would have to be filled with "unimaginables" yet to be conceived. Still, without its traditional inventory of stimuli, the artistic mimesis and its practice could not survive. As long as our physical and inner life is what it has been and, as long as old and fresh stimulative subjects and their traditional or innovative stylizations thrill living generations, literary practices—unlike fleeting theories—cannot help but remain. Naturally, new scripted genres will be born and the cyclical waves of "golden age" will follow spells of creative mediocrity, even decadence.[11] As in the past, literary tradition will blossom in the works of active authors in tune with it but who, at the same time, effectively assimilate viable stimuli invented by talented apostates. As in the past, the same tradition will be sustained by public interest in literature and its cinematic transpositions.

At the beginning of the past century, the dadaist attempt to replace the recognized practices current during the *belle époque* with creative chaos was short-lived but the successive surrealist wave made its mark, less in prose than in poetry. Its proponents were soon seen by their peers, publishers and readers as worthy successors to Rimbaud, Mallarmé, the controversial Jarry and Lautréamont. Today, no decent anthology of French poetry will ignore the politically and socially engaged poems by Paul Eluard. After World War II, one heard again and again Jacques Prévert's generation reciting his automatist elegy, "Rappelle-toi Barbara/ Il pleuvait sans cesse sur Brest ce jour-là". *Paroles*, the collection in which it appeared, had many more than 200 editions. His poetry became popular because it combined accessible surrealist techniques with the charms of the French *chanson.* Henri Michaux, sailor, painter and whimiscal poet of cryptic conjurations and cosmic visions, certainly created his original esthetic universe. Ionesco's plays and Beckett's plays and prose adapted the surrealist and automatist writing and subconscious illusions to the needs of their subject matter and stylistic accents; Harold Pinter and Edward Albee offered their own variations.

While acknowledging the significance of surrealist and postsurrealist mimesis of the irrational subconscious through radically modified means (i.e., automatist writing, immersion into dreamlike state of mind, search for the *hazard objectif,* disruption of chronology), it seems clear today that the anti-classical dadaist and surrealist mimesis (inspired by Freudian theories) merely broadened the prevalently rational classical mimesis by trying to represent the inaccessible underground of the

11 In the conclusive final chapters of his *From Dawn to Decadence 500 years of Western Cultural Life* (New York: HarperCollins, 2000), Jacques Barzun sketches a vast mosaic of the present (hopefully cyclical rather than terminal) decline of contemporary civilization, including its literature. Unfortunately Barzun's work appeared too late for me to refer more specifically to the ample valuatory comments relevant to *Literary Practice III.*

human soul. Compared with expressionist and surrealist painters and sculptors crusading against realistic representations of nature, the experimental writers had little impact. Dozens of productive contemporaries of Picasso, whose innovative practices transformed the esthetic climate in visual and even decorative arts, are today recognized as classics of modern art. On the other hand, the experimental literati who influenced poetry played only a limited role in the major literary field of modern prose. The prominent novelists satisfying their readers' expectations throughout the past century[12] overwhelmingly adhered to traditional writing techniques. Their criteria continue to be the primary gauge of literary quality today. This enduring endorsement testifies to the vitality of literary practice.

* * *

12 For example, Nobel and Pulitzer prize-winners and Prix Goncourt laureates.

APPENDIX

These addenda, like the Appendix in *LP II*, are excerpts from works in the public domain or short citations from the texts alluded to, but not quoted, in this volume. Their purpose is to illustrate and corroborate my critical comments as well as to provide specific textual guidance to students of literature.

Baudelaire, Charles (1821–67), ***Les Fleurs du Mal*** **(1857)**

The text below (banned from the collection in 1857), ties in with the comments on the poet's treatment of erotica (ch. IV, "Flaubert's and Baudelaires's Corruption of Public Mores") as well as with the reflections on the density and power of shocking antitheses (*LP II*, "Baudelaire's 'Une charogne,'" pp.81–86); it further complements the discussion on interpretations of "Sed non satiata" (*LP II*, pp. 103–110) and remarks on "Allegory" (*LP II*, 119–20, re "Spleen").

Les Métamorphoses du vampire
La femme cependant, de sa bouche de fraise,
En se tordant ainsi qu'un serpent sur la braise,
Et pétrissant ses seins sur le fer de son busc, [corset]
Laissait couler ces mots tout imprégnés de musc:
— "Moi, j'ai la lèvre humide, et je sais la science
De perdre au fond d'un lit l'antique conscience.
Je sèche tous les pleurs sur mes seins triomphants,
Et fais rire les vieux du rire des enfants.
Je remplace, pour qui me voit nue et sans voiles,
La lune, le soleil, le ciel et les étoiles!
Je suis, mon cher savant, si docte aux voluptés,
Lorsque j'étouffe un homme en mes bras redoutés,
Ou lorsque j'abandonne aux morsures mon buste,
Timide et libertine, et fragile et robuste,
Que sur ces matelas qui se pâment d'émoi,
Les anges impuissants se damneraient pour moi!

Quand elle eut de mes os sucé toute la moelle,
Et que languissamment je me tournai vers elle
Pour lui rendre un baiser d'amour, je ne vis plus
Qu'une outre aux flancs gluants, toute pleine de pus!
Je fermai les deux yeux, dans ma froide épouvante,
Et quand je les rouvris à la clarté vivante,
À mes côtés, au lieu du mannequin puissant
Qui semblait avoir fait provision de sang.
Tremblaient confusément des débris de squelette,
Qui d'eux-mêmes rendaient le cri d'une girouette [weather vane]
Ou d'une enseigne, au bout d'une tringle de fer [iron bars],
Que balance le vent pendant les nuits d'hiver.

Claude Pichois, editor of the Pleiade *O.C.*, cites the subject's precedents to stress that the vampire's metamorphosis is a characteristic Romantic theme (*O.C.*, Pleiade ed., text p. 159 and nn. p. 1356).

* * *

Le Spleen de Paris (1855–62)

The abridged poem-in-prose below characterizes Baudelaire as a traditional forerunner of sardonic male chauvinism. It ties in with ch IV, "Baudelaire's Farcical Satire of Equity à la Proudhon"; it also complements *LP II*, ch. V, "Rhythmical prose", p. 157 and *LP II*, Appendix, pp. 220–2.

La Femme sauvage et la petite maîtresse

Vraiment, ma chère, vous me fatiguez sans mesure...on dirait, à vous entendre soupirer, que vous souffrez plus... que les vieilles mendiantes qui ramassent des croûtes de pain à la porte des cabarets.

Si au moins vos soupirs exprimaient le remords, ils vous feraient quelque honneur; mais ils ne traduisent que la satiété du bien-être et l'accablement du repos. Et puis, vous ne cessez de vous répandre en paroles inutiles: "Aimez-moi bien! J'en ai tant besoin! Consolez-moi par ci, caressez-moi par là!" Tenez, je veux essayer de vous guérir...
Considérons bien...cette solide cage de fer derrière laquelle s'agite...comme un orang-outang exaspéré par l'exil, imitant...tantôt les bonds circulaires du tigre, tantôt les dandinements stupides de l'ours blanc, ce monstre poilu dont la forme imite assez vaguement la vôtre.

Ce monstre est un de ces animaux qu'on appelle généralement "mon ange!" c'est-à-dire une femme. L'autre monstre, celui qui crie à tue-tête, un bâton à la main, est un mari. Il a enchaîné sa femme légitime comme une bête, et il la montre dans les faubourgs, les jours de foire, avec permission des magistrats, cela va sans dire.

...Voyez avec quelle voracité...elle déchire des lapins vivants et des volailles piaillantes que lui jette son cornac. "Allons, dit-il, il ne faut pas manger tout son bien en un jour", et, sur cette sage parole, il lui arrache cruellement la proie, dont les boyaux dévidés restent un instant accrochés aux dents de la bête féroce, de la femme, veux-je dire.
Allons! Un bon coup de bâton pour la calmer! Car elle darde des yeux terribles de convoitise sur la nourriture enlevée... Dans sa rage, elle étincelle tout entière, comme le fer qu'on bat.

Telles sont les moeurs conjugales de ces deux descendants d'Ève et d'Adam, ces oeuvres de vos mains, ô mon Dieu! Cette femme est incontestablement malheureuse, quoique après tout, peut-être, les jouissances titillantes de la gloire ne lui soient pas inconnues...

Maintenant, à nous deux, chère précieuse! A voir les enfers dont le monde est peuplé, que voulez-vous que je pense de votre joli enfer, vous qui ne reposez que sur des étoffes aussi douces que votre peau, qui ne mangez que de la viande cuite, et pour qui un domestique habile prend soin de découper les morceaux?... [I]l me prend quelquefois envie de vous apprendre ce que c'est que le vrai malheur.

A vous voir ainsi, ma belle délicate, les pieds dans la fange et les yeux tournés vaporeusement vers le ciel, comme pour lui demander un roi, on dirait vraisemblablement une jeune grenouille qui invoquerait l'idéal...

Tant poëte que je sois, je ne suis pas aussi dupe que vous voudriez le croire, et si vous me fatiguez trop souvent de vos *précieuses* pleurnicheries, je vous traiterai en *femme sauvage*, ou je vous jetterai par la fenêtre, comme une bouteille vide.

Diderot, Denis (1713–84), *La Religieuse* (publ. posthumously 1796)

This novel is a melodramatic satire of ecclesiastic despotism in prerevolutionary convents. In his preface to the novel (Livre de Poche edition), Henri de Montherlant characterizes the fictitious abbey Longchamp as "un Dachau religieux." This establishment abuses the novice sister Suzanne, who was forced to take the veil. Diderot modelled his heroine after the daughter of a lawyer who, convinced that she was not conceived by him but by his wife's lover, banishes her to the convent. The stimulative conflicts include father against daughter, the loss of secular freedom, the desperate nun's clash with the convent regime and milieu, erotic abuse, inner conflict and, of course, the crusade against the oppressive Church.

Sister Suzanne's ordeal begins when the old Mother Superior dies and is replaced by Sister Sainte Christine, who reintroduces the "cilice" (horse-hair shirt) and monastic "discipline" (self-flagellation). She is spied on, exorcized and ultimately robbed of her modest "dowry" paid to the convent by her parents. The citation below relates Sister Suzanne's sins and punishment. Her cross-examination is triggered by Suzanne's regular requests for writing paper. Secretly, she has been keeping a personal record of her experiences, hoping that her journal could one day facilitate her return to secular life. The other nuns, however, suspect that she uses the paper to report on the Mother Superior to ecclesistic authorities.

— Ma Chère mère, lui disais-je, je n'ai rien fait qui puisse offenser ni Dieu, ni les hommes, je vous le jure.

— Ce n'est pas là le serment que je veux.

— Elle aura écrit contre vous, contre nous, quelque mémoire au grand vicaire, à l'archevêque... Madame, il faut disposer de cette créature...

La supérieure ajouta: "Soeur Suzanne, voyez..."

Je me levai brusquement, et je lui dis: "Madame, j'ai tout vu; je sens que je me perds; mais un moment plus tôt ou plus tard ne vaut pas la peine d'y penser. Faites de moi ce qu'il vous plaira; écoutez leur fureur, consommez votre injustice..."

Et à l'instant je leur tendis les bras. Ses compagnes s'en saisirent. On m'arracha mon voile; on me dépouilla sans pudeur. On trouva sur mon sein un petit portrait de mon ancienne supérieure; on s'en saisit; je supplia qu'on me permît de le baiser encore une fois; on me refusa. On me jeta une chemise, on m'ôta mes bas, on me couvrit d'un sac, et l'on me conduisit la tête et les pieds nus, à travers les corridors. Je criais, j'appelais à mon secours; mais on avait sonné la cloche pour avertir que personne ne parût. J'invoquais le ciel, j'étais à terre, et l'on me traînait. Quand j'arrivai au bas des escaliers, j'avais les pieds ensanglantés et les jambes meurtries; j'étais dans un état à toucher des âmes de bronze. Cependant l'on ouvrit avec de grosses clefs la porte d'un petit lieu souterrain, obscur, où l'on me jeta sur une natte que l'humidité avait à demi pourrie. Là, je trouvai un morceau de pain noir et une cruche d'eau...il y avait, sur un bloc de pierre, une tête de mort, avec un crucifix de bois. Mon premier mouvement fut de me détruire; je portai mes mains à ma gorge; je déchirai mon vêtement avec mes dents; je poussai des cris affreux...je me frappais la tête contre les murs; je me suis mis toute en sang; je cherchai à me détruire jusqu'à ce que les forces me manquassent... C'est là que j'ai passé trois jours; je m'y croyais pour toute ma vie. Tous les matins une de mes exécutrices venait, et me disait:

— Obéissez à notre supérieure, et vous sortirez d'ici.

— Je n'ai rien fait, je ne sais ce qu'on me demande. Ah! Soeur Saint Clément, il est un Dieu...

* * *

Having been expelled without dowry to another convent, she is adored by her new (Lesbian) superior, who visits her in her cell and tries to seduce her.

A l'instant elle ferma ma porte, elle éteignit sa bougie, et elle se précipita sur moi. Elle me tenait embrassée; elle était couchée sur ma couverture à côté de moi; son visage était collé sur le mien, ses larmes mouillaient mes joues; elle soupirait, et elle me disait d'une voix plaintive et entrecoupée: "Chère amie, ayez pitié de moi!"

— Chère mère, lui dis-je, qu'avez-vous? Est-ce que vous vous trouvez mal? Que faut-il que je fasse?

— Je tremble, me dit-elle, je frissonne; un froid mortel s'est répandu sur moi.

— Voulez-vous que je me lève et que je vous cède mon lit?

— Non, me dit-elle, il ne serait pas nécessaire que vous vous levassiez; écartez seulement un peu la couverture, que je m'approche de vous; que je me réchauffe, et que je guérisse.

— Chère mère, lui dis-je, mais cela est défendu. Que dirait-on si on le savait? J'ai vu mettre en pénitence des religieuses, pour des choses beaucoup moins graves. Il arriva dans le couvent de Sainte-Marie à une religieuse d'aller la nuit dans la cellule d'une autre, c'était sa bonne amie, et je ne saurais vous dire tout le mal qu'on en pensait. Le directeur m'a demandé quelquefois si l'on ne m'avait jamais proposé de venir dormir à côté de moi, et il m'a sérieusement recommandé de ne le pas souffrir. Je lui ai même parlé des caresses que vous me faisiez; je les trouve très innocentes, mais lui, il ne pense point ainsi; je ne sais comment j'ai oublié ses conseils; je m'étais bien proposé de vous en parler.

— Chère amie, me dit-elle, tout dort autour de nous, personne n'en saura rien. C'est moi qui récompense ou qui punis; et quoi qu'en dise le directeur, je ne vois pas quel mal il y a à une amie, à recevoir à côté d'elle une amie...

— Et ne suis-je pas votre chère mère?

— Oui, vous l'êtes; mais cela est défendu.

— Chère amie, c'est moi qui le défends aux autres, et qui vous le permets et vous le demande. Que je me réchauffe un moment, et je m'en irai. Donnez-moi votre main... Je le lui donnai. "Tenez, me dit-elle, tâtez, voyez; je tremble, je frissonne, je suis comme un marbre..." et cela était vrai... Elle me disait à voix basse: "Suzanne, mon amie, approchez-vous un peu..." Elle étendit ses bras; je lui tournais le dos; elle me prit doucement, elle me tira vers elle, elle passa son bras droit sous mon corps et l'autre dessus, et elle me dit: "Je suis glacée; j'ai si froid que je crains de vous toucher, de peur de vous faire mal."

— Chère mère, ne craignez rien.

* * *

The Mother Superior's warming-up therapy is suddenly interrupted by a knock on the door. It is her former Lesbian lover, Sister Sainte Thérèse.

...[E]lle avait écarté son linge, et j'allais écarter le mien, lorsque tout à coup on frappa deux coups violents à la porte. Effrayée, je me jette sur-le-champ hors du lit d'un côté, et la supérieure de l'autre; nous écoutons, et nous entendons quelqu'un qui regagnait, sur la pointe du pied, la cellule voisine. "Ah! lui dis-je, c'est ma soeur Sainte-Thérèse; elle vous aura vue passer dans le corridor, et entrer chez moi; elle nous aura écoutées, elle aura surpris nos discours; que dira-t-elle?..." J'étais plus morte que vive.

France, Anatole (François Anatole-Thibault, 1844–1924). "Histoire de Doña Maria d'Avalos et du Don Fabricio, duc d'Andria" (*Le Puits de Sainte Claire, O.C. X*, pp. 237–47; transl. by Margaret Brydon).

This text is related to comments on violent conflicts (ch. III) and treatment of erotica (ch. IV). This novella dramatizes a fateful meeting of Eros and Thanatos, linked with an outburst of sadistic jealousy, climaxed by a necrophilic rape. The tale opens with an ostentatious celebration of Doña Maria's wedding.

"Twelve floats pulled by horses covered with scales, feathers and furs to look like dragons, griffins,...displayed naked men women, gilded from head to foot, who represented the gods who came down from Olympus to celebrate the Venosian nuptials. On one of the floats a young, winged boy was trampling on three ugly old women. A banner above the scene proclaimed, 'Love conquers the Parcae'."

Conjugal adultery, the jealous husband's violence and an unexpected act of nocturnal eromania ultimately confirm the veracity of the ambiguous motto on the banner. Eros will win but the Parcae will have the last word.

The heroine is caught *in flagranti* with her lover, the Duc d'Andria, by her husband, Prince Venosa, and his bodyguards. Don Fabricio, fighting half naked, is stabbed to death. The prince, calling his wife "Puttana!" then "Putaccia!" and finally "Sporca puttaccia! sadistically enjoys her fear. But his adulterous wife soon regains her Spanish *sang froid* and starts whistling to irritate her husband and kisses her dead lover passionately. Prince Venosa, not quite satisfied with killing the Duke, repeatedly runs his sword through his wife's stomach and chest. He orders the naked bodies of the two lovers displayed publicly in the palace courtyard,where the dogs lick his wife's wounds. This climax seems grim enough, but France has a more disgusting gradation in store to surprise his reader:

"The bodies were left there in shameful exposure. As the night drew to a close, since the sight-seers had all disappeared, the servants went off to their quarters. But then a figure, who remained tenaciously all day before the gate, glided along the staircase... A Dominican monk crept up to the steps where Doña Maria d'Avalos had been flung; he hurled himself upon the corpse and violated it."

Other precedential or modern examples of the emotive Love/Death theme include, e.g., the myth of Orpheus and Euridice, many versions of Tristan and Yseult's tragic love, *Romeo and Juliet*, *Clarissa*, *Les Liaisons dangereuses*, *Madame Bovary*, Anatole France's *Histoire comique* (1903) etc. In his *Alexandria Quartet*, Lawrence Durrell sums up the ultimate erotic substance of Justine's and Nessim's fateful marriage: "He had conquered her in offering her a married life which was both a pretense and yet at the same time informed by a purpose which might lead them to *death*! This was all that sex could mean to her now! How thrilling, sexually thrilling, was the expectation of their death!"[1] The *Amor/Mors* antithesis fascinates Baudelaire: See above, Baudelaire, "Metamorphose," and also comments on "Une Charogne" in *LP II*, pp. 81–86. A Naturalist approach to this subject is illustrated below in Zola's *Germinal*.

Jarry, Alfred (1873–1907), *Ubu Roi* (first staged as *Les Polonais*, 1888)

To distinguish his puerile creative clowning from other decadent eccentricities, Jarry whimsically baptized his artistic ideology "pataphysics." Also whimsically, he formulated its goals in a posthumously published book of absurd parodies, *Gestes et Opinions du Docteur Faustroll, Pataphysicien* (1911). Pataphysics is the "science des epiphénomènes" (accessory, marginal phenomena) seeking solutions of apparently not particularly urgent problems. For instance, instead of spelling out the law of an object's free fall toward the centre of gravity, pataphysicians speculate on the ascension of non-objects ("unités de non densité") away from the gravity focus upward to the peripheral zones of attraction. In other words,. the pataphysical experts challengingly and absurdly seek theoretical answers to questions nobody will ever ask. Jarry's fictional ancient pataphysicians, land surveyor Ibicrates and Sophrotates, mathematically solve as follows the key theological question: Who is God? He is "the shortest way (chemin) from zero to the infinite" (my transl.).

However, similar pataphysical axioms play only a minor role in Jarry's best known work, *Ubu Roi*, which struck André Gide as "the most extraordinary thing seen in the theatre."

In the eyes of the anointed guru of French drama Sacha Guitry, it was a genuine masterpiece, however, not related to any easily identifiable literary genre. He labelled it as an "excessive caricature" and as "the most original and powerful burlesque" (cited in Barbara Wright's *Ubu King*, n.p., New Directions, 1962).

Its opening is cited and stylistically analyzed in *LP II* (pp. 42–3). In this volume I discuss *Ubu* in ch. VII, especially in "Lautréamont's nightmarish wanderings" and in several other instances, I allude to Jarry's adolescent crudity reflected in his treatment of stimulative subjects. Here is the ending of the burlesque: Père and Mère Ubu are reunited after Ubu's abortive attempt to crown himself as the Polish King.

MÈRE UBU: Raconte-moi ta campagne, Père Ubu.
PÈRE UBU: O! dame, non! C'est trop long Tout ce que j'essayais, c'est que malgré mon incontestable vaillance tout le monde m'a battu.
MÈRE UBU: Comment, même les Polonais?
PÈRE UBU: Ils criaient: Vive Venceslas et Bougrelas. J'ai cru qu'on voulait m'écarteler. Oh! Les enragés! Et puis ils ont tué Rensky!
MÈRE UBU: Ça m'est bien égal! Tu sais que Bougrelas a tué le Palotin Giron!

1 *Mountolive* (New York: E.P. Dutton, 1959), p. 205.

PÈRE UBU: Ça m'est bien égal! Et puis ils ont tué le pauvre Lascy!
MÈRE UBU: Ça m'est bien égal!
PÈRE UBU: Oh! Mais tout de même, arrive ici, charogne! Mets-toi à genoux devant ton maître (*il l'empoigne et la jette à genoux*), tu va subir le dernier suplice.
MÈRE UBU: Ho, ho, monsieur Ubu!
PÈRE UBU: Oh! Oh! Oh! Après, as-tu fini? Moi je commence: torsion du nez arrachement des cheveux, pénétration du petit bout de bois dans les oreilles, extraction de la cervelle par les talons, lacération du postérieur, suppression partielle ou même totale de la moelle épinière (si au moins ça pouvait lui ôter les épines du caractères), sans oublier l'ouverture de la vessie natatoire et finalement la grande décollation renouvellée de saint Jean-Baptiste, le tout tiré de très saintes Ecritures, tant de l'Ancien que du Nouveau Testament , mis en ordre, corrigé et perfectionné par l'ici présent Maître des Finances! Ça te va-t-il, andouille?
Il la déchire. [Not quite]
MÈRE UBU: Grâce, Monsieur Ubu!
Grand bruit à l'entrée de la caverne.

Before Ubu can liquidate Mère Ubu, the hillbilly couple is forced to flee. In the final scene, the spectators see them sailing around the Cap "Elseneur" from Poland to France. Mère Ubu hopes to amaze their countrymen with tales of their marvellous adventures and Ubu is confident of being appointed "Maître des Finances" in Paris. His final words, as the curtain falls: "S'il n'y avait pas de Pologne, il n'y aurait pas de Polonais."

La Fontaine de, Jean (1621–95), "Les Lunettes", *Contes et Nouvelles, vol IV* (1675)

This story is a typical *gauloiserie* included in the lascivious vol. IV of *Contes et Nouvelles* confiscated by Royal order in 1675 (referred to in ch. IV, "La Fontaine's *libertinage").* Its plot is inspired by Bonaventure de Périers' 62nd novella, "Du jeune garçon qui se nomma Thoinette pour estre reccu à une religion" (See ch. IV, "The Renaissance: from Rabelais to Montaigne and Ronsard"). The hero of this versified anecdote is a resourceful youngster. Before a beard appears on his chin, he disguises himself as a maiden, is admitted to the convent and becomes "Sister Colette." Soon Sister Agnes enjoys the new novice's company to the extent that she gives birth to a child. Such sins cannot be tolerated: "La prieure est en courroux [colère] extrème / Avoir ainsi souillé cette maison / Bientôt on mit l'accouchée en prison / Puis il fallut faire enquête du père."

All nuns have to strip naked to enable the prioress to find the male among them. Being thus cornered, "Sister Colette" ties his *corpus delicti* with a thin thread and holds it hidden between his thighs. But surrounded by a crowd of naked nuns, the excited flesh breaks the thread in a critical moment of inspection.

La prieure a sur son nez des lunettes,
Pour ne juger du cas légèrement,
Tout à l'entour sont debout vingt nonnettes,
En un habit que vraisemblablement
N'avaient pas fait les tailleurs du couvent.
Figurez-vous la question qu'au sire
On donna lors: besoin n'est de le dire,
Touffes de lis, proportion du corps,
Secrets appas, embonpoint, et peau fine,
Fermes tetons, et semblables ressorts,

Eurent bientôt fait jouer la machine:
Elle échappa, rompit le fil d'un coup,
Comme un coursier qui romprait son licou [halter],
Et sauta droit au nez de la prieure,
Faisant voler lunettes tout à l'heure
Jusqu'au plancher. Il s'en fallut bien peu
Que l'on ne vît tomber la lunetière [here, bespectacled woman].
Elle ne prit cet accident en jeu.

Following this discovery, the juvenile "faiseur d'enfants" is tied to a tree outside the convent and the sisters, ready to flagellate him, rush back to the convent to fetch whips and rods. During their brief absence, a miller, passing by, asks what happened. The boy tells him that the lusty nuns were trying to seduce him and, when he turned them down, they punished him by tying him to a tree. "You idiot!"says the miller, dying with desire. He unties the boy; the boy ties him to the tree and hastily disappears. When the nuns return, the new Don Juan greets them cheerfully, promising absolutely satisfactory cooperation. Unfortunately, the alleged longings of the pious flock seem to have evaporated. The young father's second ruse proves more successful than his attempt to tame his instrument of paternity.

Large d'épaule, on aurait vu le sire
Attendre nu les nonnains en ce lieu.
L'escadron vient, porte en guise de cierges
Gaules et fouets: procession de verges,
Qui fit la ronde à l'entour du meunier,
Sans lui donner le temps de se montrer,
Sans l'avertir. "Tout beau! dit-il, Mesdames,
Vous vous trompez, considérez-moi bien:
Je ne suis pas cet ennemi des femmes,
Ce scrupuleux qui ne vaut rien à rien.
Employez-moi: vous verrez des merveilles;
Si je dis faux, coupez-moi les oreilles.
D'un certain jeu je viendrai bien à bout:
Mais quant au fouet, je n'y vaux rien du tout.
Qu'entend ce rustre, et que nous veut-il dire?
S'écria lors une de nos sans dents;
Quoi! Tu n'es pas notre faiseur d'enfants?
Tant pis pour toi, tu payras pour le sire:
Nous n'avons pas telles armes en main
Pour demeurer en un si beau chemin.
Tiens, tiens, voilà l'ébat que l'on désire."
A ce discours, fouets de rentrer en jeu,
Verges d'aller, et non pas pour un peu…

Mérimée, Prosper (1803–70), *Tamango* (1829)

The following excerpts from the novella especially complement ch. V, "Grave irony in Wilde's and Mérimée's prose" and earlier reflections on the observable intensities of esthetic contrasts (*LP I*, pp. 149–51). The Romantic saga treats a universal theme of enslavement, cruelty and greed. The text reflects remarkable esthetic density (both stylistic and topical) as well as high micro- and macrostimulative intensities. Its subject matter exploits diverse domains of excitive topics and stylistic features—colorful conflicts, farcical, satirical and tragic subjects, bizarre adventure, exotic *couleur locale* of an African slave market, mimesis of a slave ship and erotic accents. Stylistically, the text relies on naval diction, Voltairean irony, compositional discipline, dramatic pace and epical unity. The thrilling suspensful plot depicts criminal business between a ruthless white antagonist and a barbaric black protagonist.

The Antagonist

Le capitaine Ledoux était un bon marin. Il avait commencé par être simple matelot, puis il devint aide-timonier [relief steerman]. Au combat de Trafalgar, il eut la main gauche fracassée...il fut amputé et congédié ensuite avec de bons certificats. Le repos ne lui convenait guère, et...il servit, en qualité de second lieutenant, à bord d'un corsaire [privateer]... Avec le temps, il devint capitaine d'un lougre corsaire de trois canons et de soixante hommes d'équipage, et les caboteurs [coasting vessels] de Jersey conservent encore le souvenir de ses exploits. La paix le désola: il avait amassé pendant la guerre une petite fortune, qu'il espérait augmenter aux dépens des Anglais. Force lui fut d'offrir ses services à de pacifiques négociants; et comme il était connu pour un homme de résolution et d'expérience, on lui confia facilement un navire. Quand la traite des nègres fut défendue, et que, pour s'y livrer, il fallut non seulement tromper la vigilance des douaniers français, ce qui n'était pas très difficile, mais encore, et c'était le plus hasardeux, échapper aux croiseurs anglais, le capitatine Ledoux devint un homme précieux pour les trafiquants de bois d'ébène [black ivory, slaves].

Espérance

Bien différent de la plupart des marins qui ont langui longtemps comme lui dans les postes subalternes, il n'avait point cette horreur...des innovations...qu'ils apportent trop souvent dans les grades supérieurs. Le capitaine Ledoux, au contraire, avait été le premier à recommander à son armateur [shipowner] l'usage des caisses en fer, destinées à contenir et conserver l'eau. A son bord, les menottes et les chaînes dont les bâtiments négriers [slave ships] ont provision, étaient fabriquées d'après un système nouveau, et soigneusement vernies pour les préserver de la rouille. Mais ce qui lui fit le plus d'honneur parmi les marchands d'esclaves, ce fut la construction...d'un brick...capable de contenir un très grand nombre de noirs. Il le nomma *l'Espérance*. Il voulut que les entre ponts [twin decks] étroits et rentrés, n'eussent que trois pieds quatre pouces de haut, prétendant que cette dimension permettait aux esclaves d'être commodément assis; et quel besoin ont-ils de se lever?

— Arrivés aux colonies, disait Ledoux, ils ne resteront que trop sur leurs pieds!...

De la sorte son navire contenait une dizaine de nègres de plus qu'un autre du même tonnage...

L'Espérance partit de Nantes un vendredi, comme le remarquèrent depuis des gens superstitieux. Les inspecteurs qui visitèrent scrupuleusement le brick ne découvrirent pas six grandes caisses remplies...de menottes... Ils ne furent point étonnés non plus de l'énorme provisions d'eau que devait porter *l'Espérance*, qui...n'allait qu'au Sénégal pour y faire le commerce de bois et d'ivoire. La traversée n'est pas longue, il est vrai, mais enfin le trop de précautions ne peut nuire.

The protagonist

Tamango, guerrier fameux et vendeur d'hommes, venait de conduire à la côte une grande quantité d'esclaves, et il s'en défaisait à bon marché... Le capitaine Ledoux...le trouva dans une case en paille qu'on lui avait élevé à la hâte, accompagné de ses deux femmes et de quelques...conducteurs d'esclaves. Tamango s'était paré pour recevoir le capitaine blanc. Il était vêtu d'un vieil habit d'uniforme bleu, ayant encore les galons de caporal; mais sur chaque épaule pendaient deux épaulettes d'or attachées au même bouton, et ballotant [dangling], l'une par devant, l'autre par derrière. Comme il n'avait pas de chemise, et que l'habit était un peu court pour un homme de sa taille, on remarquait entre les revers blancs de l'habit et son caleçon de toile de Guinée une bande considérable de peau noire qui ressemblait à une large ceinture. Un grand sabre de cavalerie était suspendu à son côté au moyen d'une corde, et il tenait à la main un beau fusil...de fabrique anglaise. Ainsi équipé, le guerrier africain croyait supasser en élégance le petit-maître [dandy] le plus accompli de Paris ou de Londres... Ledoux, après l'avoir examiné en connaisseur, se tourna vers son second, et lui dit:

— Voilà un gaillard que je vendrais au moins mille écus...à la Martinique.

The bargain

On disputa longtemps, on but prodigieusement d'eau-de-vie; mais l'eau-de-vie produisait un effet bien différent sur les deux parties contractantes. Plus le Français buvait, plus il réduisait ses offres; plus l'Africain buvait, plus il cédait des ses prétentions. De la sorte, à la fin du panier, on tomba d'accord. De mauvaises cotonnades, de la poudre, des pierres à feu, trois barriques d'eau-de-vie, cinquante fusils mal raccommodés furent donnés en échange de cent soixante esclaves. Le capitaine, pour ratifier le traité, frappa dans la main du noir plus qu'à moitié ivre... Restait encore une trentaine d'esclaves: c'étaient des enfants, des vieillards, des femmes infirmes. Le navire était plein.

Tamango...offrit au capitaine de les lui vendre pour une bouteille d'eau-de-vie la pièce. L'offre était séduisante. Ledoux...prit les vingt plus sveltes des trente esclaves.

An unforeseen erotic bonus

Alors Tamango ne demanda plus qu'un verre d'eau-de-vie pour chacun des dix restants. Ledoux prit donc trois enfants; mais il déclara qu'il ne voulait plus se charger d'un seul noir. Tamango, voyant qu'il lui restait encore sept esclaves sur les bras, saisit son fusil et coucha en joue une femme qui venait la première: c'était la mère des trois enfants.

— Achète, dit-il au blanc, ou je la tue; un petit verre d'eau-de-vie ou je tire.

— Et que diable veux-tu que j'en fasse? Répondit Ledoux.

Tamango fit feu, et l'esclave tomba morte à terre.

— Allons, à un autre! S'écria Tamango en visant un vieillard tout cassé: un verre d'eau-de-vie, ou bien...

Une des femmes lui détourna le bras, et le coup partit au hasard. Elle venait de reconnaître dans le vieillard...un *guiriot* ou magicien, qui lui avait prédit qu'elle serait reine.

Tamango, que l'eau-de-vie avait rendu furieux, ne se posséda plus... Il frappa rudement sa femme de la crosse de son fusil; puis se tournant vers Ledoux:

— Tiens, dit-il, je te donne cette femme.

Elle était jolie. Ledoux la regarda en souriant, puis il la prit par la main:

— Je trouverai bien où la mettre, dit-il.

L'interprète était un homme humain. Il donna une tabatière de carton à Tamango, et lui demanda les six esclaves restants. Il les délivra de leurs fourches, et leur permit de s'en aller où bon leur semblerait.

Slave trader handcuffed by his customer

[L]e capitaine dit adieu à Tamango et s'occupa de faire au plus vite embarquer sa cargaison... Pour Tamango, il se coucha...et dormit pour cuver son eau-de-vie.

Quand il se réveilla, le vaisseau était déjà sous voiles et descendait la rivière. Tamango, la tête encore embarrassée de la débauche de la veille, demanda sa femme Ayché. On lui répondit qu'elle avait eu le malheur de lui déplaire et qu'il l'avait donnée en présent au capitaine blanc... A cette nouvelle, Tamango stupéfait se frappa la tête, puis il prit son fusil, et, comme la rivière faisait plusieurs détours...il eut le temps de se jeter dans un canot et de joindre le négrier.

Ledoux fut surpris de le voir, mais encore plus de l'entendre redemander sa femme.

— Bien donné ne se reprend plus, répondit-il.

Et il lui tourna le dos.

Le noir insista, offrant de rendre une partie des objets qu'il avait reçus en échange des esclaves. Le capitaine se mit à rire; dit qu'Ayché était une très bonne femme, et qu'il voulait la garder... [M]ais Tamango persistait. Il offrait jusqu'à ses épaulette d'or, son fusil et son sabre. Tout fut inutile.

Pendant ce débat, le lieutenant de *l'Espérance* dit au capitaine:

— Il nous est mort cette nuit trois esclaves, nous avons de la place. Pourquoi ne prendrions-nous pas ce vigoureux coquin, qui vaut mieux à lui seul que les trois morts? Ledoux fit réflexion que Tamango se vendrait bien mille écus... Le rivage était désert, et le guerrier africain entièrement à sa merci... Ledoux lui demanda donc son fusil, comme pour l'examiner et s'assurer s'il valait bien autant que la belle Ayché. En faisant jouer les ressorts, il eut soin de laisser tomber la poudre de l'amorce. Le lieutenant de son côté maniait le sabre; et, Tamango se trouvant ainsi désarmé, deux vigoureux matelots se jetèrent sur lui, le renversèrent sur le dos... La résistance du noir fut héroïque... [M]ais, lorsqu'il vit que [tout]...était inutile, il ferma les yeux et ne fit plus aucun mouvement...

— Parbleu! s'écria le capitaine Ledoux, les noirs qu'il a vendus vont rire de bon coeur en le voyant esclave à son tour. C'est pour le coup qu'ils verront bien qu'il y a une Providence.

Uprising

Tout à coup Tamango, qui venait doucement de rompre ses fers, pousse un grand cri qui devait servir de signal, tire violemment par les jambes le matelot qui se trouvait près de lui, le culbute, et, lui mettant le pied sur le ventre, lui arrache son fusil, et s'en sert pour tuer l'officier de quart. En même temps, chaque matelot de garde est assailli, désarmé et aussitôt égorgé. De toutes parts, un cri de guerre s'élève. Le contre-maître [boatswain], qui avait la clef des fers, succcombe un des premiers... S'apercevant que Tamango était l'âme de la conjuration, [Ledoux] espéra...le tuer... Il s'élança donc à sa rencontre le sabre à la main en l'appelant à grands cris. Aussitôt Tamango se précipita sur lui. Il tenait un fusil par le bout du canon et s'en servait comme d'une massue... Tamango frappa le premier. Par un léger mouvement de corps, le blanc évita le coup. La crosse, tombant avec force sur les plances, se brisa, et le contre-coup fut si violent, que le fusil échappa des mains de Tamango. Il était sur la défense, et Ledoux, avec un sourire de joie diabolique, levait le bras et allait le percer; mais Tamango était aussi agile que les panthères de son pays. Il s'élança dans les bras de son adversaire, et lui saisit la main dont il tenait son sabre. L'un s'efforce de retenir son arme, l'autre de l'arracher. Dans cette lutte furieuse, ils tombent tous les deux; mais l'Africain avait le dessous. Alors, sans se décourager, Tamango, étraignant son adversaire de toute sa force, le mordit à la gorge avec tant de violence que le sang jaillit comme sous la dent d'un lion. Le sabre échappa de la main défaillante du capitaine. Tamango s'en saisit; puis, se relevant, la bouche sanglante, et poussant un cri de triomphe, il perça de coups redoublés son ennemi déjà demi-mort... Le lieutenant mourut avec gloire. Il s'était retiré à l'arrière, auprès d'un de ces petits canons qui tournent sur un pivot... De la main gauche, il dirigea la pièce, et, de la droite, armé d'un sabre, il se défendit si bien qu'il attira autour de lui une foule de noirs. Alors, pressant la détente du canon, il fit au milieu de cette masse serrée une large rue pavée de morts et de mourants. Un instant après il fut mis en pièces.

Lorsque le cadavre du dernier blanc...coupé en morceaux, eut été jeté à la mer, les noirs rassasiés de vengence, levèrent les yeux vers les voiles du navire, qui toujours enflées par un vent frais, semblaient obéir encore à leurs oppresseurs et mener les vainqueurs, malgré leur triomphe, dans la terre de l'esclavage.

Liberation, euphoria and aftermath

Tout à coup un nègre paraît sur le tillac: son visage est radieux. Il annonce qu'il revient de découvrir l'endroit où les blancs regagnent leur eau-de-vie; sa joie et sa contenance prouvent assez qu'il vient d'en faire l'essai. Cette nouvelle suspend un instant les cris de ces malheureux. Ils courent à la cambuse [ship store] et se gorgent de liqueur. Une heure après, on les eut vus sauter et rire sur le pont, se livrant à toutes les extravagances de l'ivresse la plus brutale. Leurs danses et leurs chants étaient accompagnés des gémissements et des sanglots de blessés... Le matin au réveil, nouveau désespoir. Pendant la nuit, un grand nombre de blessés étaient morts. Le vaisseau flottait entouré de cadavres. La mer était grosse et le ciel brumeux. On tint conseil. Quelques apprentis dans l'art magique, qui n'avaient point osé parler de leur savoir-faire devant Tamango, offrirent tour à tour leurs services. On essaya plusieurs conjurations puissantes. A chaque tentative inutile, le découragement augmentait.

Sartre, Jean-Paul (1905–80)

"Le Mur" discussed in ch. III ("Executions, Sartre") opens with a superficial but ominous interrogation of the three prisoners, after which they are led to a dank basement cell to wait their sentence. They personify three existentialist options available to humans in their vain struggle against the tragic absurdity of life. In the following microstimulative excerpt, the characters facing the death discuss the technicalities of fasscist executions. Tom, the American volunteer, tells his fellow prisoners what a Moroccan deserter told him about executions by Franco's troops: "You know what they do in Saragossa? They lay the guys on the highway and run the trucks over them...they say it is to save ammunition." "It doesn't save gas," Pablo replies. This repartee sets the scene for the arrival of a Belgian doctor who is collaborating with the Fascists and is gathering evidence of stress among the condemned prisoners. He assures them that the executed do not generally suffer, unless the firing squad has to fire a second round. In monitoring the reactions of the three doomed men, he approaches Juan, a boy who will be executed even though he is not involved in the political conflict.

"Finally, he turned to the little Juan. Did he wish to feel the boy's neck for medical reasons or was it a gesture of charity? If it was charity, it was the one and only instance of it throughout the night. He started caressing the little Juan's neck., The kid let him do it, never taking his eyes off him. Then, all of a sudden, the boy grabbed the hand, staring at it in a funny way. He held it between his two hands and there was nothing funny about those two gray pincers squeezing the fat reddish hand. I had an inkling of what was going to happen...but the doctor must have thought it was just an emotional ouburst and smiled paternally. After an instant, the kid lifted the plump paw to his mouth, ready to bite it. The Belgian jerked it away abruptly and stumbled backwards against the wall, For a second, he gazed at us with horror, realizing that we were no longer creatures like him. I started to laugh and one of the guards jumped to his feet." ("Le Mur" in the collection *Le Mur*, Paris: Gallimard, 1939, pp. 13-14 and 25-6. My transl.)

"Existentialist fantasies" (ch.VI) also examines Sartre's *Huis clos* and *Les Jeux sont faits*, offering different yet analogical visions of existentialist humanism.

* * *

Shakespeare, William (1564–1616), *Titus Andronicus* (1594)

This early and atypically gruesome Shakespearean tragedy demonstrates the density and intensity of shockingly violent subjects. (See comments in ch. III, "Cycles of Mimesis: Voltaire on Shakespeare".) The two excerpts (Act II: scene II and Act V: scene II) illustrate Renaissance representations of murder, rape, and even cannibalism on stage. The first citation relates the assassination of the Emperor's brother Bassianus by Tamora's sons, Demetrius and Chiron who, encouraged by their sadistic mother, plan to make the victim's "dead trunk pillow to [their] lust" by violating his mistress Lavinia. There follows a morbid plea from Lavinia as she confronts the bloodthirsty Tamora and her murdering sons.

Lav. O, let me teach thee! For my father's sake,
That gave thee life, when well he might have slain
Thee,
Be not obdurate, open thy deaf ears.
Tam. Hadst thou in person ne'er offended me,
Even for his sake am I pitiless.
Remember, boys, I pour'd forth tears in vain,
To save your brother from the sacrifice;
But fierce Andronicus would not relent:
Therefore, away with her, and use her as you will,
The worse to her, the better loved of me.
Lav. O Tamora, be call'd a gentle queen,
And with thine own hands kill me in this place!

For 'tis not life that I have begg'd so long;
Poor I was slain when Bassianus died.
Tam. What begg'st thou, then? Fond woman, let me
Go.
Lav. Tis present death I beg; and one thing more
That womanhood denies my tongue to tell:
O, keep me from their worse than killing lust,
And tumble me into some loathsome pit,
Where never man's eye may behold my body:
Do this, and be a charitable murderer.
Tam. So should I rob my sweet sons of their fee:
No, let them satisfy their lust on thee.
Dem. Away! For thou hast stay'd us here too long.
Lav. No grace? No womanhood? Ah, beastly
creature.!
The blot and enemy to our general name!
Confusion fall –
Chi. Nay, then I'll stop your mouth. Bring thou her
husband:
This is the hole where Aaron bid us hide him.
[*Demetrius throws the body of Bassianus into the pit; then exeunt Demetrius and Chiron , dragging off Lavinia.*
Tam. Farewell, my sons: see that you make her sure.
Ne'er let my heart know merry cheer indeed,
Till all the Andronici be made away.
Now will I hence to seek my lovely Moor,
And let my spleenful sons this trull deflour. [*Exit*.]

* * *

Having abused Lavinia, the two rapists cut out her tongue and cut off her hands. The violence escalates still further in a bloody denoument .

Enter Titus, dressed like a Cook, Lavinia veiled, young
Lucius, and others. Titus places the dishes on the table.
Tit. Welcome, my gracious lord; welcome, dread
Queen;
Welcome, ye warlike Goths; welcome, Lucius;
And welcome, all: although the cheer be poor,
'Twill fill your stomachs; please you eat of it.
Sat. Why art thou thus attired, Andronicus?
Tit. Because I would be sure to have all well,
To entertain your highness and your empress.
Tam. We are beholding to you, good Andronicus.
Tit. An if your highness knew my heart, you were.
My lord the emperor, resolve me this:
Was it well done of rash Virginius
To slay his daughter with his own right hand,
Because she was enforced, stain'd and deflower'd?
Sat. It was, Andronicus.
Tit. Your reason, mighty lord?
Sat. Because the girl should not survive her shame,
And by her presence still renew his sorrows.

Tit. A reason mighty, strong, and effectual;
A pattern, precedent and lively warrant,
For me, most wretched to perform the like.
Die, die, Lavinia, and they shame with thee;
[Kills Lavinia.]
And, with thy shame, thy father's sorrow die!
Sat. What hast thou done, unnatural and unkind?
Tit. Kill'd her, for whom my tears have made me blind.
I am as woful as Virginius was,
And have a thousand times more cause than
To do this outrage: and it now is done.
Sat. What, was she ravish'd? tell who did the deed.
Tit. Will't please you eat? Will't please your Highness feed?
Tam. Why hast thou slain thine only daughter thus?
Tit. Not I; 'twas Chiron and Demetrius:
They ravish'd her, and cut away her tongue;
And they,'twas they, that did her all this wrong.
Sat. Go fetch them hither to us presently.
Tit. Why, there they are both, baked in this pie;
Whereof their mother daintily hath fed,
Eating the flesh that she herself hath bred.
'Tis true, 'tis true; witness my knife's sharp point.
[Kills Tamora.]
Sat. Die, frantic wretch, for this accursed deed!
[Kills Titus.]
Luc. Can the son's eye behold his father bleed?
There's meed for meed, death for a deadly deed!
[Kills Saturninus. A great tumult. Lucius and others go up onto the balcony.]

Viau de, Théophile (1590–1626)

The libertine poet, who ignored the dangers of his era, died young in jail. The two poems below *La poésie érotique*, pp.126–29. See n. 54, ch. IV) broaden the illustrative citations in ch. IV, "Théophile de Viau's and Malherbe's pornography": the sonnet warns Renaissance women that masturbation is a poor substitute for the real thing. The "Épigramme" is a thumbnail *gauloiserie* portraying a typical f*abliau* womanizer and his ribald self-promotion.

Sonnet

Mesdames qui avez inventé cet usage
De vous jouer vous même à de vits de velours,
Si vous vouliez d'autrui rechercher le secours
Certes vous y auriez du plaisir davantage.

Pour apaiser d'un con la fureur et la rage,
Il lui faut un gros vit et lequel soit toujours
Bien roide et bien fourni de la sauce d'amour,

Que l'on nomme du foutre en naturel langage.

Foutez-vous tout un jour, toutes deux s'il vous plaît
De vos gaude-michis, enfin tout cela n'est
Que pardonner l'amour pour une moquerie.

Mais prendre à belle main un bon gros vit nerveux
Et en remplir d'un con le gosier chaleureux,
C'est le vrai jeu d'amour et de la fouterie.

Épigramme

Il est arrivé dans la ville,
Un personnage fort utile,
Expressément pour le déduit [love making];
Il a quinze pouces de vit
Et fait neuf coups sans déconner,
Et six après sans s'étonner,
Pourtant s'il y a damoiselle,
Jeune femme, fille ou pucelle,
Qui aye besoin d'un tel vit
Qu'elles mettent leur nom en écrit,
Le lieu, la rue et la demeure,
Le personnage ira à l'heure
Et s'il ne fait tout ce qu'il dit,
Il veut qu'on lui coupe le vit.

Zola, Émile (1840–1902), *L'Assommoir* (1877). Abridged

The shocking vision of the drunk tinsmith Coupeau, aka Cadet Cassis, husband of the heroine, Gervaise (see *LP II* , pp. 41–2), is the overture to her adultery with her first lover, Auguste Lantier, whom she meets again many years after he had left her with three sons (including Étienne, hero of the below-cited *Germinal*). Lantier becomes a drinking partner of Cadet Cassis and finally a tenant in the proletarian ménage à trois (actually a ménage à quatre, since Mother Coupeau lives in the apartment). Nana, mentioned in the citation, is the Coupeaus' daughter. Coupeau has been away for two days on an alcoholic binge and Gervaise accepts Lantier's invitation to a café-concert. When they return home, they find Coupeau snoring in bed. Zola wrote this scene in working-class slang ("la langue verte"), illustrated in *LP II*, pp. 41–2 and 89–90, as well as in *LP II,* Appendix, pp. 243–4.

— Tout le monde dort, dit Gervaise, après avoir sonné trois fois…

La porte s'ouvrit…quand elle frappa à la vitre de la loge pour demander sa clef, la concierge ensommeillée lui cria une histoire à laquelle elle n'entendit rien d'abord. Enfin, elle comprit que le sergent de ville Poisson avait ramené Coupeau dans un drôle d'état, et que la clef devait être sur la serrure.

— Fichtre! Murmura Lantier, quand ils furent entrés, qu'est-ce qu'il a donc fait ici? C'est une vraie infection.

En effet, ça puait ferme. Gervaise, qui cherchait des allumettes, marchait dans du mouillé. Lorsqu'elle fut parvenue à allumer une bougie, ils eurent devant eux un joli spectacle. Coupeau avait rendu tripes et boyaux; il y en avait plein la chambre; le lit en était emplâtré, le tapis également, et jusqu'à la commode qui se trouvait éclaboussée. Avec ça, Coupeau, tombé du lit où Poisson devait l'avoir jeté, ronflait là dedans, au milieu de son ordure. Il s'y étalait, vautré comme un porc, une joue barbouillée, soufflant son haleine empestée par sa bouche ouverte, balayant de ses cheveux déjà gris la mare élargie autour de sa tête.

— Oh! Le cochon! Le cochon! Répétait Gervaise indignée, exaspérée. Il a tout sali...Non, un chien n'aurait pas fait ça, un chien crevé est plus propre.

Tous deux n'osaient bouger, ne savaient où poser le pied. Jamais le zingeur n'était revenu avec une telle culotte et n'avait mis la chambre dans une ignominie pareille. Aussi, cette vue-là portait un rude coup au sentiment que sa femme pouvait encore éprouver pour lui... L'idée seule que la peau de ce goujat chercherait sa peau, lui causait une répugnance... Il faut pourtant que je me couche, murmura-t-elle. Je ne puis pas retourner coucher dans la rue... Elle tâcha d'enjamber l'ivrogne et dut se retenir à un coin de la commode, pour ne pas glisser dans la saleté. Coupeau barrait complètement le lit. Alors, Lantier, qui avait un petit rire en voyant bien qu'elle ne ferait pas dodo sur son oreiller cette nuit-là, lui prit une main, en disant d'une voix basse et ardente:

— Gervaise... écoute, Gervaise...

Mais elle avait compris, elle se dégagea, éperdue, le tutoyant à son tour, comme jadis.

— Non, Laisse-moi... Je t'en supplie, Auguste, rentre dans ta chambre... Je vais m'arranger, je monterai dans le lit par les pieds...

— Gervaise, voyons, ne fais pas la bête, répétait-il. Ça sent trop mauvais, tu ne peux pas rester... Viens. Qu'est-ce que tu crains? Il ne nous entend pas, va!

Elle luttait, elle disait non de la tête, énergiquement... Ah! Elle était bien plantée, avec un loupiat de mari par devant, qui l'empêchait de se fourrer honnêtement sous sa couverture, avec un sacré salaud d'homme par derrière, qui songeait uniquement à profiter de son malheur pour la ravoir! Comme le chapelier haussait la voix, elle le supplia de se taire. Et elle écouta, l'oreille tendue vers le cabinet où couchaient Nana et maman Coupeau...

-Auguste, laisse-moi, tu vas les réveiller, reprit-elle, les mains jointes. Sois raisonnable. Un autre jour, ailleurs... Pas ici, pas devant ma fille...

Il ne parlait plus, il restait souriant et, lentement, il la baisa sur l'oreille, ainsi qu'il la baisait autrefois pour la taquiner, et l'étourdir. Alors, elle fut sans force, elle sentit un grand bourdonnement, un grand frisson descendre dans sa chair. Pourtant, elle fit de nouveau un pas. Elle dut reculer. Ce n'était pas possible...l'odeur devenait telle, qu'elle se serait elle-même mal conduite dans ses draps...

— Tant pis, bégayait-elle, c'est sa faute, je ne puis pas... Ah! Mon Dieu! ah! mon Dieu! il me renvoie de mon lit, je n'ai plus de lit... Non, je ne puis pas, c'est sa faute.

Elle tremblait, elle perdait la tête. Et, pendant que Lantier la poussait dans sa chambre, le visage de Nana apparut à la porte vitrée du cabinet, derrière un carreau... Elle regarda son père roulé dans son vomissement; puis, la figure collée contre la vitre, elle resta là, à attendre que le jupon de sa mère eût disparu chez l'autre homme, en face... Elle avait de grands yeux d'enfant vicieuse, allumés d'une curiosité sensuelle.

Germinal (1885)

The novel's finale illustrates the naturalist's effective gradation uniting several macrostimulative subjects. Three overlapping conflicts culminate: the ongoing ideological clash of miners and mine owners; the starving and delirious miners' struggle for life after days in the flooded mine, and the violence of the protagonist Étienne

Lantier, who fatally smashes the skull of Chaval, his rival in love. This link between love and death reaches a gruesome climax with the first and last tryst of Étienne and the dying Catherine on a ledge above the slowly receding water carrying away the corpse of Chaval. Étienne, whose hair turns grey during the endless wait for rescue, is saved. Fate spares him to witness the tragic results of the desperate strike. Yet the survivors' bitter lessons do not destroy the strikers' hope that one day they will no longer be exploited. The title of the novel suggests that their sacrifices are the seeds of ultimate victory.

Murder in the flooded mine

Une nouvelle journée s'achevait, et Chaval s'était assis près de Catherine, partageant avec elle sa dernière moitié de la tartine. Elle mâchait les bouchées péniblement, il les lui faisait payer chacune d'une caresse, dans son entêtement de jaloux qui ne voulait pas mourir sans la ravoir, devant l'autre... Mais, lorsqu'il tâcha de la prendre, elle se plaignit.

— Oh! Laisse, tu me casses les os.

Étienne, frémissant, avait posé son front contre les bois, pour ne pas voir. Il revint d'un bond, affolé.

— Laisse-là, nom de Dieu!

— Est-ce que ça te regarde? Dit Chaval. C'est ma femme, elle est à moi, peut-être!

El il la reprit, et il la serra, par bravade, lui écrasant sur la bouche ses moustaches rouges, continuant:

— Fiche-nous la paix, hein! Fais-nous le plaisir de voir là-bas si nous y sommes.

Mais Étienne, les lèvres blanches, criait:

— Si tu ne la lâches pas, je t'étrangle!

Vivement, l'autre se mit debout, car il avait compris, au sifflement de la voix, que le camarade allait en finir. La mort leur semblait trop lente, il fallait que, tout de suite, l'un des deux cédât la place. C'était l'ancienne bataille qui recommençait, dans la terre où ils dormiraient bientôt côte à côte; et ils avient si peu d'espace, qu'ils ne pouvaient brandir leur poings sans les écorcher.

— Méfie-toi, gronda Chaval. Cette fois, je te mange.

Étienne, à ce moment, devint fou. Ses yeux se noyèrent d'une vapeur rouge, sa gorge s'était congestionnée d'un flot de sang. Le besoin de tuer le prenait, irrésistible, un besoin physique, l'excitation sanguine d'une muqueuse qui détermine un violent accès de toux. Cela monta, éclata en dehors de sa volonté, sous la poussée de la lésion héréditaire. Il avait empoigné, dans le mur, une feuille de schiste, et il l'ébranlait, et il l'arrachait, très large, très lourde. Puis, à deux mains, avec une force décuplée, il l'abattit sur le crâne de Chaval.

Celui-ci n'eut pas le temps de sauter en arrière. Il tomba, la face broyée, le crâne fendu. La cervelle avait éclaboussé le toit de la galerie, un jet pourpre coulait de la plaie, pareil au jet continu d'une source. Tout de suite, il y eut une mare, où l'étoile fumeuse de la lampe se refléta. L'ombre envahissait ce caveau muré', le corps semblait, par terre, la bosse noire d'un tas d'écaille.

Et penché, l'oeil élargi, Étienne le regardait. C'était donc fait, il avait tué.

The floating cadaver

Le septième jour, Catherine se penchait pour boire, lorsqu'elle heurta de la main un corps flottant devant elle… Elle but, mais comme elle puisait une seconde gorgée, le corps revint battre sa main. Et elle poussa un cri terrible… C'était le cadavre de Chaval, remonté du plan incliné, poussé jusqu'à eux par la crue. Étienne allongea le bras, sentit aussi les moustaches, le nez broyé; et un frisson de répugnance et de peur le secoua. Prise d'une nausée abominable, Catherine avait craché l'eau qui lui restait à la bouche. Elle croyait qu'elle venait de boire du sang… "Attends, bégaya Étienne, je vais le renvoyer."

Il donna un coup de pied au cadavre, qui s'éloigna. Mais…quelque courant le ramenait. Chaval ne voulait pas partir, voulait être avec eux, contre eux.

Love and death

L'image de Chaval la hantait, et elle…racontait leur existence de chien, le seul jour où il s'était montré gentil…les autres jours de sottises et de gifles, quand il la tuait de ses caresses, après l'avoir rouée de coups… "Oh! Renvoie-le, oh! Garde-moi, garde-moi tout entière!"

D'un élan, elle s'était pendue à lui, elle chercha sa bouche et y colla passionnément la sienne. Les ténèbres s'éclairèrent, elle revit le soleil, elle retrouva un rire calmé d'amoureuse. Lui, frémissant de la sentir ainsi contre sa chair, demi-nue sous la veste et la culotte en lambeaux, l'empoigna, dans un réveil de sa virilité. Et ce fut enfin leur nuit de noces, au fond de cette tombe, sur ce lit de boue, le besoin de ne pas mourir avant d'avoir eu leur bonheur, l'obstiné besoin de vivre, de faire de la vie une dernière fois. Ils s'aimèrent dans le désespoir de tout, dans la mort.

Ensuite…des heures s'écoulèrent. Il crut longtemps qu'elle dormait; puis, il la toucha, elle était très froide, elle était morte.

* * *

ERRATA

Obvious typographical, punctuation or spelling errors and graphical inconsistencies are not included.

Literary Practice I – Esthetic Qualities and Values in Literature

Page, Line	Incorrect	Correct
48, line 2	overall	over all
53, line 21	Menelaus Atreides	Atreides
54, n.4	Du Grobes	Du groβes
60, line 12	m lange	mélange
95, cit. line 13	tranger	étranger
99, line 23	8 (5+4)	8(4+4)
99, last line	9 (4+4)	9(4+5)
118, line 15	Pareil la	Pareil à la
121, line 37	representation	represented
121, line 38	p. 11/20	p. 120

Literary Practice II – Esthetics of Style

Page, Line	Incorrect	Correct
196, n. 5	p	p. 87.
231, line 11	pp. 109-10	pp. 120-21

*   *   *